PAYING THE PROFESSORIATE

How are professors paid? Can the "best and brightest" be attracted to the academic profession? With universities facing international competition, which countries compensate their academics best, and which ones lag behind? *Paying the Professoriate* examines these questions and provides key insights into and recommendations for the current state of the academic profession worldwide.

Paying the Professoriate is the first comparative analysis of global faculty salaries, remuneration, and terms of employment. Offering an in-depth international comparison of academic salaries in 28 countries across public, private, research, and nonresearch universities, chapter authors shed light on the conditions and expectations that shape the modern academic profession. The top researchers on the academic profession worldwide analyze common themes, trends, and the impact of these matters on academic quality and research productivity. In a world where higher education capacity is a key driver of national innovation and prosperity, and nations seek to fast-track their economic growth through expansion of higher education systems, policy makers and administrators increasingly seek answers about what actions they should be taking. *Paying the Professoriate* provides a much needed resource, illuminating the key issues and offering recommendations.

Philip G. Altbach is J. Donald Monan S.J. University Professor and Director of the Center for International Higher Education, Boston College, USA.

Liz Reisberg is Research Associate at the Center for International Higher Education, Boston College, USA.

Maria Yudkevich is Associate Professor of Economics and Vice Rector for research at the National Research University Higher School of Economics in Moscow, Russia.

Gregory Androushchak is Adviser to the Rector and Researcher at the Laboratory for Institutional Analysis at the National Research University Higher School of Economics in Moscow, Russia.

Iván F. Pacheco is Research Assistant at the Center for International Higher Education, Boston College, USA.

PAYING THE PROFESSORIATE

A Global Comparison
of Compensation and Contracts

Edited by
Philip G. Altbach, Liz Reisberg,
Maria Yudkevich, Gregory Androushchak,
and Iván F. Pacheco

Routledge
Taylor & Francis Group

NEW YORK AND LONDON

First published 2012
by Routledge
711 Third Avenue, New York, NY 10017

Simultaneously published in the UK
by Routledge
2 Park Square, Milton Park, Abingdon, Oxon OX14 4RN

Routledge is an imprint of the Taylor & Francis Group, an informa business

© 2012 Taylor & Francis

Library of Congress Cataloging in Publication Data

Paying the professoriate : a global comparison of compensation and contracts / [edited by] Philip G. Altbach ... [et al.].
   p. cm.
  Includes bibliographical references and index.
  1. College teachers—Salaries, etc.—Cross-cultural studies.   I. Altbach, Philip G.
  LB2333.5.P39   2012
  378.1'2—dc23   2011044500

ISBN: 978–0–415–89806–5 (hbk)
ISBN: 978–0–415–89807–2 (pbk)
ISBN: 978–0–203–80308–0 (ebk)

Typeset in Bembo
by Apex CoVantage

SUSTAINABLE
FORESTRY
INITIATIVE

Certified Sourcing
www.sfiprogram.org
SFI-00555
The SFI label applies to the text stock.

Printed and bound in the United States of America by
Walsworth Publishing Company, Marceline, MO.

CONTENTS

ACKNOWLEDGMENTS

A complex project like this one requires a great deal of cooperation and assistance. Our greatest acknowledgment is to our 28 country researchers. We are indebted to them for their commitment to this project over more than a year, their willingness to dig out often problematical data, and the work through several revisions. We continue to value their colleagueship.

One of the key figures involved in the project was Yaroslav Kuzminov, rector of the National Research University Higher School of Economics. He plays an active role in the reform of education in Russia and has consistently emphasized the importance of the academic profession as central to the successful modernization of the university sector. He continues to advocate for appropriate remuneration for faculty in order to ensure that an academic career is economically attractive and viable. Not surprisingly, he expressed great interest in the project on academic salaries, carried out by CIHE and published in 2008, and suggested a further study of academic remuneration and academic contracts, with a broader sample of countries from different parts of the world and deeper analysis. He participated in the design of the project, from the discussions on methodology and which countries should be included to contributing to the conclusions drawn from the results. The Higher School of Economics also provided core funding for the project.

At the Higher School of Economics' Laboratory for Institutional Analysis, Elena Shutova provided logistical support. Alexander Novikov and Anna Panova helped us to collect and analyze empirical country data. The World Bank also provided logistical and other assistance.

The Boston College Center for International Higher Education provided additional funding and support for the project. We are also indebted to the Ford Foundation for its support during the early phases of the project. We are especially indebted to Edith S. Hoshino, CIHE publications editor, for editing the final manuscript, and to Salina Kopellas for logistical support.

INTRODUCTION

This book, and the research project on which it is based, is predicated on the importance and centrality of the academic profession. Without a committed and adequately compensated professoriate, no university can be fully successful. Further, the terms of employment for the profession must provide a career structure that will attract and retain the "best and brightest" teachers as well as researchers—and encourage them to do their best work. Despite the fact that the academic profession is at the core of the university, the professoriate has suffered a decline in status and remuneration in many countries, at precisely the time when higher education has moved to the center of the global knowledge society. Our research on the related themes of academic salaries, remuneration, and contracts reflects our concern for the many challenges confronting the professoriate and the implications for the university in the 21st century.

The original research was conceived during a doctoral seminar at Boston College on the academic profession. The group was interested in how much professors were paid in different countries; they found that very little research had been done about this topic and that data were sparse. For a few countries, national statistics were available, but for most, there were none at all. The Boston College Center for International Higher Education (CIHE) undertook further research on this topic in 2006, focusing on 15 countries and Palestine. The data were collected from public sources as well as from various universities. Researchers in each the 15 countries assisted in the collection of information and data, and this effort resulted in the report—Laura E. Rumbley, Iván F. Pacheco, and Philip G. Altbach, *International Comparison of Academic Salaries: An Exploratory Study*, published by the Center in 2008. One of the findings was the fact that salaries alone do not reflect an accurate picture of academic incomes, and remuneration must be measured in broader terms.

This research attracted the attention of the Laboratory for Institutional Analysis (LIA) at the National Research University Higher School of Economics (HSE) in Moscow, Russia. Since 2002 HSE has taken part in "Monitoring of Educational Markets and Organizations (MEMO)," which is an annual study that consists of representative surveys of students and their families, school teachers, faculty and top administrators at colleges and universities, and employers. The LIA's interest was in the area of institutional plans for hiring, promotion, and the contractual arrangements and incentives for academic employment. This expanded research agenda facilitated the consideration of the broader issues of remuneration. The current study benefited from the combined expertise and funding of HSE and CIHE.

This study should not be considered a continuation of the first edition but a reconceptualized and expanded version. Many issues not considered in the first study, such as supplementary income and additional employment, are considered. Still, the quality of data in regard to those issues is still less than ideal. Additionally, in this volume, the country reports and statistical data were provided by local experts who produced better and more reliable data. Richer statistical analysis based on the new data has been conducted and included here by the LIA/HSE.

Organization of This Volume

There are 28 countries included in this research project. They represent all continents and a range of academic and societal circumstances and are presented here in alphabetical order.

Each chapter follows a similar outline and presents a brief overview of the higher education system: legal and policy frameworks related to higher education; the structure of academic hierarchy, hiring practices, and salary ranges; qualifications and contract types; procedures for promotion and other forms of rewards and recognition; nonsalary benefits; options for supplementary employment and income; and international mobility and competition.

Chapters 1 and 2 provide analyses of global trends in the academic profession and a brief comparative discussion of salaries, contracts, and remuneration across the 28 case study countries.

A few definitions are necessary. By salaries, we mean the direct monetary compensation provided by academic employers to the professoriate. Remuneration includes nonsalary funds received by the professoriate—for consulting, extra teaching, administrative tasks, or other work—including, in some cases, adjustment for cost of living and other variables not covered by the basic salaries. In some countries, while salaries may be low, total remuneration may be a more adequate measure of academic income. By contracts, we mean the specific legal and other arrangements that govern the terms and conditions of academic employment.

Research Process and Methodology

The research was guided by a common questionnaire, with the objective of collecting comparable data. Our country experts mostly found data either unavailable or inconsistent. The study hoped to include the private and public sectors, but data from the private sector proved particularly difficult to obtain.

Enormous variations in practice exist among the countries included in this study, and it is hoped that the overview and background information provided in each chapter will offer helpful context for interpreting the data provided.

The research process was quite challenging on many levels. Bringing together researchers from 28 countries to work on a common theme was itself a significant undertaking. The entire research group met once in Moscow at the invitation of the Higher School of Economics in October 2010. During this meeting draft chapters were reviewed and critiqued; revisions were then undertaken based on the feedback from colleagues and the editors of this volume. The statistical data were delivered to the LIA team for analysis and comparison. Charts and graphs compiled from these data are available in this book but in greater detail on the project website: acarem.hse.ru.

Another significant difficulty was finding a mechanism to compare salaries and remuneration across currencies and widely varied economic realities. As in the first study, we have used purchasing power parity (PPP) in a series of tables and analyses at the end of this volume. However, in the country chapters, researchers have used national currencies and have in most cases indicated a rough equivalent to U.S. dollars.

Limitations of This Study

Important topics such as differences in salaries based on gender, discipline, and other variables were not systematically collected, although in some cases information is provided. These topics were not included in the questionnaire because it would have added complexity to an undertaking that was already complex enough. We leave this additional layer of analysis for future research.

The differences in the methodology of data collection, sources, and in some cases years of the statistical information may affect the comparability of data, an issue that will be addressed in the analysis part of this book. Also, the different criteria and methods used to determine salaries across countries make comparisons a challenge and forced decisions in which consistency was sacrificed in order to compare data from all the participating countries.

This study focused on tenure track (or equivalent) full-time faculty. However, some attention was devoted to other arrangements that are now displacing the traditional full-time faculty member.

This research project remains exploratory in the sense that we do not have all of the answers, and the data sources remain inconsistent and in some cases problematical. Yet, this is the first comparative analysis of academic salaries, remuneration, and contracts of its kind ever undertaken.

Philip G. Altbach
Liz Reisberg
Iván F. Pacheco
Chestnut Hill, Massachusetts, United States

Maria Yudkevich
Gregory Androushchak
Moscow, Russian Federation

PART 1

Analysis

1

ACADEMIC REMUNERATION AND CONTRACTS

Global Trends and Realities

Philip G. Altbach, Liz Reisberg, and Iván F. Pacheco

The academic profession is at the central core of the university. Without a strong, well-educated, and committed professoriate, no academic institution or higher education system can be successful. Yet, the profession now faces enormous challenges. The massification of enrollments, privatization, growing pressures for accountability, increased global competition for talent, and the economic downturn combine to influence national policies that define higher education. Furthermore, academic staff are being asked to deal with the broad range of needs of a more diverse student population. Worsening conditions of employment, deteriorating salaries, and threats to job security have made the academic profession less attractive to young scholars in some countries, while other countries are performing a concerted effort to make salaries and working conditions more appealing.

The matters of concern mainly include key elements of salaries, remuneration, and the terms and conditions of academic work—the core of academic appointments. Without significant salaries and appropriate contracts and conditions of service, the profession cannot thrive—and indeed cannot perform quite well. Without conditions that permit a secure career, competitive with alternatives in the labor market, the entire academic enterprise will falter. In most countries, within this study as well as in much of the world, academic staff supplement their base salary with added income earned by means of teaching overloads, research productivity, nonacademic work, teaching in multiple institutions, or administrative service. The contemporary university in most countries finds itself in crisis, in part based on the risks faced by the academic profession (Altbach 2003).

This book is based on a study of the academic profession in 28 countries, on all continents. With so many new forces shaping higher education globally, the academic profession may face new challenges and serious risks. Moreover, in higher education compensation and careers are at the heart of the contemporary crisis worldwide.

The Academic Revolution and the Academic Profession

Much has been investigated about the academic revolution of the 21st century (Altbach, Reisberg, and Rumbley 2010; Task Force on Higher Education and Society 2000; Altbach 1996). The contemporary transformation of higher education presents direct implications for the academic profession. Three key forces are of special relevance for the academic profession. Massification has transformed higher education everywhere. In the first decade of the 21st century, global enrollments grew from 100 million to 150 million. Continued growth will impact India and China dramatically, along with sub-Saharan Africa. In much of Europe, parts of East Asia, and North America, however, higher education systems have matured and are no longer significantly expanding. In some countries, the age cohort that traditionally enrolled in higher education is actually shrinking. This shift formed implications for the academic profession, as well. Higher education is no longer an elite enterprise, and this new reality has had dramatic implications for the academic profession.

The global knowledge economy, made possible by the revolution in information technology, has also affected higher education and the academic profession. Research has become a key function of the top-tier universities worldwide, creating new options and challenges for academics at the top of the profession. Both massification and the knowledge economy have created diversification of higher education, with segments devoted mainly to teaching and providing access to students, while a smaller segment focuses on research.

Institutional diversification has led to a fracturing of the academic profession into many segments and to the decline of a sense of the academic community. Burton Clark, referring to the United States, wrote of the professoriate divided into "small worlds, different worlds"—the various subcultures and circumstances of the profession in a complex academic system (Clark 1987). At top research universities, the working conditions, salaries, and roles of the elite professors, in most countries, differ greatly from the jobs of staff who teach at mass-access institutions, who are lower in the academic pecking order and who now constitute the large majority of the academic workforce. Increasingly, remuneration and working conditions of faculty members in new high-demand areas—such as business studies or information technology—are quite different from those in the humanities. The academic profession of the 21st century is, without question, less of a community than it was in the past. Size alone makes the community problematical, along with the enormous diversity in the academic profession. There were at least 6 million postsecondary teachers worldwide in 2007, and the number is increasing rapidly to match growing enrollments (Altbach, Reisberg, and Rumbley 2010, 228–33).

Increased demands for accountability, greater attention to serving the vocational needs of students, the shortcomings of preuniversity education, and other pressures have added to the challenges facing the academic profession.

International competition for talent and institutional prestige has created new tensions as international pressures often conflict with local needs.

The dramatic rise of the private sector in higher education has affected the professoriate. Private higher education, for-profit and nonprofit, is now the fastest-growing segment of postsecondary education worldwide and constitutes the majority of enrollments in parts of Latin America and Asia. Although many of the faculty who teach in the private sector also hold positions at public universities, some alterations exist among academic circumstances at private universities. Globally, the terms and conditions of academic appointments in the private sector vary and are sometimes less favorable than in public universities. In some countries, the private sector will pay more but offer less attractive working conditions, demanding more teaching hours with no compensation or time allocated for research, preparation, advising, or other types of service.

Finally, globalization has facilitated the increased mobility of talent, especially for academics at the top of the prestige hierarchy. The countries in this book (for the most part) divide into two categories—brain drain and brain gain. South Africa is in the unusual position of being in both categories, gaining talent from the African region but also losing top talent to Europe and other more-developed countries. Countries with greater resources are able to draw talent from weaker economies. Traditionally, this quality has been to the advantage of institutions in Canada, the United States, and Western Europe; but new players (Saudi Arabia and China, for example) have entered the global competition for top researchers and scholars. This situation works to the detriment of weaker economies—such as, Armenia, Latvia, and Ethiopia—where resources are limited but the need for talent is at least as strong.

Confronting New Realities

As noted previously, several trends have converged to change the higher education landscape and, as a result, the conditions of academic work and the profession. With few exceptions, enrollment has expanded dramatically in the developing countries included in this book. Rapid enrollment expansion created an urgent need for more seats, infrastructure, and academic staff.

Most of the developed countries in this study—Australia, Canada, France, Norway, the United Kingdom, and the United States—were transformed by enrollment expansion several decades ago and are now relatively stable. Japan stands out as a developed country that now confronts the challenges of having expanded beyond its current needs and finds itself with excess capacity and staff.

In all countries, periods of rapid expansion increased the demand for teaching institutions and academic staff who would teach. The result has been an ongoing tension between the priorities of higher education. The greater need requires academic staff to teach the expanding numbers of students in classrooms, while prestige and value continue to be measured by research productivity. Despite the growing segment of higher education dedicated exclusively to teaching, salary, promotion, and other rewards are more often based on research productivity and rarely on teaching performance. International prestige that emanates from rankings is greatly influenced by research achievement, and this, in turn, often influences national policy and budget allocation.

In countries where higher education was historically limited to or dominated by publically supported institutions, governments have opened the door to private providers in order to address growing enrollment demand. Private universities (with rare exceptions) tend to be entirely devoted to teaching. Private universities, often for-profit, now account for a growing share of enrollment in countries where this sector was previously insignificant, if not nonexistent—including Russia, Kazakhstan, Latvia, Ethiopia, Armenia, Saudi Arabia, and the Czech Republic. As already noted, this sector has also become a source of supplementary employment for academic staff in the public sector. This research was limited by the general lack of data provided by the private sector in nearly all countries, particularly in regard to salaries and remuneration. The private sector, in general, seemed to be less transparent and less accountable than the public sector.

Patterns of Academic Appointments and Contracts

Patterns of appointment and contracts vary widely across the globe, but the academic profession remains a remarkably stable career as well as one that provides considerable social prestige—even if not always a reasonable standard of living. But the profile of the academic workforce has changed in recent decades. The academic community is not only much larger but also much more diverse than in the past.

The urgency of increasing coverage for expanded enrollment in so many countries has strained budget and human resource capacity nearly everywhere. The challenges of filling so many new positions at a time of worldwide fiscal austerity have resulted in several notable trends and patterns.

The need has generally been addressed by greater numbers of part-time or full-time, fixed-contract academic hires. Even systems with a strong tradition of hiring academic staff on a tenure track, or with permanent civil service hiring arrangements, are moving toward more fixed-term appointments. In the United States, for example, half of the new appointments to academic posts are either part-time or full-time contract employees (Schuster and Finkelstein 2006). Western Europe seems least affected by the trend toward part-time academic staff, although numbers are growing there as well.

Interestingly, although relatively few countries included in this research have formal tenure systems, most full- and part-time academic staff are renewed as a matter of course. Tenure systems tend to have well-defined norms for determining when contracts will be renewed, with a clearly defined threshold to permanence. In systems without formal tenure, surprisingly, academic staff, particularly part time, are infrequently subject to a formal and comprehensive review of their relevant activities and are rarely dismissed. In only a few countries (Germany, Japan, and the United States) are the terms of continuance clear and quite strict and are academic staff routinely forced to leave a position.

Additionally, developing countries in particular were hard pressed to fill openings for staff that held advanced degrees. In many countries in this study, entry-level positions in the academic hierarchy are filled by teachers with only a first degree. Indeed, the first university degree (the equivalent of a bachelor's degree) may be the average academic qualification for those teaching in postsecondary education worldwide today. It should be noted, however, that this was also common in the past, before massification in countries (Argentina, Brazil, and Colombia), where graduate programs were sparse. Where graduate programs have expanded nationally, more countries require new hires to have advanced degrees, and younger faculty are more likely to have such degrees. The doctorate, a requirement for almost all academic appointments—in Australia, Canada, Europe, and the United States for the past century—has now become a requirement for appointments at research universities everywhere.

Hiring practices tend to follow a similar pattern, often outlined in national legislation; opportunities are announced in the national press and open to all candidates. Typically, institutions maintain considerable autonomy in determining when they have openings and how they are promoted and filled. In a few countries (France, for example) included in the research, candidates must be reviewed at the national level before they can be considered for a specific academic position, but this is not a common practice.

Despite a trend toward making the hiring process more competitive and transparent, individuals are still often hired through personal networks or offered temporary contracts that bypass the formal public contest system. In Argentina, academic staff can be hired more quickly under "interim contracts," bypassing a public competition; Colombia does the same, by hiring temporary or occasional staff. Even when vacancies are announced publicly and where formal procedures exist for hiring new staff, positions are often filled internally, with faculty from lower ranks or with the university's own graduates contributing to "inbreeding" (i.e., hiring some of its own graduates) in many countries. In Russia, the head of a chair uses his or her considerable autonomy to make hiring choices, including often his or her own PhD students. Likewise, Armenian universities give preference to their own students, when hiring. Japan tends to rely on personal connections for appointment to entry-level academic posts. Indeed, the observation from the research data is that inbreeding in both initial hiring and in promotions is a common practice.

Conditions that encourage inbreeding constitute tradition, the lack of a national market, the absence of financial incentives to move, and significantly less attractive working conditions elsewhere. Most analysts feel that such a scheme is a detriment to academic creativity, since it emphasizes the continuity of ideas and practice rather than innovation. This practice also stresses academic hierarchy, because younger scholars, trained by their elders, simply fit into existing arrangements. At the same time, the persuasion of loyalty and a sense of solidarity in an academic system may be as beneficial as it is detrimental.

Yet, several countries resist inbreeding. The Ministry of Education in Italy provides subsidies to encourage tenured academics to move, instead, to a university in another region. The United States, Turkey, and Germany are among countries with traditions of obliging graduating students to apply to a different university for entry-level faculty positions.

Hiring in India is complicated by a quota system that reserves a percentage, sometimes approaching half, of university positions for members of specific castes or other social classifications. If qualified staff cannot be found with the required characteristics, the position remains vacant—creating additional challenges for covering rapidly growing enrollments.

In many countries, academics in public universities are part of the civil service (Brazil, Germany, Malaysia, and Saudi Arabia, for example). In these cases, staff are appointed, evaluated, and often paid according to the rules and procedures of the civil service. Soon after being appointed, academics often have strong job protection that is similar to tenure. Their salaries are typically determined by length of service and rank rather than any evaluation of job performance. Many continental European countries have applied civil service rules to academic appointments because academics are considered to be public employees, although a number of countries—such as the Netherlands—have moved away from the civil service pattern of hiring academic staff.

Academic Salaries

Defining what constitutes an academic salary in various sectors or countries proved to involve many factors. It has been manifested that academic salaries are often a complex construction of basic salary and supplements, bonuses, allowances, and subsidies—subsequently, they are extremely difficult to compare internationally. Another issue is the extent to which, in countries, salaries were sufficient to place academic staff in the middle class. Clearly, the definition of "middle class" varies depending on the economic and cultural environment. In this book, this determination is approved by each of the country experts, based on national perceptions and measures.

One of the other challenges of comparing salaries across countries is how to get an accurate idea of the purchasing power that results from a salary in each country. A simple currency conversion is not enough, because it does not take into account the diversity in the cost of living between countries. A more accurate examination is the usage of the purchasing power parity (PPP) index. The indices are based on an item or a set of items (basket of goods) whose prices are compared with the price of the same item or basket of goods in the reference country (in this case, the United States), providing a uniform tool for comparison. This study has adjusted salaries in each local currency to the PPP index, to get a comparable amount in PPP dollars, using the index from the seventh version of the Penn World Tables (Heston, Summers, and Aten 2011). The PPP index allowed quantitative comparisons across countries, but the study relied on the country authors to determine whether academic salaries were sufficient to support a middle-class standard of living in their local economic environment. This combination of quantitative and qualitative assessment provided an overview of the value of different academic salaries.

Figure 1.1 shows three levels of salaries in each of the study countries—the average for entry level, average salary for the system, and the average of salaries paid at the top of the salary scale. As with all comparisons in this study, these numbers reflect systems of different size and with varying degrees of institutional diversity. The United States, for example, presents an average salary at each level that factors in a large number of individuals at many universities that include small undergraduate teaching institutions as well as elite research universities. There is quite a large salary range reflected in the averages reported. On the other hand, Germany has a smaller number of institutions with much less diversity and, as a result, less variation in salary. In other words, the averages reported are useful for comparisons but reflect calculations pulled from quite different systems.

Figure 1.1 highlights variations in salary ranges from country to country as well as the large gaps that often exist between entry-level salaries and those paid to senior academic staff.

Table 1.1 shows more clearly the specific amounts of the average entry level and the average top-level salaries reported by each country expert, as well as the average for each system. These data are only for the public sector. China, Armenia, Ethiopia, Kazakhstan, and Russia are the five countries offering the lowest average entry-level salaries, while the United Kingdom, Saudi Arabia, Italy, South Africa, and Canada offer the best average salaries to senior staff.

Table 1.1 does not indicate the concentration of individuals at each rank, but this is demonstrated in Table A.1 in the appendix. Salary ranges reveal a great transaction. In countries where the top-level salary is high and the gap between entry level and top level is small, salaries overall are clearly attractive. Where entry-level and top-level averages are both low, it is easy to see that an academic career will be less attractive and that these countries will be vulnerable to brain drain.

China reflects the largest gap between entry-level and top-level salaries by far—Argentina, Germany, and Norway, the smallest gap. More details about the ratios between entry-level and top-level salaries are included in Chapter 2.

As noted previously—in most cases, actual median salaries are difficult to define. In systems across the globe, from India to Mexico, salaries in the public sector are a composite of base salary, bonuses, competitive awards, and allowances

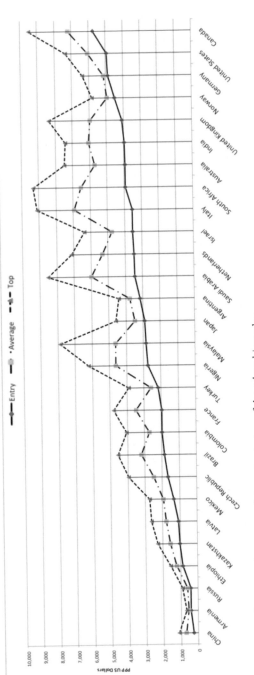

Figure 1.1 Salary range by country from entry to top of the salary hierarchy.

Source: Data collected by country experts from multiple sources and compiled for this study.

Table 1.1 Salaries at entry level and top of salary hierarchy with average salary (in US$PPP)

	Entry	*Average*	*Top*
Armenia	405	538	665
Russia	433	617	910
China	259	720	1,107
Ethiopia	864	1,207	1,580
Kazakhstan	1,037	1,553	2,304
Latvia	1,087	1,785	2,654
Mexico	1,336	1,941	2,730
Turkey	2,173	2,597	3,898
Czech Republic	1,655	2,495	3,967
Colombia	1,965	2,702	4,058
Argentina	3,151	3,755	4,385
Brazil	1,858	3,179	4,550
Japan	2,897	3,473	4,604
France	1,973	3,484	4,775
Norway	4,491	4,940	5,847
Nigeria	2,758	4,629	6,229
Israel	3,525	4,747	6,377
Germany	4,885	5,141	6,383
Netherlands	3,472	5,313	7,123
United States	4,950	6,054	7,358
India	3,954	6,070	7,433
Australia	3,930	5,713	7,499
Malaysia	2,824	4,628	7,864
United Kingdom	4,077	5,943	8,369
Saudi Arabia	3,457	6,002	8,524
Italy	3,525	6,955	9,118
South Africa	3,927	6,531	9,330
Canada	5,733	7,196	9,485

Source: Data collected by country experts from multiple sources and compiled for this study.

that tend to vary on an individual basis. Thus, total income in many countries is drawn from a combination of sources that provide a complete picture only when totaled, and the average salaries in Table 1.1 tell only part of the story. Additional employment also provides critical income for most of the academic profession worldwide. In fewer than half of the 28 countries in this study—Australia, Canada, Japan, France, Germany, India, Italy, Malaysia, the Netherlands, Norway, Saudi Arabia, the United States, and the United Kingdom—it is possible for most full-time academic staff to live comfortably on their base salary.

Even where full-time academic salaries provide an income considered to be middle class in the local context, the data show that this tends to be true mostly for full-time senior scholars and less true for younger staff. In many developed countries, academic salaries are falling behind salaries in professions that require comparable education. Countries including Japan, Germany, Israel, and the United States will find it harder to attract young talent in the future, unless salaries at the lower end of the hierarchy improve. Younger staff are also deterred by increased pressures that stem from greater teaching loads, an increased emphasis on the number of publications—in China and Colombia, among many other countries—and other demands. In other countries, academic salaries do not begin to approach a comfortable standard of living. In Kazakhstan, academic staff tend to earn half the salaries of peers with similar qualifications who work in other sectors. In Russia, young faculty earn approximately 70 percent of the average wage in the workforce; professors' salaries often fall 10 percent below the average wage of others in the workforce who have completed higher education. In most countries, a middle-class income generally depends on additional employment, either within the same institution, at another academic institution, or in nonacademic employment. All of this added pressure decreases the attractiveness of the academic career and will further deter the "best and brightest" from choosing academe.

As mentioned previously, it is difficult to generalize about salaries across all 28 countries because of the systems of bonuses, allowances, and supplements that cause actual salaries to vary widely nationally as well as within the same institution or within the same discipline. Allowances and bonuses generally compensate for poor base salaries or salaries that are too low to provide a middle-class standard of living. In some countries these supplemental payments are not included in taxable or pensionable income and are not reported, which makes it even more difficult to collect complete and accurate national data.

The value of rewards, bonuses, and allowances differ enormously; examples include a frozen turkey at Christmas in Mexico; allowances toward housing in Ethiopia, India, and Japan; family allowances for marriage and children in Germany; an allowance to compensate for inflation in India. The allowances that appear throughout the following chapters are too numerous to name and make a quantitative comparison of compensation packages nearly impossible.

Many countries provide incentives to encourage research, especially in the top research-intensive sector. In Mexico, the National System of Researchers (known locally by its Spanish acronym, the "SNI") provides a 50 percent supplement to the base pay of scholars who qualify; the National Science Institute (CONICET) sponsors a similar program in Argentina. French scholars receive important bonuses for scientific excellence. Israeli faculty can increase their salary by more than 13 percent for achievements in research. South Africa has a similar award program that provides salary supplements, ranging from $7,000 to $18,000, depending on the achievements of the individual scholar. Top Chinese universities pay their academic staff a significant bonus for each article published in internationally recognized refereed journals. These programs offer important incentives and recognition to encourage high levels of productivity, but they benefit small percentages of the total academic staff in any given nation.

For many academic staff in most of the countries studied here, a middle-class income requires additional employment. Many academics earn extra money by working in various academic and nonacademic pursuits. In most of the countries in this study academic staff accept extra teaching assignments for additional income. In some cases, this will be at the same institution but reflect a teaching overload beyond the hours specified in the contract or teaching in evening programs, professional seminars, or summer sessions; in other cases, faculty teach in different institutions. Others do consulting for industry or government, hold positions in research institutes or think tanks, write for newspapers, or have parallel careers as doctors, accountants, lawyers, or information-technology professionals.

The motivations for combining academic and nonacademic activities are difficult to analyze, since they often vary from one individual to another. While some pursue full-time professional careers and teach part time simply for the pleasure and satisfaction teaching provides, others teach part time and pursue additional professional activities out of financial necessity. Still others hold full-time academic positions and engage in professional activities part time for income, professional challenge and renewal, and/or prestige. The data are insufficient for even tentative conclusions about the degree to which academic employment is combined with nonacademic activities.

There is some debate over the advantages and disadvantages of academic staff pursuing supplementary employment. Some types of additional employment will undoubtedly contribute practical and relevant experience that will benefit classroom teaching and academic advising. However, when academic staff must pursue additional employment for economic survival, their attention will be divided, and it is unlikely that they will contribute their best work to their university. Inevitably, the university will suffer diminished quality in the long run.

In many countries, salary steps are established by state or national governments, for public institutions. In all countries, salaries for the private sector are negotiated privately and confidentially between the staff member and the administration of the hiring institution, and little data are made public. In general, private-sector salaries are composed of salary alone, with the exception of payments to retirement and health insurance programs required by law. In a few cases—Argentina and Mexico are two examples—private-sector academic staff are eligible for salary supplements offered by the national government, if they have a significant history of research and publications.

The presence and influence of unions vary considerably across the countries in our study. Academic staff are represented by unions in 12 of the 28 countries. Salary structures and working conditions are shaped by unions or collective bargaining to varying degrees. In several countries—Israel, Japan, the Netherlands, and Nigeria—national negotiations establish national benchmarks. In Australia, negotiations were formally conducted at a national level, but the trend is in the direction of actual negotiation with institutional management. Likewise, in

Canada, Norway, and South Africa, unions tend to negotiate locally with each individual institution. The pattern in Argentina is somewhat unusual, given that the public university faculty union negotiates first with the National Council of Public University rectors and the Ministry of Education before direct negotiations between local unions and university authorities take place. In Argentina, Brazil, and Canada, unions have helped to significantly improve the working conditions of part-time academic staff. Unions have only a limited influence in the United States—mainly in mass-access public colleges and universities. The extent to which negotiations between individuals and institutional management are permitted varies widely.

The factors that determine salaries tend to compose rank, seniority, academic qualifications, and publications; rank and seniority often carry the most weight. Another trend apparent in this research was the extent to which salaries vary by institution type, geographical location, and discipline. Research universities invariably offer higher salaries than teaching institutions. Public universities tend to pay better and offer superior conditions (fewer teaching hours) than private universities, although Ethiopia, France, Saudi Arabia, Turkey, and the United States offer exceptions to this pattern. Salaries are often more beneficial in urban centers; working conditions almost always are favorable. Employment alternatives in the labor market are also influential. In most countries, academic salaries vary by discipline with salaries typically higher in medicine, law, economics, and accounting, where universities have to compete with other sectors of the labor market for talent. Still, in some countries, salaries are determined almost exclusively by the government, either through civil service norms or the Ministry of Education. In these cases, salaries may not reflect market conditions, academic discipline, productivity, or any other factors.

Promotion and Career Advancement

Full-time academic careers are remarkably stable but usually with little national (or international) mobility. Careers are mostly characterized by a slow but steady march up the academic hierarchy. In some systems, only a small proportion of the profession reaches the top rank of full or chair professor.

Formal guarantees of job security are not universal, although few faculty seem to lose their jobs at any point on the career ladder. Among the 28 countries, 12 include academic staff at public institutions, in the civil service that typically provides lifetime job security. Countries with a formal tenure system—including the United States, Canada, Australia, and the Netherlands—provide a guarantee of career-long job security, along with assurance of academic freedom as part of the tenure arrangement, granted in most cases following rigorous review after five or more years of service. Only Mexico offers tenure (*definidad*) to part-time as well as full-time academic staff. Although most countries provide no formal guarantee of job security, most academic staff are able to keep their positions over the long run. They have, in a sense, de facto tenure, even if it is not written into law or institutional regulations.

Quite a few of the countries in this study—including Russia, the United Kingdom, Japan, and Latvia, to name a few—offer renewable contracts that, after several substantive reviews, are more or less automatically renewed. There is also, as mentioned previously, a certain degree of inertia in the academic culture of many systems, leading to nearly automatic contract renewal except in cases of gross negligence.

Academic hierarchies tend to be comprised in the three-to-five levels that may start with "lecturer" and advance to "professor," often with several salary steps at each level. Promotion tends to be earned most often on the basis of qualifications and seniority and also as a reward for advanced degrees and, sometimes, on research productivity. Staff is recognized less often for service or excellence in teaching. Few countries have effective evaluation systems to conduct a useful performance assessment; reappointments and advancement are often a product of inertia.

Typically, a newly hired staff is offered a term appointment at the rank of assistant professor or its equivalent and later may be promoted up the hierarchy, often obtaining tenured or permanent status after some type of evaluation. Perhaps the key element of this appointment system is that it is controlled within the university and seldom depends on governmental participation or approval. Of course, the implementation of these arrangements varies significantly by country and institution.

Advancement within academic hierarchies falls into two categories. There are systems, like Australia, Canada, Norway, and the United States, where advancement along the hierarchy at research universities is largely determined by research achievement determined by peer review. At institutions devoted primarily to teaching, other criteria are applied, but academic staff can be promoted for merit based on a range of criteria from student evaluations to administrative service.

The other system is the one followed in Argentina, Germany, and the United Kingdom—where there are a limited number of senior academic positions within a university and a position must be vacated before it can be filled. In fact, where there are limited positions at each level of the hierarchy, internal candidates do not receive preferential consideration when a senior position is vacated and are obligated to apply in an open competition with external candidates.

Data from 28 countries show some significant variations in career patterns. Mainly, academics once hired remain at the same university throughout their career. In most countries there is surprisingly little job mobility between institutions. Russia, Japan, and China are good examples of countries with simply no tradition of individual academic mobility among local institutions. Only in a few countries, notably the United States and Canada (largely in the more prestigious universities), there is considerable mobility during the course of a career. Globally, the rule tends to be that where one starts an academic career is where one finishes it. As the exception, individual scholars, the most talented, tend to accept positions outside of their country in pursuit of better income, academic freedom, better infrastructure, and more opportunities to collaborate with international peers.

The Growing, Yet Obscure, Private Sector

The expansion of private higher education institutions has greatly affected the academic profession. Yet, in nearly all countries, data from the private sector are unavailable. Much of the information included in the country chapters in this project is based on surveys with limited responses or anecdotal information. Globally, the regulation and reporting obligations of this sector are quite uneven. The private higher education sector is, typically, far from transparent and until recently largely free from accountability requirements.

While the data do not provide much certainty about the private higher education sector, academics in this sector have less secure terms of employment, are more likely to be part time, and enjoy less autonomy in their working conditions. Employment conditions and salaries of academic staff in the private sector vary considerably by institution type. At elite private universities, a minority of institutions globally, faculty are more likely to be employed full time and earn more than their counterparts in the public sector. This environment is viewed at a growing number of high-profile business schools—such as, INSEAD in France and SDA Bocconi in Italy, and the well-established private colleges and universities in Colombia, Japan, and the United States, where there is a long tradition of private education. But these schools tend to be exceptions, and academic staff in the private sector tend to earn less.

In much of the world, the private sector survives by hiring academic staff from public universities, who teach part time at private institutions. Retired professors are frequently hired as well. This moonlighting provides many individuals with needed additional income but reduces the time and attention available for research or other work at their primary institution of employment.

The private sector is extremely diverse, with a growing number of for-profit institutions (many owned by corporations), particularly in developing countries. Private institutions rarely encourage or support research. As a result, academic staff are usually hired only to teach. They often employ professional management, so academic staff are rarely expected to assume administrative responsibilities and therefore carry heavier teaching loads than the norm in the public or nonprofit sector.

International Mobility

Local and international academic and economic trends encourage the mobility of talent. This is, after all, the era of globalization, and universities and the academic profession are deeply involved. Shifting political and economic patterns provide a "push/pull" for academic staff, in pursuit of the best working conditions and salary to pursue their scholarship and research. In recent years, it has not only been lesser-developed countries that lose talent. Economic and academic circumstances have, for example, pushed scholars in Italy and Israel to look for employment abroad. The United Kingdom has suffered a modest brain drain to Canada and the United States. Economic and political conditions have pulled talent from countries throughout Africa to South African universities and, at the same time, from South Africa to Europe and elsewhere.

This research project illustrates one of the central contributors to global academic mobility. The significant inequalities in salaries, remuneration, and the terms and conditions of academic work benefit the wealthier academic systems and institutions and contribute dramatically to flows of talent from the less well-endowed systems to those with more resources. While money is not the only factor involved—academic freedom, good facilities, and a meritocratic academic culture are also relevant—salaries and remuneration are certainly key elements.

National policies are in some cases formulated to repatriate scholars or attract international talent. Israel provides financial incentives for Israeli scholars willing to return home. Nigeria adjusted salaries to be competitive with other countries in the region and added a generous sabbatical program to allow mobility but in the hope of not losing staff permanently. China has implemented several ambitious programs to entice Chinese academics settled elsewhere to return home. In keeping with a national strategy to become an education hub, Malaysia is offering differential remuneration packages to foreign scholars with an international profile. In no cases, however, have these and other programs yielded major success. As illustrated in this research, the significant divergence in salary and remuneration, as well as in the terms and conditions of academic life, make it quite difficult for such efforts to achieve significant major results.

Conclusion

For most members in the academic profession, this period is not the best of times. Salaries have not kept up either with inflation or with incomes for similarly qualified professionals. The security of tenure or lifetime employment is less assured, and accountability has diminished professional independence and added supervision. A dominant concern is that the best and brightest are no longer attracted to academe.

The dramatic expansion of the part-time labor force to meet the demands of massification has created "second-class" academics, whose salaries and benefits are significantly lower than those of full-time staff. Yet, there are always exceptions to rules, and this research noted anomalies—in Mexico, part-time staff are eligible for tenure; in Canada, part-time staff are often represented by their own union; in Argentina, part-time staff are considered members of the permanent workforce and are often paid on a par with full timers.

The growth of private higher education has further diversified higher education, and there is considerable variation within the private sector. The salaries and working conditions tend to vary between the for-profit and nonprofit segments. On the whole, the rapidly expanding private sector has provided additional employment opportunities for academics. However, with the exception of a few elite private colleges and universities in a small number of countries, the private sector offers only part-time and low-paid teaching positions and supports little, if any, research or knowledge production.

The academic profession, within countries and globally, is divided as never before. The increased diversity of higher education is reflected in a diverse spectrum of employment conditions for scholars. There are sharp distinctions in salaries, contracts, and working conditions by country, institution type, rank, and academic discipline. "Mandarins" (top-level bureaucrats) exist at the top of the system, with many full- and part-time teachers at the bottom. Even more stark variations exist between academics in the developed and developing countries.

The pressures of massification make it quite likely that current inequalities will persist or get worse in many countries, and the many academics worldwide will continue to see deteriorating income and working conditions. In numerous countries, the ratio of full-time to part-time positions is shrinking; rather, part-time positions dominate the academic labor market today. At the same time, the global knowledge economy has created a class of "super professors" who will continue to enjoy better salaries, working conditions, and prospects for mobility.

Without definitive data, it can be estimated that most academics worldwide hold only a first university degree—and thus have limited leverage to improve their salaries or working conditions. The production of PhDs has not been able to keep pace with the enrollment expansion in the developing world, during recent decades.

Yet, some of the countries in this study have increased salaries in order to compensate for buying power lost during years of salary stagnation, to make the academic profession more attractive to young scholars, to encourage productivity, and to stem the tide of brain drain. In some cases, such as India and Malaysia, salary levels have improved overall. In other cases, such as Nigeria, the benefits offered often compensate for low-base salaries and make the total remuneration quite reasonable. In still other systems, there are incentives and rewards for (mostly) research productivity that can lead to a reasonable standard of living.

An essential question was whether academic salaries provided a middle-class income. Based on the data collected for each country study, many countries—including, Argentina, Brazil, Canada, the Czech Republic, France, Germany, India, Italy, Japan, Malaysia, the Netherlands, Nigeria, Norway, South Africa, the United States, and the United Kingdom—reported that full-time faculty salaries, particularly those for senior faculty, did indeed offer a middle-class standard of living. A middle-class income often depends on allocation of additional allowances, incentives, and bonuses or further teaching in "extra sessions"—such as summer school or professional seminars.

Some countries—Ethiopia and Kazakhstan, for example—reported that an academic salary would not provide a comfortable standard of living (and significantly lower than professionals with comparable education), regardless of the level in the hierarchy. In very few countries included in this study were academic salaries competitive with professional positions that required comparable education. Interestingly, the United States, where employment conditions for the academic profession have been among the most attractive in the world, salaries overall are losing ground (Schuster and Finkelstein 2006).

Precise comparison of academic remuneration across 28 countries proved nearly impossible. Each country presented its own idiosyncratic patterns for calculating how academic staff are paid, with complicated systems of supplementary pay and benefits that might be awarded to all academic staff or only a few. In addition, country norms complicated comparison further. Some countries have national health care and national pension plans, while other countries include these elements as compensation. Cases range from systems where salaries were established by the national government to systems where each salary is an individual negotiation between a person and an institution. And, finally, the size of higher education systems across these 28 countries varies enormously, which also distorts comparisons.

Academic contracts, the arrangement for hiring, evaluating, and promoting the profession, have undergone a good deal of change. In general, there is a slow move away from the highly bureaucratic civil service system toward more flexible hiring and contracts. Yet, the data show that the large majority of academics have remarkable career stability despite the varied terms of appointments.

Most generalizations are impossible to make without noting a myriad of exemptions, but the data collected here yield significant insights about the realities of the academic profession globally. It is doubtful that many people pursue an academic career because of the potential income the profession offers. The country experts confirmed that, even where salaries are poor, the academic profession provides social status, independence, and flexibility—with generous vacations and (often) attractive benefits.

With shifting patterns in the global economy, greater investment in higher education, generally, and in academic staff, specifically, is more likely to improve the circumstances of academics in emerging economies such as Brazil, China, India, Malaysia, and South Africa, rather than the "titans" of the last century.

References

Altbach, Philip G., ed. 1996. *The international academic profession: Portraits from 14 countries.* Princeton, NJ: Carnegie Foundation for the Advancement of Teaching.

Altbach, Philip G., ed. 2003. *The decline of the guru: The academic profession in developing and middle-income countries.* New York: Palgrave Macmillan.

Altbach, Philip G., Liz Reisberg, and Laura E. Rumbley. 2010. *Trends in global higher education: Tracking an academic revolution.* Rotterdam, Netherlands: Sense.

Clark, Burton R. 1987. *The academic life: Small worlds, different worlds.* Princeton, NJ: Carnegie Foundation for the Advancement of Teaching.

Heston, Alan, Robert Summers, and Bettina Aten. 2011. Penn World Table Version 7.0, Center for International Comparisons of Production, Income and Prices at the University of Pennsylvania.

Schuster, Jack H., and Martin J. Finkelstein. 2006. *The American faculty: The restructuring of academic work and careers.* Baltimore: Johns Hopkins University Press.

Task Force on Higher Education and Society. 2000. *Higher education in developing countries: Peril and promise.* Washington, DC: World Bank.

2

QUANTITATIVE ANALYSIS

Looking for Commonalities in a Sea of Differences

Gregory Androushchak and Maria Yudkevich

Often when people start to examine how university life is organized, their understanding progresses through several stages. The first stage is understanding that academic cultures are different from the external "real world" of nonacademic life. University faculty and researchers typically operate with different incentives, interests, and remuneration than participants in other sectors of the workforce. In this respect, the academic labor market and academic contracts represent a subsector of the broader traditional labor market; they are more homogeneous and subject to more uniform rules. When examined internationally, it becomes apparent that wage and contract-related practices in the academic world are quite varied, as are policies and opportunities for earning additional income outside the university. Such practices are described in detail in each of the chapters in this book. It is clear that the academic profession today is not only affected by the salary, contract, and remuneration schemes that operate in each country but increasingly by international trends in a globalized academic world.

After reviewing these differences, one begins to look for what items different national practices have in common. Are there typical models? What features do they share? The analysis in this chapter reflects a review of common elements and differences observed in the data collected by this book's 28 country experts. This analysis will summarize and compare several characteristics of contemporary higher education. The focus will include data relating to the academic profession—the percentage of faculty that constitute a total labor force, the workload in terms of students per full-time faculty, and distribution of faculty by academic rank. The analysis of faculty salaries is based on international PPP (purchasing power parity) U.S. dollars, in relation to gross domestic product per capita and the differentiation by academic rank. Finally, the chapter summarizes a survey of these country experts, concerning the importance of different fringe benefits as components of remuneration packages beyond basic salary.

One of the central questions of this analysis was whether the academic profession remains attractive enough to entice and retain talent within different countries. This central issue is broader than whether academic and nonacademic salaries are comparable. Indeed, as the study has shown, academic earnings often include supplemental compensation for extra activities (e.g., teaching overload, research, consultancy, and industry collaborations), as well as nonpecuniary benefits (prestige, social benefits—including health care, long vacation, etc.). In some countries, salary alone will not even provide a middle-class income (allowing for the fact that the middle class is defined differently in each country). In some countries (Mexico and Ethiopia are examples) the basic salary may not support an individual, let alone a family, but provides a professional and social status that can be leveraged to earn additional income by teaching in multiple institutions or through a nonacademic professional activity.

Data Collection and Research Protocol

The data provided by the authors of the case study chapters in this book defined a list of indicators that describe the public and private academic sectors in each country (such as the number of universities, of students, and of faculty). In addition, each expert provided descriptions of the academic hierarchy in their country, defining formal academic ranks. The country experts also collected detailed information on average faculty salaries by academic rank, which presented the unique opportunity to explore income differentiation in academia across 28 countries. Wage figures were retrieved either from official statistical information, publications related to faculty remuneration, or interviews and/or surveys. In some cases, reliable data were quite difficult to obtain, and the researchers delivered the best ones available. The information is provided in terms of average monthly salaries of faculty on average and by academic rank.

Data were requested from the 2008 calendar year or the 2008/09 academic year—taking into account the two-year data-collection lag common in most countries, although accepted the statistics for the most-recent year available. Inflation in these countries was rather moderate (not exceeding 8.5% per year). Thus, the salary data are overall comparable after conversion to international U.S. dollars by PPP exchange rates.

Our choice of PPP exchange rates for conversion of academic salaries is due to the fact that it provides the best basis for direct comparison of salaries, by tying them to their purchasing power. Other choices that had been considered included real exchange rates and the *Economist*'s Big Mac index. The former choice—real exchange rates—is suitable to estimate nominal differences in academic salaries and does not take into account the amount of real goods and services available in the economy. For example, in recent years the official Russian exchange rate in terms of rubles per dollar is 75 percent higher than a PPP exchange rate (that takes into account the availability and relatively low prices of locally produced goods). So, if the official exchange rate was used, that term would understate significantly the relatively low salaries of Russian faculty. Having that in mind and also taking into account the fact that the previous study of faculty salaries, published by the Boston College Center for International Higher Education,[1] used PPP U.S. dollars in 2008, here that methodology will be worked with to ensure comparability of salary data.

To formulate generalizations about fringe benefits and to put academic remuneration into a more complete context, each country expert was asked to report the common types of fringe benefits (e.g., health plans, coverage of housing costs, provision of low interest loans, paid vacations, provision of retirement plans) and to estimate their importance as a component of faculty contracts. However, since it is possible that neither academic salary nor fringe benefits are the most important sources of income for some faculty, the experts provided additional data with regard to other sources of income available to faculty in their countries. Assessments about the relative significance of academic salary, fringe benefits, and supplemental earnings were made by country experts based on their knowledge of the local academic system.

This research project reflects data and analysis primarily from public universities. Private higher education is rapidly expanding globally, and some analysis of private universities is included. However, information and statistics from the private sector are generally less available. Yet, it is observed that salaries and working conditions in the emerging private sector globally are, with some exceptions, inferior to those in public universities, and that employment security, fringe benefits, and other factors lag behind public institutions.

This analysis is based on two additional sources of statistical information. The share of faculty in the total labor force can be estimated on the number of faculty provided by the country experts and the total labor force data from the World Bank.[2] To examine faculty salaries in local context, the GDP per capita can be used, as reported by the Center for International Comparisons at the University of Pennsylvania.[3] The year of data provided by the country experts was matched with the data from the latter two sources for the same year. However, for countries where data more recent than 2009 were reported, they were matched with the 2009 data from these external sources.

Comparative Overview of Higher Education Systems

Discussing faculty remuneration requires placing the analysis within the context of a higher-education system. In this respect, the situation varies substantially from country to country. For example, countries differ by the total number of degree-granting universities (from about 30 in smaller countries, such as Latvia and Saudi Arabia, to almost 2,500 in Brazil, and 3,000 in Mexico), and by the size and role of the private sector (from no private universities in Australia to about three-fourths of all the universities in Brazil and Mexico).

The major challenge of this research, and of most comparative studies for that matter, is finding identical variables to compare. Each of the 28 countries defines and organizes its higher-education sector differently. In some cases, higher education includes universities and institutes of applied science, which tend to be more technically or employment oriented—as in the case of Germany and the Netherlands. India's system of postsecondary education is divided between universities that provide graduate instruction and colleges that teach mainly at the first-degree level. Contracts, working conditions, qualifications, and salaries generally vary by sector. Because of the diversity within each country as well as between countries, quantitative averages and generalizations have limitations that should be kept in mind.

Faculty in Different Types of Universities

The size of the public higher-education sector and the number of people employed vary substantially from country to country (see Figure 2.1). China is by far ahead of all the other countries in respect to the total number of public university teachers—more than twice the number in the United States, second in the list, and nearly three times the number of faculty in Russia, which is third on that list.

No correlation exists between the number of institutions and the number of academic staff employed to teach in any given country, as there are no national or international norms for class size or teaching load. While in some countries teaching loads for each rank are determined by legislation, in others they are subject to individual bargaining and determined by individual contracts. Student-to-faculty ratios also vary considerably, by sector and institution type.

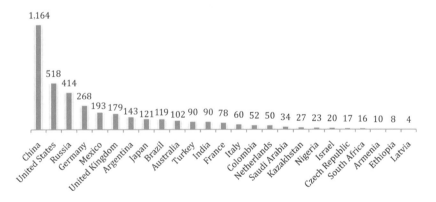

Figure 2.1 Number* of total faculty in public degree-granting universities.

Source: As reported by country experts and based on national statistics.

Note: Data for total faculty for Canada (41,000 full-time faculty), Malaysia (22,000 full-time faculty), and Norway (11,000 full-time faculty) are unavailable.

*Numbers equal thousands.

The private sector includes both for-profit and nonprofit institutions, where salary level, teaching loads, the number of contact hours within an academic program, and class size vary a great deal. According to the data that have been reported by the country experts, the countries with the greatest number of faculty employed in the private sector are the United States, China, Brazil, and Japan.

Despite the central role of universities in a modern knowledge society, the academic sector constitutes less than 1 percent of the total labor force in these case study countries (see Figure 2.2). The countries with the largest percentages are Armenia and Russia, closely followed by Germany and Norway. In the rest of the countries, this indicator is close to 0.4 percent.

The ratio of students per teacher is another important characteristic of higher-education institutions. Generally assumed, the lower the ratio, the more attention each student gets and, subsequently, the better the quality of educational services provided. Figures 2.3 and 2.4 show the ratio of the total number of students to full-time faculty in degree-granting universities in public and private universities, respectively. Conclusions from these figures should be made with caution because of variations in the way countries report data and how each country defines full-time faculty. For example, in many countries, PhD students are part-time faculty and play a significant role in higher education; they are often not included when these ratios are calculated.

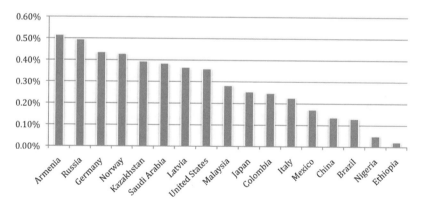

Figure 2.2 Percentage that full-time faculty in degree-granting universities constitute in total labor force.

Source: Calculations based on total number of full-time faculty in degree-granting universities as reported by country experts.

Note: The calculations are based on national statistics and World Bank data on total labor force; data on total number of full-time faculty in degree-granting universities for Canada, Czech Republic, France, India, Israel, Netherlands, South Africa, Turkey, and United Kingdom are unavailable.

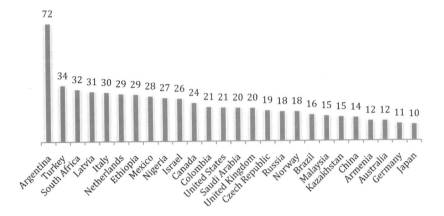

Figure 2.3 Number of students per full-time faculty in public universities.

Source: Calculations based on total number of full-time faculty in degree-granting public universities and total number of students in degree-granting public universities as reported by country experts based on national statistics.

Note: Data either on total number of full-time faculty or on total number of students in degree-granting public universities for France and India are unavailable.

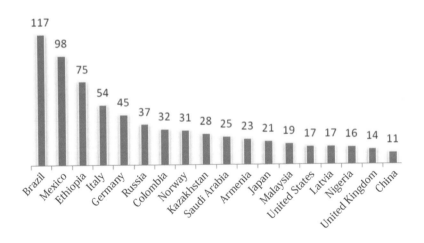

Figure 2.4 Number of students per full-time faculty in private universities.

Source: Calculations based on total number of full-time faculty in degree-granting private universities and total number of students in degree-granting private universities reported by country experts, based on national statistics.

Note: Data either on total number of full-time faculty or on total number of students in degree-granting private universities for Argentina, Australia, Canada, Czech Republic, France, India, Israel, Netherlands, South Africa, and Turkey are unavailable.

Academic Hierarchies

Countries differ significantly in the way the academic hierarchy is structured (see Figure 2.5). In some countries, it is rather flat, and there are just three levels (as in India, Italy, or the United States). In others, there can be up to six hierarchical levels (e.g., in Australia or Ethiopia). Differences also reflect whether a country includes PhD students and part-time lecturers in the academic profession. People in these positions may be considered to be part of the academic hierarchy, but in some countries they are considered staff.

In many systems, while universities may not have the autonomy or flexibility to increase salaries for better performing faculty members, they can use promotion of higher academic ranks to increase compensation. That is a case in Russia. In contrast, in some countries, where there is more freedom and funding (as in the United States), productivity and teaching effectiveness can be rewarded. In these cases, the system of academic ranks tends to be flatter.

Bearing these differences in mind, for the efficiency of comparison, this research has organized positions into a top and bottom and combined the remaining ranks into a middle group. Splitting faculty ranks into three levels highlights important differences between higher education systems in different countries (see Figure 2.6). For example, in Italy and Norway the distribution of faculty among top, middle, and lower ranks is virtually equal. In others, the middle level comprises the majority of positions (e.g., Argentina, China, Russia, or Germany),

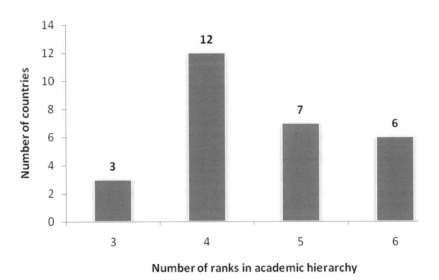

Figure 2.5 Number of ranks in academic hierarchy in the countries studied.
Source: Calculations based on data as reported by country experts.

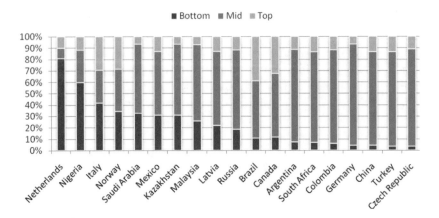

Figure 2.6 Distribution of faculty by academic ranks.★

Source: Calculations based on data as reported by country experts.

Note: Data for the countries not included are not available.

★Top-rank faculty refer to the highest-rank faculty; bottom-rank faculty refer to the lowest-rank faculty. The only exception is Brazil, for which bottom-rank faculty refer to the lowest and second-lowest rank—due to insignificantly small proportion of those in the lowest rank.

and only few make it to the top level (professor status). In some countries, almost all academics reach the top level in the course of their career, while in others, only a small proportion reach the rank of full professor. The data shown in Figure 2.6 may reflect not only a large percentage of academic staff concentrated in the middle of the hierarchy but may also be the result of a hierarchy with many intermediate steps. In China, for example, there are so many levels in the academic hierarchy that academic staff can progress along the ladder for many years, without reaching the level of full professor.

Faculty Remuneration

One of the central questions of this study is how academic remuneration is correlated to socioeconomic development of a country; there is a correlation between faculty salaries to gross domestic product (GDP) per capita. Faculty compensation is also compared to the remuneration of professionals outside academia with comparable education and qualifications.

Separate comparisons were made regarding GDP for academic staff at the top of the hierarchy and those at the beginning of their career. Also, there is a positive correlation between the economic level of the country (based on GDP per capita) and compensation for academic staff at both the lowest and highest

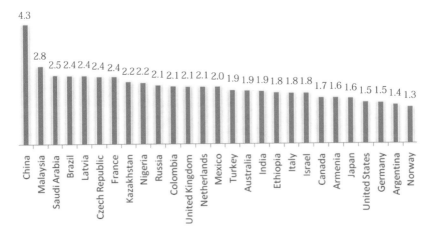

Figure 2.7 Ratio of top- to bottom-rank faculty salaries.
Source: Calculations based on data as reported by country experts.

levels of the salary hierarchy. At the same time, while average academic salaries are positively related to GDP per capita, a positive correlation also exists between GDP per capita and salary gap between high- and low-rank faculty.

The progression to better salaries varies enormously from country to country, with widening ratios from the bottom of the scale to the top in some countries— creating large gaps between top- and low-ranking faculty (see Figure 2.7). For example, in China, salaries quadruple from the lowest to the top level of the salary scale. In contrast, the top of the scale in the United States and Norway reflects smaller increases for academic staff, as they progress in the hierarchy. This probably reflects the fact that salaries are not determined strictly by the academic rank.

Direct comparison of academic salaries in PPP U.S. dollars reveals that in the countries with a higher level of economic development, as defined by GDP per capita, on average academics should expect to earn more than in the countries with a lower level of economic development. However, higher nominal salaries do not necessarily mean that they permit a higher level or a better quality of consumption. For example, particular items of consumption in different countries may vary in cost due to differences in supply, tax regime, and other factors. So, to assess the relative well-being of faculty, as compared to average employees' well-being in the country, one needs to analyze relative remuneration—as compared to any measure of income differentiation across countries.

The best choice would be to use average salaries across the countries. However, due to differences in definitions of average salary, as reported in national statistics and data availability, another option is relevant. By one of the definitions, GDP

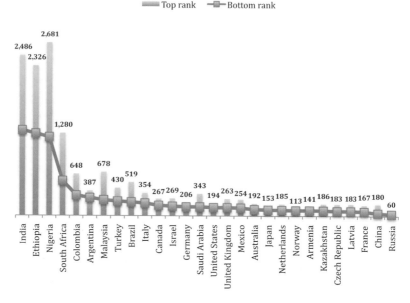

Figure 2.8 Relative academic salaries in degree-granting public universities (ratio of yearly faculty salaries to GDP per capita), percent.
Source: Calculations based on data as reported by country experts.

can be viewed as a measure of value added (i.e., output) of a country. By greatly simplifying the matter, it may be admitted that value added is the sum of incomes received by all the economic agents in the economy. Therefore, differences in GDP per capita across countries capture the differences in average incomes. Hence, relating yearly academic salaries to GDP per capita provides a simple measure of relative academic salaries that shows actual well-being of faculty in different countries.

Relative academic salaries vary from country to country (see Figure 2.8). In most countries—Russia is one exception—the annual wage of top-ranking professors exceeds GDP (sometimes threefold), and the wages of employees at the beginning of an academic career are significantly lower than GDP.

Structure of Salaries and Fringe Benefits

In most of the university systems studied here, fringe benefits are offered in addition to salary. The benefits offered most frequently included health plans, housing (use of a university-owned residence, mortgage assistance, etc.), low-interest loans, and paid vacations. In most of the countries, university teachers obtain retirement benefits and paid vacations (as would employees in other sectors), because these benefits are stipulated in law. However, there are some notable exceptions from that rule; for example, in the United States, paid summer vacations are not included explicitly in academic contracts; faculty are generally paid on a 12-month basis but are not expected to work during the summer months. In 86 percent of the countries, pension contributions are also required by law.

A number of countries offered benefits related to housing—providing a residence or a housing subsidy or attractive terms on mortgage, which is often important for younger faculty. On the whole, the country experts reported that benefits are rarely effective as a means of attracting the best professionals. Figure 2.9 indicates which benefits are offered by what percentage of the countries.

As mentioned previously, an academic salary does not provide a middle-class income for university teachers in many countries. The analysis highlighted several

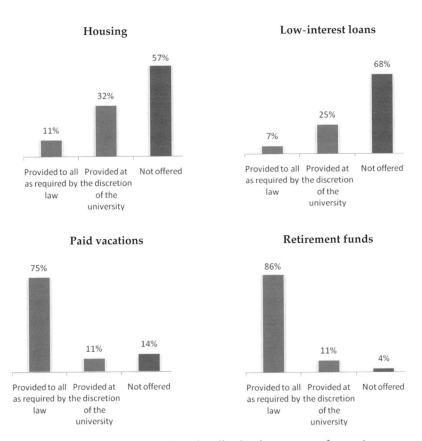

Figure 2.9 Supplementary contract benefits offered and percentage of countries awarding them.

Source: Calculations based on data as reported by country experts.

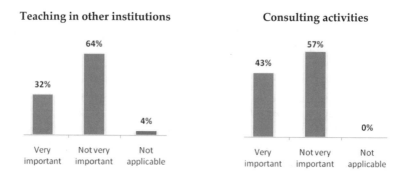

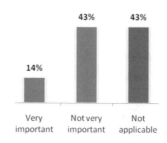

Figure 2.10 Different sources of additional income for faculty, by percentage of countries surveyed.

Source: Calculations based on data as reported by country experts.

common sources of additional income. Figure 2.10 shows the different kinds of income-producing activities and indicates (by percentage) how many of the countries see academic staff pursuing additional income.

Conclusion

When this research was initiated, it was considered that by collecting comparable data, we could compare countries on the basis of a universal data-collection methodology. However, by the end of the project it was realized that the task was much more difficult. Basic characteristics of academic contracts vary significantly from country to country, making comparisons very difficult, even when the terminology is the same. For example, the concept of "teaching loads" can be defined and calculated in different ways. In some places, it is common to talk about the weekly teaching load and in others about an annual load. Sometimes a teaching load only includes contact hours; in other cases it also includes the hours spent preparing for class and grading examinations and papers. Nor is it always clear what is meant by academic staff, whether this includes doctoral students or lecturers. Likewise, it is not always obvious what constitutes "full time" or "full time equivalent."

Another example, perhaps more important, is related to the discussion of tenure—an essential element of academic contracts in the United States, Canada, and Australia—although in all three countries the proportion of the faculty enjoying tenure-track career paths has declined. Tenure, as defined, represents a type of contract that guarantees job security and a certain level of academic freedom. The initial assumption was that all countries would fall into one of two groups—where some form of tenure exists or where faculty do not have an assurance of permanence. However, the situation is more ambiguous. While some educational systems award tenure as defined, other countries incorporate faculty into the civil service by providing job security similar to tenure but not necessarily including the other benefits of a tenure system. Job security is a critical element in the comparison of contracts and working conditions, but it proved difficult to determine where and to what extent this was assured.

Many of the differences discovered may be attributed to the diversity in the objectives, necessities, and priorities of various education systems—inevitably shaping contracts and norms. In some systems or institutions, teaching is emphasized and research plays a less significant role. In these cases, research plays little if any role in performance evaluation or promotion. In other systems and institutions, where research is a priority, productivity is critical to career advancement. Expectations of academic staff vary accordingly and are reflected in both formal contracts and unspecified expectations.

Academic contracts and the expectations of academic staff, to a certain degree, reflect academic culture. Informal academic norms are often as influential as the provisions of formal contracts. In some countries, contracts are more specific than in others.

There is a correlation between a country's economic level and faculty salaries. For the most part, richer countries provide better conditions for universities and tend to reward academic staff more generously. At the same time, the data do not allow broader generalizations about the connections between the development of a nation's universities, national welfare, or the society's sustainable development. Additional materials and empirical data collected during the project are available at the project's webpage: http://acarem.hse.ru.

The assumption when this research began was that we would develop fairly clear patterns of salaries, remuneration, and contracts and that common denominators would emerge. It was discovered, however, that there is a great deal of complexity regarding total salary packages and that only limited generalizations are possible. Some cross-national patterns emerged, but it is clear that the realities of the academic profession remain embedded in national circumstances and result in increasingly varied patterns of salaries, remuneration, and the terms and conditions of academic work.

Notes

1. L. E. Rumbley, I. F. Pacheco, and P. G. Altbach, *International Comparison of Academic Salaries: An Exploratory Study* (Chestnut Hill, MA: Center for International Higher Education, Boston College, 2008).
2. http://data.worldbank.org/indicator.
3. http://pwt.econ.upenn.edu/.

PART 2

Case Studies

3

LABOR CONTRACTS AND ECONOMIC INCENTIVES FOR ARGENTINE UNIVERSITY FACULTY

Ana García de Fanelli

Salary and benefit decisions at public universities are fixed by collective bargaining between the faculty union and the Council of Public University rector. Wages are determined by the category, the workload, and seniority. Benefits include health plans, paid vacations, and retirement funds. The merit-pay system exists only at a few elite private universities and at public universities, as bonuses for faculty members who conduct research activities. Thanks to increased wages in real terms from 2004 to 2010, faculty with full-time posts at public universities—around 22 percent of the professors and 7 percent of the junior teaching assistants—enjoy a middle-income standard of living. Non-full-time public university faculty earn their living thanks to professional and academic activities at other public or private organizations or are self-employed as, say, consultants and physicians. Part-time faculty enjoy the same conditions as full-time faculty regarding their labor contracts (stable positions) and fringe benefits. Academic salaries in private institutions are determined via individual negotiation; those with stable contracts also enjoy fringe benefits.

Overview of Higher Education

The Argentine higher education sector, which awards undergraduate and graduate degrees, is composed of 107 public and private universities and almost 1.7 million students, 80 percent of whom are concentrated in the public sector. The undergraduate enrollment level is quite developed, while the graduate level is relatively incipient, accounting for only about 6 percent of the total (see Table 3.1). This overall trend is a by-product of the Spanish-French academic organization of the curricula, with lengthy professional first degrees awarded by universities. As a consequence, academic posts are mainly available at the undergraduate level,

Table 3.1 Argentine university sector, 2008

University Sector*	Undergraduate students	Graduate students	Institutions
Total	1,600,522	97,939	107
Public	1,283,482	79,678**	48
Private	317,040	18,261	59

Source: Ministry of Education 2008.
*Includes university institutes. In the private sector, the figure includes one international university and one foreign university
**Official data plus the estimation of graduate students of Universidad de Buenos Aires (UBA)

unlike professors for the master's or doctoral degrees, who are generally hired on an hourly based contract.

Another important characteristic of the university sector is the high concentration of students and public and private institutions in the metropolitan area of Buenos Aires—the country's wealthiest region. This concentration enables faculty to combine their professional activities in the public or the private sectors with part-time teaching.

Public and private universities are quite heterogeneous at the institutional and school levels. Within the public university sector, there are few research-intensive schools (or *facultades*)—most of which target the basic and agronomic sciences—at some traditional institutions. All the others are primarily teaching schools, devoted mainly to professional training.

Like the public sector, the private university sector is also quite varied. The majority are comprised of teaching-oriented institutions, devoted to professional fields, with faculty hired on an hourly basis. Also, a few elite-type private universities show a much higher than average proportion of full-time posts and faculty with PhDs.

Part-time faculty posts were designed to cover increased demand in professional fields (e.g., law, accountancy, medicine). They enabled these professors to maintain their professional jobs while carrying out teaching activities. During the 1980s and 1990s, as a consequence of stringent public budgets, part-time posts also became a mechanism to hire professors at lower costs in a context of enrollment expansion. Thus, public universities offered few opportunities to work as full-time faculty. Moreover, the average academic wages at that moment were quite low. This context contributed to Argentina's "brain drain" problem. An estimated 6,500 Argentine researchers resided abroad (especially in the United States) in 2003. These researchers represented about 18 percent of the total number of researchers residing in Argentina (Luchilo 2011).

The circumstances changed dramatically from 2000 to 2008. The public-sector enrollment increased an average rate of 1.5 percent, quite below the private sector average rate of 5.8 percent (Ministry of Education 2008). The financial situation of public universities also changed. From 2004, public university education expenditures climbed from 0.48 to 0.87 percent of the gross domestic product in 2009, while the public university expenditure per student increased from (an estimated) US$1,382 to US$3,254 in PPP (purchasing power parity).

Academic Labor Contracts

While some similarities exist, academic labor contracts do vary between the public and the private sectors.

Labor Contracts at Public Universities

Table 3.2 presents the level of state or university regulation in academic personnel decision making. Direct state regulation refers to a set of rules, such as those defined by the 1995 Higher Education Act. The article of the 1995 act regarding human-resource management only affects the public university sector. Indirect regulation refers to government influence on faculty and organizational behavior about certain academic matters through the use of quality assurance (accreditation and evaluation standards) and funding instruments (incentives, rewards, and total amount of funds). All these regulations impact especially on public universities, whereas the quality-assurance mechanisms also exert some indirect influence on private ones.

The Argentine constitution recognizes the academic and institutional autonomy and administrative autarchy of public universities, enshrined in their individual

Table 3.2 Argentine government and national university regulations on academic personnel issues

Issues	Government Regulation		Self-regulation (National universities)
	Direct	Indirect	
Number of posts and types of contracts	+	+	+
Staff classification system	−	−	+
Hiring process	+	+	+
Working hours	−	+	+
Allocation of teaching/ research activities	−	−	+
Appraisal systems	−	−	+
Moonlighting	−	+	+
Salaries	−	+	+

Source: Based on the 1995 Higher Education Act (Ministry of Education 2010).

charters or statutes. Thus, public universities control the serious matters concerning academic contracts and enjoy the constitutional status of *autonomic organizations*. Among other things, this status implies that academic employment should be considered *public employment* under the rules of each university statute.

Faculty can be hired on a full- (40 hours weekly), half- (20 hours weekly), or part-time (10 hours weekly) basis. Full-time professors conduct research in addition to their undergraduate teaching activities. Half-time faculty are usually hired with the expectation that their primary activity will be teaching and their secondary activity will be research. Finally, part-time faculty only teach, with the exception of those part-time faculty that also belong to the research career of the National Council for Scientific and Technological Research.

In 2008, full-time faculty at public universities represented only 13.1 percent of the total (see Table 3.3).

An essential element to align faculty objectives with those of the university is obviously the level and structure of the remuneration that they receive. However, in certain types of labor markets, like the ones that prevail for professors at most Argentine public universities, pay is tied to rank within the hierarchical structure of the chair model. So, promotion opportunities are just as relevant as monetary rewards within the incentive structure.

Faculty positions with a full-, half-, or part-time workload usually comprise two broad categories: professors (full, associate, and assistant professors) and junior teaching assistants (senior assistant, assistant, and, in some cases, volunteer advanced students). Table 3.3 shows the distribution of academic posts in these positions and their workload.

Table 3.3 Argentine Faculty Occupational Structure,* National Universities, 2008 (%)

Rank	Total rank	Gender			Workload			
		Female	Male	Total	Full-time	Half-time	Part-time	Total
Professors	38.7	41.8	58.2	100	21.8	23.5	54.7	100
Full professor	11.5	35.7	64.3	100	24.7	25.9	49.4	100
Associate professor	4.0	39.1	60.9	100	34.9	20.2	44.9	100
Assistant professor	23.3	45.2	54.8	100	18.1	22.9	59.1	100
Junior teaching staff	61.3	52.0	48.0	100	7.6	18.0	74.5	100
Senior assistant	27.3	52.2	47.8	100	12.3	26.8	60.9	100
Assistant	26.6	54.2	45.8	100	4.8	13.9	81.4	100
Teaching assistant	7.3	42.8	57.2	100	0.0	0.0	100	100
Total	100	48.0	52.0	100	13.1	20.1	66.8	100

Source: Ministry of Education 2008.

*Corresponds to faculty posts, not to persons. N = 142,767 faculty posts

The only prerequisites for hiring faculty on a full-, half-, or part-time basis are that the candidates hold at least an undergraduate degree and are qualified for holding a public office. Some universities also state that candidates must meet a minimum seniority when applying to each category. In general, holding a PhD degree and having seniority in the previous rank position are major factors for upgrading a position.

The pyramid of academic ranks presents a huge base and a narrow top. About 6 in 10 faculty are junior teaching assistants. Moreover, 58 percent of the professors rank in the lowest category: assistant professors. These data document the lack of academic mobility in the public university academic market. Another characteristic of this pyramid is that male faculty are overrepresented at the professoriate rank, although the participation of women in the public university labor market matches that of men (see Table 3.3).

The traditional career pattern consists of starting as a volunteer advanced student or directly as an assistant, transitioning to the position of senior assistant, then to assistant professor, and finally to the position of full or associate professor. Nonetheless, in the pyramid chair model that predominates at most Argentine public universities, few posts are available at the top (full and associate professors).

According to the legal framework of the traditional public universities, progression from one of these positions to the other (despite the workload) is based on an open competitive procedure and must be renewed after a fixed period of time. Academic posts are announced publicly and applicants are evaluated by the competition jury. Faculty appointed through this modus operandi are called "regular" or "ordinary" faculty. A dismissal proceeding involving a faculty member in a regular position is rare and only justified based on just and sufficient cause.

Nonetheless, this procedure is difficult to carry out—owing to financial, bureaucratic, and political issues. Thus, the real functioning of the faculty career takes the form of an informal internal labor market managed by chairholders and other university authorities. Barely 40 percent of the professorial positions and 29 percent of the junior teaching assistant positions at public universities in 2004 were obtained via an open competitive procedure (García de Fanelli 2008). Hence, a large proportion of faculty are currently employed as interims, under contracts that are generally renewed automatically once a year or every six months. Although these are not formal permanent contracts, these interim agreements enable faculty members to be promoted to higher ranks should the position become available and until the open competitive procedure can take place. They also receive social security benefits and health insurance. Since this process seldom leads to the loss of the position; interim professors, especially chairholders, also enjoy a de facto tenure.

The stable (tenure-like) positions, both de jure obtained through open competitive contests and de facto achieved via the interim contracts, usually correspond to the undergraduate level. At most schools of public universities, the graduate teaching activity is carried out through special individual contracts with a fixed duration and wages, according to the number of hours devoted to the teaching activity. The appointment procedure is generally up to the director of the graduate program and its academic committee. The candidates must have a master's or a PhD degree, be formally approved by the school council, and be authorized by the university council.

According to the 1995 Higher Education Law, the government can impose only two restrictions directly on academic contracts at public universities: first, at least 70 percent of the total faculty must be appointed through open competitive contests and, second, faculty must have attained the highest educational credential of the level they teach. Additionally, future faculty should have a PhD background. Nonetheless, conformity to rules is not easy to monitor or feasible to control. In contrast, the state exerts influence mainly through indirect mechanisms: definitions of salary scales in collective bargaining agreements, standards and criteria employed in institutional evaluation and accreditation of undergraduate and graduate programs, and the total amount of public funding allocated to public universities.

Regarding quality-assurance impact on academic contracts, standards and criteria used in accreditation reviews and in institutional evaluation strongly consider full-time posts, appointments via competitive contests, and faculty with PhD degrees. As a consequence, these mechanisms influence public and private organizational behavior.

Finally, the financing that the government allocates to each public university, as a lump sum, defines the budget constraints on public universities' ability to carry out their human resource policies. Note that nearly 85 percent of these funds are distributed to cover salaries for faculty and other staff.

The government also affects public university salaries via special rewards, like the lump sum faculty receive if they also conduct research, as well as recently granting bonuses to those who have PhD and master's degrees.

In sum, each public university has total control over matters concerning the personnel. However, the government influences the academic contracts directly via legal regulations—although it lacks the power to enforce them—and indirectly, through signals, incentives, and rewards produced by the quality-assurance and funding instruments. The quality-assurance instruments influence both the public and private university sectors.

Labor Contracts at Private Universities

Like the public sector, the private one is also quite heterogeneous. Of the 59 private universities and university institutes, only a few fit the elite type—with increased tuition and fees, a greater proportion of full-time professors and full-time students, research activities, higher-quality facilities, and updated libraries.

Private universities depend almost entirely on student tuition and fees and private funding (donors, the church, firms). Some private institutions also receive public institutional grants as research centers, and their professors compete for public research funds.

Information about faculty contracts in the private university sector as a whole is unavailable. In particular, no global data exist on the proportion of faculty by workload. Nonetheless, data gathered from institutional assessment reports and some interviews with experts in higher education show that private universities generally hire their academic staff under two main types of contracts. First, a group of faculty, especially but not only those with full-time contracts, is hired under a wage relationship—that is, stability regulated by private law and the inclusion of social benefits like a health plan, paid vacation, and retirement plans. These contracts usually provide faculty with some stability for a minimum of three years. Second, another group of faculty, particularly those hired on an hourly basis, has a fixed-term contract, falling under the legal form of service contracts or an autonomous relationship. Under a fixed-term contract, the professor has no right to any social benefits or severance pay.

Faculty positions in the private sector usually comprise the categories of professors and junior teaching assistants, although the latter represent a smaller proportion than at public universities. The hiring process is also quite diverse and fragmented. The appointment procedure at private universities does not usually follow an open competition mechanism. The decision is generally taken by the governing board upon the recommendation of the faculty staff based on the candidate's academic and professional qualifications and personal contacts (Del Bello, Osvaldo, and Jiménez 2007).

Full-time academic contracts generally imply that faculty should teach and conduct research. However, this depends on the relevance of the research or teaching activities within the institutional mission. At elite-type private institutions, for example, the selection mechanisms employed consider the candidate's research activity quite important, thus reflecting his or her academic background and publications. On the contrary, hourly faculty are only hired to carry out teaching activities (Rabossi 2008).

Academic Remunerations

As with academic labor contracts, the wage determination and its structure vary between the public and private sectors.

Wage Determination at Public Universities

The faculty at Argentine public universities generally support a structured remuneration system. In this labor market, wages are associated with the academic position and seniority and not with individual productivity. In particular, faculty are not financially rewarded for their teaching performance. Additionally, since wages are mainly funded via public budgets, institutions do not have the latitude to offer better salaries to attract accomplished scholars.

The mechanism for fixing salaries, a responsibility of the national government until 1992, was modified with the introduction of the collective bargaining procedure in 1998. However, it has acquired special importance since 2004, when this procedure was put back in place after the collective-bargaining agreement had been interrupted for a period of almost six years.

Overall, a global agreement is first signed between the public university faculty union and the Council of Public University rectors with the participation of the Ministry of Education. Afterward, other direct negotiations are held between each university trade union and the university authority (the university council and the rector). Although all faculty unions negotiate the acceptance of a basic common wage structure, the final negotiation takes place between each university authority and the corresponding faculty union. Some new smaller public universities have introduced new remuneration structures.

Salaries are based on rank, workload, and especially seniority (see Table 3.4). For example, full professors with a full-time workload and medium seniority earned AR$10,145 (approximately, US$2,500) monthly in October 2010, whereas professors in the same category and seniority but with a part-time workload earned only AR$2,170 (approximately, US$500) monthly. Seniority could mean a 120 percent increase over the basic salary after 24 years of work, independently of the rank (professor or assistant).

Table 3.4 Argentine faculty average monthly gross salary (medium seniority), October 2010

Rank and workload	Argentine Pesos
Full-time Faculty	
Full professor	10.145
Associate professor	9.214
Assistant professor	8.252
Senior assistant	7.228
Assistant	6.205
Part-time Faculty	
Full professor	2.170
Associate professor	1.971
Assistant professor	1.765
Senior assistant	1.546
Assistant	1.327

Source: Ministry of Education 2011.

Note: These data do not include additional bonuses, such as research incentives, extra month's salary, zones or specific union agreements established at certain public universities.

In October 2010, US$1.00 was equivalent to AR$3.96.

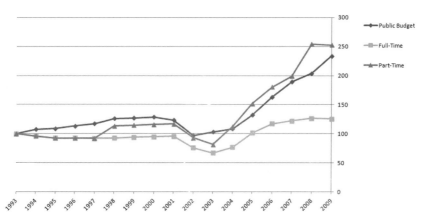

Figure 3.1 Budget trends in public universities and in full-time and part-time full professor salaries.

Source: Ministry of Education 2008, 2011.

Note: The budget and salary trends are measured in real terms; the influence of price changes from the base year (1993 = 100) has been removed, using the Consumer Price Index.

Non-full-time faculty earn their living thanks to professional and academic activities at other public or private organizations or self-employment as consultants, physicians, or other experts.

Unlike the aforementioned homogenization procedure to set the faculty pay scale, other processes contribute to income differentiation. First, the Program of Incentives for Research-Teachers offers professors and junior teaching staff at public universities extra income if it is proved that they not only teach but also do research. To be favored by this program, faculty should first be categorized as "research teachers." To achieve this status, faculty apply for periodic evaluation procedures carried out by external judges. These judges evaluate publications, teaching activities, and other relevant academic background. Faculty are categorized on five levels from the lowest (5) to the highest (1). Additionally, faculty must demonstrate that they have been awarded competitive public research grants to carry out the research project. Hence, these research awards are not permanent but depend on the possibility of obtaining research grants. Around 20 percent of the total faculty at public universities receive this bonus (Ministry of Education 2008), and it represents between 5 and 10 percent of the total monthly fixed wage.

Second, many professors teach at the graduate level on an hourly contract basis, receiving on average better hourly wages than at the undergraduate level. Finally, faculty earn extra income from external activities, such as consulting and technical assistance to businesses, the government, social organizations, communities, and individuals.

Income from graduate courses and the external consulting and research activities vary greatly according to the field of study. Business professors, economists, and engineers tend to benefit most. Unfortunately, none of these external funds—including the Program of Incentives—affects fringe benefits, especially retirement and seniority. This means that the pension or the seniority benefit only takes into account the regular wage an undergraduate faculty member receives.

An additional fringe benefit was incorporated in 2010. Faculty retirement benefits now amount to 82 percent of the average real wage earned during their last 10 years of teaching.

Regarding the wage evolution, academic wages increased in real terms from 2004 to 2009 (see Figure 3.1). This situation explains why those faculty with full-time posts at public universities—around 22 percent of the professors and 7 percent of the junior teaching assistants—enjoy a middle-income standard of living.

Part-time salaries have risen far more rapidly than full-time salaries owing to the influence of the faculty unions, which had demanded a solution to the previous distortion in the remuneration structure. According to the 2003 remuneration structure, full-time faculty earned six times more than part-time faculty. Full-time faculty work 40 hours per week, and part-time faculty work 10 hours per week. Thus, full-time faculty work four times more hours.

The current public university structures of remuneration present some features that act as a disincentive to good quality teaching and research activities. First, the average salary levels are compressed in relative terms; only a 1.6 difference exists in earnings between the lowest and the top academic positions. Second, as wage determination in professional fields does not take into account the opportunity costs of working in other private or public settings, there are fewer economic incentives for the most competent professionals to remain at the public university.

This last finding highlights the importance of comparing the mean hourly faculty wages with those in the labor market, regarding a similar educational background. An augmented wage equation was estimated to determine the hourly wage premium paid to university professionals employed outside the university sector for the period of 1996–2003 (Groisman and García de Fanelli 2009). The main finding was that the faculty's hourly mean wage was lower than that of others employed with a similar educational background, as controlled by the traditional variables of this type of income function (age, gender, position in the household, and occupational category). The results of the regression confirmed that the hourly income of university faculty was lower than the average for other relevant university graduate groups used for comparison. The estimated average gap between the hourly income of university faculty and the earnings of other professional workers was 20 to 25 percent. This penalty was higher in fields like accounting, engineering, and law and lower for human-science fields. Also, the penalty increases when compared with university graduates who work in high-skilled jobs, such as senior-management positions. These findings call attention to the probable impact wages have on the quality of higher-education teaching as they do not take into account the opportunity costs of faculty in the professional fields.

Wage Determination at Private Universities

Academic salaries in private institutions are determined via individual negotiation; unlike the faculty remuneration structure at public universities, seniority is not a component within the wage structure.

Some private universities offer faculty bonuses based on their research and teaching productivity. A study conducted at a *research-oriented* private university and another *teaching-oriented* one revealed that both implemented an incentive structure aligned with their core missions. Wages of full-time professors at the research-oriented private university reflect productivity and opportunity costs and show major salary differences. These elite private universities offer better salaries to attract the best professors. Faculty receiving bonuses at the teaching-oriented private university are assessed for their teaching commitment to the institution as well as their teaching ability and student-teacher relationship. That is, these universities value loyalty to the pedagogical model (Rabossi 2008).

Conclusion

Among the main challenges Argentina faces in the design of a new incentive structure to align the university objectives with those of the faculty, three issues deserve special attention. The first is whether the career structure for recruitment and promotion of the faculty should be based on an open competition or on an internal competence evaluation if the objective is to improve quality, efficiency, and guarantee academic freedom. This also implies revising the rigid chair system to create more open alternatives to promotion of unfilled professorships.

The second issue is to analyze how best to pay faculty so as to appropriately motivate teaching and research activities. In particular, one concern is whether to maintain the prevailing structured salary scheme or to introduce some merit-pay system based on faculty productivity. The merit-pay system also poses a dilemma. It is far easier to measure research than teaching productivity. Merit pay that rests mostly on research productivity can cause adverse specialization—that is, faculty focusing more on publishing than on teaching. The compensation scheme to resolve this problem depends on whether the university considers teaching and research as substitute or complementary activities.

Finally, at most of the public universities, no explicit faculty management policy exists to align faculty objectives with those of the university organization. As Paul Milgrom and John Roberts (1992, 16) say, "The study of organizations is not about how berries are arranged on a tree of authority but about how people are coordinated and motivated to get things done." With regard to the Argentine case, merely increasing wages, as has happened since 2004, without a plan to coordinate and motivate faculty to accomplish the institutional objectives cannot guarantee improved teaching and research activity at public universities.

References

Del Bello, Juan Carlos, Barsky Osvaldo, and Graciela Jiménez. 2007. *La universidad privada Argentina*. Buenos Aires, Argentina: Libros del Zorzal.

García de Fanelli, Ana. 2008. Estructura ocupacional docente y esquema de incentivos en las universidades Argentinas: Transformaciones desde los años ochenta. *Desarrollo Económico: Revista de Ciencias Sociales* 48 (189): 31–60.

Groisman, Fernando, and Ana García de Fanelli. 2009. Incentivos a la profesión académica: Los salarios de los docentes universitarios en la Argentina. *Revista Latinoamericana de Estudios del Trabajo* 14 (21): 1–35.

Luchilo, Lucas. 2011. *Argentina: Una estimación de la emigración de científicos e ingenieros*. Buenos Aires, Argentina: Centro Redes.

Milgrom, Paul, and John Roberts. 1992. *Economics, organization and management*. Englewood Cliffs, NJ: Prentice-Hall.

Ministry of Education. 2008. *University yearly statistics, 2008*. Buenos Aires, Argentina: Ministry of Education.

Ministry of Education. 2010. Consejo Federal de Educación: Ley de Educación Superior Nro. 24.521. http://www.me.gov.ar/consejo/cf_leysuperior.html. Accessed June 12, 2010.

Ministry of Education. 2011. Recuperación del Sueldo Docente Universitario. http://www.me.gov.ar/spu/salarios/ay1_dexc.html. Accessed February 21, 2011.

Rabossi, Marcelo. 2008. "Agency costs and labor contract design in the university market: Public and private cases in Argentina." PhD diss., University at Albany, State University of New York.

4

THE ACADEMIC CAREER IN A TRANSITION ECONOMY

Case Study of the Republic of Armenia

Arevik Ohanyan

This chapter provides an overview of the contemporary higher education system in the former Soviet republic of Armenia, with a specific focus on faculty remuneration and the factors shaping compensation in academia. Through the use of surveys and data collected during this research, the results presented here highlight the determinants and sources of faculty compensation; discuss formal and other sources of income, as well as teaching, research roles, and expectations; and discuss current trends in these areas.

In general, faculty wages compare unfavorably with those of professionals in comparable fields who work in the private sector. For example, the compensation of entry- or mid-level economists and computer scientists in the private sector possessing master's degrees was found to be similar to that of the highest-ranking professors in those fields in academia. Income potential for university faculty was revealed to be significantly lower than in the private sector. Starting salaries and benefits for young faculty at a single institution are below levels associated with the middle class in Armenia. Thus, many academics—particularly young faculty—seek to supplement and diversify their incomes by concurrently teaching at more than one institution or, less often, by engaging in entrepreneurship, consulting, nongovernmental organization activities, private tutoring, or in nationally and internationally sponsored research programs.

This study reflects a comparative analysis of survey results, with a particular focus on distinctions between public and private institutions, across urban and regional settings, and among institutions of varying reputation and perceived prestige. A general lack of transparency and accountability in the sphere of higher education was a challenge that needed to be overcome for data collection. The acquisition and aggregation of empirical material, particularly statistical information, was in many ways original—due to the paucity of comparable studies in

Armenia. The National Statistical Service of the Republic of Armenia and the Ministry of Education and Science were used as primary sources of statistical data on the national education sector. A separate study was designed and implemented to acquire data on compensation levels and sources of income for faculty.[1]

Contemporary Higher Education in Armenia

The higher education sector in Armenia broadly comprises public and private universities—as well as state-associated institutes, academies, and conservatories—as defined by Armenian legislation regulating graduate and postgraduate education (National Information Center for Academic Recognition and Mobility 2010). Prior to 1991, under the Soviet system, the higher education sector consisted entirely of public institutions; education was considered a public good and was completely financed by the state. Currently, the higher education system is increasingly competitive, with the presence of both private local and international universities as well as institutions established by intergovernmental agreements. As of 2010, of the 114,629 student cohort in Armenia, 91,890 (about 80 percent of total enrollment) were enrolled at 23 public institutions (including 12 branches in provinces outside the capital); and 22,739 were enrolled at 54 private institutions (National Statistical Service 2010). Public institutions are primarily affiliated with the Ministry of Education and Science, with the exception of military academies, which are under the supervision of the Ministry of Defense.

Qualifications for Academic Appointments

Degree Levels

In 2005, Armenia formally joined the Bologna Declaration and enacted changes in the degree structure. Previously, a five-year program in higher education would lead to the Specialist Diploma. This structure has changed, with the following main degree categories: (1) bachelor's degree—generally, four years of study; (2) master's degree—two years of study; (3) intern degree—a minimum of one year of postgraduate study in *internatura* leads to a certificate for professional activity in medicine; (4) *ordinatura*—two to three years of professional education leads to a clinical residency degree; (5) candidate of sciences degree—three to five years in *aspirantura* (postgraduate study); and (6) doctor of sciences degree—after postgraduate studies, the student has the option to continue his or her research in *doctorantura* (doctoral study) (National Information Center for Academic Recognition and Mobility 2010).

Faculty Ranking

The ranks of faculty in the public higher education system include professors, docents, assistants, and lecturers (Ministry of Education and Science 1996). Some universities also maintain the rank of senior lecturer, but this rank generally is no longer in practice. In contrast with public universities, three levels of academic ranks and positions are used in the three private universities studied in this research—lecturer or assistant, docent, and professor. In the Armenian higher education system, graduates with a master's degree or with a diploma of specialist (received under the previous system) are eligible to begin a career as a "lecturer," although with limited responsibilities and teaching load. Professionals who have completed postgraduate studies (*aspirantura*) and have passed qualifying examinations for candidate of sciences degrees are eligible for the position of "assistant." A candidate of sciences, having a relevant scientific-pedagogical experience throughout the last three years of his or her career and also having at least three scientific publications after becoming a candidate of sciences, may apply for the position of "docent" within the higher education institution. A doctor of sciences is eligible to apply for the position of professor—with at least five years of scientific-pedagogical experience at the granting institution and having continued research after attaining the degree as evidenced by a significant number of publications in the area of expertise (at least five scientific articles, a book, etc.).

Among public universities in Armenia as of 2010, 8.6 percent of faculty hold the degree of doctor of sciences, and 38.6 percent hold candidate of sciences. In private universities the percentages are 6.8 percent and 39 percent, respectively (National Statistical Service 2010). The percentage of doctors of sciences and candidates of sciences in different institutions is one of the primary minimum licensure requirements: 50 percent of the overall faculty of a university should have at least a degree of the candidate of sciences (Ministry of Education and Science 2000). These requirements are a major factor regarding the decision for hiring the faculty member or prolonging a member's contract; this is currently adding pressure and increasing the competition among institutions for attracting candidates with the requisite qualifications.

These general policies constitute the most common experiences and requirements to advance in professional academia in Armenia today, but there are a number of variations on this outlined structure. Nevertheless, as previously discussed, the primary qualifications for advancement of faculty are the academic degree, title, experience, and demonstrated research productivity.

Academic Contracts

Types of Academic Contracts

Four main types of academic contracts are currently in use at public universities of Armenia: (1) hourly based: these contracts are used when the number of teaching hours is relatively small and offer relatively little job security; (2) joint appointments: the faculty member teaches courses, while also having administrative duties or teaching in another institution; (3) full-time noncompetitive: the contract between the faculty member and the university is signed for up to one year; and (4) full-time competitive: the contract between the faculty member and the university is signed for up to five years. There is no tenure system in public institutions—in the last case the contract is terminated or not prolonged only in exceptional cases; and the faculty member typically stays in the same institution for the duration of the academic career.

In almost all public universities, professors teaching on an hourly basis, as well as those holding proportional positions (0.25 percent or 0.5 percent of the full-time faculty load), are appointed to their positions by the rector without any competition. If an opening for a teaching position occurs in a public institution, at least two months prior to hiring, an announcement concerning the position is made in the media. Some of the main qualifications include the academic degree and the rank, record of publications, and inventions. The practice of open competition is generally superfluous, although the five-year contracts of professors are generally renewed automatically without rigorous mechanisms of assessment, evaluation, or accountability. In addition, a graduate from the same university will generally be offered a position in that university at the expense of other possible candidates, if any. The reality of internal promotion in most public universities decreases the possibility of an external candidate having much success in an open competition to start or continue a career in the public sector.

The picture is much different in the case of private institutions, where small or medium-sized institutions rarely serve defined regulations for faculty recruitment or promotion, and many decisions may be characterized as based on current needs. In private universities, the selection and compensation of professors is subjective and nonuniform across institutions: compensation is established by the rector through direct negotiations with each professor. In larger private universities, however, policies and deviations are often established from such guidelines and observed only in exceptional cases.

Both public and private universities enjoy significant autonomy to attract better-qualified professors and are free to compete with one another for such candidates. In reality, however, aside from salary levels, institutions rarely offer additional types of inducements or compensations. The decision for a professor to move from one university to another is often primarily determined by the level of salary, the rank, and the prestige of the institution.

Teaching Loads

In nearly all universities, a faculty member's formal workload—the total time and output that an institution expects from the faculty member—is calculated by administrators following the institution's internal regulations. The workload tends to vary from one institution to another and is also contingent on the rank and tenure of each individual faculty member. Faculty workload is typically not reflected in the formal employment contract and is often determined individually for each professor or faculty member.

Teachers employed on an hourly basis or holding joint appointments are generally not expected to engage in administrative work, supervise student research projects, or conduct original research. In contrast, such activities are mandatory for full-time ("basic") faculty members in almost all public universities. Approximately 75 percent of faculty are employed on a full-time basis in public institutions, although this figure has been decreasing in the recent past (National Statistical Service 2010). The time for research is typically not included in calculations of faculty workload and is rarely formally remunerated. In general, conditions and infrastructure at many universities are not tailored to meet the needs of faculty research agendas, and research is often conducted outside the formal realm of the home university. With little or no financial compensation or resources available from their home institutions, faculty rely on funding from national and international agencies to advance their research interests and agendas toward career advancement and academic growth.[2]

Currently, some of the public universities, particularly ones that have adopted the mission of a research institution, are striving to review internal regulations and explicitly allocate time and budget for research conducted by faculty members. These institutions are also in the process of reviewing and changing faculty-evaluation mechanisms. One of the universities that has formally initiated a new evaluation and compensation mechanism is Yerevan State University, the largest public university in Armenia. At Yerevan State University, the typical faculty workload is 700 academic hours (usually 80 minutes per academic hour) per year, of which the minimum classroom-based hours (lectures, seminars, laboratory supervision, etc.) are 128 and 256 hours for a professor and a docent, respectively. By this new regulation, 80 hours for a professor, 60 hours for a docent, 40 hours for an assistant or a lecturer are formally allocated to research activities. The remainder of the workload is allocated toward supervising and grading examinations and related student assignments; consulting with and advising students, supervising master's theses, doctoral dissertations, and other student research projects; directing internship programs, developing teaching materials, and the like. Having implemented a new evaluation mechanism, Yerevan State University is also attempting to incorporate time for service, a relatively new category among Armenian higher education institutions. The total workload of a full-time faculty member at other universities ranges from 600 to 1,080 hours per year (the maximum permitted limit), which is typically divided into 40 academic weeks per year and is allocated among the mentioned activities except for research and service.

In contrast to public universities, in private universities, faculty are primarily focused on teaching; approximately 40 percent of faculty are employed on a full-time basis. In most private universities, faculty are paid on an hourly basis for teaching and other academic activities; rarely is the formal workload calculated or projected at the beginning of the academic year. As in public universities, the major incentive for faculty in private institutions to conduct research is personal and academic growth and not financial compensation.

Academic Salaries

Average Salaries in Academia

Factors affecting faculty salary include the academic degree, rank, and record of publications and research. The quality of teaching is the primary factor when a faculty member's contract is being reviewed for renewal; increasingly, in some institutions student evaluations of professors are considered. According to data collected for this research, the average monthly salary levels for full-time professors in public universities in 2010 were approximately US$420 monthly (156,000 Armenian dram, at a US$374 exchange rate), US$300 (AMD 112,000) for docents, US$250 (AMD 95,000) and US$210 (AMD 80,000) for assistants and lecturers, respectively. The average monthly nominal wage in the country for the year 2010 was US$290 (AMD 108,840). The findings are similar among private universities, as well.

Disparities

As indicated in Figure 4.1, the sharp fluctuations observed between highest and lowest levels of compensations in public institutions are partly explained by the inclusion of branches of higher education institutions based in Yerevan (the capital city) and those in the provinces. It is particularly interesting to note that faculty

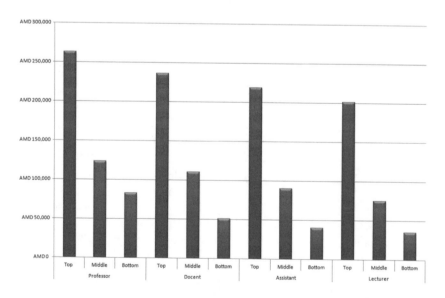

Figure 4.1 Academic salaries (monthly) at public universities.
Source: Data collected for this research report.
Note: AMD 374 = approx. US$1.00.

compensation in public institutions often differ across branches in different provinces and the capital city depending on the profitability of the branch. In some cases, compensation in the regions was nearly 50 percent lower than in Yerevan.

The variation in salary can also be explained by the diversity of thematic directions and curricular choices made by the institution, including but not limited to emphasis on economics, law, medicine, and international relations. In addition, higher levels of compensation were observed in more prestigious and well-known institutions, where higher numbers of student applications correlated with larger budgets and larger compensation funds. Only 25 to 30 percent of a public higher education institution's total budget is subsidized by the state (Economy and Values Research Center 2010, 56).

In institutions considered to be more prestigious and that offer faculty higher levels of compensation, faculty members were able to increase their compensation by 24 percent on average by advancing their graduate studies and academic rankings. The picture was quite different in universities perceived to be less prestigious, with lower levels of compensation. The corresponding differential in the levels of compensation between junior and senior faculty members in such contexts was approximately 58 percent. It should also be noted that the possibility of dramatic increase in this case is not necessarily guaranteed; indeed the professor in the less prestigious university (bottom of scale) earns on average 70 percent less than the entry-level lecturer in the prestigious university.

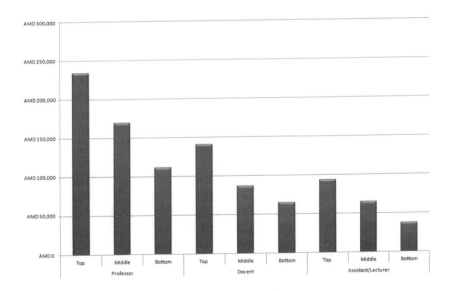

Figure 4.2 Academic salaries (monthly) of private universities.

Source: Data collected for this research report.

AMD 374 = approx. US$1.00

Among private institutions that are comparatively less well-known in the country and have a limited income base, the difference in salary between entry-level and highest-ranking faculty members is 60 percent; in relatively more prestigious private universities and relatively larger universities, that difference is 50 percent (see Figure 4.2).

Public versus Private Institutions

Because the rank and titles of faculty members are not directly comparable across public and private universities, a comparison of compensation levels in both types of institutions merits some caution. One exception is that of the highest-ranking faculty (i.e., professors) in both types of institutions. At that rank, professors in public institutions earn on average approximately 11 percent more than their colleagues in the private sector. It should be noted that state universities receive state subsidies, which provide for a minimum faculty-compensation level (AMD 30,000, or approximately US$80, monthly), and the remainder of salary is derived from university funds raised by the student tuitions, national and international research funds, donations, and charitable foundations as well as for-profit course offerings (extension schools) and programs of the university. In both public and private sectors, student tuition constitutes a disproportionately large share of income to the institution's budget; around 79 percent of the total student body in public universities pay for their education.

Nonsalary Benefits and Further Compensation

Almost all higher educational institutions in Armenia, both public and private, offer little or no additional benefits to their faculty, apart from salary. At this point the only formal additional benefit received by faculty are paid vacations, maternity leave benefits, and pensions—as stipulated by relevant national regulations. In some universities, a form of year-end bonus payment, referred to as the "thirteenth month's salary," is conventionally offered.

In an effort to provide incentives to young professors, the Armenian government is implementing a special program that subsidizes apartments in newly constructed buildings for junior faculty and provides subsidized home mortgage loans with lower than market rates and longer periods of repayment. Junior faculty members of all public universities are eligible to take advantage of this governmental initiative.

Supplementary Employment

Employment in More Than One Institution

With the growth in the number of private universities, the practice of being employed concurrently at more than one institution has expanded among faculty members in Armenia. As part of the present research, in-depth interviews with faculty members indicated that this prevailing trend has become an essential source of income for many.

Generally, faculty teach at one public university, which they consider important to acquire or maintain a certain social status and professional prestige; and this employment is in parallel with additional positions at several private institutions. This trend, however, is changing as private universities develop further and are able to offer attractive work environments. In many private universities professors enjoy academic liberty and an atmosphere where creative thinking is valued with many opportunities for self-expression and self-realization. These universities are also increasingly able to offer an atmosphere of realizing initiatives and ideas with ease, which is valued by academic professionals. It should be noted that there are no legal limitations to the number of employment positions a faculty member may have; however, increasingly, public institutions are discouraging this practice of working simultaneously in a multitude of institutions.

Research as an Opportunity for Income Diversification

In general, professors have been able to generate additional income by joining various research initiatives. Research funds for such projects are derived from governmental as well as international entities. Professors who are proficient in foreign languages have been primarily able to take advantage of international research grants. Mainly, research is carried out in specialized scientific research institutions that may be outside of the university; this approach to academic research is analogous to German and Russian models. The link between universities and these research institutes (often called academies) is poorly developed, although faculty are included in both types of institutions.

Consulting as a Source of Income

Engaging in professional consulting is also common among faculty in certain fields. The marketplace demands more for consulting services in the areas and professions of management, economics, financial analysis, auditing, medicine, architecture, and law. For instance, when working with small and medium enterprises, a professor may provide consulting services and counseling but may also engage in writing business plans and securing funding for the enterprise from banks and other sources.

Business Owners, Nongovernmental Organization Founders, and Private Tutors

A number of professors interviewed for this research discussed instances of professors who are business owners of a small or medium enterprise, which they considered to be an additional source of income. However, this practice does not appear to be very widespread in Armenia. Another source of income for professors is leading or founding a nongovernmental organization. Using this organization as an institutional umbrella, professors have been able to secure additional grants and thereby diversify their sources of income. A number of professors and other faculty members also engage in private tutoring, while others have been involved in various alleged corruption schemes in universities, as mentioned by some respondents of this study. The respondents, however, emphasized that such activities are already in decline, a trend at least partly related to recently implemented educational reforms and new governmental policies.

International Competition

There are only a few internationally oriented universities or institutions, created by international agreements, that are able to offer salaries sufficient to attract international faculty. The low-compensation levels, in addition to forming a disincentive for international faculty, is in many cases cited as the motive for local researchers and faculty members to seek employment in other countries or to leave the teaching profession. For the most part, higher education holds no systematic or strategic policies to increase the involvement of international scholars or Armenian academics with international experience to the Armenian higher education system. The opportunities presented by the substantial Armenian diaspora and expatriate communities worldwide, which together total a population approximately three times that of Armenia itself, are mainly poorly exploited in the higher education fields, with few exceptions.

Conclusion

Adequately trained human resources—primarily, professional academic faculty—are arguably the most critical factor in addressing the new demands of the Armenian higher education sector. Among surveyed institutions of higher education, a significant diversity was found in faculty remuneration levels, recruitment and retention policies and practices, expected responsibilities, and levels of educational innovation as well as in prevalence of faculty engaged in secondary jobs and activities to supplement income. These differences were often a function of type of institution, such as public or private, urban or rural, perceived level of prestige, and extent of reform or progress particularly relative to a Soviet-era baseline. In general, limited opportunities for competitive and merit-based recruitment, low-remuneration levels, challenging work conditions, and general difficulties in fostering innovation, dynamism, and academic freedom have made attracting qualified talent into academia difficult in the post-Soviet period. Reforms have been inconsistent or slow, with many institutions of higher education in Armenia yet to overcome legacies of the past organizational culture. More aggressive reforms and revisions in recruitment, selection, assessment, training, and development—as well as the creation of compensation and employee benefit systems to support employee motivation in both public and private institutions—have only recently started to emerge at specific institutions. Such sustained reform is essential to keep the academic profession vital and to make it attractive to younger generations as well as international faculty, and in order to keep pace with international developments in higher education.

Notes

1. To determine the levels of faculty compensation, 23 existing public higher education institutions were contacted, of which 15 provided data to determine levels of faculty compensation. Interviews with accountants and financial specialists were also carried out. In terms of geographical coverage, institutions from various regions in Armenia have been included in addition to those based in the capital of Yerevan.

   Considering the specificities and the diversity among private higher-education institutions, data from the 54 of them included in this study have been categorized in terms of the number of students and the number of majors (or specialties) that are accredited relative to the total number of majors in the system. Three cases have been included for more in-depth examination: two extreme cases that are highest and lowest in terms of the criteria discussed above and a third case that is representative of more frequently occurring types (median). In-depth interviews with the rectors (presidents) of the selected universities were conducted. The results were integrated in terms of the three main case studies covered in this research.

   In addition, information concerning the ranking of professors, sources of income, and compensation for faculty, beyond the compensation of higher education institutions, as well as fringe benefits, was collected through 13 in-depth interviews—including two professors, three docents, four aspirants, and four lecturers.

2. Despite the low absolute-funding levels, the research productivity of Armenian scientists is relatively high. In the United Nations Educational, Scientific and Cultural Organization Science Report of 2010 (UNESCO 2010), Armenia was ranked second, after Israel, among central and west Asian counties between 2001 and 2008 in the number of scientific publications in leading academic journals, outranking immediate neighbors—such as Georgia, Azerbaijan, and Kazakhstan.

References

Economy and Values Research Center. 2010. *National competitiveness report of Armenia: Higher education challenge.* http://www.caps.am/UserFiles/File/ACR_2010_eng%281%29.pdf. Accessed January 15, 2011.

Ministry of Education and Science. 1996. *Government decision of Republic of Armenia on regulation on formation of faculty members at state universities, N 372.* http://www.arlis.am/DocumentView.aspx?docid = 15677. Accessed August 29, 2010.

Ministry of Education and Science. 2000. *Government decision of the Republic of Armenia, N 372.* http://www.edu.am/DownloadFile/409arm-Licenzavorman_karg.pdf. Accessed December 5, 2010.

National Information Center for Academic Recognition and Mobility. 2010. *The law on graduate and postgraduate education of the Republic of Armenia.* http://www.armenic.am/?laid = 2&com = module&module = menu&id = 97. Accessed August 28, 2010.

National Statistical Service. 2010. *Higher professional education: 2009–2010 academic year.* http://armstat.am/file/article/sv_03_10a_5200.pdf. Accessed September 15, 2010.

UNESCO (United Nations Educational, Scientific and Cultural Organization). 2010. *UNESCO science report 2010: The current status of science around the world.* http://www.euromedalex.org/sites/default/files/UNESCO%20SCIENCE%20REPORT%20 2010.pdf. Accessed January 15, 2011.

5

ACADEMIC SALARIES, MASSIFICATION, AND THE RISE OF AN UNDERCLASS IN AUSTRALIA

Anthony Welch

Australia highlights some key issues that have been pointed to in various studies of the professoriate and at times associated with the massification of higher education. In this period, a relative decline in public funding has lead to a significant rise in part-time and casual appointments, as well as worsening student–staff ratios.

These elements have led to a significant bifurcation of the professoriate, with associated salary differentials. On the one hand, a declining proportion of older, tenured staff—especially at the higher levels—enjoy salaries that are comparable anywhere. Most of the staff in this category are male. On the other hand, a growing number of younger and nontenured staff do not enjoy either decent salary levels or associated benefits such as superannuation (pension plans) or sabbatical leave. More staff among this category are female. Data regarding the extent of casualization—in Australia, casual staff are those with short-term, sessional appointments—are, however, incomplete.

Development of the Higher Education System

The higher education system in Australia is relatively young and can be said to have begun with the founding of the University of Sydney, in 1850. Subsequently, universities opened in each of the colonial capitals; Australia did not become a nation until 1901. Such institutions still largely dominate most contemporary performance indicators in higher education and may offer higher salaries.

The initial era was characterized by several elements. Perhaps the first was the derivative nature of the institutions, based on the British model. In one sense this was perfectly predictable: regarding British colonies, adopting models from anywhere else was highly unlikely.

In at least two other senses, however, it was arguably a limitation. The persistence of the British model meant that chairs were dominated by expatriate British academics until the 1950s, and British nomenclature persisted with the ranks of tutor, lecturer, senior lecturer, reader (or associate professor), and professor being widely used (although tutor has been replaced by lecturer A). One small private university (Bond) adopted the more American-style nomenclature of assistant professor, associate professor, and professor. The rank of professor is still reserved for a small percentage of academic staff, albeit less so than in earlier eras.

Copying the great British universities also ignored Australia's realities, at the heel of Southeast Asia. Equally, no real attention was paid to the significance of Australia's widespread and diverse indigenous people in the curriculum of the earliest universities.

A third feature also followed from this cultural dependence. Like their older British cousins at the time, Australia's first universities were much more characterized by teaching than research. A generous sabbatical leave scheme, a common response to the *Tyranny of Distance* (Blainey 1982), was one faculty benefit that sustained international research networks, in the days before mass travel and communications.

In 1939, 0.2 percent of Australia's total population attended a university. Total student enrollment was 14,236, (of which 8,240 were at the two oldest universities: Sydney and Melbourne). Currently, enrolled students number around 1 million, while equivalent full-time academic staff numbers totaled 33,496, in 2007. But of late, growth in student numbers substantially outstripped growth in academic staff. While in 1989 there were 26,104 equivalent full-time academic staff, this had risen to 33,496 by 2007, and 37,472 by 2008—a rise of 43.5 percent (Coates et al. 2009). Over the same period, however, for such staff, enrollments rose from 350,000 to 726,000, a rise of 107.4 percent. Such significant disparities worsened staff-student ratios by over 60 percent—from 1:13.41 in 1989 to 1:21.67 in 2007, nationally (Coates et al. 2009, 5). While some differences are evident within and across institutions, the pattern is broadly observable in all Australian universities. While the trend is by no means unique to Australia, the impact on both working conditions and salaries has been significant, leading, inter alia, to a significant fracturing of the profession (Welch 2005b).

Adding to the pressures on the profession is the aging of the academic workforce. While this, too, is by no means unique to Australia, the fact that around one-quarter of academics in Australia are age 55 or over is of concern. When this is paralleled by a declining proportion of academics under the age of 40, the issue of replenishment becomes even more pressing (Hugo 2005). As a country of migration (like Canada, where the proportion of academics over age 55 is 35 percent), migration has helped blunt the greying of the professoriate, especially when schemes began to target the highly skilled. The research by the Organization for Economic Cooperation and Development (OECD) showing Australia with the highest net brain gain of all OECD member states, as well as its proximity to Asia and reputation as an open society, led to a rise in the numbers of academics from East and Southeast Asia, most notably mainland Chinese (Welch and Zhang 2008a, 2008b; Yang and Welch 2010).

Gendering of the academic profession has long been pointed out (Sheehan and Welch 1996; Coates et al. 2009). More women were clustered among casual (with short-term, sessional appointments), contract staff (who hold employment contracts of specified duration rather than being tenured), and at the lower echelons in the earlier study. Proportions of men and women with contract (or limited-term) lectureships have recently equalized, but more men than women are still tenured (59.3 percent and 53.5 percent, respectively), and more men still occupy chairs. While most Australian academics gained their higher degrees domestically, more men earned their PhD degrees abroad than women.

Prima facie, the Australian university system remains overwhelmingly public (Rumbley, Pacheco, and Altbach 2008)—of the 39 universities, only two are private, both rather small. However, higher education funding fell from 1995 to 2004 among OECD member countries, intensifying the effective privatization of public-sector universities (OECD 2007). Underfunding drove public universities to aggressively diversify their income sources, most notably via recruiting full-fee-paying international students, who now comprise about one in four students, overall. On average, Australian universities now earn around 15 percent of their total budgets from international students. In some cases, it is significantly higher. Without international student income, no Australian universities could sustain the current level of resources, including academic salaries (Welch 2002; Altbach and Welch 2010).

Salaries: The Current Picture

Australia is a federal system, with almost all universities established by state legislation. Nonetheless, the academic profession in Australia was a long part of the centralized wage-fixing system. Like 95 percent of Australian workers, academics were thus subject to salary awards. Industrial awards—legally binding documents that specify salaries and conditions—resulted from negotiations, usually national, on particular issues between unions and management, occasionally accompanied by industrial action. If the differences proved irresolvable, the dispute went to an industrial court, which arbitrated the matter.

National Negotiations

Academic staff are widely represented by unions, of which the National Tertiary Education Union is by far the largest, with some 25,000 members. The union has a substantial proportion of academic staff in Australian universities as members. Employers are represented by the Australian Higher Education Industrial Association, established in 1990 (AHEIA, n.d.). As paymaster, the federal government often intervened directly in the process of arbitration, notwithstanding that direct grants to universities from the federal government now account for a much smaller, and declining, proportion of institutional budgets.

The dissolution of the former Academic Salaries Tribunal (1974–1988), which in the past set wages independently, heralded a move toward enterprise bargaining. The workers at each university, largely represented by their unions, bargain directly with management, regarding salaries. Negotiations center on both wages and conditions, with some aspects of current industrial awards remaining in place. The key legislation from 1998 to 2005 was the Higher Education Conditions of Employment Award. After its abandonment, awards were simplified; but the goal remained to tie improved salaries and conditions to productivity gains, especially in an era of tight budgets. Each institution also now negotiates a mission-based compact with the federal government, specifying individual performance targets, although the precarious result of the federal election of August 2010 placed some existing arrangements under a cloud.

Some senior academics, particularly in the sciences, or in areas of shortage (such as accounting, where wages in the profession are higher than in the academy), may now negotiate individual contracts, sometimes with significant salary loadings or bonuses. An alternative sometimes practiced is to appoint academics in such "hard-to-staff" areas at a level higher than would apply in other areas, where academics are more plentiful. The majority of academics, however, work within a five-band, minimum-rates salary range, as indicated in Table 5.1.

At each level, salaries vary by around 10 percent according to institution, with the most established universities paying the most. Medical academics attract a

Table 5.1 Salary information, by level, 2010 (A$)*

Level	Step	Year (2010)
Level A	Top	$5,811
	Middle	$5,067
	Bottom	$4,323
Level B	Top	$7,248
	Middle	$6,683
	Bottom	$6,119
Level C	Top	$8,611
	Middle	$8,046
	Bottom	$7,482
Level D	Top	$9,894
	Middle	$9,446
	Bottom	$8,998
Level E		$11,546

Source: Data collected in January 2010 from Department of Employment, Education, and Workplace Relations Higher Education Statistics.

*A$1.00 = US$1.08

clinical loading—if paid at the full level around A$25,000 (US$27,000) or more. Paraclinical and dental attract a lower loading; perhaps half or two-thirds of the above. Moonlighting does not occur, but lower-paid (casual or part-time) academics often work across more than one university.

Salaries and Living Standards

Most Australian academics are full-time employees, but part-time and casual (or sessional) appointments have been growing. Assessing the living standards that academic salaries yield is complex, especially given issues of purchasing power parity and major changes in exchange rates; at the time of writing, the Australian dollar was around US$1.08. A recent Association of Commonwealth Universities survey saw Australian salaries rated as the world's highest (Maslen 2010).

The past two decades have eroded salary relativities at all levels, however. In some universities, positions at level A are now not always advertised, since salaries are not competitive enough to warrant advertisement (Horsley, Martin, and Woodburne 2005). The 2008 salary data in Table 5.2 show that the average annual wage in Australia was A$65,300 (US$70,200). Using a somewhat different measure of average weekly earnings (arguably somewhat inflated), some declining relativities have been showed: while average weekly earnings increased by 1.47 over the years 2001–2008, academic salaries increased by 1.37 (Coates et al. 2009; Horsley, Martin, and Woodburne 2005). Using that baseline, average weekly earnings increased from A$938 in 2001 to A$1,381 in 2008 (US$1,013–US$1,491), whereas the earnings of a level A lecturer rose from A$685 to A$940 (US$740–US$1,015) over the same period, and a (full) professor from A$1,858 to A$2,552 (US$2,007–US$2,756) (Coates et al. 2009, 13). Academic salaries at all levels declined relative to average weekly earnings, as illustrated in Table 5.2.

Even if the average weekly earnings levels may be somewhat inflated, a clear pattern emerges of a gradual erosion of academic salary relativities. Also, the issue of living standards depends significantly on specific employment conditions. Of the salary bands A–E, all except E have several steps within the band. As seen in Table 5.1, at level A (the lowest), full-time employment delivers an income that, even at the top of the band, is little beyond the average weekly earnings. Most academics are at levels B and C (56.3 percent of the total) and are thus somewhat above those weekly levels, while full professors' salaries are more than double the average weekly earnings levels. But, as Australian Bureau of Statistics data show, this ratio has eroded significantly; it was 2.9 in 1992, compared with around 2.3 currently—based on an assumed professorial annual salary of A$150,000 (US$162,500) (ABS, n.d.). While there has been some erosion of academic salary relativities over time, it should also be pointed out that long service leave (of three months after 10 years of service, prorated after that), superannuation benefits (of 17 percent) and generous sabbatical leave (full salary, plus a modest

Table 5.2 Comparison of academic salaries and average weekly earnings, 2001–8 (A$)

	2001	2002	2003	2004	2005	2006	2007	2008
Assistant lecturer (Level A)	685	712	739	753	780	831	886	940
Lecturer (Level B)	978	1,017	1,055	1,076	1,114	1,118	1,266	1,343
Senior lecturer (Level C)	1,198	1,246	1,292	1,318	1,365	1,455	1,551	1,646
Associate professor (Level D)	1,442	1,500	1,556	1,587	1,643	1,752	1,868	1,981
Professor (Level E)	1,858	1,932	2,005	2,045	2,117	2,257	2,406	2,552
Average weekly earnings	938	1,901	1,145	1,196	1,260	1,316	1,325	1,381

Source: Coates et al. 2009, 13.

Note: By end 2010, the Australian dollar had reached parity with the U.S. dollar and by mid-2011 was at approximately US$1.08. This is likely to increase the attractiveness of Australian salaries to overseas staff seeking academic appointments.

travel allowance) complicate any comparison with average weekly earnings. (See the section on supplementary benefits for details.) While long service leave is a feature of public-sector employment, superannuation benefits vary significantly, and sabbatical leave provisions are reserved for tenured academics.

A further complication relates to significant differences in living costs. Middle-class expectations in Australia have traditionally included home ownership, something with steeply rising prices—particularly in Sydney, Perth, and Melbourne. The fact that housing prices are much higher in the major capital cities not only affects living standards of academic staff but also led some universities to offer modest, once-only incentive payments to academic staff who transfer from a less costly location.

A third element complicating any single assessment of academic living standards is the major trend toward casual employment of academic staff (see the definition above) that has occurred within the system. Perhaps three decades ago, around 80 percent of academic staff at Australian universities were tenured, with effective employment until the age of 60 or 65 years. Recent estimates are that this proportion has now declined to little more than 60 percent in equivalent full-time terms (Coates et al. 2009, 24). By contrast, casual staff numbers grew by 125 percent over the past two decades. From 12.7 percent of the total workforce in 1989, casual staff accounted for 22.2 percent of equivalent full-time staff totals by 2007 (Coates et al. 2009, 7). The extent of casualization, the fact that many work at more than one university, and the high turnover of casual contracts renders it impossible to know with accuracy the numbers of casual staff within the Australian academic system; but some estimates present a compelling case:

> Sessional teachers are the hidden part of massification that has taken place in higher education in Australia over the last 30 years…Between 40 and 50 per cent of teaching in Australian higher education is currently done [by casual staff]. This has been largely unacknowledged.
>
> *(Percy et al. 2008, foreword)*

Given this uncertainty, it is impossible to know with accuracy the average-earning levels of the significant numbers of casual staff in the Australian system; but it is clear that this trend represents the development of significant underclass staff, who are effectively "teaching only."

Academic Employment

The PhD remains the standard entry point for the profession, although widespread casualization has undermined this to an extent. The Australian academic system is open and international, with an impressive record of employing academics with PhDs from a variety of overseas locations (Welch 2005a, 2005b, 2010a). A more recent pattern consists of the employment of academics from a variety of countries, who have first taken their PhDs in Australia (Welch and Zhang 2008a, 2008b; Yang and Welch 2010).

Standard employment practices traditionally consisted of placing an advertisement in the national and international press—commonly the *Chronicle of Higher Education* and *Times Higher Education,* each of which is widely read overseas. Electronic sources are also now commonly used for recruitment purposes, and for senior appointments recruitment firms ("headhunters") may be used. Once short lists have been finalized, based on criteria specified in the advertisement, interviews are used to select the successful candidate. While interviewees were traditionally invited to appear before the interview panel, Skype or telephone interviews are now sometimes replacing face-to-face interviews, especially for applicants in another country or at the lowest levels. Given the larger size of the current system and a significant turnover, dispensation may be occasionally granted for more junior or short-term appointments—to be made on nomination or internally, especially if the need is urgent.

As indicated above, the proportion of academics who now have tenure has declined sharply over the past two decades. While tenure was once deemed to be continued until the age of 65, legislation to outlaw age-related discrimination has long been in effect. Appointments now commonly include a probationary period of up to three years followed by a careful review. Most of these academics qualify for a continuing appointment. In some universities this practice is all-inclusive, except for the precise allowance of the vice-chancellor or nominee (UNISA n.d.). Where fixed-term contracts are for a period shorter than three years, the period of probation is specified; for contracts of longer than three years, the probation period may form three years.

Appointees are effectively civil service employees. Annual performance assessment procedures are now universal, at all levels, and a less than satisfactory assessment may well inhibit salary progression or promotion to the next level (from level A to B, B to C, etc.).

The traditional assumption that all academics are expected to be research active has now been overtaken by an increasing division within the profession, between those who teach more and those who are more devoted to research. While evidence of this bifurcation has been pointed to internationally for some time (Welch 2005a), this practice is having an impact on newer recruits to the profession. In effect, numerous senior members of the academy tend to research more and teach less, relative to their younger and more junior peers. "Teaching-only" positions have grown in recent years, and as universities compete for research-active staff who are highly productive and able to attract significant research funding, a parallel if less general trend involves the appointment of "research-only" academics. In the contest for highly research-active staff, the older, more well-established universities tend to leverage their status, thereby adding to their existing advantage. For such academics, or for particularly distinguished level E staff (professors), a salary bonus may be negotiated, of perhaps 20 percent. For the latter, the title of university professor is used at some institutions. For science faculty, for example, who may have developed a process, patent, or product that has commercial potential, a contract may be negotiated with the university—by which an agreed proportion of any income earned is allocated to the inventor. In the context of massification and more intense competition for research-active staff, mobility has increased significantly.

Supplementary Benefits

Salaries and benefits for academic appointments as dean, pro-vice-chancellor and higher levels are usually individually negotiated, outside the enterprise bargaining agreement arrangements (Horsley, Martin, and Woodburne 2005). For such senior managers, the practice of salary sacrifice (a process that confers tax advantages by sacrificing some salary and hence lowering tax liability) may be used to cover lease of a vehicle and mobile communications packages. Housing benefits are reserved for the vice-chancellor (president), but pension savings (known in Australia as superannuation) are compulsory for all but casual staff (who earn a bonus of 25 percent, in lieu). For most staff, a total superannuation of 17 percent, some of which is paid by the employee but the majority of which is paid by the university, is standard; and for academics over the age of 60, recent national legislation allows them to sacrifice an additional quantum of their income, up to A$50,000 per annum, into superannuation (pension) funds, thereby effectively reducing the level of income tax for which they are liable. While academic staff on casual contracts are paid an additional amount of 25 percent, in lieu of the pension and long-service leave benefits that apply to tenured staff, the increasing casualization pointed to earlier means that universities are saving considerable amounts in salaries:

> Between a third and a half of teaching is now performed by casual staff, which means universities actually save the significant costs of leave entitlements and full superannuation for these "sessional" employees.
>
> *(Gregg 2009; see also Brown, Goodman, and Yasukawa 2006)*

Some branches of the National Tertiary Education Union have now implemented procedures to limit the exploitation of casual staff (Knight and Horrocks 2010).

Joint appointments are much less common than in Europe, for example, except for casual or fractional appointments, which are much more dependent on multiple appointments to sustain a reasonable income. Moonlighting is uncommon, and consulting relatively unusual, especially in the humanities and social sciences. It is somewhat more prevalent among those in professional faculties and science faculties—but still uncommon. Most staff depend on their salaries.

Qualifications

For some decades, the PhD has been the entry-level qualification; yet, as indicated above, for professional faculties, especially in hard-to-staff areas such as accounting or law, exceptions are made. In other areas, notably the sciences and social sciences, where PhDs are more plentiful, the situation is very different:

> A book, multiple journal articles and a history of grant funding is now usually necessary on top of a completed dissertation to make a shortlist after graduating.
>
> *(Gregg 2009)*

In disciplines such as chemistry, a PhD is no longer considered adequate; a postdoctoral appointment, often overseas, is also expected.

Promotion is based on demonstrated performance, against specified criteria. While teaching, service, and research productivity are all expected, the increasing emphasis on amassing of performance data on every aspect of academic performance means that candidates for promotion are now faced with increasing demands for more detailed data. Particularly at research-intensive institutions, demonstrated research performance is, in practice, valued more than teaching excellence or service record; but all three criteria must be satisfied. At many institutions, an "outstanding" grade on two of the three areas of achievement is necessary for the promotion application to succeed.

Conclusion

The Australian academic profession is highly international, and its situation in the most dynamic area of the world, the Asia Pacific, bodes well for continued diversity and excellence among the professoriate. As seen above, academic salaries for full-time faculty are also generally competitive when seen internationally, and the practice of advertising internationally also acts as a guarantor of continued quality. The fact that the system is part of the English-speaking community also confers a wider capacity to draw talent from around the world. At the same time, a number of issues will challenge the ongoing capacity of the system to recruit and retain the best individuals and factors—the greying of the professoriate, the decline in funding in per-student terms, increasing workloads, and the increasing casualization of the profession, if not addressed. While, as indicated above, the OECD estimated that Australia has the highest net brain gain of all member nations (Docquier and Marfouk 2006; Welch 2010b), it also suffers from a degree of brain drain that is both a vindication of the quality of the system and a challenge to its future development.

References

ABS (Australian Bureau of Statistics). n.d. *Average weekly earnings, states and Australia, August 1992*. http://www.ausstats.abs.gov.au/ausstats/free.nsf/0/75A5825F3E9A9D19C A2574FA00165580/$File/63020_AUG1992.pdf. Accessed April 20, 2010.

AHEIA (Australian Higher Education Industrial Association). n.d. http://www.aheia.edu. au. Accessed July 8, 2010.

Altbach, P. G., and A. Welch. 2010. *Australia: The perils of commercialism*. http://www.univer sityworldnews.com/article.php?story=20100820152350449. Accessed July 17, 2010.

Blainey, G. 1982. *The tyranny of distance: How distance shaped Australia's history*. Melbourne, Australia: Macmillan.

Brown, T., J. Goodman, and K. Yasukawa. 2006. "Getting the best of you for nothing." *Casual Voices in the Australian Academy*. Melbourne, Australia: National Tertiary Education Union.

Coates, H., I. Dobson, D. Edwards, T. Friedman, L. Goedegebuure, and L. Meek. 2009. *The attractiveness of the Australian academic profession: A comparative analysis*. Melbourne, Australia: Australian Council for Educational Research.

Department of Employment, Education, and Workplace Relations. n.d. "Higher education statistics." Department of Employment, Education, and Workplace Relations. http:// www.deewr.gov.au/HigherEducation/Publications/HEStatistics/Publications/Pages/ Staff.aspx. Accessed January 2010.

Docquier, F., and A. Marfouk. 2006. "International migration by educational attainment, 1990–2000." In *International remittances and the brain drain*, ed. Çaglar Özden, and Maurice Schiff, 151–200. Washington, DC: World Bank.

Gregg, Melissa. 2009. "Why academia is no longer a smart choice." *New Matilda*. http://new-matilda.com/2009/11/24/academia-no-longer-smart-choice. Accessed June 12, 2010.

Horsley, M., G. Martin, and G. Woodburne. 2005. *Salary relativities and the academic labour market*. www.dest.gov.au/sectors/higher_education/publications_resources/profiles/ salary_relativities.htm#publication. Accessed March 15, 2010.

Hugo, G. 2005. "Demographic trends in Australia's academic workforce." *Journal of Higher Education Policy and Management* 27 (3): 327–43.

Knight, N., and L. Horrocks. 2010. "The impact of casualisation on teaching, marking and other academic activities." *The Advocate* (March): 18.

Maslen, Geoff. 2010. "Australia and South Africa pay top salaries." *University World News* 152. http://www.universityworldnews.com/article.php?story=20101217224942899. Accessed December 26, 2010.

OECD (Organization for Economic Cooperation and Development). 2007. *Education at a glance 2007*. Paris: OECD.

Percy, A., M. Scoufis, S. Parry, A. Goody, M. Hicks, I. Macdonald, K. Martinez, N. Szorenyi-Reischl, Y. Ryan, S. Wills, and L. Sheridan. 2008. *The red report: Recognition, enhancement, development*. Lismore, Australia: Council of Australian Directors of Academic Development.

Rumbley, L. E., I. F. Pacheco, and P. G. Altbach. 2008. *International comparison of academic salaries: An exploratory study*. Chestnut Hill, MA: Center for International Higher Education, Boston College.

Sheehan, B., and A. Welch. 1996. "Australia." In *The academic profession: Portraits from fourteen countries*, ed. P. G. Altbach, 51–94. Princeton, NJ: Carnegie Foundation for the Advancement of Teaching.

UNISA (University of South Australia). n.d. *Procedures on probation—Academic staff*. http://www.unisa.edu.au/policies/codes/academic/probation.asp. Accessed September 20, 2010.

Welch, A. 2002. "Going global? Internationalising Australian universities in a time of global crisis." *Comparative Education Review* 46 (4): 433–71.

Welch, A. 2005a. "The peripatetic professor: The internationalisation of the academic profession." In *The professoriate: Profile of a profession*, ed. A. Welch, 71–96. Dordrecht, Netherlands: Springer.

Welch, A., ed. 2005b. *The professoriate: Profile of a profession*. Dordrecht, Netherlands: Springer.

Welch, A. 2010a. "Cultural difference and identity." In *Education, change and society*, ed. R. Connell, C. Campbell, M. Vickers, A. Welch, A. Foley, N. Bagnall, and D. Hayes, 130–67. Melbourne, Australia: Oxford University Press.

Welch, A. 2010b. "Nation-state, diaspora and comparative education." In *Changing educational landscapes*, ed. D. Mattheou, 285–308. Dordrecht, Netherlands: Springer.

Welch A., and Z. Zhang. 2008a. "Communication networks among the Chinese knowledge diaspora: A new invisible college?" In *Geographies of knowledge, geometries of power: Higher education in the 21st century. World Yearbook of Education 2008*, ed. R. Boden, R. Deem, D. Epstein, and F. Rizvi, 338–54. London: Routledge.

Welch, A., and Z. Zhang. 2008b. "Higher education and global talent flows: Brain drain, overseas Chinese intellectuals, and diasporic knowledge networks." *Higher Education Policy* 21 (4): 519–37.

Yang, R., and A. Welch. 2010. "Globalisation, transnational academic mobility and the Chinese knowledge diaspora: An Australian case study." *Discourse: Australian Journal of Educational Studies (Special Issue on Trans-national academic mobility)* 31 (5): 593–607.

6

BRAZIL

The Widening Gap

Simon Schwartzman

Brazilian legislation assumes that all higher education institutions should evolve to become full-fledged universities, with well-qualified, tenured, well-paid, and full-time staff—doing good-quality teaching and research. In fact, some institutions, particularly in the public sector, are moving in this direction, with some limitations. However, most of the private institutions, which account for 75 percent of the student enrollment, are not undergoing such changes. Few of their teachers have advanced degrees; most work part time and have no job stability; and this reflects a wide gap in salaries and working conditions, when compared with those in the first group.

Overview

Brazil has a highly differentiated system of higher education, with a relatively small number of well-funded public institutions and a large number of private, for-profit, and philanthropic institutions. Brazil is a federation, with 27 states and more than 5,000 municipalities, and some of the public institutions are maintained by the federal government, others by states, and a small number by municipalities (Schwartzman 2004).

Traditionally, higher education institutions were organized in the European tradition, with faculties providing diplomas legally valid as licenses for the learned professions—medicine, law, engineering, architecture, and dentistry—and later in new professions such as business administration, psychology, communications, and pedagogy. In the European tradition, without undergraduate courses in the North American or English pattern, all students are admitted to professional degree programs. In 1968, new legislation introduced several features of North American higher education, including regular master's degrees and doctoral programs, the credit system, the replacement of chairs by academic departments, and strengthening the role of university rector.

The 1968 reform led to two divergent sectors. Higher education teaching in public universities became a career in the civil service—with competitive salaries and other benefits for full-time employment and promotions, based on academic criteria. Besides lecturing, higher education teachers are expected to do research and extension work; new graduate education programs were created to grant the advanced degrees required for these careers (Balbachevsky and Schwartzman 2010). This was followed by the creation or expansion of several research support agencies, both by the national and state governments.

This public system did not grow fast enough to accommodate the expanding demand for higher education, which was mostly absorbed by private institutions (Durham 2004). Today, about 75 percent of the enrollment in higher education in Brazil takes place in private institutions. The limited growth of public institutions can be explained given their high cost, due to the relatively high academic salaries and selective admission of students, based on *numerus clausus* and competitive entrance examinations for the different course programs. This was different from what has been happening in most other Latin American countries, where the rule was open admissions and the lack of well-paid careers for the academic staff in public institutions.

Private institutions, however, could not adopt the same organization model and career patterns of the public ones. Public institutions are fully supported with budgetary resources and legally forbidden to charge tuition. Private institutions, with few exceptions, cannot receive public subsidies and depend on tuition to survive. Since public institutions attract the best-qualified students—coming usually from richer families—private institutions (with some exceptions) have to cater to low-income sectors that cannot pay much. Most of their students need to work; and because of that, most of their courses are provided in the evening. The Brazilian legislation still assumes that all higher education should be organized in universities or eventually evolve into one—centered on high-quality academic research and Humboldt's ideal of integration between research and teaching. But in practice, few institutions—even in the public sector—can meet the standards of what a research university should be.

Currently, legislation allows for the existence of three main types of institutions: fully autonomous universities with graduate education and research; autonomous "university centers," with no graduate education and research but, supposedly, good-quality teaching in different fields; and isolated faculties, with limited autonomy to create new courses and expand admission. To become a university, a private institution must demonstrate the existence of graduate education programs and research, among other criteria. Public universities, however, can be created by law. Formally, no difference exists in the standing of the degrees provided by these different types of institutions, once they are allowed to function. There are also a small number of technical institutes supported by the federal government, but Brazil never developed an extended system of technical, shorter higher education programs, such as the French Institutes Universitaires de Technologie.

In recent years, this picture has been changing in many ways. In the public sector, the federal government has been pressing public institutions to admit more students and to open evening courses. A program provides additional resources for federal universities willing to expand, many institutions are introducing quotas for low-income or minority students, and private universities are granted tax exemption if they admit a certain number of low-income students for free (MEC 2010). For some years, a tendency has been under way for the public sector to bring in more students from low-income sectors, in less competitive careers, and for some private institutions to cater more to richer students.

According to the Ministry of Education, in 2008 there were 2,252 institutions, 90 percent private, 5.1 million students in regular first-degree courses, and 75 percent in private institutions. Of these institutions, 183 had university status and 1,911 were isolated, nonuniversity institutions. The size of these institutions varies enormously. A small, isolated institution would have about 1,700 students on average—a university, 15,000. The largest private universities, with locations scattered in many cities, may enroll above 200,000; the largest public university, the University of São Paulo, has about 55,000 graduate (undergraduate) and 25,000 postgraduate students in 11 locations.

In 2009, there were 88,286 students in master's degree programs, 53,237 students in doctoral programs, and 9,122 students in professional master's degree programs. Of the 150,000 graduate (undergraduate) students, 80 percent were in public universities, one-third of them in the state of São Paulo. Some graduate programs are offered by public research institutes that are usually not classified as higher education institutions—such as the Institute of Applied and Pure Mathematics in Rio de Janeiro, the Brazilian Center for Physics Research, or the Oswaldo Cruz Institute in public health.

Academic Qualifications

In 2008, there were 338,900 higher education teaching posts in the country, or about 15 undergraduate (first university degree) students per teacher, with large variations among sectors: 10.6 students per teacher in the public sector and about 17.3 in the private sector. Approximately 76 percent of the academics in public institutions had full-time contracts, compared with just 18 percent in the private sector (see Table 6.1).

In federal universities, the academic career is comprised of five ranks—auxiliary, assistant, adjunct, associate, and full professor (*auxiliar, assistente, adjunto, associado, titular*). Each of these ranks, up to full professor, is divided into four levels. In principle, access to a university career should require a doctoral degree and success in an open formal competition (*concurso*). However, in federal

Table 6.1 Academic posts and contracts in higher education

	Public universities	Private universities	Total
Number of faculty	119,368	219,522	338,890
Full time	91,608	40,774	132,382
Part time	27,760	178,748	206,508

Source: Ministry of Education, Higher Education Census (MEC, INEP 2008).
Note: Data refer to teaching posts, not persons. The same person can have multiple posts.

institutions, a doctoral degree is not required for the first two rank levels. In the past, many teachers with just a first university degree were hired through provisional contracts, which were later transformed into permanent appointments. Promotion up to associate level is achieved by seniority and also by the acquisition of graduate degrees; promotion to full professorship, in principle, should also depend on success in an open competition. The government has stimulated academics in public institutions to get higher degrees by improving their salaries and, in the private sector, by including academic qualifications of the staff as a criterion in assessment procedures.

In the state universities of São Paulo the ranks are auxiliary, assistant, doctor professor, associate, and full professor (*auxiliar, assistente, professor doutor, associado, titular*). A doctorate is required for the doctor professor's rank. To be promoted to associate professor, it is necessary to pass a *livre docência* exam, reminiscent of the German *Privatdozent* exam. To be promoted to a full professorship, it is necessary to pass a competitive exam. Other states have similar career structures, except for *livre docência,* which is a peculiarity of the São Paulo institutions.

Most private institutions do not have career ladders, but salaries are paid according to the academic degree held by the faculty member. Salaries vary according to academic qualification and seniority. In public institutions, job stability applies to all teachers, regardless of their formal qualification or rank. In the private sector, there is no stability; anyone can be dismissed at any time according to the employer's will, under the private-labor legislation.

Although in principle it is necessary to have a doctorate to teach in higher education, only 22 percent of the teachers have it, ranging from 48.1 percent in public universities to 8.3 percent in private institutions, and there are still a few teachers without a higher education degree at all. The best situation is in the public universities in the state of São Paulo, where 86 percent of the academic staff hold doctoral degrees. The presence of a large number of teachers without a doctoral degree is usually interpreted as a provisional condition, to be corrected as the qualifications of Brazilian academics improve and the old generation is replaced by the new. In the meantime, lesser degrees, such as a master's and specialization or training certificates, are accepted by the institutions as academic credentials.

Currently, Brazilian universities graduate about 10,000 PhDs a year—a very significant number but still small compared with the need to fill in the 287,000 teaching positions still staffed by lesser-qualified personnel. Moreover, since private, low-cost teaching institutions are not able to pay for full-time staff with advanced degrees, this picture is not likely to change in the foreseeable future.

Contracts

In public institutions, besides the basic salary, remuneration may include benefits related to academic degrees and current or past administrative activity. Full-time, exclusive-dedication academics cannot have other regular employment but may receive research fellowships and additional payment for research and technical activities done within the university. Many public universities have established autonomous foundations that are used to sign research and technical-assistance contracts with public and private agencies and firms that pay additional money for researchers involved in their projects. This practice is not allowed in other branches of the civil service but has been tolerated in the universities. Finally, the actual income of an academic may be increased by court decisions regarding acquired rights affected by changing legislation.

A full-time contract usually means 40 hours of work per week, which should be dedicated to teaching, research, and class preparation. Part-time contracts can be half time or less, for teaching and other activities; per-hour contracts pay only for the number of classes actually delivered by the teacher, not allowing time for class preparation, office hours, research, or institutional activities. In practice, union bargaining and jurisprudence have reduced the difference between these two types of part-time contracts in terms of rights and benefits. In most cases, teachers with part-time or hourly contracts work in more than one institution or combine teaching with other professional activities, facilitated by the fact that most teaching in private universities takes place in the evenings.

Academics in public universities, as civil servants, cannot be dismissed except for grave misconduct. In the private sector, private labor market legislation allows the employee to be dismissed at any time, with some limited compensation. Salaries are the same in all federal universities, according to academic qualifications and rank—regardless of merit, except the acquisition of formal credentials; in the private sector, in principle, salaries can be negotiated case by case.

In public universities, full-time contracts are usually, but not always, exclusive-dedication contracts. A full-time contract without exclusive dedication means that, outside an academic's 40 hours in the institution, the teacher can have a private practice, teach in the evening in another place, or do external consulting. In principle, none of these external activities are allowed for those with exclusive dedication. In practice, this rule is not fully implemented.

Salaries

Table 6.2 gives the range of monthly salaries for academics in full-time, exclusive-dedication contracts in federal universities; it ranges from R$36,000 to R$153,000 (reais) a year (about US$20,000 to US$87,000, based on an exchange rate of R$1.75 = US$1.00). State universities have their own pay scale. In the state of São Paulo, the corresponding range is from R$3,435 to R$10,216 per month, or between US$25,000 and US$76,000 per year. The admission procedures, promotion rules, and benefits in state universities are similar to those of the federal government.

Although pay scales are the same in all federal universities, there is no national academic mobility; each person is attached to the institution where he or she works. One consequence of this system is little mobility of teachers from one institution to another and no mechanisms for public universities to compete for talent in the country or abroad. There are resources for paying visiting professors for short periods, but it is difficult, although not impossible, for a public university to hire a foreign-born academic for its permanent staff.

Most private institutions do not publish their salary levels or career paths. However, an informal enquiry among several private institutions showed that they pay between R$20 and R$50 per hour for teaching (US$11–US$28), depending on the teacher's academic degree. This means, for a 20-hour, part-time job between US$260 and US$590 a month; but many teachers work only 12 or even fewer hours per week in an institution, which means that they have to work in different institutions or combine teaching with other professional activities to reach a reasonable income.

Table 6.3 presents the main data on income, based on the National Household Survey of the Brazilian Institute of Geography and Statistics (IBGE 2008). The figures refer to monthly income in Brazilian reais in 2008. The estimated number of teachers in the survey is much smaller than the figures reported by the Higher Education Census—96,000 in the public sector against 119,000 in the census; and 112,000 in the private sector against 219,000 in the census (MEC, INEP, n.d.). One possible explanation for the differences is that the census gives information on posts, while the household survey gives information on people who may hold one or more teaching posts; and there may be also sampling errors. As one could expect, this difference is much higher in the private sector, where part-time contracts are the rule.

These data do not distinguish between civil service at the federal, state, or municipal levels. Although most higher education teachers in public institutions are civil servants, and most of those in the private sector have private working contracts, there are many exceptions to these rules. About 17 percent of those working in the public sector do not have a formal job contract, and 12.6 percent are hired according to the private-law legislation. There is no additional information

Table 6.2 Academic monthly salaries in federal universities in Brazil, 2010

	Graduation	*Training*	*Specialization*	*MA*	*Doctoral degree*
Full professor	4,786.62	5,221.96	5,580.63	7,818.69	11,755.05
Associate				7,448.09	11,424.45
Adjunct		3,945.91	4,241.00	5,793.14	7,913.30
Assistant	3,275.82	3,525.01	3,730.17	4,985.00	
Auxiliary	2,814.48	3,001.80	3,190.30		

Source: Ministry of Education, Higher Education Census (MEC, INEP 2011).
Note: Values in Brazilian reais (US$1.00 = R$1.75).

Table 6.3 Mean income of teachers in higher education

	Main work	*All activities*	*% of income from main work*	*Number of cases*
Public sector, civil servant	R$ 4,358.80	R$ 4,967.37	87.7	65,756
Private sector, regular contract	R$ 3,442.72	R$ 4,201.20	81.9	98,835
All public sector	R$ 3,762.73	R$ 4,271.81	88.1	96,000
All private sector	R$ 3,209.21	R$ 3,911.95	82.0	112,026
Total	R$ 3,447.17	R$ 4,062.51	84.9	208,026

Source: Brazilian Institute of Geography and Statistics, National Household Survey (IBGE, PNAD 2008).
Note: Values in Brazilian reais (US$1.00 = R$1.75).

about the kind of jobs they hold, but they may be, for instance, graduate students working as research or teaching assistants or replacement teachers with temporary contracts, or they may work in municipal institutions that do not have civil service careers. In the private sector, about 9 percent of the higher education teachers do not have a regular working contract. Incomes of those in the public sector are higher than those in the private sector, and incomes of those with regular contracts are higher than those without these contracts. Also, for the civil servants in the public sector, their main salary represents 87.7 percent of their income from all activities; while for those with regular contracts in the public sector, it is only 82 percent, with another 18 percent coming from other sources. One-fourth of the teachers who hold civil servant status earn additional income from a secondary job; for those with private-law contracts, 32 percent do. This proportion is likely to be still higher, given the propensity of persons not to fully report the income earned outside their main job.

Table 6.4 compares higher education teacher salaries with those of other occupations requiring higher education. To be a higher education teacher in Brazil

Table 6.4 Mean income by occupation

	Mean income
Employers	6,356.13
Medical doctors	5,836.52
Analysts, operation engineers	5,290.66
System analysts	4,044.02
Teachers in higher education, public sector	3,762.73
Managers	3,710.33
Dentists	3,692.37
Administrator, business adviser	3,542.71
Agronomist	3,502.74
Accountant	3,458.64
Police officer	3,365.51
Lawyer, attorney, judge, prosecutor	3,296.23
Teachers in the private sector	3,207.21
Architects, civil engineers	3,082.18
Total with higher education	2,780.04

Source: Brazilian Institute of Geography and Statistics, National Household Survey (IBGE, PNAD 2008).

Note: Monthly salaries in Brazilian reais (US$1.00 = R$1.75).

means to have income above average for persons with higher education. For those in the public sector, the income is not as good as that of medical doctors, top-level engineers, and of those in business; but is better than the income of those in other, less prestigious occupations. Earnings for those in the private sector are closer to the average for persons in higher education, similar to architects, civil engineers, and data-processing specialists. It allows for comfortable middle-class lifestyle, particularly if there are two higher education salary earnings in the family.

Distribution of Academic Activities

This section deals with what the academics actually do with their time in terms of teaching, research, and other activities. The information comes from the International Comparative Survey on the Academic Profession, carried out in Brazil in 2007 (Balbachevsky and Schwartzman 2009; Balbachevsky et al. 2008). The sample of 1,200 respondents included academics in public and private institutions as well as in nonuniversity scientific research centers and institutes. For the analysis, the respondents were divided on five strata, based on the characteristics of the institutions in which they worked—public, research-intensive universities; other public universities; private, elite institutions; other private institutions; and research institutes (see Table 6.5).

Table 6.5 Hours worked per week in different activities, by type of institution

Type of institution	Public, research intensive	Public, other	Private, elite	Private, others	Research institutes	Total mean
Teaching[a]	17.11	19.82	21.17	22.76	12.03	19.87
Research[b]	12.84	9.14	9.3	5.86	20.41	9.36
Extension[c]	2.78	2.6	3.55	2.17	1.09	2.53
Administration[d]	5.41	4.77	6.34	3.24	6.09	4.64
Other academic activities[e]	3.03	2.36	2.17	2.73	2.24	2.54
Total respondents	195	614	60	270	53	1,192

Source: Balbachevsky et al. 2008.
[a]Preparation of instructional materials and lesson plans, classroom instruction, advising students, reading and evaluating student work.
[b]Reading literature, writing, conducting experiments, fieldwork.
[c]Services to clients and/or patients, unpaid consulting, public or voluntary services.
[d]Committees, department meetings, paperwork.
[e]Professional activities not clearly attributable to any of the categories above.

Teachers generally devote half of their time to teaching and related activities, with the heaviest teaching load at private institutions. Research-related activities consume half of the time in research centers but less than 6 percent in private institutions. The third activity is administrative work, about 5 percent of the time; and other activities take another 2 to 3 percent of the time.

In public universities, full-time contracts assume that the teachers will spend half of their time on research. As Table 6.6 shows, the percentage reported by the teachers is closer to 10 hours, or 25 percent of their time, except at research institutes. Still, there are many indications that only a fraction of those reporting to do research are actually engaged in research activities.

Table 6.6 shows that, in the private sector, most teachers have a secondary job; and even among those in the public sector, 18.3 percent have an additional job, either in another teaching institution, a nongovernmental organization, or in private practice. Since the salaries in public institutions are fairly satisfactory, why would those teachers look for additional work? One explanation is the natural desire of every person to raise his or her standard of living; the other is that the demand on one's time in a public university is not very high, creating a space and a longing for other activities.

Given the expectation that all academics should do research and publish, the number of persons reporting to have done research and published is relatively high in all groups. However, in research centers and research-intensive universities, research is done with external funding, more articles are published in international publications and in peer-review journals, and international collaboration is more frequent. In nonresearch public and private institutions, external funding is

Table 6.6 Teachers holding second jobs (%)

	Institutions					
	Public, research intensive	*Public, other*	*Private, elite*	*Private, others*	*Research institutes*	*Total mean*
Additional work or job	18.3	30.7	50.6	66.5	24.5	45.7
Secondary work						
Teaching or research institution	6.6	14.5	24.0	39.2	16.3	24.7
Company	2.5	6.4	7.0	18.9	2.0	19.8
Nongovernmental organization	4.6	5.1	6.4	7.8	2.0	6.2
Autonomous, self-employed	6.6	11.8	21.6	19.8	2.0	15.2

Source: Balbachevsky et al. 2008.

much more limited, most of the publications are in Portuguese, and international cooperation is much reduced.

Conclusion

This overview of the academic salaries in Brazil shows that there are two main types of higher education institutions in the country—public and private. Public institutions operate within limitations and policies set by the government and are supported with public funds; private institutions may be for profit or not and depend mostly on tuition fees. Within the public sector, it is possible to distinguish research-intensive institutions from those that are mostly teaching places. There is little research done at private institutions, but it is also possible to distinguish a small number of private, elite institutions, catering to high-income groups, from a larger sector of low-cost, teaching-only institutions, which comprises the bulk of higher education in Brazil today.

The salary conditions of teachers working in public and private institutions are quite different. Salaries in the public sector are higher, and there are more fringe benefits and a lighter teaching load. Most contracts are full time, but the teachers also have the possibility of earning additional income by participating in research projects, doing consultancy, and other activities—even when their work contract is for exclusive dedication. Teachers in public institutions cannot be fired or move to other institutions, and promotion is based primarily on seniority and acquired credentials. Salaries are the same for all federal universities and for all state universities within a state and cannot be negotiated individually. It is difficult for a non-Brazilian to enter the university career in a public institution, although it is allowed by legislation.

In the private sector, most contracts are part time, income is lower, and teachers have to work in more than one place to make ends meet. In all institutions, it is assumed that teachers in higher education should do research, but, in practice, most of those in nonresearch institutions do not receive external support for their projects and are not linked to international research networks.

Compared with other groups, teachers in public institutions are relatively well off, while teachers in private institutions, although earning relatively less, are still above the country's average income for persons with higher education degrees.

References

Balbachevsky, Elizabeth, and Simon Schwartzman. 2009. "The academic profession in a diverse institutional environment: Converging or diverging values and beliefs?" In *The changing academic profession over 1992–2007: International, comparative and quantitative perspectives,* ed. University of Hiroshima's Research Institute for Higher Education, 145–64. Hiroshima, Japan: Hiroshima University Press.

Balbachevsky, Elizabeth, and Simon Schwartzman. 2010. "The graduate foundations of research in Brazil." *Higher Education Forum* (Research Institute for Higher Education, Hiroshima University) 7 (March): 85–100.

Balbachevsky, Elizabeth, Simon Schwartzman, Nathalia Novaes Alves, Dante Filipe Felgueiras dos Santos, and Tiago Silva Birkholz Duarte. 2008. "Brazilian academic profession: Some recent trends." *The Changing Academic Profession in International Comparative and Quantitative Perspectives, RIHE International Seminar Reports* 12 (September): 327–44.

Durham, Eunice. 2004. "Higher education in Brazil: Public and private." In *The challenges of education in Brazil,* ed. C. Brock and S. Schwartzman, 147–78. Oxford, UK: Triangle Journals.

IBGE (Instituto Brasileiro de Geografia e Estatistica), PNAD (Pesquisa Nacional por Amostra de Domicilios). 2008. *Síntese de Indicadores 2008.* http://www.ibge.gov.br/home/estatistica/populacao/trabalhoerendimento/pnad2008/. Accessed December 22, 2011.

MEC (Ministry of Education and Culture). 2010. *University for all (ProUni).* http://siteprouni.mec.gov.br/.

MEC, INEP (Instituto Nacional de Pesquisas Educacionais Aníso Teixeira [National Institute of Educational Studies]). 2008. *Censo da educação superior.* http://portal.inep.gov.br/web/censo-da-educacao-superior.

MEC, INEP. (Instituto Nacional de Pesquisas Educacionais Aníso Teixeira [National Institute of Educational Studies]). 2011. *Censo da educação superior.* http://portal.inep.gov.br/web/censo-da-educacao-superior.

MEC, INEP. (Instituto Nacional de Pesquisas Educacionais Aníso Teixeira [National Institute of Educational Studies]). n.d. *Censo da educação superior.* http://portal.inep.gov.br/web/censo-da-educacao-superior.

Schwartzman, Simon. 2004. "Equity, quality and relevance in higher education in Brazil." *Anais da Academia Brasileira de Ciências* 26 (1): 173–88.

7

THE ORGANIZATION OF ACADEMIC WORK AND FACULTY REMUNERATION AT CANADIAN UNIVERSITIES

Glen A. Jones and Julian Weinrib

Decisions concerning faculty remuneration in Canadian higher education are highly decentralized. Faculty are employed by individual institutions, and almost all full-time faculty are unionized—with salary and benefit decisions emerging from collective bargaining between the university and a local faculty association. Benefits include pensions, sabbatical entitlements, supplemental health insurance, and a range of other items. Full-time, tenure-track faculty in Canadian universities are reasonably remunerated for their work, particularly when compared to the majority of their international peers, but substantial differences run in average salary levels by institution, institutional type, region, and gender.

The Canadian Context

Canada's approach to higher education policy is quite decentralized, with the provinces and territories assuming the major role in the legislation and regulation of higher education policy. The federal government plays a major role in the support of research and development—including university research—working in cooperation with the provinces in the provision of student financial assistance and operating a range of programs and initiatives that indirectly impact the university sector. It is the provinces that create, regulate, and—in the case of public institutions—fund universities (Jones 2006).

Canada's universities are generally established under provincial legislation as private, not-for-profit corporations. Most universities are considered public institutions, in that they are autonomous legal corporations that receive government operating support and are regulated as part of a provincial higher education system (Jones 2002). A small number of universities are considered private in that they do not receive government operating support. Although as this public/ private distinction is not captured by Canada's national data systems, it is difficult to systematically compare private and public university salaries. On the other hand, the data that are available suggest that faculty salaries at private universities are lower than salaries at publicly supported institutions.

Unionization and Faculty Appointments

Canada's federal political structure and the legal foundation of Canada's universities have obvious implications for the organization of academic work. As independent corporations, each university has the legal authority to hire its employees and determine the conditions of employment. While most universities may be considered public institutions, university professors are employees of the university, not the state, and there are differences in the remuneration and working conditions of faculty by institution. These employment relationships are also regulated by provincial labor laws, and there are differences in legislation by jurisdiction.

This chapter focuses primarily on full-time tenured and tenure-stream faculty. The phrase "tenured and tenure-stream" defines the traditional, full-time professoriate, where individuals are expected to engage in some combination of teaching, research, and service and where, following a successful review of performance during a probation period of between three and seven years, a professor would be granted tenure and a permanent contract with the university. Frequently, other categories provide university teachers and research with quite different conditions of employment, but this chapter focuses on the "traditional" tenure-stream faculty.

University professors have organized associations at every institution to represent their common interests in discussions with the central administration of the university. Beginning in the 1970s, a number of these institution-based faculty associations sought and obtained legal status under provincial legislation as labor unions (Tudivor 1999). While the history of unionization differs by province, the full-time faculty in almost all Canadian public universities are now members of recognized labor unions, and it has been suggested that higher education may be the most highly unionized sector in Canada (Dobbie and Robinson 2008). Salaries and other important conditions of employment, including tenure and promotion policies, are defined by collective agreements negotiated between the university (the administration of the university operating under the authority of the university board) and the faculty (represented by the faculty union). In addition to salaries, these agreements frequently define a range of benefits provided to university faculty as employees of the institution—including tenure, retirement pension plans, sabbatical entitlements, medical benefits to supplement provincial public health care plans, maternity/parental leaves, stipends for overload teaching, and vacations. The value of the total benefits provided under these employment arrangements obviously varies by institution, but universities usually spend an additional 20 to 30 percent of total salary costs to cover benefits. While salary is the most significant element in attracting most faculty to academic positions, the offer of employment might also include support for moving costs, research start-up funds, or housing loans—all of which would have been negotiated between the candidate and the university under the framework of the collective agreement. There are also differences in the history and tenor of collective bargaining by the institution; some universities have had protracted faculty strikes in order to resolve an impasse in the negotiations between the faculty association and the university.

There were approximately 38,300 full-time faculty employed by Canadian universities in 2007–8 (CAUT 2010a). Based on incomplete 2003–4 data, David Dobbie and Ian Robinson (2008) estimated that 55 percent of all Canadian faculty held full-time, tenure-stream appointments, while approximately 9 percent held full-time (non-tenure-stream) appointments; and 36 percent held part-time appointments. It is important to note that Dobbie and Robinson's estimate does not include data from Quebec and essentially extrapolates the share of appointment categories based on the ratio identified in a 1997–98 study by Statistics Canada.

While most full-time, tenure-stream faculty are unionized and covered by negotiated agreements with the university, the situation can be quite different for university teachers who are not full time or have been employed under other categories of academic work. The salary and benefit data provided in this study focus on full-time, tenure-stream faculty, but at many universities other categories of individuals engaged in teaching and/or research are remunerated in quite different ways—in some cases, unionized as members of bargaining units that are quite dissimilar from the full-time faculty union. Once again, considerable variations exist in how non-full-time, permanent faculty are categorized, organized, and remunerated by the university; but it has been noted that these individuals are usually paid far less and seldom receive the range of benefits or the level of job security associated with full-time, tenure-stream faculty (Rajagopal 2002). Some part-time faculty aspire to tenure-stream positions and struggle to find enough teaching assignments to support a family as well as maintaining some level of research activity (Muzzin 2009). While Statistics Canada collects and reports basic demographic and salary data on full-time faculty, there is no systematic collection and analysis of data on part-time faculty.

Comparable salary and benefit arrangements are offered in publicly assisted universities that are not unionized. In fact, it is common in these institutions for the faculty association and university administration to negotiate salaries and benefits through an approach that closely resembles collective bargaining. However, the faculty do not have the legal right to strike, and there are other important differences in the legal authority of the association. Unionized and nonunionized universities exist in the same job market, and universities and faculty associations closely monitor salary and benefit changes taking place within peer institutions (Anderson and Jones 1998).

Appointments, Contracts, and Promotion

Candidates for a faculty position are generally expected to have completed a doctoral degree. Three commonly accepted and defined ranks are provided for tenure-stream faculty: assistant professor, associate professor, and full professor. All new academic positions are widely advertised, and the process usually involves an elaborate search process—including a public lecture, meetings with professors and students, and an interview by a search committee of faculty. Junior faculty are hired at the assistant professor level, and promotion to associate professor frequently takes place in parallel with a successful tenure review following a probationary contract period of three to seven years, depending on institutional policy. Tenure provides tremendous job security, and it is assumed that a tenured faculty member will continue to hold the position until retirement. Given the differences in tenure and promotion policies by an institution, including the criteria for making these decisions, these processes generally begin with a review of the candidate's teaching, research, and service by a committee of peers. Promotion to the rank of professor takes place some years after tenure, following a systematic review of the candidate's work by a committee of peers. Unlike these three traditional ranks, no common definition is used for the term *lecturer* in Canadian universities; the term is used in different ways at different institutions, to denote a range of employment categories—including part-time appointments, junior faculty who have not yet completed a doctorate, or faculty who have an appointment primarily focusing on teaching.

Salary Information

As already noted, the Canadian higher education system is highly decentralized. Canadian universities are autonomous institutions, and salary and benefit arrangements are determined at the institutional level, frequently as a function of collective bargaining. Average national salaries, therefore, hide important differences by institution.

Data on faculty salaries were obtained from the Statistics Canada 2010 report *Salaries and Salary Scales of Full-Time Teaching Staff at Canadian Universities, 2007/2008* (Statistics Canada 2010). From this data set, salaries from 52 institutions and 39,295 full-time staff were compiled for analysis. Furthermore, salary data by rank include full-time teaching staff with senior administrative responsibilities—including assistant, associate, and vice deans; department heads; coordinators; and chairpersons—all of whom receive additional remuneration to their basic teaching salary.

Pan-Canadian monthly salary averages are summarized in Table 7.1, while calculations based on the three major institutional types are summarized in

Table 7.1 Full-time teacher average monthly salaries (C$),★
Pan-Canadian

Full professor (top level)	10,704
with administrative duties	11,578
without administrative duties	10,567
Associate professor	8,377
with administrative duties	9,190
without administrative duties	8,415
Assistant professor (entry level)	6,928
Male	9,116
Female	8,113

Source: Statistics Canada 2010.
★C$1.00 = about US$1.02 (2011).

Table 7.2. Junior faculty receive salaries that allow them to live a middle-class lifestyle, while senior salaries would be considered well above average, compared to national average-income levels.

Salary levels are specified under the union contract, and the degree to which salaries will vary by field of scholarship will differ by institution. According to national data, salaries are lower in the social sciences and humanities than in the sciences and professions, but these data mask differences by institution (CAUT 2010a, 7). Salaries will increase by rank and seniority and, in some institutions, based on an assessment of merit through an annual review of performance. Department chairs, deans, and other academic administrators receive an additional stipend as compensation for their additional responsibilities. In unionized environments, department chairs are considered members of the faculty union, and the chair stipend level is specified in the collective agreement. Deans and other academic administrators are considered management.

Institutional policies govern the degree to which faculty can obtain remuneration through external contract activity. Institutional policies generally limit externally paid activities to a specific number of days each year. According to data from a recent survey, approximately one-third of faculty reported engaging in some form of external contract activity during a one-year period (Metcalfe et al. 2008).

Canadian faculty salaries for junior positions are generally perceived as internationally competitive, and this was confirmed by an earlier study (Rumbley, Pacheco, and Altbach 2008). Concerns about brain drain have tended to focus on more senior positions, since few Canadian universities can compete with the salary levels offered to research stars by top American research universities. The federal government has created several programs (such as the Canada Research Chairs Program and the more recent Canada Excellence Research Chairs initiative) designed so that universities can retain leading researchers in Canada and attract leading international scholars in strategic fields.

While there is no formal categorization system for Canadian universities, *Maclean's* magazine, which publishes annual rankings of Canadian universities, classifies institutions into three groups: medical/doctoral universities, comprehensive universities, and primarily undergraduate universities. This categorization system is increasingly used in Canadian higher education research, including reports by Statistics Canada (Orton 2004). Medical/doctoral institutions offer the broadest range of PhD and research programs, as well as housing research-intensive medical schools. Primarily, undergraduate institutions focus on undergraduate education—with minimal or no graduate-level programming—and as an extension, low levels of external research grants. Comprehensive institutions offer a range of graduate, professional, and undergraduate education.

Table 7.2 illustrates the variation in average salary levels by the category of institutions. It is clear that the average salaries of full-time teachers at primarily undergraduate institutions are lower than the average salaries at comprehensive and medical/doctoral institutions. This is particularly true for assistant professors at primarily undergraduate universities, who earn, on average, 81 percent of the average at medical–doctoral institutions and 83 percent of the national average for this rank (Statistics Canada 2010). In addition, the average salaries at comprehensive institutions are lower but comparable to those in the same rank at medical/doctoral institutions; average salaries at comprehensive universities are 91 percent of average salaries at medical/doctoral institutions for full professors, 95 percent for associate professors, and 95 percent for assistant professors.

These data illuminate a broader trend in the Canadian higher education landscape, concerning the increasing emphasis placed on research and research-related activities. Canadian institutions and academics have been reported as increasingly dependent on revenues from provincial, federal, and private research funding (Polster 2007; Metcalfe and Fenwick 2009; Jones and Weinrib 2011). The huge differences in the level of research support by institution serve an impact on the budgetary flexibility of institutions, on their ability to support and attract highly productive research faculty, and on their access to federal research chairs and infrastructure support, which are frequently allocated on the basis of past success in research grant competitions.

Table 7.2 Full-time teacher average monthly salaries (C$),* by institutional type and rank

	Medical-doctoral	*Comprehensive*	*Undergraduate*
Full professor (top level)	11,110	10,127	9,905
Associate professor	8,769	8,357	8,004
Assistant professor (entry level)	7,112	6,774	5,786
Other	6,718	6,257	5,982

Source: Statistics Canada 2010.

*C$1.00 = about US$1.02 (2011).

A final variable in this analysis is the salary differentiation between academic staff with and academic staff without administrative duties. Across all 52 Canadian universities, included in this study, both full and associate professors holding positions with senior administrative duties (chairs, deans, etc.) receive, on average, roughly 10 percent more than their peers.

Differences in Salary Levels by Province and Gender

The second major subcategory in the analysis of remuneration trends for full-time teaching staff at Canadian universities is cross-provincial variation. A wide variance consists in cost of living, both regionally and subregionally, within a country as geographically large and diverse as Canada.

While few quantitative metrics are available to analyze the most and least expensive cities and provinces in Canada, or the correlation between cost of living and faculty salaries, average salaries across all ranks are highest in each of the three provinces with cities highly ranked on national and international cost-of-living surveys: Toronto, Ontario; Vancouver, British Columbia; and Calgary, Alberta. As seen in Table 7.3, Ontario, Alberta, and British Columbia represent the only provinces with average monthly faculty salaries above the national average of C$8,776.

One example of how provincial variables may impact staff salaries, beyond the general numbers portrayed in Table 7.3, is the variance in full-time teaching salaries at medical/doctoral institutions across provinces. Ontario and Quebec are home to 9 of the 15 medical/doctoral universities in Canada: 5 in Ontario and 4 in Quebec. These 9 institutions house 12,585 of the 21,316 total full-time teaching staff at all medical/doctoral institutions—7,077 in Ontario and 5,506 in Quebec (Statistics Canada 2010). As detailed previously, full-time faculty at this university type receive the highest-average remuneration across the three institutional types in Canada. However, while medical/doctoral institutions generally have higher salaries, these salaries are higher in Ontario than they are in Quebec.

The final category for analysis is in regard to what is commonly referred to as the "gender gap," or the discrepancy between male and female salaries, at and across the three primary faculty ranks. This examination will take root in a gendered analysis that considers gender to be a cultural, rather than a purely biological, category. Through such an analysis, emphasis will be placed on "social and cultural expectations associated with gender and the ways they are incorporated" in academia (Acker 2003, 394). While a quantitative analysis of salary trends grounds this study, it is important to attempt a more complex understanding of how and why the current situation is as it is and where Canadian universities can go from here.

Female representation and remuneration practices in the higher education sector remain pressing issues in Canada. While much progress has been made over the past 40 years in terms of working conditions for female staff, some critical scholars argue that "the underlying structures and ideologies that work

Table 7.3 Full-time teacher average monthly salaries (C$),* by province

	Alberta	B.C.	Manitoba	N.B.	Neuf.	N.S.	Ontario	P.E.I.	Quebec	Sask.	Canada
Full prof.	11,786	11,341	10,317	9,564	9,107	9,705	11,273	9,690	9,853	10,618	10,704
Assoc. prof.	8,925	8,623	7,724	7,456	7,514	7,595	9,102	7,983	7,894	8,404	8,377
Assist. prof.	7,305	7,284	6,326	6,024	5,849	6,297	7,236	6,393	6,406	7,083	6,928
Average	9,544	9,143	8,140	7,797	7,551	7,795	9,118	7,851	8,336	8,624	8,776

Source: Statistics Canada 2010.

*C$1.00 = about US$1.02 (2011).

to the disadvantage of women in academia continue to exert a strong, if increasingly unheralded, impact" (Acker and Armenti 2004, 4). As a starting point, female full-time teachers across the 52 universities summarized in this study earn 89 percent of what their male counterparts earn. This percentage remains steady at each of the three institutional levels. A major source of this continued discrepancy is a top-heavy representation of males against females across the three major professorial ranks. Drawing from the Canadian Association of University Teachers 2009–10 almanac (CAUT 2010a), an argument can be made that the major impediment to decreasing the overall salary gap between genders is to increase the representation of female staff at the full professor rank. According to CAUT Almanac data, female full professors earned 95 percent of their male counterparts, associate professors earned 97 percent, and assistant professors earned 96 percent (CAUT 2010a). However, "in 2007, only 20 percent of full professors in Canadian universities were female," compared to a 35 percent representation at the associate professor level, 43 percent at the assistant professor level, and 34 percent representation across all ranks (CAUT 2010b, 5).

The current situation is not without progress. One study concludes that the "amount of the gender earnings gap that is 'unexplained,' or due to the differences in the pay of women and men with the same education, rank and field, has declined from more than 30% to less than 20%" (Warman, Woolley, and Worsick 2010, 348), and "on average, the female and male salary structures are more similar than they once were" (369). In addition, the 2010 CAUT Almanac summarizes that, in 2007, 41 percent of new full-time university teachers in Canada were female, a 6 percent increase from 2001, and 42 percent of full-time female university teachers were in tenure-track positions, up from 28 percent in 1987 (CAUT 2010a, 5).

This analysis indicates that until the current senior cohort retires and can be replaced by staff with more equitable earning differentials, the raw data will continue to portray a significant gender gap in Canadian universities. What the above analysis has highlighted is that to a great extent gender and age are inextricably linked as significant contextual variables of full-time faculty remuneration trends in Canadian universities. As a greater number of teachers are being hired at younger ages and a greater number of teachers are continuing to hold positions past the previous mandatory retirement age of 65 (CAUT 2010b, 2), this correlation will become increasingly important for researchers to monitor. Unfortunately, at this time, limitations in the Canadian data-collection apparatus and a lack of studies on these issues limit the depth of analysis that this report can carry out on the relationship between age, gender, and remuneration. What data are available makes it clear that progress is being made to redress past inequities, but it is also clear that the process is dependent on both the passing of time and the continued development of more equitable hiring and promotional practices in Canadian universities.

Conclusion

The organization of academic work in Canadian universities is characterized by highly decentralized employment arrangements. Canadian universities are chartered and regulated as non-for-profit corporations by provincial governments, and most receive provincial government operating support and are considered public institutions. Faculty are employed by individual institutions, and the vast majority are members of institution-specific labor unions. Based on the previous iteration of this study, full-time, tenure-stream faculty receive internationally competitive salaries (Rumbley, Pacheco, and Altbach 2008)—despite variations in average salary levels by Canadian province, institutional category, and gender.

While there are national data on full-time faculty salaries, relatively little national data are available on part-time faculty and other employment categories of teachers and researchers in Canadian universities. This gap—combined with the fact that academic work is largely defined and constructed at the institutional level, plus the absence of studies that have systematically compared and analyzed these institutional arrangements—means that relatively little is known about academic work in Canada. This study has reinforced previous conclusions that current national data-gathering systems are inadequate for the task of analyzing the conditions of employment for full- and part-time teaching staff in Canadian universities (Canadian Council on Learning 2007; Jones et al. 2008). Additional data are needed in order to understand and analyze the implications of the differentiation and fragmentation of academic work through the creation of new employment categories, the existence of multiple unions representing differently defined university teachers and researchers, and the challenges that these changes represent for collegiality and academic community.

References

Acker, Sandra. 2003. "The concerns of Canadian women academics: Will faculty shortages make things better or worse?" *McGill Journal of Education* 38 (3): 391–405.

Acker, Sandra, and Carmen Armenti. 2004. "Sleepless in academia." *Gender and Education* 16 (1): 3–24.

Anderson, Barb, and Glen A. Jones. 1998. "Organizational capacity and political activities of Canadian university faculty associations." *Interchange* 29 (4): 439–61.

Canadian Council on Learning. 2007. *Measuring what Canadians value: A pan-Canadian data strategy for post-secondary education.* Ottawa: Canadian Council on Learning.

CAUT (Canadian Association of University Teachers). 2010a. *CAUT Almanac of post-secondary education in Canada: 2009–2010.* http://www.caut.ca/uploads/2009_CAUT_Almanac.pdf. Accessed May 17, 2010.

CAUT (Canadian Association of University Teachers). 2010b. Education review: The changing academy? A portrait of Canada's university teachers. *CAUT Education Review* 12: 1–8. http://www.caut.ca/uploads/EducationReview12-1-en.pdf. Accessed May 21, 2010.

Dobbie, David, and Ian Robinson. 2008. "Reorganizing higher education in the United States and Canada: The erosion of tenure and the unionization of contingent faculty." *Labour Studies Journal* 33 (1): 117–40.

Jones, Glen A. 2002. "The structure of university governance in Canada: A policy network approach." In *Governing higher education: National perspectives on institutional governance,* ed. Alberto Amaral, Glen A. Jones, and Berit Karseth, 213–34. Dordrecht, Netherlands: Kluwer Academic.

Jones, Glen. A. 2006. "Canada." In *International handbook of higher education,* ed. J. J. F. Forest and Philip G. Altbach, 627–45. Dordrecht, Netherlands: Springer.

Jones, Glen, Theresa Shanahan, Lucia Padure, S. Lamoureux, and Emily Gregor. 2008. *Marshalling resources for change: System-level initiatives to increase accessibility to post-secondary education.* Ottawa: Canada Millennium Scholarship Foundation.

Jones, Glen A., and Julian Weinrib. 2011. "Globalization and Canadian higher education: A case study." In *A handbook on globalization and higher education,* ed. Roger King, Simon Marginson, and Rajani Naidoo, 222–40. London: Edward Elgar.

Metcalfe, Amy S., and Tara Fenwick. 2009. "Knowledge for whose society? Knowledge production, higher education, and federal policy in Canada." *Higher Education* 57: 209–25.

Metcalfe, Amy S., Donald Fisher, Kjell Rubenson, Yves Gingras, Glen A. Jones, and Iain Snee. 2008. "Changing academic profession: Canadian survey." Unpublished raw data.

Muzzin, Linda. 2009. "Equity, ethics, academic freedom and the employment of contingent academics." *Academic Matters* (May): 19–22.

Orton, L. 2004. A new understanding of postsecondary education in Canada. Presentation at the Annual Meeting of the Canadian Society for the Study of Higher Education, Winnipeg, May 31.

Polster, Claire. 2007. "The nature and implications of the growing importance of research grants to Canadian universities and academics." *Higher Education* 53: 599–622.

Rajagopal, I. 2002. *Hidden academics: Contract faculty in Canadian universities.* Toronto, Canada: University of Toronto Press.

Rumbley, Laura E., Iván F. Pacheco, and Philip G. Altbach. 2008. *International comparison of academic salaries.* Chestnut Hill, MA: Center for International Higher Education, Boston College.

Statistics Canada. 2010. *Salaries and salary scales of full-time teaching staff at Canadian universities, 2007/2008: Final Report.* http://www.statcan.gc.ca/pub/81–595-m/81–595-m2010082-eng.pdf. Accessed May 17, 2010.

Tudivor, N. 1999. *Universities for sale: Resisting corporate control over Canadian higher education.* Toronto, Canada: James Lorimer.

Warman, Casey, Francis Woolley, and Christopher Worsick. 2010. "The evolution of male-female earnings differentials in Canadian universities, 1970–2001." *Canadian Journal of Economics* 43 (1): 347–472.

8

A STUDY ON ACADEMIC SALARY AND REMUNERATIONS IN CHINA

Wanhua Ma and Jianbo Wen

Faculty salaries in Chinese universities are composites of a base salary, further remuneration, and fringe benefits. Information about faculty salaries in China is hard to obtain—partly because of the complex structure as well as the absence of national statistics. Previous studies reflect similar complexities (Wang 2005; Rumbley, Pacheco, and Altbach 2008; Mohrman, Geng, and Wang 2011). The information in this chapter is based on a case-study methodology to assess the current situation of Chinese academic salaries and remuneration, hiring practices, contracts, and promotions. The case university selected for this study is highly specialized in economics and finance, research oriented, and located in one of the country's largest cities. Data were collected from various disciplines, at several faculties. This case reflects salary and remuneration of English department professors, since these are the most representative of Chinese academic salaries and remuneration—in general, because the majority of universities are teaching oriented.

Overview of Higher Education in China

Higher education in China includes public universities, nonstate colleges and universities, adult universities, short-cycle colleges, advanced vocational institutions, as well as alternative forms of higher learning. The higher education system includes those universities and colleges that are under local and provincial governments and the Ministry of Education. This system includes 1,079 four-year institutions and 1,184 three-year vocational or technical institutions. Some of the 1,079 institutions are related to the 211 Project and 985 Program universities. The 211 Project is a venture of National Key Universities and colleges initiated in 1995 by the Ministry of Education of the People's Republic of China. The numerals reflect an abbreviation of the 21st century and approximately 100 universities. The 985 Program was launched in May 1998, when former president Jiang Zemin announced China's goal of creating "world-class" institutions. After his announcement, millions of renminbi (RMB) were pumped into the most promising research universities. Both programs underscore China's seriousness about improving the quality of its higher education institutions and building world-class universities.

As a result of these two programs, Chinese universities could be classified into three tiers. The first and second tiers include the 39 universities in the 985 Program, followed by the 211 Project universities; state or provincial universities, the local public, and private universities are considered the third tier.

All public four-year institutions award a bachelor's degree. A smaller group of institutions offer graduate degrees. The Academy of Science and the Academy of Social Sciences both have graduate schools and award master's and doctoral degrees.

The Chinese higher education system is now the largest in the world—with 29,070,000 students as of 2008; the gross enrollment rate was 23.3 percent. According to the newly published document *The Outline for Mid- and Long-Term Higher Education Development Plan for China (2010–2020),* the number of students in higher education is estimated to be 33,500,000 by 2015 and 35,500,000 by 2020 (Ministry of Education 2010). The gross enrollment rate will become 36 percent and 40 percent, respectively. Following the growth of the system, one would expect Chinese higher education to have another leap forward during the coming decade, with an increased number of faculty in the near future. According to *China Education Statistics,* until 2008 there were altogether 1,309,799 full-time teachers—1,237,451 registered in regular higher education institutions, 53,227 in adult institutions, and 19,121 in nonstate/private institutions (Ministry of Education 2009).

Two important events have supported China's higher education development in the past. One is the presidential call for building world-class universities at the centennial of Peking University in May 1998, where the 985 Program was launched. The other benefit is the enrollment increase mandated by the Ministry of Education in 1999. In terms of finance and governance, a two-level provision has been in place since then. The two-level provision system means the central government is responsible for policymaking, development plans, system reforms, quality controls, and the core funding of the governmental universities, and the local government or provincial government is responsible for managing admission, funding, and job placement of graduates in accordance with national policies and laws for local and provincial universities and colleges. Currently, the central government provides core funding to the 211 Project and the 985 Program universities. Other universities are funded mainly by provincial and local governments and supplemented with the central government funding.

Faculty Hierarchy and Remuneration

In China, faculty positions progress from assistant professor, to associate professor, and to full professor. Generally, an assistant professorship involves only one level.

The associate professorship consists of three levels or ranks, and the full professorship consists of four levels or ranks, with a member of the Academy of Science considered as the top rank. In China, a member of the Academy of Science enjoys not only a high social status but also higher salary, extra research grants, and many other subsidies and bonuses.

A newly hired faculty with a fresh PhD always begins as an assistant professor. An assistant professor has only one salary level, but after being promoted to associate professor, he or she will be ranked according to the year of services, teaching performance, and research/publications. A newly promoted full professor is always paid as a fourth-rank professor, with some exceptions. The base salary for faculty in this rank is relatively the same countrywide.

The academic progression would begin with assistant lecturer, lecturer, associate professor, and full professor. At the case university, an assistant lecturer's salary is around RMB 2,000 (US$307), a lecturer's around RMB 2,500 (US$385); an associate professor's around RMB 2,900 (US$446); and a professor's about RMB 3,400 (US$523)—not including additional remuneration or fringe benefits. This scale does not reflect actual earnings, given all the variations. Usually, the fringe benefits in Chinese universities include different subsidies and bonuses. In the case university, full professors are divided into four ranks: the fourth-rank refers to the starting position of a full professor, and the member of the Academy of Science is considered as the first-rank professor. Throughout this chapter, most information relates to beginning full professors.

For example, a beginning fourth-rank (English) full professor's income from the case university is around RMB 9,807 (US$1,509), as shown in Table 8.1. This amount of salary is before income tax and after the deduction of public reserve fund. In China, the public reserve fund is a mandated faculty retirement plan that is directly deposited by the university into the teacher's reserve account. The university is also mandated to provide matching funds; the matching fund should form 10 percent of the faculty member's monthly basic salary. It becomes apparent that subsidies can expand the base salary by three to four times.

After the public reserve fund and the tax deduction, this professor would take home around RMB 8,500 (US$1,307). A further condition is that a faculty member who before has received a lump-sum distribution for public housing cannot receive an additional cost-of-living subsidy. In the data shown in Table 8.1, the professor did not previously receive a housing benefit and so will receive the monthly cost-of-living subsidy. The living subsidy is a form of welfare provided by the central and local governments; it is offered only at public universities. This kind of welfare will usually last three to five years. After that, there will be other kinds of living subsidies, but the amount will be reduced. If the optional living subsidy is deducted, the professor's take-home pay should be about RMB 7,500 (US$1,153) monthly.

This particular fourth-rank full-professor's payment includes subsidies for telephone use and transportation. These two subsidies are not required by the

Table 8.1 Monthly salary of a fourth-rank professor★
(renminbi), 2010

Items	RMB★★
Base salary	1,420
Scale salary	555
Teaching subsidy	50
Duty subsidy	1,995
Food subsidy	50
Telephone	100
Laundry	10
Transportation	315
Book and magazine	27
Housing subsidy	115
Living subsidy (optional)	1,100
Internal subsidy	3,900
Unemployment insurance	12
One-child subsidy	50
Price subsidy	10
Public reserve fund	(817)
Other subsidies	100
Total	8,992

Source: The data are from the pay slip of the case university.

★Starting position as full professor.
★★US$1.00 = RMB 6.5.

central government but are offered at the discretion of the university. If the university or the school of the university has the money to provide those subsidies, it is fine; but if not, nobody can complain. The position subsidy for this fourth-rank (English) full professor is RMB 3,900 (US$600); at other universities, it should be around RMB 2,500 to RMB 3,000 (US$416). The case university is particularly self-sufficient in financing matters. However, this is not a general phenomenon, because at different universities the amount of government grants varies, as does the university's own financial situation; thus, subsidies vary among institutions.

Some universities provide training programs organized by individual faculty. Individuals who teach those training classes receive a bonus, about four- to six-times higher than what a person earns for regular, mandated teaching classes. This will never appear in the university's regular payment statement, because it is optional and not all faculty are involved. Who obtains the opportunities to teach those highly paid classes is the dean's decision at each school or college.

So with additional bonuses, one can estimate that this beginning fourth-rank full professor's monthly take-home income would be higher than the RMB 7,500 (US$1,153).

Fringe Benefits and Additional Subsidies

Fringe benefits vary between the ranks of professors. A number of direct subsidies are included in the monthly payment, as demonstrated in Table 8.1. Usually, the largest benefit provided by the university is the internal subsidy—with a great difference between assistant professor to full professor. Subsidies for each rank are determined by each university, and the subsidies can range from RMB 3,000 (US$416) to RMB 50,000 (US$7,728) annually (Chen 2002). This represents a striking 17-fold divergence. This scale applies to the faculty, staff, and administrators of the whole university personnel system. Few, if any, academic faculty are awarded the lowest-level subsidy. The lowest level is designed for lower-level staff. Subsidies to academic faculty at the assistant level generally begin at RMB 10,000 (US$1,538).

For clarification, a comparison is made between an associate professor and a lecturer in Table 8.2 to show the variations in subsidies. The main gap lies in the duty subsidy and public reserve fund. The duty subsidy forms welfare benefits for specific work posts, and the public reserve fund serves as the faculty and staff retirement plan. The base salary and scaled salary are shown in Table 8.2. All faculty in the public system receive some of subsidies shown in Table 8.2. As mentioned previously, the case study was conducted at a typical public, research-oriented institution that specialize in finance and economics. Since this university is in a strong financial position, it can provide extra subsidies to faculty and staff, while other universities may be unable to do so. The variations in categories and

Table 8.2 Variations of monetary subsidies, 2010

Subsidy	Associate professor RMB[*]	Lecturer RMB[*]
Teaching	50	50
Duty subsidy	1,675	1,240
Food subsidy	50	50
Telephone	100	100
Laundry	10	10
Transportation	325	315
Book and magazine	27	27
Housing subsidy	95	80
Living subsidy[**]		1,100
Internal subsidy	2,800	1,800
One-child subsidy	10	
Price subsidy	10	10
Public reserve fund	743	505
Total (before taxes)	5,895	5,287

Source: The data are from the pay slip of the case university.
[*]US$1.00 = RMB 6.5.
[**]Living subsidy refers to the welfare benefits provided by the university to the faculty for their house buying or renting.

amounts of subsidies at different universities make it difficult to generalize about the whole system.

Other Monetary Bonuses

As mentioned earlier, bonuses are sometimes paid by individual departments and schools or from a bonus fund of the university; since they are optional, bonuses are not included in the salary or fringe benefits listed above. They also depend on the annual performance of the schools in the university. Mainly, bonuses are calculated on the basis of additional teaching loads, faculty compensation from research grants, rewards for publication, and consulting services.

In the case study, if a beginning full professor faculty member meets the standard of the university teaching loads, the person will get RMB 50 (US$7.70) for each class taught. Then this particular school will pay the faculty an additional RMB 80 (US$12.30) as a bonus. Thus, the two payments, together, would total RMB 130 (US$20) for each class the professor taught.

Participation in transnational or local training, for which fees are charged, produces additional income at multiple levels. The university takes a percentage for administrative costs; the schools take a percentage for the bonuses mentioned above; and the training centers that run those programs keep the majority of the income for salaries, classroom rent, and lecture fees and further elements. All faculty members in the school will obtain some basic bonuses, but the amounts will differ. School deans may also gain extra rewards from this fund.

Additional Factors on Salary and Remuneration

Many factors influence faculty salary in public universities—the number of years worked, academic field, rank, teaching load, research grants, seniority, number of publications, among others. To increase faculty income, universities tacitly consent to faculty engagement in a range of ancillary activities, such as consulting, teaching night classes, or other remunerative activities. In research universities, faculty are more likely to engage in consulting and cooperative research activities. Thus, faculty in 985 Program universities have more opportunities to earn extra income compared with peers in non-985 universities. Nearly all persons who hold membership in the Academy of Science in Higher Education serve at 985 Program universities and are the individuals most eligible for the first-rank professorship salary.

To attract and retain top-level scholars, the Chinese government has initiated programs—such as the special-subsidy program—for faculty who have made special contributions. The professors who receive this honor are awarded RMB 20,000 (US$3,077) in one lump sum. Another government program is the Changjiang scholars program. Professors in this program receive RMB 100,000 (US$15,385) annually, plus their basic salary and other subsidies and bonuses. Recently, local governments in conjunction with the national government and universities initiated a special program to attract talent by launching the 111 Program with RMB 500,000 (US$76,923) annually and a lump sum of RMB 1,000,000 (US$153,846) for home settlement. These programs include a small percentage of Chinese faculty.

In China, while faculty and staff in higher education institutions belong to the public-unit staffing system, they are not civil servants and do not have lifetime employment until receiving tenure. They receive their base salaries from the central or provincial government and other subsidies from their respective institutions. Institutions are now given more autonomy to tap particular resources for institutional development, and universities have their own sources of income. Thus, they all can use some of their own resources to increase compensation to faculty and staff. It should be noted that new specialized universities may do better than traditional comprehensive universities; so, there are gaps among universities in levels of faculty compensation. Even within the same university, the gap could be significant between schools. In the well-known business schools at the 985 Program universities, faculty income would become 10 times higher than that of faculty in humanities or social sciences, because business schools can charge much higher tuition and fees for a master of business administration, executive master of business administration, or short-term executive training programs. Base salaries tend to be similar and fall within a rather narrow range; it is typically the variations in fringe benefits and bonuses that differentiate faculty's income.

Generally, national institutions have more channels for generating funds than local ones. First, per capita–fiscal allocation at the national level is higher than at the local level, due to better fiscal conditions; second, there are several dedicated projects supported by the central government's budget, which direct additional funding to national institutions; third, national institutions receive more research funding due to their mission and stronger capacity (Yan 2009). Local institutions have limited opportunities to generate extra funds except for government grants. For example, faculty at local universities may gain less in subsidies and bonuses. Additionally, due to contrasts in local economic conditions, the financial situation of institutions in various provinces differs considerably. In the southeast coastal areas of the country, local universities seem to do better than other local universities, which affects faculty benefits and bonuses.

Salaries at Private Universities

In contrast, faculty in the private sector are employees of a particular university, where salary and fringe benefits depend solely on the university or, more specifically, the income from student tuition. Thus, salary or income may form a much lower level in comparison with counterparts in the public sector. These universities are almost entirely teaching oriented. Thus, teachers always face a heavy teaching load; if they want to receive bonus pay, they need to teach more classes. Due to a current lack of data, little information is available about faculty remuneration or contracts at private universities.

Supplemental Employment

There are opportunities for most faculty to teach or consult outside their university and, for the services they provide, to earn additional lecture and consulting fees. Teaching in private universities and colleges in the evening and offering courses for self-study programs are other ways to earn extra salary. How much an individual could earn from those activities is not known, and it is difficult to learn the percentage of professors who teach in more than one institution, because those activities are usually ad hoc in nature.

Academic Promotions and Assessment

Requirements or educational qualifications for a faculty position differ among universities. The Higher Education Law provides some guidelines for minimum requirements. The law prescribes that to obtain a qualification to teach in a higher learning institution, one faculty member shall be a postgraduate or university graduate. In practice, to enter the academic profession, at the minimum a master's degree is required; at top-ranked universities, at the minimum a doctorate degree is required. In fact, some schools or research institutes in the 985 Program universities have a minimum requirement of a foreign PhD for faculty members. A master's degree holder will start at the lowest rank of teaching assistant, and a PhD holder will start as an assistant professor. To be promoted to associate professor or professor, a PhD degree is generally essential. Besides the education requirement, a qualification certificate is also necessary. All teachers in national, provincial, local, and private universities must obtain the certificate to be a teacher at a higher learning institution. This credential is awarded by the Ministry of Education.

Universities are now establishing their own internal quality mechanisms to evaluate individual faculty performance. In most universities, the criteria for faculty promotion focuses mainly on research and publications in core journals, which is dramatically different from the old system, which was based on years of work and seniority. Of course, teaching and years of service are also considered for promotion.

For an assistant professor with a PhD degree to be promoted to a full professor, the process would take at least take seven years—generally two years for an assistant professor to be promoted to associate professor and five years from associate professor to full professor. Not many associate professors can be promoted in five years, so in practice, it takes longer. In Peking University's personnel reform structure, if an associate professor cannot be promoted to full professor within four contracts, this faculty member cannot be contracted for further employment.

Each contract involves three years. Thus, if not promoted to a full professor in 12 years, an associate professor is automatically terminated.

At Chinese universities, 38.3 percent of the professoriate now hold a doctoral degree, 23.1 percent have a master's degree, and 38.3 percent have a bachelor's degree. Most of the faculty with PhD degrees are in 211 Projects and 985 Program universities. At Peking University, over 70 percent of its faculty have PhD degrees and over 40 percent hold foreign a PhD degree. How education background affects faculty salary is unknown. Yet, generally speaking, a good education background forms quicker promotion, which in turn means higher salary. Some universities now rigorously recruit faculty from the international academic labor market. The recent efforts to recruit top foreign-trained Chinese from overseas through the 111 Program may attract back some scholars.

Conclusion

The research results reported here illustrate the general situation of Chinese faculty salaries in public four-year institutions. Since universities are given more autonomy in tapping different resources, some universities may do better than others, financially. Thus, there are differences in faculty's income from one institution to another, even among schools or colleges within the same university. The extreme cases would always be related to business schools. This chapter has used a beginning (English) full professor's salary and remunerations in a well-known specialized university to demonstrate how Chinese faculty are paid. The discussion highlighted the complexity of faculty salary and remuneration in China, and many issues related to faculty compensation need further investigation.

For lack of national data in regard to fringe benefits of other professions in the country, it is hard to determine how well academic faculty are paid compared to other professions. Only recently, the *Chinese Statistics Yearbook* (2009) showed that among 19 sectors in 2008, higher education are well above the average at the national level, which allows Chinese faculty life to be considered much better off. According to national statistics, the average income in the education sector in the city where the case university is located is RMB 55,200 (US$8,532) annually; the salary of a (English) full professor is very much above average.

References

Chen, X. 2002. "The academic profession in China." In *The decline of the guru: The academic profession in developing and middle-income countries,* ed. P. G. Altbach 107–34. New York: Palgrave.

China Statistics Yearbook. 2009. *Average wage of staff and workers by sector and region.* Beijing: China Statistics Press.

Ministry of Education. 2009. "The number of faculty and staff in higher education institutions." In *Yearbook of China education statistics (2008),* sec. 11. Beijing: People's Education Press.

Ministry of Education. 2010. *The outline for mid- and long-term higher education development plan for China (2010–2020)*. Beijing: People's Publishing House.

Mohrman, K., Yiqun Geng, and Yingjie Wang. 2011. "Faculty life in China." In *The NEA 2011 ALMANAC of higher education*, 82–99. Washington, DC: National Education Association.

Rumbley, Laura E., Iván F. Pacheco, and Philip G. Altbach. 2008. *International comparison of academic salaries: An exploratory study*. Chestnut Hill, MA: Boston College, Center for International Higher Education.

Wang, Weiping. 2005. "The reviving academic profession in China: The case of Zhejiang Shu Ren University." PhD diss., Boston College.

Yan, F. 2009. "China's academic profession in the context of social transition: Institutional perspective." *Economics of Education Research* (Beida) 7 (2): 9.

9

ACADEMIC SALARIES IN COLOMBIA

The Data Tell Only a Small Part of the Story

Iván F. Pacheco

The salary for a *profesor titular* (full professor) in Colombia is certainly enough to afford a middle-class livelihood, but full-time professors are a minority in the country, in which more than 69 percent of the professoriate holds a part-time contract. Between 3 percent and 8 percent of the numbers of the professoriate have a PhD, but a trend to improve faculty's qualifications is already evident. Data on academic salaries are not regularly collected for either public or private universities. International academic mobility is not a major concern in the country.

Overview of Colombian Higher Education

There are 282 higher education institutions in Colombia: 43 technical institutes, 51 technological institutes, 109 university institutes and technological schools, and 79 universities (Ministry of Education, n.d.b). The classification of higher education institutions was initially based on the type of programs each institution was allowed to offer; however, recent regulations have confused the differentiation among higher education institutions in Colombia and the variations that distinguish them. For the purpose of this chapter, universities, university institutes, and technological schools concentrate on the large majority of professional programs (bachelor's level, four to five years), while the rest of the institutions offer mostly vocational (two- to three-year) programs equivalent to the associate level in the U.S. system. Universities are also allowed to offer master's and doctoral programs.

Enrollment levels in Colombia have been growing constantly since the 1960s, and from 2000 to 2010, the growth rate improved dramatically, from 977,243 to 1,570,000 students—most of them in undergraduate university programs. For decades, Colombian higher education has been mostly private, based on the number of institutions and students; but since 2002, public institutions have been expanding their enrollment faster than private ones. In 2002, public higher education accounted only for 37 percent of the total enrollment; six years later, in 2008, it provided about 55 percent of the total enrollment (Ministry of Education, n.d.b).

Academic Contracts

The modest requirement to become a public university professor is a *profesional* (bachelor's) degree. Exceptionally, the university's superior council board can authorize hiring a professor with lesser qualifications. While in this regard no regulation applies to private higher education institutions, the same minimal requirement is effective in most of these institutions.

By 2005, the highest degree that most professors held was a specialist (36.9 percent), a postgraduate degree typically corresponding to one year of additional studies and no thesis, followed closely by a bachelor's degree (*profesional*), which accounted for 36.8 percent. While 21 percent of the Colombian professoriate had a master's degree, only between 3.3 and 8 percent (depending on the source) held a doctoral degree (Ministry of Education, n.d.b; Borrero 2006)—a rate extremely low compared with regional and international standards. The requirements for hiring more and better-qualified faculty have been rising, and the master's degree is becoming the lowest entry requirement for full-time faculty in public and private universities.

Academic Ranks

Four academic ranks consist in public universities: auxiliary professor, assistant professor, associate professor, and full (*titular*) professor. Specific regulations, applicable only to the National University, serve as a special category for instructors who do not have a bachelor's degree. University bylaws must determine the process and specific requirement for faculty evaluation and promotion in each university. Seniority is usually the key element to ascend from one category to the next. However, according to the law, to become an associate professor, the candidate requires a significant contribution to teaching sciences, the arts, or humanities, which has to be defended in front of peers from other institutions. To become a full professor, the candidate must have produced and justified several contributions. All these elements are left for each university to define. A specific degree (master's or doctorate) is not a requirement to become *profesor titular*.

The requirements for an academic promotion must be stipulated in the university's bylaws. While there is great variation across private universities, seniority is usually the most relevant requirement. In some private universities, the rank is based on a point system described below.

Types of Contracts

Based on a resolution, academic contracts can constitute a full-time (40 hours per week), half-time (20 hours), or hourly (less than 20 hours) condition. Full-time professors are not forbidden to work for other employers as long as the number of weekly hours of their first contract is covered. There is a special category called *docentes de tiempo completo con dedicación exclusiva* (full-time professor with exclusive dedication), the conditions of which vary among universities. Sometimes professors of this type of contract are expected to work up to 46 hours per week; sometimes they are expected to contribute to specific projects like the drafting of internal bylaws or the organization of an international conference. In some cases, such a contract is a temporary agreement, and it is the rector who can grant and retire such status. In other cases, the public call to fill a vacancy may be made for a full-time, exclusive position. Interestingly, in public universities the bylaws usually do not mention the prohibition of working for another employer while having an exclusivity agreement.

Hourly based contracts represent 64 percent of the total contracts in the private and public sectors, followed by full time—including exclusive and nonexclusive dedication (25 percent)—and half time (11 percent) (Ministry of Education, n.d.b).

Professors at public universities can be *de planta* (permanent) and *temporales* (temporary). Permanent professors can be full time or half time and are considered public servants; hence, the structure of salaries and benefits is based on a special law for public servants and each university's bylaws. Permanent professors get their positions through a competitive process, taking into account experience, production, and credentials. A typical hiring process includes a public call, the evaluation of the candidate's resume and academic or related production (sometimes by peers), and, in some cases, an interview. A trial period, the duration of which must be defined in each university's bylaws, can also be part of the process.

Public servants enjoy more stability than most workers in the country, and they are hired for an indefinite term. The National University is in many regards a special case, as only full professors have indefinite-term contracts; all the other contracts are signed for a five-year period. Nonetheless, most get their contract renewed after the five-year period. So, in general, permanent professors at public universities enjoy de facto tenure.

Public universities also can appoint a nonofficial category called "temporary professors," which includes nonpermanent professors (*profesores ocasionales*) and professors with hourly based contracts (*profesor de cátedra*). Temporary professors are not covered by the labor regulations for public servants but by those applicable to private workers.

The form of a nonpermanent professor does not create an ongoing relationship between the university and the professor, and it allows universities to impose a heavier teaching load than what applies to permanent professors. Nonpermanent professors can serve full-time or half-time positions; they can be hired for less than a year; and the rank system does not apply to them. However, several universities define a temporary professor's salary, based on a system of equivalencies, in which they are paid similarly to those with public-servant status. The format of nonpermanent professor was initially created to allow the flexibility to hire faculty for shorter periods, particularly guest professors. An unforeseen result of this new hiring policy was that it allowed universities to skip the legal require-ments in the faculty recruitment process and also to avoid hiring staff as public servants, which would have a long-term impact on the finances of the university.

In what seems to be a contradiction, some institutions have made public calls to hire nonpermanent professors through meritocratic processes and define in their bylaws what is necessary to renew these contracts. Despite the legal limit of one year for the duration of these contracts, some nonpermanent professors have been hired by the same university for 10 consecutive years, using contracts of less than a year that are regularly renewed after their expiration (Arboleda 2004). However, job security for temporary professors is precarious.

Official data do not discriminate between permanent and nonpermanent pro-fessors (Ministry of Education, n.d.a), but many believe that today the majority of teaching staff at public universities are nonpermanent professors.

Private universities have more freedom to hire and fire staff than public uni-versities. They generally do not award tenure, and promotions are usually based on seniority. Academic contracts in private universities are usually signed for a year or less (sometimes, for a semester). No standard procedure exists for hiring academic personnel in private universities. Some universities use open calls and merit-based processes, while in others, without a specific process, positions are filled based on the rector's and dean's networks or other informal functions.

Research is not a central issue in most academic contracts, nor is the amount of time that professors should dedicate to research or teaching. In some public and private universities, the allocation of faculty time and performance expecta-tions are discussed by the university senate, or another equivalent body, and may (or may not) influence institutional policy. Some research universities may have faculty positions with exclusive or preferential dedication to research. Research subsidies as a mechanism to attract faculty are a rarity in the Colombian system. Part-time teachers (hourly based and half time) are usually not expected to do research, and they are usually compensated on the basis of teaching hours.

Moonlighting

Individuals are forbidden to have two simultaneous jobs in government institu-tions (including universities) or to receive payment from two different institutions financed with money from the national treasury. But there are some excep-tions—like the honoraria received by public servants who also teach as adjunct professors under hourly based contracts; the compensation that university pro-fessors may receive for working as advisers to the legislature; and honorariums received for services related to health professions. Professors from public uni-versities are allowed to work in private universities, with the exception of those with an exclusivity agreement. In fact, some professors build their prestige on the number of institutions they work for. Some prestigious private universities, in their bylaws, may include exclusivity as a requirement for permanent professorships, may negotiate exclusivity with some professors, or demand fidelity to the institution.

In public universities, when professors are assigned administrative functions they are entitled to receive additional salary benefits. In private universities, professors can get additional compensation for teaching executive courses or graduate courses, but the remuneration model varies in these universities.

Academic Salaries

Salaries at public universities are based on a complex system of scores with four main elements: academic degree, career rank, experience, and academic production. Salary is obtained by the multiplication of the allocations to each professor multiplied by the monetary value of the salary point. The value of the benefits is defined annually by the government; for 2010, this value was COL$9,313 (about US$5.17).

Academic degree points are determined on the basis of the type of degree and the duration of studies; career rank takes into consideration the four ranks defined by the higher education law; experience covers the trajectory of the professor both in academia and in other positions; and academic production takes into account several products—including articles, books, patents, video films, and others (see Table 9.1). Academic productivity is the factor that allows higher accumulation of points; the difference between the salary of a professor with high productivity and one with less accomplishment can be significant.

This salary model has created a big impact in public universities. It has stimulated academic productivity in such a way that the number of articles published has more than doubled between 2002 and 2010. Likewise, academic salaries are more competitive, especially with respect to industry. On the other hand, it has also promoted purely academic tasks, which means that other products related to social or industry-related work have not grown as fast because they are not rewarded. Some observers indicate the scheme's negative impact on teaching, given that more credit is given to professors for research and publishing than for teaching. It has also increased, in some cases significantly, the income of the universities in a way that is difficult to forecast. It might also have created perverse stimuli, since quantity has become more influential than quality or long-term projects. Some professors become experts at gaining credits, not always with the expected scientific or technical impact on their productivity.

Salaries presented in this chapter are based on the allocation of benefits to ideal profiles corresponding to the average professor for each ranking. They are not based on data provided by the universities.

Each university has an Internal Points Committee for the Allocation and Acknowledgment of Points. When a public university hires a professor, the

Table 9.1 Salary point system for public universities

Academic degrees: (maximum of 323 points)	
Undergraduate degree	178
Undergraduate degree (medicine or musical composition)	183
Specialization (each year of a specialization program finished)	10
Master's degree	40
Second master's degree	20
Doctoral degree	80
Career rank: (maximum of 96 points)	
Top level (*profesor titular*)	96
Level 2 (*profesor asociado*)	74
Level 3 (*profesor asistente*)	58
Level 4 and lower (*profesor auxiliar o instructor*):	37
Experience	
Years of research experience	6
Years of teaching experience	4
Years of other professional experience at the executive level	4
Years of other professional experience	3
Academic productivity★	
Article, depending on the level of the journal	Up to 15
Multimedia productions (Video, film or soundtrack)	Up to 12
Books from research	Up to 20
Textbooks	Up to 15
Books of essays	Up to 155
National or international appraisals	Up to 15
Patent	25
Translation of a book	Up to 15
Artistic creation	Up to 20
Original musical or artistic interpretation	Up to 14
Technological innovation	Up to 15
Original software	Up to 15

Source: Ministerio de Educación Nacional 2002.

★Maximum of five items of work per year.

committee evaluates the four factors (academic degree, career rank, experience, and academic production) and determines the number of points granted to determine the professor's remuneration. Professors are entitled for an update when a change in any of the factors described above occurs. Other factors can improve professors' salaries—such as by assuming administrative positions within the university or having the professor's activities of teaching or service acknowledged as outstanding. Without a national standard among the points committees across universities, the differences in the evaluation and allocation of points from one university to another can diversify salary between two people with an identical trajectory.

In addition to the salary scores, which have a permanent effect on a professor's salary, faculty can also earn bonus points that are paid only once. Bonuses are based mainly on academic production, which is not certified to define a professor's salary. At the National University, there is a bonus for professors with an exclusive agreement, consisting of an additional 22 percent of the full salary.

Universities are also free to specify the value of "an hour" in hourly based contracts. Some have defined it as a percentage of the monthly allocation for a professor with similar qualifications; others calculate it based on the national minimum wage; while others pick an accurate amount of pesos that is updated every year. In all cases, a professor's qualifications are considered to determine the amount of salary.

Public university institutes do not practice this scheme. The government establishes their salaries in the same way as for nonacademic public servants—that is, based on the legal classification of the position. Salaries at these institutions are not competitive at all; they are, on average, one-third of salaries in public universities.

Academic salaries in private institutions vary even more than in public institutions. They depend on many factors, such as location, type of institution, accreditation, and size of the institution. Most institutions now have academic regulations and rules that establish ranks with the corresponding salary ranges, but, in most cases, salaries are confidential.

Private universities with a tradition of research (about six or seven in the country) have salary schemes similar to public universities, with the variation that all points given are paid only once. In some universities, faculty are evaluated based on either a teaching portfolio; the attainment of goals in teaching, research, and service; or students' surveys.

Information about salaries from private universities is hard to obtain. For this study, eight private universities provided information, under the condition of anonymity. The sample included universities from three cities, some of them with branch campuses elsewhere. The values presented in Table 9.1 and Figure 9.1 are an average among these institutions.

Two main elements can help explain the variation in academic salaries in private universities: the size of the city in which they are located and the accreditation of the institution and its programs. Institutions with voluntary institutional accreditation located in larger cities tend to have better salaries, while institutions without voluntary accreditation in smaller cities tend to pay lower salaries.

Private universities can compete for faculty by offering better salaries, lower teaching loads, and better working conditions. Some of them have additional benefits, such as extra-monthly salaries per year and longer-paid vacations than the minimum established by law.

Figure 9.1 shows a comparison of salaries at public and private universities. In general, public universities appear to pay better salaries than the private ones, except in the case of full professors, who are slightly better paid at private universities.

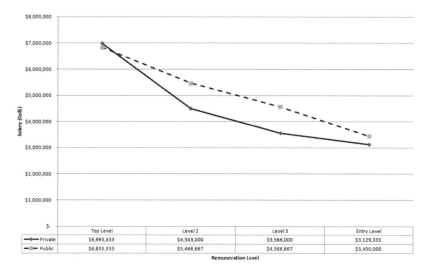

Remuneration Level	Top Level	Level 2	Level 3	Entry Level
Private	$6,993,333	$4,503,000	$3,566,000	$3,129,333
Public	$6,833,333	$5,466,667	$4,566,667	$3,450,000

Figure 9.1 Academic salaries in public and private universities.

Source: For public universities, calculations are based on ideal profiles; for private universities, the survey includes six undisclosed universities.

Note: The September 13, 2010, market exchange rate was US$1.00 = COL$1,801.04.

Nonetheless, the sample was not representative for all private universities and was based on estimations for the public ones.

Taxes and Benefits

Only salary earners whose gross annual income is more than COL$66,888,000 (US$37,131) per year are obliged to declare income taxes. This excludes most of the professoriate. However, workers with earnings above COL$3,463,000 (US$1,922) per month are subject to withholding tax (*retención en la fuente*) ranging from 0 to 33 percent (Redacción Económica 2009). In most cases, there is no tax refund.

In addition, every worker in Colombia must contribute to the pension system and the mandatory health plan—with 4 percent of their salaries for each of these components—while the employer (university) needs to provide an additional 12 percent for pensions and 8.5 percent for the health plan.

Colombia has a universal health care system that provides basic health care to its citizens, and public universities may have their own health care system. Complementary health care plans with better services are also available and are usually paid by the beneficiary.

Academic staff in public universities have additional benefits. While most Colombian salary earners acquire 14 monthly salaries per year, academic staff get 17;

and while a regular worker in the country earns 15 working days of paid vacation, academics get 30 days—15 working and 15 calendar days—of paid vacation. The retirement age for public servants is 60 years for women and 62 years for men. However, professors in public universities enjoy special treatment that allows them to retire 10 years later (Republic of Colombia 1996). During the last decade, a change in the structure of retirement funds stimulated faculty to retire earlier, because otherwise their pension would have been reduced significantly. Private universities often absorb several of those professors who make use of the early retirement option so that they can enjoy both their pension from the government and the salary (or compensation) from the private university.

Additional benefits—like free housing, low-interest credit, and others—are not typically used to attract faculty in public or private universities.

Competitiveness of Salaries

Given the scarce information available, comparisons of salaries between the academic profession and other professions in Colombia are unreliable. The Ministry of Education created the Labor Observatory for Education (Observatorio Laboral para la Educación, n.d.), which keeps track of higher education alumni during the five years following graduation. The most recent results showed that faculty with a bachelor's degree earn an average of COL\$1,378,027 (US\$765); specialists would make an average of COL\$2,396,839 (US\$1,331); with a master's degree, COL\$3,007,488 (US\$1,670); and those with a doctoral degree, an average of COL\$4,904,102 (US\$2,722). In general, salaries paid both in public and private universities are comparable.

In the international context, Colombia is neither an exporter nor an importer of faculty. Despite the awareness that the percentage of professors with a doctoral degree is quite low, even within the region, there are no governmental or institutional policies designed to attract faculty from other countries. While public research universities complain about the difficulty of attracting highly qualified faculty, either nationally or internationally, because of the low entry-level salaries, the main competitors for local talent are not foreign universities but rather industry. Brain drain is still considered a problem, more in terms of students who get their degrees abroad and do not come back to the country than in terms of faculty who migrate to other countries.

Conclusion

Full-time professors can earn a good, middle-class standard of living with salaries that compete with industry in most cases—especially those who are active in research and therefore earn more points. The level of income will vary, depending on several elements; the institution's accreditation status and its geographical location have significant weight. However, staff with a full-time position, supporting a middle-class living, represent only about a quarter of the country's total faculty.

Entry-level salaries for full-time faculty at public and private universities are also competitive with the rest of the labor market. However, public universities need to deal with the rigidness of government-defined remuneration scales, which make working for a public university unattractive for young highly qualified scholars. According to the ministry's data, specialist faculty and those with bachelor's degrees are still the majority of the professoriate. However, universities now tend to prefer candidates with at least master's degrees as new hires.

Private universities have more flexibility to compete for faculty with salaries and benefits; however, public universities tend to provide more stability than private ones.

Part-timers are a majority in the country (64 percent), but there is a huge gap on information about this type of professor. Working for more than one university is a common practice, and it is neither forbidden nor encouraged by legislation.

Complete and accurate quantitative information on academic salaries is not easily available in Colombia. Reliable and systematically collected information is imperative to inform the discussions on academic salaries that are held both in the public and the private sector.

References

Arboleda, Gloria Cecilia. 2004. *De los profesores ocasionales y los catedráticos.* http://www.as pucol.org/15-viicongreso/15-eje4/De%20los%20profesores%20ocasionales%20y%20 catedr%E1ticos.doc. Accessed September 11, 2007.

Borrero, Margarita. 2006. *Educación: Visión 2019.* Bogotá, Colombia: Ministerio de Educación Nacional. http://desarrollo.ut.edu.co/tolima/hermesoft/portal/home_1/rec/arc_13436.pdf.

Ministry of Education (Ministerio de Educación Nacional). n.d.a. *Glosario de la educación superior.* http://www.mineducacion.gov.co/sistemasdeinformacion/1735/articles-213912_glosario.pdf. Accessed September 9, 2010.

Ministry of Education (Ministerio de Educación Nacional). n.d.b. SNIES—Sistema Nacional de Información de La Educación Superior. http://200.41.9.227:7777/men/. Accessed September 8, 2010.

Ministry of Education (Ministerio de Educación Nacional). 2002. *Decreto 1279 de 2002.* http://www.mineducacion.gov.co/1621/article-86434.html.

Observatorio Laboral para la Educación. n.d. *Salario de entrada de recién graduados por nivel de formación.* http://www.graduadoscolombia.edu.co/html/1732/article-195068.html. Accessed September 12, 2010.

Redacción Económica. 2009. Se pagará retención en la fuente desde $2,3 millones. *Colombiano,* December 30. http://www.elcolombiano.com/BancoConocimiento/S/se_pagara_retencion_en_la_fuente_desde_$23_millones/se_pagara_retencion_en_la_fuente_desde_$23_millones.asp.

Republic of Colombia. 1996. *Ley 344 de 1996.* http://www.alcaldiabogota.gov.co/sisjur/normas/Norma1.Jsp?i=345. Accessed September 9, 2010.

10

THE CZECH REPUBLIC

High Estimation for the Academic Profession

Helena Sebkova

Czech higher education institutions own the right to hire academic staff and to determine the number of academic positions. A higher education institution determines academic salaries, which should be described in the Internal Salary Regulations (part of the institutional statute). Nonsalary benefits provide health and retirement insurance, paid vacations, and sabbaticals. Some additional benefits can include supplementary pension insurance, low-interest loans, contributions toward boarding expenses, and other items. A contract can be concluded for limited or indefinite time; tenure does not exist. The salaries of higher academic ranks (associate professors and professors) are comparable with those of the best-paid job categories, but they can differentiate significantly by institution, field, and gender.

This chapter examines Czech higher education and the focus on the academic career and salaries. The specific sections address the academic contracts and salaries of various ranks of academics and their qualifications, nonacademic salaries, and supplementary employment as well as international competition. The final section discusses both the attractiveness of an academic career and its problems and tackles the possible changes in the near future.

Overview of Higher Education

Czech higher education has been significantly reformed during the 1990s and 2000s. The system has gone through a period of substantive expansion, transforming from an elite to a mass system. These changes were accompanied by a decrease in state control in favor of institutional self-governance, autonomy in decision making, and new accountability measures. The higher education system is composed of two basic sectors, distinguished according to the establishing party—public higher education institutions (a total of 26) and private

Table 10.1 Overall size of the Czech higher education system

Type of institution	No. of institutions 1989–90	No. of institutions 2008–9	No. of students 1989–90	No. of students 2008– 9	% of total no. of students 2009
Public *	—	26		319,615	85.3
State	23	2	113,417	4,445	1.2
Private	—	45		50,659	13.5
Total	23	73	113,417	374,719	100

Source: Institute for Information in Education 2009.
*The former state higher education institutions were changed to public ones in 1998 (the new status was connected with the transfer of assets, change of economic rules, and change of institutional management).

higher education institutions (a total of 45). Private higher education institutions have been developed from 1998, in accordance with the Higher Education Act of 1998; prior to this, private institutions did not exist (Beneš, Beseda, and Roskovec 2009).

The subsequent typology differentiates between higher education institutions of a university type (providing bachelor's, master's, and doctoral degree programs) and nonuniversity type (focusing primarily on bachelor's degree programs).

In addition to higher education, the Czech Academy of Sciences, composed of 53 research institutes (4,350 research workers, in 2009) and carrying out research over a broad spectrum of areas, provides strong research capacity. Institutes of the Czech Academy of Sciences are completely independent from higher education institutions, but cooperation on both a formal and informal basis is quite frequent. Jointly provided doctoral degree programs and common research projects are examples of such formal cooperation. On the other hand, the part-time employment contracts of researchers at various higher education institutions (or, vice versa, the employment contracts of higher education teachers at the academy's institutes) are mostly based on informal contacts between individuals from both sides.

As is clearly visible in Table 10.1, the private higher education sector is developing very dynamically, and in the 2008–9 academic year students of private higher education institutions already made up 13.5 percent of the total enrollment.

The rapid expansion in the numbers of students has been accompanied by an increase in the numbers of academic staff, but at a much slower rate. The figures in Table 10.2 relate only to the public sector, as data on staff in private higher education institutions are not available.

Academic Staff and Contracts

The academic staff consists of professors, associate professors, senior assistants, assistants, lecturers, and scientific workers, based on the Higher Education Act

Table 10.2 Number of employees* and number of students**

	Year			
	1990	*2000*	*2008*	*2009*
Employees (total)	28,247	26,979	32,903	33,277
Academics	11,839	12,791	16,977	17,272
Number of students (total)	113,417	190,194	319,615	333,580

Source: Institute for Information on Education 2001a, 2001b, 2009.

*Full-time equivalent.

**Public higher education institutions.

of 1998. Public higher education institutions have significant autonomy in their personnel measures, and they can compete for academic staff without external regulation. Their employees are not civil servants—that is, the government does not have the right to determine the number of academic positions. The individual institution can determine the number of academic staff within all ranks, without any external influence or regulation.

The general and obligatory rules for a public higher education institution, when hiring academic staff, are stipulated by the 1998 act. The academic staff of an institution is hired through tenders/selection procedures open to all who meet the qualification requirements. The rules for the organization of such tenders should form part of the internal regulations of an institution. The internal regulations include (in accordance with the 1998 act) statute, electoral rules, scholarship rules, study examination rules, and others—including, internal salary regulations and tender rules used when filling positions with academic staff, senior assistants, assistants, lecturers, and scientific workers.

A private higher education institution is not bound by the act when hiring academic staff. It has the right to form its own hiring procedures, and it is not obliged to publish statistical data regarding its staff.

General basic rules for employment contracts are given by the Labour Code, and the Higher Education Act determines certain time limits regarding the contract, concluded with lower ranks of academic staff (for both public and private institutions). A time-limited contract (2 to 5 years) can be settled with the same academics (senior assistants, assistants, lecturers, and scientific workers), at most, for two consecutive time periods. After that, the next consecutive contract should provide employment for an indefinite time. No legitimate time limitations involve employment contracts with professors and associate professors. These contracts are created upon mutual agreement and, usually, for an indefinite time.

An academic may continue working until any age, if an institution agrees to extend his or her contract. Likewise, time-limited contracts can be used repeatedly for academics over 65 years of age. In Czech higher education, *tenure* does not exist, because a contract arranged for an indefinite time also allows its termination, in accordance with the conditions given by the Labour Code.

A higher education institution is fully responsible for the specific content of a contract. In general, the contract is an agreement between two parties—the institution and its employee. Thus, the content can vary significantly, based on what the parties want to include (workload, salary including nonsalary benefits, various reductions in duties, obligations, and other issues). A contract for part-time staff includes the agreed workload (usually expressed as a percentage of the full-time position).

Each academic is expected to teach and participate in research (Ministry of Education, Youth and Sports 2005). The ratio of teaching to research duties for academic staff is not prescribed by any standard regulation and varies significantly from case to case. The contract can specify how much time should be allocated to research and teaching. Yet, each higher education institution is responsible for these details, and no exact verification of these requirements is available. The estimated average ratio of teaching and research activities is about 2:1 (derived from the proportion of financial means spent on teaching and research). This ratio also differs between various higher education institutions. For example, apparently nonuniversity higher education institutions primarily focus on teaching and perform less research than university-type institutions.

Academic Salaries

Each public higher education institution has the right to determine the salaries of all its employees, which gives it the possibility (the institutional budget can be the limit) to make the offered position more attractive than comparable positions elsewhere. It is bound by the Higher Education Act to produce its own internal salary regulations that are part of its internal regulations (see the previous section).

A private higher education institution is not governed at all by the Higher Education Act, in setting the academic salaries. It is not obliged to publish data on academic staff salaries, and thus no information about this is available, except from results of a sociological survey.

Main Determinants of Academic Salaries

In general, the salary categories and their ranges given by internal rules can vary among various public higher education institutions. In reality, most institutions take into account the categories and ranges of salaries valid for civil servants, modifying them for their own purposes. One of the main determinants of the salary is usually the academic rank to which the individual academic belongs (professor, associate professor, etc.), as Table 10.3 confirms.

It must be stated that the average salaries are informative only to a certain extent, because the ranges of salaries in separate categories are quite wide. The real monthly salaries for professors and associate professors can vary at individual higher education institutions by up to (+/−) 50 percent from the average salary

Table 10.3 Numbers of employees and monthly average salaries at public higher education institutions

Type of faculty	2008 Number (FTE)*	2009 Number (FTE)*	2008 Monthly Average Salary in CZK**	2009 Monthly Average Salary in CZK**
Employees (all workers)	32,903	33,277	29,357	30,498
Academics total	16,977	17,272	35,529	36,889
Professor	1,890	1,977	57,596	60,800
Associate professor	3,384	3,455	44,409	45,902
Senior assistant	8,914	9,046	30,306	31,309
Assistant	1,653	1,660	23,843	24,585
Lecturer	592	625	24,032	25,161
Other	544	509	37,198	36,560
Scientific worker	1,756	1,807	29,297	29,421
Other employees	14,171	14,198	21,970	22,861

Sources: Institute for Information on Education 2001a, 2001b, 2009.
*Full-time equivalent.
**The exchange rate in December 2010 was US$1.00 = CZK 19.003.

levels (Ministry of Education, Youth and Sports 2008), while the variability of salaries for the lower ranks of academic staff (senior assistants, assistants, lecturers, and scientific workers) is slightly lower.

The important salary determinant is the official position at the institution (rector, dean, chief of department, project manager, etc.). Research activities, productivity/work performance and quality, and similarly, teaching activities and teaching performance can play significant roles as far as the salary is concerned. However, these issues are subject to various internal evaluation mechanisms and the relationship of their results to the internal regulations on salaries of the particular higher education institution.

Seniority (experience) also often plays a significant role in the salary level. Research results (Survey, Consulting & Care 2009), involving all types of institutions, show that professors aged 40 to 50 years have the highest salaries—CZK 61,300 (US$3,226)—and senior assistants and lecturers aged up to 30 years the lowest salaries—CZK 26,700 (US$1,405) and CZK 23,100 (US$1,216), respectively.

The research data confirm the differences between the salaries of men and women. For example, a female professor's salary is only 88 percent of a male professor's, in the same position. Determining the reasons for this situation is more or less speculation, given the absence of any relevant qualitative data. In any event, it is quite common for women to have more family-related responsibilities, and they commonly take maternity leave. Thus, women miss out on time experience, compared to men, which means that they cannot produce, for example, a comparable quantity of research results.

The Adequacy of Academic Salaries

The average monthly salary (calculated using data from public higher education institutions) of the two lowest academic ranks—assistant, CZK 24,585 (US$1,294) and lecturer, CZK 25,161 (US$1,324)—is only slightly higher than the average gross monthly salary in the country; which was CZK 22,691 (US$1,194), in 2008. These figures show that full-time positions of assistants and/or lecturers are financially viable for a quite modest standard of living. The higher academic ranks, especially those of associate professor and professor are approximately 2 to 2.5 times higher, and a full-time contract can be expected to provide a good or even very good standard of living.

In addition, living expenses can differ significantly between Prague and other locations (smaller towns in various rural regions and villages in the countryside). Living expenses in Prague are much higher (especially housing) than outside the capital, which is a significant disadvantage for middle-class people.

Salaries to Other Professionals and Various Research Fields

Before presenting concrete examples of salaries outside the sector of public higher education institutions, it should be pointed out that the average data can often provide a problematic insight concerning the highest and the lowest salaries. For example, the average gross monthly salary for professors, across the whole public higher education sector, was CZK 57,596 (US$3,031), in 2008 (see Table 10.3). More details are available in the *Annual Report on the Management of Higher Education*: the highest average salary of professors at one higher education institution was CZK 86,846 (US$4,571), which is well above the national average, while the lowest average salary at another institution—CZK 30,153 (US$1,587)—was only 52 percent of the national average.

The Czech Statistical Office collects data on gross monthly salaries in the Czech Republic, and it uses several types of classification. Taking into consideration various sectors, employees in finance and banking earned the highest-average monthly salary in 2008—CZK 45,683 (US$2,404). This was followed by salaries in the information and communications sectors—CZK 41,817 (US$2,201)—and the production and distribution of electricity, gas, heat, and conditioned air—CZK 35,329 (US$1,859) (Czech Statistical Office 2010).

Another Czech Statistical Office classification uses groups of different occupations. The top/management employees of large companies and establishments enjoy the highest salaries—CZK 62,229 (US$3,275); followed by lawyers and top officials—CZK 42,136 (US$2,218); and then physicists and architects—CZK 42,001 (US$2,211). Just for comparison, the lowest salaries—CZK 12,645 (US$666)—were earned by nonqualified workers in sales and other services (Czech Statistical Office 2010). It is common for the highest salaries to be connected with high qualifications (e.g., a higher education degree), but this is not always the case.

The average gross monthly salaries of professors and associate professors are easily comparable with both of the above-mentioned examples of attractive salaries and best-paid job categories. The salaries of academics in other positions are significantly lower.

Nonsalary Benefits

Health and retirement insurance and paid vacations are the obligatory financial benefits provided to employees by every employer, and this includes all public and private higher education institutions. Public higher education institutions should create several special funds (an obligation arising from the Higher Education Act), among them a social fund of up to 2 percent of the overall financial resources determined for the wages of a certain institution. The social fund can be used for further nonsalary benefits: contributions toward boarding expenses, cultural and sports activities of employees, holidays (usually for children), and others. Nonsalary benefits such as support to cover housing expenses, low-interest loans, supplementary pension insurance, and further education can be provided, using either the social fund or some of the other funds created with the financial surplus. Details about funds and their use should be included in the internal regulations of each public higher education institution. A private higher education institution may behave similarly but is not externally regulated, in any way, with regard to nonsalary benefits.

A six-month sabbatical for the academic staff at all higher education institutions once every seven years is an important nonsalary benefit, because academic staff on sabbatical are entitled to a salary, based on the 1998 Higher Education Act. The nonsalary benefits of higher education institutions are quite diverse, and the percentage of the salary that such nonsalary benefits represent cannot be estimated. Some of them may serve elements in attracting new academics. For example, housing support can attract qualified young candidates to an academic job. Except for health and retirement insurance and paid vacations, nonsalary benefits are not obligatory, and many of them are not provided to all staff members (e.g., housing support).

Supplementary Employment

Academics at public higher education institutions (mostly, professors and associate professors, less frequently academics of lower ranks) commonly have more than one job, usually not at the same institution. In the case of more than one job at the same institution, the academic has separate contracts and salaries for each position. These supplementary activities mostly involve part-time employment. Frequently, the reason for such supplementary employment is an effort to earn more money, yet there are also other reasons—to gain more experience, higher prestige, or to complete a working team.

As relatively new institutions, private higher education institutions suffer from a lack of highly qualified staff. Thus, they quite often offer supplementary employment (part-time contracts) to qualified people from public higher education institutions. Consequently, perhaps a relatively high percentage of staff work part time at private higher education institutions. There are no legal restrictions on working at multiple institutions. Individuals can arrange jobs on their own without the permission of their main employer. For this reason, until recently it was not possible to estimate the percentage of academics who teach in more than one higher education institution. In 2010, an amendment to the Higher Education Act introduced the Register of Professors and Associate Professors, under the responsibility of the Ministry of Education, Youth and Sport. This new obligation will dramatically change the situation, based on information on multiple working positions.

Teaching at multiple institutions is not encouraged in general, and limitations can be set by the Accreditation Commission, which does not consider part-time contracts for professors and associate professors a sufficient guarantee of the quality of degree programs. The newly introduced Register of Professors and Associate Professors will provide the commission with a tool to reject accreditation in the case of multiple jobs held by professors responsible for particular degree programs. It is not possible to estimate the percentage of academics (at both public and private institutions) who supplement their academic salaries with consulting or nonacademic work. Based on experience, such activities are quite common—in particular, in law, business administration, and computer sciences. Furthermore, in the hard sciences (e.g., civil engineering) and some life sciences, it is easier to find supplementary nonacademic jobs than jobs in the humanities.

Qualifications

The academic hierarchy is regulated by the Higher Education Act and is valid for all higher education institutions. As already mentioned, academic staff consist of professors, associate professors, senior assistants, assistants, lecturers, and scientific workers (who usually take part in pedagogical activities). While no legal requirement exists on the minimum degree level required to enter an academic profession, usually a master's degree is expected. Exceptions can occur only in the field of the arts.

Promotion between the lower levels (from assistant to senior assistant) is also not legally regulated, and mainly the higher education institution decides what criteria are used and if they are incorporated in the internal regulations. Promotion to the category of senior assistant tends to depend on acquiring a PhD degree.

The process of gaining the academic title of associate professor (habilitation, which requires the second doctoral thesis) and the appointment of professors are quite demanding and are stipulated in detail by the Higher Education Act. The habilitation applicant is expected to hold a PhD degree. Habilitation is required as the basic condition for promotion to the rank of professor. The appointment of professors requires that the applicant is able to present accurate research results and long-term teaching experience, and he or she must present a lecture at an open meeting. Associate professors are appointed by the rector, while professors are appointed by the president of the Czech Republic. Both academic titles are awarded forever, and they are acknowledged at all Czech higher education institutions.

In spite of open competition for posts, higher education graduates commonly remain, with their further qualifications, at the same higher education institution, and it is not exceptional for them to continue working there until retirement.

International Competition

Academic salaries in the Czech Republic may be considered attractive at a national level (at least those of associate professors and professors), but they are not competitive with the academic salaries in more mature countries (e.g., the "old" countries of the European Union, the United States, Canada, and others). Hence, salaries can attract foreign academics from some countries in eastern Europe and other regions. Particular higher education institutions certainly focus on attracting international scholars, but this policy cannot rely only on salaries, which perhaps may not be particularly attractive. Unfortunately, no national survey has been carried out in this field, so more detailed qualitative information is unavailable.

The open job market in many countries, as well as various international programs and other offers, encourage outstanding Czech academics to find positions abroad. International collaboration enables them to gain important international experience and, consequently, supports international competition. The educational programs of the European Commission (Tempus at the beginning of the 1990s, the Socrates program, and the Lifelong Learning Programme) have played a significant role for students as well as for academics. Similarly, the European research programs and various international research centers contribute to the international competitiveness of Czech academics.

International collaboration is beneficial via acquiring important experience, but it is also dangerous in terms of brain drain, which is, of course, occurring. The opportunity to work abroad is particularly attractive to young academics. They can respond to job offers in a field like informatics or medicine (common in Europe, in recent years) and decide not to return. On the other hand, the time-limited positions in various projects as well as the newly established national projects tend to encourage Czech academics to return and might limit brain drain.

The number and/or percentage of young academics who have left the country to work abroad cannot be estimated because there is no data and/or research results on this topic.

Conclusion

The academic profession is highly valued in the Czech Republic. Professors and associate professors have commonly ranked second or third in the hierarchy of occupations in various national and international surveys (Průcha 2010). The salaries of these highest academic categories are comparable to those of other attractive professions, in spite of the fact that academics with the same academic rank might earn different salaries at various higher education institutions and research fields. However, the salaries of young academics are only slightly above the average national salary, which constitutes a barrier to higher education graduates who would like to commence an academic career.

The relatively old age of academics with the highest hierarchical ranks—more than 86 percent of professors are aged above 50 years (Matějů and Fischer 2010)—is seen as a significant problem, while the demanding and complicated nature of an academic career is considered to be one of the main reasons for this situation.

The academic career and possible changes to it are themes in the debate on the new Higher Education Act, currently being prepared within the framework of broader reform in higher education, which is intended to support the competitiveness of Czech higher education.

References

Beneš, Josef, Jan Beseda, and Vladimír Roskovec. 2009. *Higher education in the Czech Republic*. Prague, Czech Republic: Ministry of Education, Youth and Sports.

Czech Statistical Office. 2010. *Labour and earnings*. http://www.czso.cz/eng/redakce.nsf/i/labour_and_earnings_ekon.

Institute for Information on Education. 2001a. *Statistická ročenka školství, 2000/01: Pracovníci a mzdové prostředky* [Statistical Yearbook, 2000/01: Employees and wages]. Prague, Czech Republic.

Institute for Information on Education. 2001b. *Statistická ročenka školství, 2000/01: Výkonové ukazatele* [Statistical Yearbook on education, 2000/01: Performance indicators]. Prague, Czech Republic.

Institute for Information on Education. 2009. *Statistická ročenka školství, 2008/09: Výkonové ukazatele, Zaměstnanci a mzdové prostředky, Ekonomické ukazatele* [Statistical Yearbook on education, 2008/09: Performance indicators, employees and wages, economic indicators]. http://www.uiv.cz/clanek/512/1857.

Matějů, Petr, and Jakub Fischer. 2010. *Výzkum akademických pracovníků vysokých škol: Hlavní výsledky a závěry* [Survey of academics in higher education institutions: Main results and conclusions]. http://ipn.msmt.cz/data/uploads/projekt_3/Hlavni_vysledky_a_za very_vyzkumu_akademickych_pracovniku.pdf.

Ministry of Education, Youth and Sports. 2005. *The long-term plan for educational, scientific, research, development, artistic and other creative activities of higher education institutions for 2006–2010*. Prague, Czech Republic. http://www.msmt.cz/vzdelavani/dlouhodoby-zamer-vzdelavaci-a-vedecke-vyzkumne-vyvojove-umelecke-a-dalsi-tvurci-cinnosti-pro-oblast-vysokych-skol-na-obdobi-2006-2010.

Ministry of Education, Youth and Sports. 2008. *Výroc̆ní zpráva o hospodar̆ení vysokých škol* [Annual Report on Higher Education Management]. Prague, Czech Republic. http://www.msmt.cz/vzdelavani/vyrocni-zprava-o-hospodareni-vysokych-skol-za-rok-2008.

Průcha, Jan. 2010. *Pedagogická psychologie* (Pedagogical Psychology), Portal, Prague.

Survey, Consulting & Care. 2009. *Výzkum akademických pracovníků vysokých škol* [Survey of academic workers of higher education institutions]. Results of the National Project "Reform of Tertiary Education." Prague, Czech Republic.

11

SALARY AND INCENTIVE STRUCTURE IN ETHIOPIAN HIGHER EDUCATION

Elizabeth Ayalew

With tertiary institutions being knowledge centers, the effort of enhancing the knowledge environment is embedded in the structure of valuing faculty contributions to research and scholarship. However, the existing low salary and remuneration structure in Ethiopia, coupled with provisions of meager resources, is seen to result in an inadequate pool of qualified and satisfied staff. This study describes salary and remuneration structure in the system and calls for the need to institute a reward scheme that would provide such institutions with much-needed intellectual expertise.

Overview of Higher Education

Since 2003, the Ethiopian higher education system has undergone an extensive reform, although a lot remains to be done to reach the returns. While developments are often expressed in figures, there are also challenges related to issues of quality provisions.

Context and Recent Developments

The modern and secular higher education system in Ethiopia started in 1950—with the establishment of Haile Selassie I University, known as Addis Ababa University (Wondimu 2003, 316). Until the early 1990s, Ethiopia had two additional public universities and 16 affiliated and independent junior colleges. However, recent developments witnessed the expansion of the enterprise, both in the public and private sector (Ashcroft 2003). Currently, the system includes 22 public, slightly more than 49 accredited private institutions, and 26 regional teacher education colleges (Ministry of Education 2010)—mainly offering courses at the undergraduate level. Such data, however, must be interpreted in the context of a developing country with a fast-growing population, at present about 80 million, a gross domestic product per capita of US$900 (World Factbook 2009), and a constantly increasing demand for higher education.

Generally, an increasing trend in student enrollment has been under way—the growing number of graduates as well as teaching staff, since 1994. The rise in student matriculation is verified by the fact that between 1994 and 2009 gross student enrollment had increased by 3,195 percent, while the number of graduates (both from graduate and undergraduate programs) had increased by 2,782 percent. Regarding the size of faculty, however, the increase of staff size was only from 1,937 in 1994 to 11,028 in 2009 (Ministry of Education 1996, 2007, 2010), which shows a growing trend in the pupil-to-teacher ratio. In addition, less than 30 percent of undergraduate enrollment and barely 10 percent of graduate enrollment in public institutions are female (Ministry of Education 2007).

Challenges in the System

Despite the huge expansion, the system has been in a constant state of change, and subsequently it suffers from a lack of quality. Although the government has increased its education expenditure as a proportion of the overall government budget since 2000, it still falls below the general range of many developing countries (World Bank 2004). The share of the budget allocated to higher education has increased from 14.9 percent to 23 percent, despite the frail resource-management system of public institutions (HERQA 2004). Ethiopian universities have been fully subsidized by the state budget, and the system provided free education to all full-time students. A recently implemented cost-sharing scheme requires newly employed graduates to repay their education from a monthly graduate tax taken from their salaries.

Expenditure per student is bound to decline annually, given the constantly increasing cost of living in Ethiopia, where the rate of inflation is 8.5 percent (World Factbook 2009). The system has also been suffering from a shrinking infrastructure, as enrollments constantly increase and tax existing facilities. A significant amount of the budget for the expansion of graduate programs is drawn from international aid (HERQA 2004).

Finally, most of the highly qualified staff have left academia for better opportunities abroad or better-paying jobs in the country. Besides this, the trend to move from rural toward urban centers, and thus to improve earning potential, is an additional cause for the lack of expertise and experience at the newer rural institutions. In fact, most regional public universities are dependent on new graduates for full-time teaching positions. In general, rapid expansion has been costly, as a result of which the system is challenged by a shortage of experienced and motivated academic staff, inadequate infrastructure, weak research output, and declining educational quality.

Academic Contracts

Recruitment, selection, and placement of full-time academic staff follow the human resource procedures of the national Civil Service Commission, specifying that academic contracts in Ethiopian public institutions are generally on a permanent contractual basis. Such contracts are theoretically signed for two years, with the understanding that renewal is based on a performance evaluation of the staff. However, implementation of strict and timely evaluation varies among institutions, depending on management culture and practice. Employment issues are typically governed by university senates and institutional human resource manuals. In theory, institutions are given some space for flexibility in policy implementation, as specified in the proclamation for higher education—which calls for benchmarking of such practices: "Institutions shall introduce rules and procedures on employment and promotion of the academic staff, consistent with international good practices" (FDRE 2009, 4994). In line with this, the need to institute the tenure system in the recruitment of academic staff has also been clearly stipulated in the higher education proclamation: "Institutions can grant tenure on permanent basis on proof of efficiency" (FDRE 2003, 2240). However, this policy has never been implemented.

The common procedure of recruitment requires that public posting of vacant positions is made, depending on requests from recruiting departments. A departmental committee reviews applications and selects candidates to be interviewed, based on the required level of qualification, academic rank, years of experience, publications, and, in some cases, the specific specialization. Such a committee has to include staff from the human resources office of the university to conduct interviews. Finally, the department's recommendation for employment is approved by the academic commission of the faculty/school and finally by the academic vice president of the university. Through less stringent but similar procedures, university departments have the autonomy to employ part-time staff (on the payment of an hourly rate), whenever there is shortage. The senate legislation of public institutions also gives room for employment of adjunct and visiting professors, particularly in fields with a scarcity of staff.

As specified in the national proclamation for higher education and in academic contracts, staff are expected to teach and do research, although the proportional combination of these duties depends on the type of the employing institution. For a full-time teaching position, the staff is expected to spend 75 percent of their time teaching and 25 percent on research; while research institutions require that 75 percent of a faculty member's time be given to research and the rest (25 percent) to teaching duties. Generally, contract agreements at public institutions entail responsibility for teaching, research, advising students, serving on committees, and performing professional and university services. However, contracts do not specify how the above duties are linked to the performance evaluation of staff. Technically, university legislation stipulates that every semester an academic staff's performance should be evaluated by students, peers, and heads and the average point of eight semesters (two years) be considered for the decision for the renewal of contracts and increase in salary level. In reality, however, strict implementation of this procedure may not be followed, and, particularly during the last few years, there has been no increase in salary levels at any of the public institutions.

Academic Salaries, Qualification, and Promotion

Academic salaries in public institutions are determined by the salary scale set by the government—based on formal qualifications and research activity, combined with years of teaching experience in tertiary institutions. At Addis Ababa University, the pioneer institution that many others emulate, the employment and promotion criteria set in the university's legislation require that the entry academic rank be the graduate assistant level (AAU 2007, 73–85). All other public universities use the same qualification and promotion system. As can be seen in Table 11.1, there are specific requirements for promotion to the various ranks. Generally, the faculty profile at public institutions shows most teachers at the lecturer rank (36.2 percent) and the fewest at the full professor rank (3 percent) (Ministry of Education 2007).

The salary revision made in the 2006–7 academic year granted a 100 percent increase across faculties—except for the medical science faculty, which had a 120 percent increase. This rise was made in an effort to maintain the drastically declining number of medical doctors, as more and more of them migrated to local private hospitals or abroad. There was another recent revision of salary for public servants in early 2010 that provided a 36 percent increase. However, none of these revisions considered implementation of the two-year steps increase set in the scale. In addition, due to uniformity of salary scale, benefits, and requirements for promotion— public institutions cannot technically compete for faculty, and the system is not flexible to prevent faculty turnover. As a result, institutions are dependent on the preferences of potential hires. Such a choice is usually influenced by the desire for an appointment in a specific field or discipline available at a certain institution or for a particular geographic location. In a few cases, executive decisions were based on individual negotiations where someone was coming from another country, either a native Ethiopian (returning from the diaspora) or a foreign citizen.

When one tries to map such a provision in line with the general salary context of the country, it is essential to consider three major areas of employment: public (civil service and public enterprise), private, and nongovernment. Average figures obtained through cursory assessment of sample organizations from these sectors of employment show that academic staff salaries are only better than subprofessionals in the civil services (without taking a year of service and fringe benefits into account). While BA/BSc holders at the entry level of the subprofessional position earn a monthly 1,100 birr, academics earn 1,650 birr, professionals in public sectors earn 2,000 birr, professionals in private organizations earn 3,000 birr, and those in nongovernment organizations earn between 4,000 birr and 5,000 birr.

Table 11.1 Summary of qualification and other requirements for promotion in public institutions

Academic rank	Graduate assistant	Assistant lecturer	Lecturer	Assistant professor	Associate professor	Professor
Qualification requirement	BA/BSc	BA/BSc and one year of service	MA/MSc or one year of service as assistant lecturer	PhD or four years of service as lecturer and two publications★	PhD or four years of service as assistant prof. and four publications★	PhD and four years of service as associate professor and six publications★

Source: AAU 2007.
★Publications generally refer to: textbook/articles/teaching materials.

An unpublished study, conducted by Addis Ababa University to support a new salary scheme for all staff at public institutions, claims that staff's actual level of expenditure is greater than earnings from salary (AAU 2006, 26). This discrepancy is compensated by additional income from extrahour classes and other sources, but it verifies the low level of income in academia. There are variations among disciplines, but staff in the fields of medicine, business, and technology are more likely to have access to other sources of income from better-paying jobs. Generally, faculty in the capital city and emerging urban areas have greater opportunities for more and better sources of additional earnings—a factor contributing to the migration of academic staff toward larger cities.

Nonsalary (Fringe) Benefits

In public institutions, staff at the rank of assistant professor and above obtain a yearly book allowance equivalent to US$15. In addition, a monthly housing allowance ranges from US$27 to US$30, depending on the academic rank, which by most standards is rated as meager. In fact, in urban areas of Ethiopia, a decent two-bedroom home can rent in the range of US$100 to US$200, monthly (US$1.00 = 16.6 birr). Therefore, these benefits cannot be considered as serious incentives. Perhaps the exemption from tuition fees for a staff member's spouse and children attending evening classes (an amount worth US$30 to US$260 per semester) is worth mentioning.

Supplementary Employment (Moonlighting)

Despite the difficulty of measuring nonsalary income, nearly all the staff of public institutions earn extra income by taking on contractual responsibility for additional duties. Many individual staff teach more than the 12 hours per week obligatory assignment. This extra teaching could be in regular programs or in evening and summer (*Kiremt*) classes. Appointment to senior academic-administrative positions in public institutions, often made through informal recommendations, also grants various privileges depending on the authority and responsibility of the place held in the organizational structure. These options include a reduced teaching load, monthly position allowance, easy access to office facilities (like landline telephone, fax, and printer), university apartments at a subsidized rental, personal vehicle with fuel allowance, and others.

Apart from this, depending on the field of study, staff may also be engaged in consulting and/or research for private, public, international, and civil society organizations; they also teach in private universities. It could fairly be estimated that more than 80 percent of the staff of public institutions are engaged in moonlighting, though their commitment of employment could be temporary and seasonal. However, recently, the government has suspended, for an unlimited time, distance-program provisions of tertiary institutions. This is likely to deter the growth of private universities, since most of them spotted their niche through this type of delivery.

So far as legal restrictions are concerned, the earlier (FDRE 2003, 2240) as well as the revised proclamations (FDRE 2009, 4998–99), and particularly the university senate legislation, give the provision for joint appointment of staff to participate in social organizations, civil societies, professional associations, and general consultancy services, but not in a manner that might cause conflict with their university commitment (AAU 2007, Article 51.2 and 51.3). However, such cases are rare in practice, and they require the approval of university vice presidents.

International Competition

The current study concludes that academic salaries are inadequate for sustaining a reasonable standard of living for academic staff, as confirmed by other studies (Assefa 2008). Thus, most of the highly educated citizens look for positions in international and multinational corporations in the country or abroad, although the reason for migration may not only necessarily be better pay but may also involve the increased likelihood of pursuing a successful career. Particularly in some fields, such as information technology and medicine, the chance of securing a competitive professional job in the international market is high. According to the International Organization for Migration's report (Solimano 2003, 6), around 300,000 professionals from Africa live and work in Europe and North America, and Ethiopia is second in the list of major sending countries. Between 1991 and 2004, the rate of physicians' emigration from Ethiopia (medical brain drain) has grown from 15 percent to 25 percent, which increases the total number of physician emigrants from 275 to 638 (Bhargava, Docquier, and Moullan 2010).

Due to high migration and the implementation of the higher education expansion scheme, some effort has been made to recruit academics from the international market. A recruitment team organized by the Ministry of Education has made visits to different countries to recruit expatriate staff, especially for post-graduate programs. As a result, many Indians and Nigerians have been recruited by some faculties for a minimum of US$1,500 monthly salary. However, this effort has not been sustained for sheer inadequacy of the funding needed to attract such staff; instead, the strategy has created dissatisfaction among local faculty who deliver similar standards of output but are paid less than US$300 a month. This, along with other problems associated with attracting qualified staff, has led to assigning new graduates to teaching positions (HERQA 2009, 17).

Private Higher Education

The 2003 and 2009 proclamations grant provisions for private institutions, resulting in a significant expansion in the sector within the last decade, starting from almost nothing to absorbing about 22 percent of all higher education learners—one of the highest rates in Africa (Tamrat 2008). This constraint on quality has been reflected in the imbalance between growth of enrollment versus faculty size, available infrastructure, and government-fund provision for higher education (Reisberg and Rumbley 2010). Especially in their early years, many of the staff of public institutions were lured to the private institutions; however, in the last couple of years, the increase in the number of public institutions is adversely affecting growth and expansion of the private sector—characterizing the latter mainly as demand absorbing (Altbach, Reisberg, and Rumbley 2009, xiv). In addition, private universities were recently prohibited from offering their regular full-time programs in two specific disciplines (law and teacher education) due to an alleged provision of substandard quality. Thus, the number of faculty from public universities, migrating to private universities for both full-time and part-time teaching, appears to be declining. Instead, staff from the private sector are likely to look for openings at public universities.

Many of these institutions focus on offering certificate and diploma-level training (Tamrat 2008), rarely graduate programs, with few of them having the institutional capacity to engage in research. As is the case with many institutions at the global level (Altbach, Reisberg, and Rumbley 2009, 80), research is not a common academic practice in private universities, but they have always tried to attract qualified staff from public institutions by offering attractive remuneration. Most such institutions are located in urban centers and are owned by individuals or shareholding companies, which often characterize them as being profit oriented.

Employment at private universities is governed by the national labor law; it is typically contractual, and the salary structure is market driven. Private universities pay more than public universities (see Table 11.2), and they also offer a better benefit scheme; but they are not generally willing to disclose salary data as they compete for faculty, based on what they offer. Compared to public universities, the private ones have room for negotiation, and many offer differential salaries across disciplines, which they separate as critical in areas like law and information

Table 11.2 Academic salary standards by type of institution and academic rank

Type of institution	Full professor	Associate professor	Assistant professor	Lecturer	Assistant lecturer	Assistant graduate
			*Ranges of monthly salary (before tax) in ETB**			
Public	5,400–6,900	4,700–6,000	4,000–5,500	3,400–4,500	2,800–3,800	1,650
Private	From 5,200 onward	5,000–15,000	5,000–10,000	3,000–6,000	2,000–4,500	1,800–2,000

Source: Ethiopian Civil Service Commission, Interoffice memo and data collected from sample private higher education institutions.

Note: The range for public institutions shows the gap in the scale (top–bottom level), while it shows the institutional and interinstitutional variation (by discipline) in payment for private.

*ETB: Ethiopian birr (ETB 16.6 = US$1.00).

technology (where trained experts are relatively limited) and noncritical. When it comes to benefits—apart from paid vacation, which is a common benefit across all institutions—they have diverse fringe benefits for their staff. However, private institutions are generally known for imposing a requirement of higher teaching load, 15 to 18 hours per week, as compared to the 12 hours per week load of public institutions. In line with this, academic contracts do not demand that staff engage in research. In most of the sample institutions considered for this study, contract agreements specify only that salary increases are based on job performance.

As has been explained earlier, salary provisions at entry points depend on the market rate and discipline. Private institutions are believed to be more demand driven and flexible in attending to the needs of their customers, from whom they collect the majority of their income, in terms of fees. As a result, most of their functional orientation is geared toward delivering teaching in more popular disciplines (like business, law, and information technology). The orientation toward more teaching and less research is because promotion to higher academic ranks is a rare phenomenon. Staff employed at a certain rank are likely to remain at the same level for years, except for a few institutions that have recently started initiating research activities. Instead, private institutions motivate staff by offering better rates of payment, frequent increases in steps of salaries, various fringe benefits, and a better working environment. Table 11.2 shows the salary provisions in these institutions, with reference to the public institutions.

Taking the upper limit of the salary range for all academic ranks, private institutions have a higher salary scale than public institutions. This variation is further exaggerated by the fact that public institutions do not have a step of increase on salaries, while private institutions do. Besides, unlike administrators at public universities whose position allowance is dependent on the academic rank, most private institutions offer significantly higher salaries to administrative officers—irrespective of an academic rank.

In addition, private universities have more part-time staff, compared to public institutions. Since their major function is teaching, the majority (about 95 percent) of the staff is reportedly at the midlevel of the academic hierarchy (lecturer) and most are employed by more than one institution concurrently. Managers/owners of private universities are aware of this tendency and estimate that 60 percent of their staff hold multiple positions.

Almost all of these institutions use certain fringe benefits: life and medical insurance; higher institutional contribution to the provident fund (an obligatory savings plan that employees can withdraw when they leave or retire); a salary increase through steps of the scale; and allowances for housing, transport, mobile use, and so forth. A few of the private institutions use reduced teaching obligations, research subsidies, and yearly bonus payments to attract and retain their academic staff. Moreover, institutions with opportunities to provide consultancy services engage their staff in activities such as the formation of teaching materials or manuals, design and conduct of exams, and preparing and giving short-term training to other organizations to allow supplementary income for staff. In some of the cases, staff are given the option to set their own class schedule (without a frequent alternation), with the tacit understanding that staff could be engaged in teaching duties in other institutions at the same time. A flextime arrangement is believed to enhance staff retention but with the adverse effects of dividing the professor's attention and commitment.

Conclusion

This chapter indicates that academic contracts, particularly in public institutions, are not effective—given the limited (if any) evaluation of performance and the noncompetitive remuneration. Academic salaries, particularly for public institutions, are too low to curb the flow of qualified personnel to other organizations.

Certain differences between public and private institutions are clear—the institutional focus in terms of primary function (teaching versus research), and a significant gap in salary amount, contract type, terms of recruitment, and salary structure (based on academic output versus market demand). Moonlighting is a common practice in both, although the type of external engagement varies.

Therefore, given the expansion of the system and the need for provision of quality education through better remuneration in particular, the current salary and benefit scheme fails to prevent faculty dissatisfaction and apathy; neither does it enable the existing faculty to live a life worthy of their professional status. Tertiary institutions need faculty engaged with a sense of commitment and belonging, not those who make it a springboard to better opportunity elsewhere. In general, the higher education enterprise can neither retain local human resources nor attract international staff unless a solution is offered to change the current dismal state of affairs.

References

AAU (Addis Ababa University). 2006. *New salary scale and benefit scheme for the academic staff of public higher education institution.* Proposal document.

AAU (Addis Ababa University). 2007. *Senate legislation.* Addis Ababa, Ethiopia: Addis Ababa University Press.

Altbach, P. G., L. Reisberg, and L. E. Rumbley. 2009. *Trends in global higher education: Tracking an academic revolution.* A report prepared for the UNESCO 2009 World Conference on Higher Education. Paris: UNESCO.

Ashcroft, K. 2003. "Emerging models of quality, relevance and standards in Ethiopia's higher education institutions." *Ethiopian Journal of Education* 23 (2): 1–25.

Assefa, T., ed. 2008. *Academic freedom in Ethiopia: Perspectives of teaching personnel.* Addis Ababa, Ethiopia: Forum for Social Studies.

Bhargava, A., F. Docquier, and Y. Moullan. 2010. "Modeling the effects of physician emigration on human development." In *Revised panel data set on physician emigration (1991–2004),* World Bank's Social Protection and Labor unit (contract 7152391). http://siteresources.worldbank.org/INTINTERNATIONAL/Resources/1572846-1283439445793/7368291–1283443649876/MBDDataSet.xls. Accessed November 20, 2010.

FDRE (Federal Democratic Republic of Ethiopia). 2003. *Higher education proclamation, no. 351/2003.* Addis Ababa, Ethiopia: Negarit Gazeta.

FDRE (Federal Democratic Republic of Ethiopia). 2009. *Higher education proclamation, no. 650/2009.* Addis Ababa, Ethiopia: Negarit Gazeta.

HERQA (Higher Education Relevance and Quality Agency). 2004. *Higher education systems overhaul (HESO), Report of the committee of inquiry into governance, leadership & management in Ethiopia's HE system.* http:// www.ethiopia-ed.net/images/1581754547.doc. Accessed December 23, 2011.

HERQA (Higher Education Relevance and Quality Agency). 2009. *Quality assurance for enhancement of higher education in Ethiopia: Challenges faced and lessons learned.* http://www.nuffic.nl/international-organisations/international-education-monitor/country-monitor/africa/ethiopia/documents. Accessed December 23, 2011.

Ministry of Education. 1996. *Education statistics annual abstract.* Addis Ababa: Federal Republic of Ethiopia.

Ministry of Education. 2007. *Education statistics annual abstract.* Addis Ababa: Federal Republic of Ethiopia.

Ministry of Education. 2010. *Education statistics annual abstract.* Addis Ababa: Federal Republic of Ethiopia.

Reisberg, L., and L. E. Rumbley. 2010. "Ethiopia: The dilemmas of expansion." *International Higher Education* 58: 23–24.

Solimano, A. 2003. "Globalizing talent and human capital: Implications for developing countries." Manuscript prepared for the fourth annual World Bank Conference on Development Economics for Europe, Norway, June 2002. www.andressolimano.com /.../Globalizing%20Human%20Capital,%20manuscript.pdf. Accessed December 23, 2011.

Tamrat, W. 2008. *The anatomy of private higher education in Ethiopia: Current landscape, challenges & prospects*. Addis Ababa, Ethiopia: Saint Mary's University.

Wondimu, H. 2003. "Ethiopia." In *African higher education: An international reference handbook*, ed. D. Teferra and P. G. Altbach, 316–25. Bloomington: University of Indiana Press.

World Bank. 2004. *Higher education development for Ethiopia: Pursuing the vision*. Washington, DC: World Bank.

World Factbook. 2009. *The world factbook*. http//:www.cia.gov/library/publications/the-world-factbook/. Accessed August 22, 2010.

12

CHANGING THE RULES OF THE FRENCH ACADEMIC MARKET

Gaële Goastellec

Historically managed at a national level by discipline and uniformly organized, the French academic profession today faces a process of slow status, activity, and salary differentiation through broader reforms aimed at increasing the competitiveness of the French higher education sector on the international market. This chapter analyzes these ongoing changes.

Overview of Higher Education: A System Deeply Challenged

During the last few years, the French higher education system has been seriously challenged. The Shanghai rankings underscore the distance between national expectations and the international situation of French higher education institutions and have favored some transformation of the higher education system. In 2006, a research programming law created the hub of research and higher education (PRES—Pôles de recherche et d'enseignement supérieur), which combines higher education and research institutions. The aim is twofold—improving the international visibility of the higher education and research institutions and favoring the integration of quite diverse institutions. Simultaneously, another law (no. 2007–1199) provides more autonomy to universities regarding the management of funding and human resources. In 2008, another reform—the "Plan Campus"—was aimed at identifying and financially sustaining 12 centers of university excellence.

With a plurality of ongoing reforms aimed at restructuring the higher education system, redefining its configuration by providing more power to the universities, and introducing differentiation between universities, the higher education system can thus be described as facing important challenges, including changes in the organization and management of the academic market. These reforms reflect the abandonment of a historical doctrine—pretending that all universities, diploma, and (to some extent) academics were equal on French territory. These reforms served also as the catalyst that ended the traditional structure of the academic profession. This chapter is an attempt to frame and explain these changes, focusing on the public universities, which account for the largest part of the higher education system.

Changes in Context

The French higher education system is mainly public. Access to universities is free and nonselective for all high school graduates. The public higher education sector is composed of a large number of universities (79); the *grandes écoles* (public or private institutions) (25), which represent the highly selective sector of the system; and engineering schools (113), often university based. These higher education institutions register around 2 million students. The private sector registers 14 percent of the higher education enrollment (Ministry of Education 2009) and is composed of engineering schools, business schools, and a few university institutions (Chartier 2005). In the public sector, a national framework exists that defines the status and salary of academics. Traditionally, academics work full time in a single institution and enjoy a middle-class economic status, while their social status and cultural capital are perceived as higher. The situation is much more complex in the private sector, which is characterized by more diversity regarding lecturers' status and more opacity regarding its functioning.

The French higher education system is now massified: 54.5 percent of the relevant-age-group graduates from high school and 45.1 percent access higher education (FQP 2003). This expansion has been accompanied by a growing academic profession. In 2008–9, students in the public sector were taught by 72,733 academics: 17,772 professors—senior position, tenured; 28,984—junior, tenured faculty (*maîtres de conference*); 14,926 temporary academic staff, attached for teaching and research, untenured, who are mostly PhD students or new PhD holders (ATER—*Attaché temporaire d'enseignement et de recherche*), and PhD students with a national fellowship (*Allocataires-Moniteurs*); 4,549 heads of clinic or hospital; and 6,802 "others"—including high school teachers and specific functions in the *grandes écoles* (prestige university-level institutions with competitive entrance exams) (Ministry of Education 2009, 207). These statistics do not include an unknown number of part-time nontenured lecturers. With massification, not only has the number of academics increased, but their activities have changed, too, from the education of elite scholars for specific professions to the education of a diversified student body to various types of professional roles.

Academic Contracts

Hiring Academics: Changing Rules

The hiring of academic personnel is highly centralized and organized through a national law in specific stages. A first round of recruitment occurs at the national level. Every PhD or habilitation holder aspiring to a tenured academic position in a French university must first present an academic file to the National Universities Council (Conseil National des Universités), where disciplinary commissions—composed of French academics—meet once every year to decide whether a candidate has a profile (research, teaching, publications, etc.) strong enough for authorization to apply for a position. Candidates for junior, tenured faculty positions—to some extent, comparable to lecturer positions in the United Kingdom and a tenured position with the expectation of research, teaching, and administrative responsibilities—and for the professoriate have to go through the same process. Twice a year, all the academics' positions available are published on a national website, with the profile required for each position. During the past few years, this national advertisement also includes, off the academic calendar, a few positions that come available during the year. The first level of selection is thus nationally centralized and managed by discipline.

A second round of recruitment is organized at the institutional level. Academic position seekers must send a letter of candidacy and their academic file to the department, announcing a position they want to apply for. The recruitment commission of the department then examines each candidate. A short list of candidates is invited for a presentation discussion with the commission. After these auditions, the commission decides on a ranking that is validated or modified by the university administration council and formally submitted to the Ministry of Higher Education. Traditionally, the department level represented the main power in the recruitment process, with the validation at university and ministry level being largely a formality. But in recent years the recruitment monopoly has been challenged by the university management; the selection commissions in charge of academic hiring are now nominated by the university president and the administration council, compared to being elected by their peers in the previous system. Half of the members must come from outside the universities and do not necessarily belong to the discipline. A specific number of professors and junior, tenured faculty in a commission are not necessary anymore. Additionally, selection commissions are now temporary recruiters—created to examine the candidacies for a single position, while historically they were active for all recruitments during a six-year period.

These changes in the organization of the recruitment commission introduce uncertainty in the distribution of power between disciplines and higher education institutions. The transition interrupts the collective memory of the criteria used and makes it easier for commission presidents to build up commissions adapted to specific recruitments. The meritocratic dimension of the recruitment process seems more at risk than in the previous system. A real issue considers the imbalance between the number of candidates for each position. In 2008, 8,865 candidates applied for junior, tenured faculty positions, and their success rate was around 19.5 percent. The rate pressure varies a lot, depending on the position: it reaches 2.2 percent for the university professors, compared with 4.7 percent for the junior, tenured position (Observatoire de l'emploi scientifique 2009, 80).

Civil Servants Are the Rule

In all public higher education institutions, academics are public servants, as defined by the Decree of 1984. The organization of the hiring process is determined by national legislation, as well as for the types of contracts issued and remunerations. Lecturers and professors are civil servants, hired for a lifetime, and their remuneration is determined at the national level. Doctoral students with a research fellowship and compulsory teaching hours (*allocataires moniteurs*) and nontenured faculty (PhD students or new PhD holders) are hired on short-term contracts (three years for the first one, one to two years for the second one) that are linked to the completion of a PhD. The French model is characterized by a hierarchy of salaries established nationally that does not allow separate institutional salary policies (Musselin 2005).

No information is available for the *grandes écoles,* but the situation for faculty is quite heterogeneous and varies with the status of the institution. Most of the faculty combine academic status within universities with additional temporary part-time contracts, characterized as a comparatively high remuneration. Specific contracts and conditions remain a black box.

The situation is quite different at private institutions, exempt from the national framework; contracts can be short term or part time, and no common remuneration scheme exists. This can lead to a precarious employment situation but also to a higher level of salaries than in the public sector, depending on the prestige and situation of the private institution—based on the national and international higher education landscape.

Redefining Academic Activities

It is a common perception that academics are first hired to teach. Research has traditionally been thought to take place outside of universities. The French state, suspicious of its universities, localized research in specific research institutions, such as, in 1650, the Collège de France and, in 1939, the Scientific National Research Center (Centre National de la recherché Scientifique). The national intellectual identity is built outside universities that are subsequently deprived of research. The higher education landscape is structured, first with universities training teachers, lawyers, and doctors; and, second, *grandes écoles,* places of innovation and educating the elite, that enroll the best secondary education students.

This paradigm has changed over time with the recognition of research as a decisive activity for academics and with the development of university research centers. Thus, pressure has increased on all academic staff to do research, with the exception of the high school teachers teaching first-cycle university students.

Work contracts specify the number of teaching hours per year—128 hours of plenary classes or 192 hours of seminars, with a possible reduction for specific administrative duties. The rest of the time is dedicated to research and to administrative tasks (the latter not, generally, specified in a contract). The contract specifies that teaching-related activities are supposed to account for 50 percent of the working time, the other half being dedicated to research (for a supposed total amount of around 1,600 hours per year). No specific level of research productivity was stipulated, but things are starting to change. Until recently, no evaluation of job performance existed, except for the informal pressure of the peers.

Since 2009, only 192 hours represent a standard level. A university president can vary the number of teaching hours, without upper or lower limits. Theoretically, this modulation depends on the evaluation by the National Universities Council. Every four years, each academic has to submit his or her file to the university, and it is then forwarded to the council. A research-active academic should see his or her teaching load reduced, while another academic doing little or no research would see the teaching load increased up to twice the previous hours. As the number of total teaching hours at a university must remain stable, an overall equilibrium must be maintained institutionally with the distribution of research and teaching loads.

If the criteria remain unclear in regard to research productivity, one can carry out the standards used by the Agency for the Evaluation of Research and Higher Education, to classify researchers and academics as a "publishing researcher" for each discipline—where a target number of publications is set as the goal to be reached within four years.

Higher education institutions do not possess the autonomy to compete for individual academic staff, so choices are made on the basis of their relative prestige and the research and teaching environments they offer. The law of 2007 introduced some flexibility in the recruitment and remuneration of higher education staff; in some cases, it is possible to abandon the hiring procedures for a public servant/tenured position in favor of a short-time contract that permits the negotiation of wages as well as research and teaching obligations. This law anticipates the possibility of hiring lecturers and researchers outside the classical framework, while the Scientific National Research Center develops new contracts for researchers on a six-year basis. These new contracts can be considered tools to improve the competitive position of a higher education institution hoping to attract foreign scientists.

Academic Salaries: From Homogeneity to Differentiation

Salaries: A Complex Calculation

In the public sector, academic salaries are defined by law. A professor earns €2,557 monthly, initially; €4,111 at the middle of the scale; and €5,129 at the top of the scale. For a junior, tenured faculty position, the bottom of the scale is around

€1,764 a month; the middle of the scale is around €3,190; and the top of the scale is €3,742 (Tentillier 2011).

For nontenured faculty (PhD students or new PhD holders), salary is about €1,699 per month for a full-time position and around €1,150 for a half-time position. PhD students who are selected to receive a national fellowship earn around €1,650 a month when their contract in cludes teaching (64 hours), but €1,350 when it does not.

For each status (junior, tenured faculty, or professor), the salaries calculation system is a highly complex one without mentioning that salaries for newcomers were increased in 2007 by the French Ministry of Higher Education, producing inequalities, meaning, in some cases, that new hires can earn more than those hired previously at the same level.

Merit has almost no role in assigning salaries; salary first depends on seniority and then on a promotion resulting from an academic file evaluation by the National Universities Council. There are a limited number of promotions available each year.

Bonuses: The Introduction of Evaluations

Besides salaries, bonuses represent an important part of faculty income and are increasingly used to offer institutions some flexibility with the distribution of salaries. While most of the bonuses were previously awarded on the basis of responsibilities assigned to different teachers, since 2009 they tend to be merit based. The criteria of bonus evaluations are elaborated by the main steering bodies of the universities. Bonuses fall into two categories—task-based bonuses, such as the traditional bonus for doctoral and research supervision (around €3,400 for a junior, tenured faculty; €4,800 for a professor, second class; €6,350 for a professor, first class), and for administrative duties (€2,000, on average). There are two new bonus categories—first, an evaluation of pedagogical responsibilities (from €3,500 to €15,000 a year) and, second, for scientific excellence (a doctoral and research supervision bonus [Prime d'encadrement doctoral et de recherché, PEDR], €3,500–€15,000 per year). The bonus system allows universities to reward academics for performance.

Salaries in Private Higher Education: A Kaleidoscope of Practices

In private higher education, without a governing framework, huge salary differences exist, depending on the institution and the status of the lecturer. Lecturers might earn from €1,624 to €2,740 a month (SNPEFP-CGT 2007). In the most prestigious business schools, a professor of finance can earn from €10,000 up to €14,000 a month (L'Express 2008). At the same time, lecturers can be paid very little. These institutions may hire "affiliated professors" (persons having a principal job elsewhere, usually in the private sector) or full professors. To attract full professors, private institutions have the flexibility to offer research teams, research budgets, and other options.

Nonsalary Benefits: The Tiny Part

Salary remains the most important element in attracting academics to the public sector, along with civil-servant status that guarantees long-life employment and a decent retirement pension. If someone has worked in the public sector for 40 years and at least until 65 years of age (university professors can remain until 68 years of age), their retirement pensions correspond to 75 percent of the salaries received during the last six months of their professional activities.

The health plan associated with the civil service offers good lifetime coverage, including for the family. It is also possible to benefit from low-interest loans available to the civil service.

Supplementary Employment: Framing the Rules

In a large majority, academic professors work at a single institution and under a single, full-time—lifetime—contract. It is not possible to estimate the number of professors who teach in more than one institution. Supplementary employment is regulated for employees in the public sector. While salaries are the same, regardless of the discipline, supplementary employment is more likely in areas such as economics and law. In May 2007, Decree No. 2007–658, which guides the possibilities for civil servants to develop moonlighting, ruled that ancillary activities are allowed in the case of assessments, consulting, or teaching in the individual's academic field. However, these activities must be authorized by the academic hierarchy and must not detract from the primary activities and functions outlined in a person's contract. Participation in these activities must not exceed 20 percent of the working time, normally dedicated to research.

Generally, when compared with salaries for professionals with similar qualifications and education in the private sector, academic salaries remain above average.

Qualifications

At public higher education institutions, the academic hierarchy progresses in the following order—beginning with PhD students who are teaching, temporary teaching and research assistants; junior, tenured faculty; and professors. Junior, tenured faculty must be PhD holders, while professors must hold a habilitation in addition to their PhD. In disciplines—such as law, political science, economics, or management—one must also hold the aggregation, a status obtained through a national and public exam. For these categories, a scale of classes and grades exist that are based on seniority and merit. Promotion within a status is earned on the basis of seniority, while promotions between classes are based on the evaluations of academic achievement.

At private higher education institutions, no uniform academic hierarchy exists; the qualifications required are not always the same as in the public sector, but, for the most part, substitute teachers compose the lower level, associate professors populate the middle tier, and full professors are at the highest level.

International Competition

French academic salaries are not particularly attractive to international scholars. Foreign academics account for 13 percent of researchers and 7 percent of lecturers. As a result, incoming mobility tends to involve short research stays. In 2008, more than 5,000 visas for non-European foreign researchers were granted, but 55 percent of those visas were for less than three months. Nevertheless, PhD students are quite international. In 2008, two out of five PhD students were from abroad; 39 percent came from Africa (mainly former colonies); 30 percent were from Asian countries; and 17.3 percent from the European Union (Observatoire de l'emploi scientifique 2009).

In terms of "outward mobility," one-third of new PhD graduates do postdoctoral research, and one-half do this abroad. Generally, French researchers are less likely to relocate to the United States, compared with their counterparts in the United Kingdom, Germany, Spain, and Italy. Yet, it seems that the United States does attract the elite of the French researchers (Kohler 2010).

French universities are not particularly attractive to foreign professors—because of the national career framework, the noncompetitive salaries, and the language barrier. But the new possibility of hiring a contract-based lecturer allows more flexibility in wages and thus can be adapted to increase institutional attractiveness. The highly selective private and public sectors have more advantages to offer—including prestige, better working conditions (colleagues and infrastructure), and salaries (in the private sector)—and the possibility to modulate the work schedule to allow for other remunerative activities.

In 2009, the government introduced new opportunities to encourage the return of the best French researchers working abroad, including the creation of 130 chairs positions at universities and research institutions. These positions are characterized by a reduced teaching load (one-third of the normal one) and an annual premium as well as research funding for young researchers (Observatoire de l'emploi scientifique 2009, 83).

Conclusion

The increased internationalization of higher education and proliferation of rankings have had considerable impact on the French higher education system.

Multiple reforms have been implemented that address the rigid structure of the higher education system and encourage differentiation among higher education institutions, as well as between academics. These reforms reflect a trend to reconfigure French higher education. Historically, universities were weak actors, compared with the internal disciplinary units of the schools and colleges or with public authorities; but they are becoming more autonomous, which has provided the latitude for the development of a stronger institutional identity.

Recognizing the importance of a diversity of roles, activities, and resources in what was formerly and traditionally a more uniform sector defines the present trend. The differentiation of higher education institutions has been supported by reforms attempting to introduce more differentiation among academics. Historically, all academics were assigned the same tasks; their professional status and remuneration were determined by a complex national structure that emphasized seniority and qualifications. In the past, merit had little bearing on a person's career. By comparison, the new system introduces and encourages differentiation of professional activities, as well as the means to evaluate and reward these activities with more flexible contracts and additional income. The process of increased differentiation is opened. It remains to be seen to what the results of this new autonomy will be.

References

Chartier, Jérôme. 2005. Cinq verbes pour l'enseignement supérieur "privé." *Rapport au Premier Ministre*. Paris: La Découverte.

FQP (Formation et Qualification Professionelle) [Training and Professional Qualification]. 2003. *Formation Salaires. Enquête sur la formation et la qualification professionnelle 2003*. Paris: INSEE.

Kohler, Ioanna. 2010. *Gone for good? Partis pour de bon? Les expatriés de l'enseignement supérieur français aux Etats-Unis* (November). Institut Montaigne. Available at: http://www.institutmontaigne.org/les-expatries-de-l-enseignement-sperrieur-francais-3251.html. Accessed June 25, 2011.

L'Express. 2008. *Profs de finance: les transferts commencent*. http://www.lexpress.fr/emploi-carriere/profs-de-finance-les-tranferts-commencent_472135.html. Accessed June 25, 2011.

Ministry of Education. 2009. *Repères et références statistiques sur les enseignements, la formation et la recherché*. Paris: Ministry of Education.

Musselin, C. 2005. *Le marché des universitaires. France, Allemagne, Etats-Unis*. Paris: Science Po Les Presses.

Observatoire de l'emploi scientifique. 2009. *L'Etat des lieux de l'emploi scientifique en France, Rapport 2009*. Paris: Ministère de L'Enseignement Supérieur et de la Recherche.

SNPEFP-CGT (Syndicat National des Personnels de l'Enseignement et de la Formation Privés-Confédération Général du Travail). 2007. *Convention collective nationale*. Paris: SNPEFP-CGT.

Tentillier, Nicolas. 2011. *Traitements des maîtres de conférences et professeurs des universités*. http://nicolas.tentillier.free.fr/Salaires/index.html. Accessed June, 25, 2011.

13

THE INCOME SITUATION IN THE GERMAN SYSTEM OF HIGHER EDUCATION

A Rag Rug

Marius Herzog and Barbara M. Kehm

A binary system with universities and universities of applied sciences, academic staff dominated by research assistants without doctoral degrees, limited contracts or opportunities for promotion, and an ongoing salary reform in Germany's 16 states make the salary conditions comparable to a rag rug. Due to social insurance and benefits, the income of these academics is quite good, related to other countries, though uncertain career prospects make universities appear less attractive employers—especially for young researchers.

The German Higher Education System

Most universities in Germany are registered as legal public entities under the supervision of the states. According to the Constitution of the Federal Republic of Germany, the states have sovereignty in cultural and educational matters and are responsible for higher education legislation. The responsible authority is the state Ministry for Education or Higher Education. After a far-reaching reform of German federalism in 2006, the German federal government was left with hardly any responsibilities for higher education. It is only engaged in the support and promotion of research and guarantees certain framework conditions.

There are 410 higher education institutions in Germany—including 105 universities, 203 universities of applied sciences, and 102 other institutions of higher education. In 2010, a total of 2,119,485 students were enrolled (Statistisches Bundesamt 2010, 6). About two-thirds of the students are enrolled at universities. In 2008, German higher education institutions employed 274,769 academics and among them 38,564 professors (Statistisches Bundesamt 2009, 37, 99).

Germany has a binary higher education system with universities and universities of applied sciences. The latter provide a more applied and professionally oriented education and mainly do not have the right to award doctoral degrees. They focus more on teaching and not on research. Most students in universities of applied sciences are enrolled in engineering, business studies, social work, and public administration programs. Other higher education institutions are teachers colleges, theological seminaries, and art academies. The distance university in Hagen is the only state-supported, distance-teaching university in Germany.

In addition to state universities, the system also has nonstate universities. Apart from a number of private higher education institutions legally created as foundations, seven (previously) public higher education institutions have become foundations. It is important to distinguish between for-profit and nonprofit institutions in the private sector.

Private and, especially, private commercial universities play a minor role in Germany, although their number has increased considerably in recent years (Goll 2009). Among the total number of higher education institutions, the proportion of private universities is about a quarter, but the proportion of students enrolled in them is rather low, with 4.9 percent of the overall student enrollment (Lenhardt, Reisz, and Stock 2009, 738; Frank et al. 2010). While private universities have become an integral part of the German higher education landscape, they do not have a long tradition in Germany and often lead a niche existence (Dilger 2009). Private full universities do not exist in Germany. The modern universities, emerging in Germany in the 19th century, were—in contrast, for example, to the United States—under state control.

Overview of the Academic Profession

The academic profession in German higher education is clearly divided into two status groups: (1) professors who are normally tenured civil servants and (2) nonprofessorial academic staff also responsible for teaching and research. The majority of the latter are employees in the civil service, having fixed-term contracts mostly until the age of 40. This group includes junior academic staff in the process of getting their PhD. In the German context they are not considered to be students but, rather, early-stage researchers. Their contracts are typically for 50 percent of the regular weekly working hours. Postdocs and senior researchers can obtain full-time positions more easily, but unlimited contracts are rare even for young professors, initially. These conditions make the young researchers' future unpredictable, as there is no guaranteed career progress. The basic principle is "up or out," and applicants who do not manage to earn a professorship will eventually have to leave the university and find a job elsewhere. By that time, they are typically around 40 years old or sometimes older.

In terms of salaries, the situation of the professors is less attractive than it at first seems, since a professor in Germany usually does not get his or her position before the age of around 40. On the other hand, there is an ongoing reform of professorial salaries, consisting of a clearly reduced basic salary and performance-related components. In financial terms, universities are less-attractive places of employment, when compared to positions in the German industry (where much higher salaries are found for higher education graduates or PhD holders) or public administration (where much more job security is found, with full-time and permanent lifetime contracts).

In Germany, civil service appointments dominate the working contracts in the higher education system. Nearly all academic staff at universities and universities of applied sciences work in the civil service of the states. The difference between professorial and nonprofessorial positions is that professors are civil servants with permanent lifelong positions, while the other academic staff members are mostly employees in the civil service—with permanent positions or fixed-term contracts. Though both groups are characterized by relatively good social benefits that make academic jobs generally attractive, civil servants have the highest job security, better income and health insurance conditions, as well as the highest pensions.

In general, the salaries of academic staff (professors, as well as others) are defined by each state and for each specific positional category—so individual negotiations for the nonprofessorial academic staff are not possible. In contrast to this, professors are allowed to top up their personal salary in negotiations, as well as the infrastructure of their chairs, academic units covering a professor with secretary, and their academic staff and facility.

Most professors are civil servants, although fixed-term contracts are increasing. So, in contrast to the nonprofessorial academic staff, they generally have greater job security and work under privileged conditions. However, more than two-thirds of the other academic staff are temporary employees with fixed-term contracts, some of whom cannot be renewed under certain conditions. Apart from differences in academic ranks, these are the main issues that distinguish professorial and nonprofessorial academic staff.

Nonprofessorial Academic Positions

The academic career ladder in German universities normally starts with graduates (master's degree level) performing as research and teaching assistants, while working toward the completion of their PhD. An individual might be a member of the human resources assigned to the chair or a member of the research team on third-party-funded projects. This phase, which can last as long as six years, rarely offers full-time jobs. After being awarded a doctoral degree, young researchers can work on their habilitation on the basis of a similar contract—up to six years in duration, but with the possibility of a full-time position and a somewhat higher teaching load. The habilitation is a formal postdoctoral qualification (usually earned after the publication of a major book and a public lecture), which does not guarantee a professorship but is a prerequisite for eligibility. This progression is possible at the same institution, although a university change is common for the qualification phase, after the doctorate. The formal habilitation has been criticized for quite some time. Also, the junior professorship, a new academic category, has been created to enable earlier independence—with the intent of abolishing the habilitation qualification (see the next section).

The number of professors is small compared to the numerous lower-level academic staff. This higher rank has a relatively high teaching load (eight hours per week, in the semester); but, since student numbers have increased considerably, additional teaching capacity is required. This has been accomplished by integrating the following new categories of instructors (Kehm 1999, 84). University staff, funded through external (research) resources, may receive part-time contracts as lecturers (often doing this without payment). Practitioners, from professional fields outside higher education institutions, may also be hired as part-time lecturers. Recent graduates or doctoral candidates may receive short-term contracts for service as teaching assistants. Persons of high professional, public, and academic esteem may be appointed as honorary professors, with an obligation to teach without remuneration. Teachers for special tasks or secondary school teachers may work for the university as technical teachers or specialist-subject teachers (especially in teacher-training fields).

In recent years, an increasing number of lecturers have been employed by universities. These are frequently postdocs, contracted exclusively only for teaching positions and having a weekly teaching load of up to 12 hours.

Professors

A new pay scale, introduced in 2005, divides professors into three groups, which are to some extent comparable with the categories of the American system, although German higher education does not signify a tenure model: junior professors (assistant professors), associate professors, and full professors. It is typical for the German higher education system that position and income become stable at a rather late stage in an academic career. The recent introduction of the junior professorship is supposed to remedy this situation. Eligibility for a junior professorship is based on having a doctoral degree and some experience in research and publications. The latest studies have revealed that the average age of gaining a professorship could be reduced. Nevertheless, most junior professors (around 800 currently in Germany) still try to obtain their habilitation, to gain a competitive edge when applying for higher-level professorships.

Junior professorships are always temporary (typically 3 + 3 year appointments). The probation initially consists of three years, then an evaluation of the performance is carried out and, assuming a positive conclusion, extended for another three years, with a slight salary increase. Only a minority of junior professorships earn a professorship. It is a general rule that junior professors need to apply for a position at a different institution after six years to avoid inbreeding. It is not possible to become a professor at the same university from which one gets the relevant qualification.

The typical way to acquire a professorship, or a promotion to a higher professorial position, or to increase one's salary involves applying for a professorship at a different university. If the application is successful, it is sometimes possible to negotiate salary supplements and additional resources in order to stay at one's old university or as a condition for accepting the new position. In contrast, professors at universities of applied sciences can be promoted to a higher position, without the need to change institutions. However, the holders of the highest professorial ranks at universities of applied sciences are not entitled to negotiate salary supplements or additional resources. Beyond that, they rarely change their institutions.

Associate professors and full professors are effectively tenured if they were already appointed to these ranks by the time the new pay scale came to force. However, in the framework of the new pay scale, the associate professor positions are also limited to six-year contracts if the candidate is recruited to a professorship for the first time.

The Payment System

A major pay-scale reform was introduced in 2005 and, since then, is applied to all new hires in Germany. The reform reduces basic salaries of professors and introduces performance-related salary components. The traditional salary categories are still in force for all professors who were hired before 2005.

The former pay-scale system in the public service had become too complicated over the decades. In 2006, the states, paying nonprofessorial academic employees, signed a collective agreement for the public-sector employees. Different scales are still used, some new and others based on old categories. Additionally, there is still an income gap between western and eastern Germany, with eastern Germany salary scales being somewhat lower than western ones.

Under the ongoing salary reform, the income of junior professors, associate professors, and full professors does not increase for the duration of employment, but there are bonuses for good performance combined with detailed control. Performance bonuses are given in cases of appointment and tenure, for special achievements in research, teaching, art, further education, and training or supporting junior researchers, as well as for functions or specific tasks relating to university administration or management—based on section 33 of the Federal Remuneration Act (BBESG 2011). However, in addition to these regulations each university has budgetary autonomy to allocate a certain percentage of its budget for such bonuses and to establish its own criteria for the award.

Salary Information

Data Limitations

Although the Federal Statistical Office provides a lot of data covering the entire country systematically, there is hardly any information about the real income of the academic staff, especially of professors. This is related to the fact that professors can negotiate their salary if they apply to another university, receive a call, and then carry out negotiations with both institutions. Furthermore, it is a taboo in Germany to talk about the results of such negotiations, at least with respect to the actual salary. Additionally, no data are available on average real-income differences between the academics employed at the individual universities. But it can be assumed that they differ by less than 5 percent for public universities of the same type (Janson, Schomburg, and Teichler 2007, 104). Since data about the real incomes of the academic profession are not available, the statistical information provided for Germany relies on averages and thus should be used with some caution. While full-time academics' basic salaries have become similar, there are considerable differences.[1] However, income tables from the homepages of the trade unions can help constitute the minimum salaries. In addition, information from individual universities, of average staff costs, provides an indication of the situation in each state. Another option for salary information is to ask universities or the academics themselves. As a whole, these studies are currently rare, so only estimates can be provided (Hartmer 2009; Jacob and Teichler 2011).

It is difficult to obtain specific data about the salaries paid by private universities (Academics.com 2008). Estimates are not possible because the salaries are freely negotiated. Inquiries to determine the scale or limits, while working on this chapter, were unsuccessful.

Professors

In 2008, the average gross monthly income of full professors in Germany was €6,108 (about US$8,626). These are the findings across all subjects that apply to traditional and new professorial positions (Hartmer 2009, 890). Junior professors receive a basic salary of €3,405 (about US$4,808). Associate professors receive a salary of €3,890 (about US$5,493) and full professors, a basic salary of €4,724 (about US$6,671).

The basic salary is pensionable and subject to the general salary adjustments. A seniority promotion—as was customary in the former scale—is absent in the new scale. Salary increases can be granted if there are children. The family allowance in stage one (married) is €105. The family allowance for the first and second child is €90 (about US$127) each. For the third and each additional child, the family allowance is €231 (about US$326) for each, as of August 2004 (Deutscher Hochschulverband 2008a, 2008b).

The improvement of income due to salary reform, as it was promised by the politicians, is seen as critical. Approximately 75 percent of all university professors receive no performance bonus after the new scale, and only an unexpectedly small number of the university professors have a higher income—due to their negotiations concerning the change of their university (Hartmer 2009, 890).

Professors at universities of applied science mainly receive a salary lower than university (full) professors (Jacob and Teichler 2011, 138).[2] Therefore, it is surprising that their mean annual gross income of about €60,000 (about US$84,390) is just 4 percent, below the corresponding average of professors at universities. However, the additional income (earned, for example, in industry) is higher by 13 percent on average than those of university professors.

The income of associate professors is 21 percent below that of full professorships. The same study also showed that university professors from the humanities and social sciences are remunerated 16 percent less for their activities at the university than their colleagues from the natural sciences.

Nonprofessorial Positions

Academic employees in the civil service on nonprofessorial positions with full-time contracts receive salaries of between 55 percent and up to 75 percent of the average salary of a full professorship (Janson, Schomburg, and Teichler 2007, 105).

The average gross income of academic staff in 2007 was €35,800 (about US$49,430)—about €3,000, monthly (about US$4,236) (Jacob and Teichler 2011, 139). The full-time gross income average is €42,000 (about US$59,316)—that is, 53 percent of the income of full professors. Academic staff employed at universities of applied sciences receive €40,000 (about US$56,492), as average annual gross income. Here, the much higher proportion of full-time employment and mostly longer occupations of the academic staff working for universities of applied sciences becomes evident, while in universities there are mainly half-time positions.

The salaries of the nonprofessorial academic staff at universities in Germany are comparable to the salaries of employees with university degrees in the public service. Junior academics without a doctorate earn less, because they mainly work part time. Contract lecturers who teach university courses without employment have a particularly low income, because they are paid in the form of hourly fees for teaching. There are, however, a few studies on the incomes of these groups (Banscherus et al. 2009, 38). They are paid on a fee basis or carry out their work free of charge. The primary idea behind these positions was to allow practitioners with a full-time job to volunteer for university teaching. Therefore, employment or welfare benefits were not needed. Meanwhile, teaching is the main source of income for a significant proportion of this group. Although they play an important role in university teaching, the majority of contract lecturers live in rather precarious conditions. Monthly incomes below €1,000 (about US$1,412) are the rule rather than the exception, and it is practically impossible to cover the costs of living without additional income.

Additional Income

Considering the late stabilization of income, combined with a late entrance into the pension system of civil servants—as well as a relatively low income, compared to earnings in industry—about 10 percent of the professors are involved in contract research and development, consultancy, professional activities, or continuing education outside the institution.

Reviews of extra income are not carried out frequently. According to a representative survey at the beginning of the 1990s, extra income varied from 9 percent in the case of university professors to 13 percent for professors at universities of applied science and 5 percent for other nonprofessorial academic staff in universities (Enders and Teichler 1995, 104). More recent data show the percentage of the additional income on total income, including nonprofessorial staff: 10 percent for university professors, 7 percent for professors at universities of applied science, but only 3 percent for research assistants at universities and 1 percent for research assistants at universities of applied science (Jacob and Teichler 2011, 138).[3] During their qualification phase the additional income of nonprofessorial academic staff is usually very low.

Taxes and Additional Salary Deductions

The taxes for civil servants amount to 30 to 45 percent of gross income, depending on the tax bracket. Civil servants neither pay unemployment insurance nor do they contribute to their pensions, because this is taken care of by the state as the official employer. In addition, health-insurance costs are shared equally between the employee and employer. The costs of health insurance depend on gender, age, health status, income, occupation, and the chosen insurance.

Employees in the civil service pay half the social security contributions (i.e., unemployment, health insurance, and pension rights); the other half is paid by the state. Employees currently pay about 7 percent of their gross income for health insurance, about 10 percent as contribution to their pension, 1.4 percent for the unemployment insurance, and 1 percent for care in old age.

The level of pension is determined by a person's lifetime income. It does not matter whether somebody became a civil servant at an early age or later in life. The first difference is the pension fund from which the pension will be paid. So, if a professor has worked outside academia for the first 20 years of the working life and was a civil servant for the last 20 years, the pension claims from both phases are combined. Changing one's position or employer does not result in a loss of pension claims. The second difference is that people who are not civil servants pay contributions to the federal pension fund for employees and workers who are automatically deducted from their monthly salary. Also, people who are civil servants do not need to pay a contribution to a pension fund for civil servants. In these cases the state pays the contributions.

Both civil servants and employees in the civil service also must pay 5.5 percent of their income tax as a solidarity contribution that was established to support German Reunification. Depending on age, every employee gets between 26 and 32 working days per year as paid leave (vacation). The minimum retirement age is 65 years.

Conclusion

The different conditions in the German higher education system—concerning the institutional level and the individual circumstances of university's academics as well as an ongoing salary reform—present "a rag rug" of academic salaries.

The following trends in the organization of academic work in German higher education institutions have to be considered (Bloch and Burkhardt 2010). While the workforce has grown, the basic structure of academic staff hardly changed. Part-time employment has grown in importance, and limited contracts for academic staff are the rule. Doctoral and postdoctoral researchers are significant for teaching and research, whereas the number of junior professorships falls short of the original expectations, despite the fact that student numbers continue to grow and many professors are nearing retirement age.

Compared with international standards, at least from the occupational point of view, employment conditions within the German higher education system show some positive as well as some negative trends.

On the positive side is the attempt to abolish habilitation and enable talented young researchers to become independent at an earlier point in their career and shorten the time, until eligibility for a professorship has been reached. Furthermore, academic staff, and especially professors, have good fringe benefits and—while employed—good social security in terms of health care and pension. Finally, it should be emphasized that being part of the academic staff of a higher education institution implies a relatively high social standing.

On the negative side we find an increasing number of fixed-term contracts, reduced basic salaries for professors that can be topped up with performance related, though often not pensionable, salary components, and a lack of institutional promotion systems. The last issue, taken together with the increasing number of fixed-term contracts, implies risks in terms of periods of unemployment or a lack of progress along the career ladder.

Notes

1. The payment of the academic staff is determined by a complex system of rules pertaining to different levels (federal, state, and university regulations), the age of the employees, the marital status, the number of their children, and so forth. With regard to professorial positions, individual negotiations (e.g., appointment and tenure) also play a role in determining individual salaries. Further differences are related to full-time or part-time positions and old or new salary scale.
2. While there are no differences in appointment and tenure between professors at universities and professors of applied sciences, the latter do not have the staff category of "chair." The highest position is equivalent to an associate professorship. A change of position from being a professor at a university of applied sciences to becoming a university professor and vice versa is extremely rare.
3. Full professors earn 11 percent, associate professors, 9 percent of their total income as extra income. Professors of the humanities and social sciences earn 3 percent, but their colleagues from the natural sciences earn 13 percent of their total income as additional income.

References

Academics.com. 2008. *Questions and answers about salaries.* http://www.academics.com/science/questions_and_answers_about_salaries_30640.html?unpaged=true. Accessed March 25, 2011.

Banscherus, Ulf, Klaus Dörre, Matthias Neis, and Andrä Wolter. 2009. "Zum Wandel von Arbeit und Beschäftigung in der" unternehmerischen Universität." WISO Diskurs. Expertisen und Dokumentationen zur Wirtschafts- und Sozialpolitik Arbeitsplatz Hochschule. Arbeitskreis Dienstleistungen. Bonn, Germany: Friedrich Ebert-Stiftung.

BBESG (Bundesbesoldungsgesetz). 2011. Bundesbesoldungsgesetz in der Fassung der Bekanntmachung vom 19. Juni 2009 (BGBl. I S. 1434), das durch Artikel 28 des Gesetzes vom 20. Dezember 2011 (BGBl. I S. 2854) geändert worden ist. http://www.gesetze-im-internet.de/bbesg/BJNR011740975.html. Accessed January 5, 2012.

Bloch, Roland, and Anke Burkhardt. 2010. "Arbeitsplatz Hochschule und Forschung für wissenschaftliches Personal und Nachwuchskräfte." Demokratische und Soziale Hochschule, Arbeitspapier 207. Düsseldorf, Germany: Hans-Böckler-Stiftung.

Deutscher Hochschulverband. 2008a. *Die W-Besoldung.* http://www.hochschulverband.de/cms1/fileadmin/redaktion/download/pdf/info_blaetter/info0205.pdf. Accessed March 25, 2011.

Deutscher Hochschulverband. 2008b. *Salaries in academia: What academics earn in Germany.* http://www.academics.com/science/salaries_30543.html?unpaged=true. Accessed March 25, 2011.

Dilger, Alexander. 2009. "Privathochschulen als Nischenanbieter. Anpassungsstrategien an die Dominanz staatlicher Hochschulen." *Forschung und Lehre* 16 (10): 732–34.

Enders, Jürgen, and Ulrich Teichler. 1995. *Der Hochschullehrerberuf im internationalen Vergleich.* Bonn, Germany: Bundesministerium für Bildung und Wissenschaft, Forschung und Technologie.

Frank, Andrea, Solveigh Hieronimus, Nelson Killius, and Volker Meyer-Guckel. 2010. *Rolle und Zukunft privater Hochschulen in Deutschland.* Essen, Germany: Stifterverband für die Deutsche Wissenschaft.

Goll, Dietmar. 2009. "Sprunghaft gewachsen: Privathochschulen in Deutschland: Bestandsaufnahme und Perspektiven." *Forschung und Lehre* 16 (10): 724–26.

Hartmer, Michael. 2009. "Was verdient ein Universitätsprofessor? Ergebnisse einer empirischen Untersuchung." *Forschung und Lehre* 12 (9): 890–92.

Jacob, Anna K., and Ulrich Teichler. 2011. *Der Wandel des Hochschullehrerberufs im internationalen Vergleich: Ergebnisse einer Befragung in den Jahren 2007/08.* Berlin: Bundesministerium für Bildung und Forschung.

Janson, Kerstin, Harald Schomburg, and Ulrich Teichler. 2007. *Wege zur Professur. Qualifizierung und Beschäftigung an Hochschulen in Deutschland und den USA.* Münster, Germany: Waxmann.

Kehm, Barbara M. 1999. *Higher education in Germany: Developments, problems and perspectives.* Bucharest, Romania: CEPES/UNESCO; Wittenberg, Germany: Institut für Hochschulforschung.

Lenhardt, Gero, Robert D. Reisz, and Manfred Stock. 2009. "Weder anspruchsvoller noch elitär Private Hochschulen in Deutschland, USA, Chile und Rumänien: Ergebnisse einer vergleichenden Studie." *Forschung und Lehre* 16 (10): 738–39.

Statistisches Bundesamt. 2009. *Bildung und Kultur: Personal an Hochschulen 2008,* Fachserie 11, Reihe 4.4. Wiesbaden, Germany.

Statistisches Bundesamt. 2010. *Bildung und Kultur: Studierende an Hochschulen. Vorbericht,* Wintersemester 2009/2010, Fachserie 11, Reihe 4.1. Wiesbaden, Germany.

14

ACADEMIC SALARIES AND CAREER ADVANCEMENT

Tuning the Professoriate for a Knowledge Economy in India

Narayana Jayaram

The dawn of the 21st century saw India witnessing competing demands for talent in the knowledge economy, occasioned by globalization and the turning away of the best of talents from the academic profession. To arrest this trend, the salaries of teachers have since been upwardly revised to an extent unthinkable a decade back. The professoriate is now comfortably placed in the middle class, and the academic profession has again become attractive in the employment market. Simultaneously, to tone up the quality of the profession, requirements for both recruitment and career advancement within it have been redefined. This chapter discusses the salient features and key issues in the recruitment and remuneration of the professoriate in India.

Diversity in Higher Education

India has witnessed a rapid growth of higher education since independence: from 20 universities and 496 colleges, in 1947, to 496 universities and university-level institutions and 29,951 colleges, by the end of 2009. Broadly, there are five types of higher education institutions—namely, (1) central universities (40), (2) institutions of national importance (21), (3) state universities (239), (4) grant-in-aid colleges (29,951), and (5) unaided (purely private) universities/colleges (numbers not available).

Central universities are established by an act of Parliament and are financed by the government of India's Ministry of Human Resources Development, through the University Grants Commission (UGC). They are multidisciplinary, combining postgraduate teaching (mainly) with research (secondarily). State universities are established by acts of State Legislative Assemblies. They receive five years of financial assistance (up to 85 percent) for all development initiatives (including teaching positions), from the UGC; thereafter they will have to be funded by the respective state governments. They have a central campus, housing departments of study offering instruction at the postgraduate level (mostly), and undertake (little) research. Most state universities have colleges affiliated to them, whose academic work they regulate and oversee. Grant-in-aid colleges are funded to the tune of 85–90 percent by the state governments concerned. They generally offer first-degree-level education and are affiliated to the state universities. These colleges may be run either by the government through its department of higher education or by private management bodies. Institutions of national importance include the 16 Indian Institutes of Technology, three institutions specializing in medical sciences, and each one specializing in statistical techniques and the Hindi language. These university-level institutions enjoy the special status accorded them by the central government, and they are all funded directly by the Ministry of Human Resources Development. Unaided (purely private) universities and colleges are privately run institutions; they do not receive any financial support from the government. As universities, they are either "deemed-to-be" under the UGC Act or established by an act of a State Legislative Assembly. As colleges, they are established and managed by private trusts: While trust laws govern their administration and finance, their academic programs are determined and overseen by the university to which they are affiliated. Reliable data on the purely private institutions are hard to come by, as there is no designated body monitoring them.

Types of Teaching Positions

The higher education institutions in India have different types of teaching positions. The most coveted type is the permanent teaching position in a public-funded university or college. Appointees to permanent positions are placed on probation for a period of two years and, on successful completion of probation, are confirmed in the post and earn the equivalent of tenure. The age of superannuation varies from 65 years (as in central universities and centrally funded institutions) to 60–62 years in state universities and grant-in-aid colleges. Teachers holding permanent positions can voluntarily retire from their post with full-pension benefit, after completing 20 years of uninterrupted service. They can also be compulsorily retired (as a penalty) or prematurely retired (in "public interest") or retired on medical grounds (after 50 years of age or 30 years of service). In centrally funded institutions, superannuated teachers may be reemployed for one year at a time for up to five years. Permanent positions are nonexistent in purely private universities and colleges.

Both permanent and contractual teaching positions involve full-time engagement in teaching and research in the institution. A different situation involves the part-time teaching position. In India, the concepts of part-time teachers (who teach for a specified number of teaching hours in a week) and guest faculty (who help the college/department "to complete portions of the syllabus") originated as a result of the unmet demand for teachers in particular disciplines. For some positions, full-time teachers are either not available (in narrow fields of specializations) or it is not viable to appoint full-time teachers (as they would not have a sufficient workload). Typically, part-time teachers and guest faculty are paid a consolidated sum, based on remuneration for the number of hours of teaching work they are assigned. They are not entitled to any statutory employment benefits—leave, medical insurance, pension, gratuity, and other options.

Qualifications for the Professoriate

Since January 2006, a three-tier academic hierarchy—namely, professor, associate professor, and assistant professor—has been standardized in public-funded higher education institutions. To maintain quality in those institutions, the UGC has prescribed the minimum qualifications for appointment to various teaching positions in public-funded institutions (UGC 2010). For appointment to the post of an assistant professor in nonprofessional courses (commerce, languages, science, social sciences, etc.), a candidate must have (1) a good academic record, with at least 55 percent marks (or an equivalent grade in a point scale) at the master's level in the relevant subject, and (2) qualified in the National Eligibility Test conducted by UGC or an accredited test certifying proficiency in the subject. Candidates having a PhD are exempt from the requirement of the National Eligibility Test qualification.

For appointment to the post of associate professor through direct recruitment, besides a good academic record with at least 55 percent marks (or an equivalent grade in a point scale) at the master's level in the relevant subject, a PhD in the concerned/allied/relevant discipline is a mandatory qualification. In addition, the candidates must have a minimum of eight years of experience of teaching and/or research in an academic/research position equivalent to that of assistant professor in a university or college. They must (1) show evidence of being engaged in research and have a minimum of five publications as books and/or research/policy papers to their credit; (2) have contributed to educational innovation, designing new curricula and courses and technology-mediated, teaching-learning process; and (3) have successfully guided doctoral candidates. Finally, they must have secured a minimum score as stipulated in the Academic Performance Indicator–based Performance Based Appraisal System (UGC, 2010, appendix 3).

For appointment or promotion to the post of professor, the candidate must be an eminent scholar with PhD in the concerned/allied/relevant discipline. Candidates for professorship must have 10 years of teaching experience in a university/college and/or experience in research at the university/national-level institutions/industries—including experience of guiding candidates for research at a doctoral level. They need to their credit at least 10 publications as books and/or research/policy papers. Other qualifications prescribed for associate professorship are also applicable to professorship.

Almost all professors and associate professors in universities now possess doctoral degrees. A majority of assistant professors in the universities also possess doctoral degrees. In colleges, the percentage of assistant professors with doctorates is low. Generally, in recruitment to university departments, as compared with colleges, greater emphasis is laid on research and publications. Incidentally, in public-funded institutions, the regulations governing minimum qualifications can hardly be violated. The slightest doubt that an appointment constitutes flouting a regulation is challenged in a court of law, and such appointments are struck down by the courts. The institutions have also become more careful after the enactment of the Right to Information Act, whose provisions will invariably be invoked by unselected applicants.

The purely private universities and colleges have greater flexibility in the matter of qualifications of teachers. However, they also ensure the minimum standards as regards the academic qualifications of the faculty such as the marks/grade in the master's level and the doctorate. As for unaided private colleges, the university to which they are affiliated would act as the watchdog.

Recruitment to the Professoriate

In all public-funded higher education institutions, direct recruitment to teaching and other academic positions is based on merit. As per constitutional mandate, 49.5 percent of the posts are reserved under the policy of protective discrimination (affirmative action): 15 percent for "scheduled castes," 7.5 percent for "scheduled tribes," and 27 percent for the "other backward classes." Besides this so-called vertical reservation, there is "horizontal reservation" to the extent of 3 percent (across categories) for "people with disability" and 1 percent each for candidates with auditory, visual, and orthopedic disabilities. All vacancies have to be compulsorily advertised, and the advertisement should specify the posts that are reserved for specific categories of candidates. If candidates from the specified groups are not available, the vacancies will have to be readvertised.

All appointments in public-funded institutions are made on the recommendations of duly constituted selection committees. The composition of such committees for various posts is prescribed by the UGC (2010, 32–36) and incorporated under the statutes/ordinances of the universities and institutes. The scoring system developed by the UGC, with the Academic Performance Indicator–based Performance Based Appraisal System gives a quantitative dimension to the selection procedure (UGC 2010, Tables 1 to 9 of appendix 3).

Appointments to the posts of assistant professor and associate professor are invariably made through interviews. Although appointment to a professor's post is generally made through interviews, in exceptional cases a scholar may be invited to the position. However, such invitees must already hold a professorship in another institution, and the decision to invite somebody as a professor requires a duly constituted selection committee.

While the elaborate guidelines suggested by the UGC underline the importance of transparency and credibility of recruitment to teaching positions, in actual practice rules are bent and appointments are often manipulated and fixed. Not infrequently, complaints of favoritism, nepotism, and corruption are heard, even as most institutions go through the process of recruitment with a veneer of legality and fairness.

By law, appointment to teaching positions in public-funded institutions is open to all citizens of the country. While there is provision for inclusion through reservation of posts, no candidate can be excluded on sociocultural or regional considerations. However, in most state universities and colleges affiliated to them, candidates from the state are preferred, as many of them offer instruction and conduct examinations in the official language of the state. Inadvertently, this has hindered mobility among teachers across states.

The private universities and unaided private colleges are not bound by the UGC guidelines for recruitment to teaching positions. They are not obliged to advertise their vacancies, and their advertisements are frugal on details. Their recruitment procedures are not transparent.

Terms of Appointment

In public-funded institutions, once the recommendations of the selection committee are approved by the executive body of the university/institute, a letter offering the appointment and terms thereof is sent to the selected candidate. In case the selected candidate does not accept the offer or does not report for duty within the stipulated period, the offer is treated as withdrawn, and the candidate on the waiting list is offered the post.

In some state universities, the recommendations of the selection committee as approved by the executive body must be ratified by the chancellor, who is ex officio as governor of the state. The appointments in grant-in-aid private colleges have to be approved by the state government's department of education. Appointments to teaching positions in the government-run colleges are made by a statutory authority called the state public service commission.

The terms of appointment are specified in the appointment order, and they are enforceable in a court of law. Among other things, the order specifies the pay in the highest and lowest pay band relative to the post and other allowances and benefits based on the rules of the government as adopted by the institution. Generally, in the universities, there is no negotiation on salary or other benefits, but higher starting pay is given to candidates with better qualifications and achievements. In private universities, theoretically, the terms of appointment are negotiable. In reality, however, such negotiations take place only in the case of faculty of high caliber or faculty in specializations where shortages exist.

While announcing the revised pay scales in 2008, the UGC prescribed a workload of 40 hours a week for 30 working weeks in an academic year for teachers in full employment, besides 14 working weeks of admission, examination, and extracurricular activities (UGC 2010, 60). The number of contact (teaching-learning process) hours for assistant professor is 16 per week, and for associate professor and professor, 14 per week. Professors who are actively involved in extension activities and administration obtain a concession of two hours.

The UGC-prescribed workload is strictly enforced only in grant-in-aid colleges, and teachers with inadequate workload are required to teach in another college to complete the schedule. If in any subject the workload falls well below the prescribed 16 hours, it is farmed out to part-time teachers. There is no standardized workload in private universities, and the workload in private colleges is exploitatively higher than in grant-in-aid colleges.

The main responsibility of college teachers is to teach the prescribed curriculum to the students and prepare them for examinations conducted by the university. Besides teaching, university teachers are also required to be engaged in research. In only a few university departments/centers and institutions of national importance is the primary emphasis is on research. As such, publication as an academic activity is more a characteristic of university teachers than college teachers. In private universities, the emphasis is almost exclusively on teaching. In all universities and colleges, teachers are expected to assist the university/college in such administrative activities as processing applications for admission, counseling students, assisting the conduct of examinations (supervision, invigilation, and evaluation), and participating in extension, co-curricular, and extracurricular activities.

Career Advancement

For several decades, the job performance of teachers in higher education institutions remained unevaluated, and any attempt at evaluation was either resisted or done perfunctorily. However, as part of the package of pay revision, the UGC has now introduced performance evaluation of teachers in all public-funded universities and colleges. Appointments and promotions (under the Career Advancement Scheme) to associate professor's and professor's positions are now based on a minimum score as stipulated in the Academic Performance Indicator–based Performance Based Appraisal System. Purely private institutions do not have a mandatory or standardized self-appraisal system.

The Indian professoriate is pyramidal in structure, and this is more so in colleges. To address this built-in structural rigidity of the professoriate and as an incentive to performance, the Career Advancement Scheme has been introduced. This project envisages six stages in a teacher's career, spread across three levels (see Table 14.1): an entry-level assistant professor (stage 1) can move up through two successive stages (stages 2 and 3), an associate professor (stage 4) can move up to stage 5, and a professor (stage 5) can move up to stage 6. Generally, in higher

Table 14.1 Career advancement scheme for the professoriate

Designation (level)	Stage	Duration of service	Academic grade pay per month	
			Rs	US$
Assistant professor (bottom)	Stage 1	Entry level (direct recruitment)	6,000	135
	Stage 2	After 4 years in stage 1 with PhD	7,000	155
		After 5 years in stage 1 with master of philosophy		
		After 6 years in stage 1 with master's		
	Stage 3	After 5 years in stage 2	8,000	175
Associate professor (middle)	Stage 4	After 3 years in stage 3 or entry level (direct recruitment)	9,000	200
Professor (top)	Stage 5	After 3 years in stage 4 or entry level (direct recruitment)	10,000	220
	Stage 6	After 10 years in stage 5	12,000	265

Source: Adapted from UGC 2010.

Notes: (1) All promotions under the Career Advancement Scheme are subject to the candidate obtaining a minimum score as stipulated in the Academic Performance Indicator–based Performance Based Appraisal System. (2) Figures in US$ calculated at $1.00 = Rs 50 and rounded off to the nearest US$5.00.

education institutions in India, incumbent teachers have no voice or influence in the recruitment or promotion of teachers.

Salaries of the Professoriate

Salaries and service conditions of teachers in universities and colleges are fixed by the UGC, as approved by the Ministry of Human Resources Development. The central universities and centrally funded institutes adopt these salaries and service conditions in totality with effect from the stipulated date. The state governments, however, adopt them with modifications regarding age of superannuation and allowances, the date of implementation of the new salaries, and the payment of arrears that may accrue because of the delay in implementation. The ministry fixes the salaries and service conditions of teachers in institutions of national importance.

The gross monthly salary of a teacher consists of five components: (1) pay in the pay band (assistant professor, Rs 15,600–39,100 or US$345–870; associate professor, Rs 37,400–67,000 or US$830–1,490; professor Rs 37,400–67,000 or US$83–1,490); (2) academic grade pay; (3) transport allowance; (4) dearness allowance (to compensate for inflation); and (5) house rent allowance. The gross monthly salaries—drawn by different cadres of teachers at the top, middle, and bottom levels of the pay band—are shown in Table 14.2.

Table 14.2 Salary of faculty, December 31, 2010

	Professor		Associate professor		Assistant professor	
Pay details	Rs	US$	Rs	US$	Rs	US$
Top of pay band						
Pay	67,000	1,490	67,000	1,490	39,100	870
Grade Pay	10,000	220	9,000	200	6,000	135
Transport allowance	3,200	70	3,200	70	3,200	70
Dearness allowance	36,090	800	35,640	790	21,735	485
House rent allowance	23,100	515	22,800	505	11,910	265
Gross salary	139,390	3,095	137,640	3,055	81,945	1,825
Middle of pay band						
Pay	55,000	1,220	52,200	1,160	27,350	610
Grade pay	10,000	220	9,000	200	6,000	135
Transport allowance	3,200	70	3,200	70	3,200	70
Dearness allowance	30,690	680	28,980	645	16,448	365
House rent allowance	19,500	435	18,360	410	10,005	220
Gross salary	118,390	2,625	111,740	2,485	63,003	1,400
Bottom of pay band						
Pay	43,000	955	37,400	830	15,600	345
Grade pay	10,000	220	9,000	200	6,000	135
Transport allowance	3,200	70	3,200	70	3,200	70
Dearness allowance	25,290	560	22,320	495	11,160	250
House rent allowance	15,900	355	13,920	310	6,480	145
Gross salary	97,390	2,160	85,840	1,905	42,440	945

Source: Adapted from UGC 2010.
Note: Figures in US$ calculated at US$1.00 = Rs 50 and rounded off to the nearest US$5.00.

In public-funded institutions, irrespective of the academic field, all professors are paid similarly. However, teachers in centrally funded institutions secure relatively higher gross salaries than those in state-funded institutions. Teachers in the institutions of national importance (like the Indian Institutes of Technology and Indian Institutes of Management) are paid marginally better salaries than university teachers.

Over the decades, the gap in salaries between academic and other professions has narrowed considerably. Nevertheless, professionals in the management, information, and communications technology and biotechnology sectors and well-established lawyers, chartered accountants/financial consultants, and medical practitioners/surgeons earn considerably more than academics in the same fields. However, in India, in regard to teachers' salaries, the general comparison is with that of the bureaucrats, and the salaries of these two professionals are now more or less comparable, though the bureaucrats get better perquisites.

There is a minimum salary for each level of the professoriate, though the minimum gross salary may vary between centrally funded institutions and state-funded institutions, and between universities in general and the institutions of national importance. In all public-funded institutions, teachers are entitled to get an annual increase of 3 percent in their basic pay (i.e., pay in the band plus academic grade pay) irrespective of their performance. Apart from this, teachers get a bigger hike in salary if they are promoted under the Career Advancement Scheme. However, no negotiation occurs on salary size or service conditions, and teachers' associations have no role to play in the matter of pay and perquisites. In purely private institutions, renegotiation is possible; most often, such negotiations are to the advantage of the management. On an average, the professoriate's pay and service conditions are revised once in 10 years, based on the recommendations of a governmental committee.

Nonsalary and Service-Related Benefits

For the Indian professoriate, salary is the most important component of income. It constitutes the key element in attracting faculty. Location of the university/college, reputation of the institution, availability of facilities for research, and other factors could also be influential for the few who have a choice. The non-salary benefits that teachers get are all as per the government provisions, and they have no bearing on the choice of teaching as a career or of a particular institution.

For those who were appointed to permanent positions before January 2004, the governmental superannuation pension scheme was an attraction. Those appointed to permanent positions since January 2004 have to contribute 10 percent of their basic pay to the pension fund, and the government makes a matching contribution. Teachers in public-funded institutions are also eligible for gratuity (a lump-sum terminal benefit, based on the years of uninterrupted service).

Teachers are eligible for a variety of paid leave, but none of them can be availed as a matter of right. Every academic year, a teacher can avail eight days of casual leave, and this leave cannot be accumulated. She or he can get one day of earned/privilege leave for 11 days of work, and this leave can be accumulated to a maximum of 300 days. Part of the earned leave can be cashed during specified block years or fully at the time of superannuation/retirement. The most attractive part of the academic profession is the fully paid vacation for eight weeks in a year.

Female teachers obtain a maximum of one year of maternity leave during their career, and their spouses get a maximum of 15 days of paternity leave for each child born (and for not more than two children). Besides maternity leave, female teachers are entitled to two years of child-care leave, provided they have exhausted all other leaves to their credit. This leave can be availed anytime, until the child attains 18 years of age; it can be split between two children.

Teachers can avail the benefit of "leave travel concession" (return fare for self and dependents) once in two years by using their vacation or applying for leave to go on a holiday. In lieu of this, teachers hailing from outside their place of work can avail "home travel concession" to visit their "hometown" (as declared at the time of joining the service).

Teachers are eligible for medical leave and medical assistance, both for themselves and for their dependents. They are entitled to the use of central or state government health-service facilities. In lieu of this, some institutions have extended medical insurance coverage to teachers, or they reimburse medical expenses up to a particular amount. To check misuse of this facility (by the hospitals, insurance companies, and teachers alike), there are elaborate norms governing medical assistance.

As part of their salary, teachers are given a percentage of their basic pay as house-rent allowance. In case the university provides housing (no college does that), teachers will not get the house-rent allowance; they will have to pay a small sum as maintenance charges.

As an incentive for promoting the small family norm, male teachers undergoing vasectomy or female teachers undergoing hysterectomy are given one increment in pay on production of a certificate from a medical authority. Such teachers must have one surviving child and not more than two children, and they must for within the specified age range.

Supplementary Employment

A teacher occupying a permanent position in a public-funded university or college cannot take up supplementary employment. However, with the permission of the institution, a teacher can undertake a teaching assignment in another university/college as a visiting/guest faculty for a brief period (by availing up to 30 days of "duty leave," to which teachers are entitled in a year). They can undertake long-term teaching assignments in another university/college by availing "extraordinary leave," during which period they are not entitled to any salary or increment benefits. Teachers can adjust this period against any leave credits they may have earned (which, however, does not exceed 300 days). The restriction on working in more than one institution does not apply to part-time teachers. In purely private institutions, the relative provision may be part of the contract.

The percentage of university teachers doing consultancy work is negligible, and consultancy is largely unknown in colleges. Professors in science, technology, and management departments in universities and teachers in institutions of national importance do consultancy work. Where consultancy is permitted, there are clear norms governing the duration for which a teacher can engage in such work and the sharing of fees accruing from it.

Moonlighting by university and college teachers is not totally unknown. Some teachers undertake consultancy and run insurance, transport agencies, or even retail trade. To circumvent institutional regulations, these are mostly done in their spouse's name. One source of additional income for some college teachers (rarely for university teachers) is private tuition. Since they are formally employed on full-time permanent positions, this raises the question of professional ethics, and in some states it is even declared illegal. Another source of supplementary income for a few college teachers is writing guidebooks (in question-answer format) for students appearing for university examinations.

Conclusion

India has one of the largest and most diverse systems of higher education in the world. Expectedly, the diversities in its higher education institutions are reflected in the varying systems and practices of recruitment of the professoriate and its remuneration packages. The institutions of national importance (like the Indian Institutes of Science, Indian Institutes of Technology, and Indian Institutes of Management) have developed the most effective systems and best practices of recruitment, even as they work under the broad regulations of the central government. They also pay higher gross salaries and offer better service conditions. Closely following them are the well-established central universities and centrally funded university-level institutes that come under the umbrella of the UGC. But the vast majority of teaching positions prevail in the state universities and grant-in-aid colleges. For teachers working in these universities and colleges, the salary and allied benefits could not be better. Regarding the purely private universities and colleges, the vagaries of the market for higher education will continue to mediate their recruitment practices and remuneration packages.

Given the rapid expansion of higher education institutions and the imminent entry of foreign education establishments into the country, the competition for well-qualified and experienced faculty is sure to increase. Only institutions offering the best remunerations and service conditions can expect to receive the best teaching talents. Viewed in this light, the prospects for state universities and grant-in-aid colleges, which constitute the largest segment of the higher education system in the country, do not appear to be bright.

Reference

UGC (University Grants Commission). 2010. *UGC regulations on minimum qualifications for appointment of teachers and other academic staff in universities and colleges and measures for the maintenance of standards in higher education.* New Delhi, India: UGC.

15

ISRAEL

Academic Salaries and Remuneration

Sarah Guri-Rosenblit

This chapter examines the salary and remuneration mechanisms of academic faculty in the Israeli higher education system. It analyzes the impact of a uniform pay scale for academics in all public higher education institutions and the continuing budget cuts in the last two decades—on the gradual erosion of the working conditions of academics in Israel, the inability of universities to compete for faculty, and an immense brain-drain phenomenon. Also highlighted are some unique features of the Israeli higher education system, such as a clear differentiation between academic faculty employed at universities as compared to those employed in colleges, an inherent entitlement of sabbaticals for university academic faculty, and some other nonsalary benefits for productive faculty as well as a plan to establish 30 research-excellence centers from 2011 onward, to attract hundreds of leading Israeli researchers to repatriate back to Israel.

Overview of Higher Education

The Israeli higher education system was composed in 2011 of 66 higher education institutions: 8 universities, 45 public colleges, and 13 private colleges (Council for Higher Education, n.d.). Israel is a relatively young nation, and the growth rate of its higher education institutions since its existence has been remarkable. Israel had in 1948 a total population of 825,000 and two universities: the Hebrew University in Jerusalem (established in 1925) and the Technion in Haifa (established in 1924). These institutions were teaching 1,635 students in 1948. Within the next two decades, five additional major research universities were established, based on the model of the two veteran ones. By 1973, these universities were teaching over 50,000 students. The total number of students rose to 140,608 in 1995 and to 264,986 in 2008 (Central Bureau of Statistics 2009, 427; Guri-Rosenblit 1996).

The first nonuniversity institute to obtain academic recognition in Israel was the Rubin Academy for Music and Dance in Jerusalem, in 1974. Since then, the nonuniversity sector has expanded immensely. In 2010, the nonuniversity sector comprised 57 institutions: 26 teacher-training colleges and 31 colleges and higher education institutions that teach toward a variety of bachelor and master's degrees. Thirteen of the 31 colleges are private. No colleges are authorized to award doctoral degrees. The number of students studying at colleges has increased dramatically in the last decade. In 2008, 101,543 were studying at the public colleges—compared to only 19,567 in 1995 (Central Bureau of Statistics 2009, 427; Guri-Rosenblit 1996).

Until 1986 there was no private sector in Israeli higher education. As in many parts of the world, private higher education institutions offer studies in areas believed to have a direct market payoff. Since the private providers must cover their costs mainly out of tuition fees, they usually concentrate on low-cost subjects that are in high demand—such as law, business administration, economics, communication, and other fields. This also holds true for Israel, where 29,049 students studied at 10 private colleges in 2007, about 42 percent of the total student body in colleges (Stav and Eizman 2008, 93).

Academic Contracts

Academic contracts in Israel follow a standard practice for hiring academic personnel by the public posting of positions, interviews, and public seminars given by candidates. Given that the number of academic posts has decreased in the last decades, today a fierce competition is under way for any opening of an academic post at a university or at a college. There are many more young PhDs than the actual jobs available.

The requirements for young PhD candidates have grown in the last years. They are usually requested to submit a list of three to four publications in leading international research journals in addition to the accomplishments in their doctoral studies and postdoctoral period. Reference letters are requested from at least three professors either in Israel or from abroad. A special committee is nominated at each university or college to short-list the applicants (to three to eight potential candidates), review their reference letters and published articles, interview the candidates, and schedule their invited talks or seminars.

Academic faculty at universities are hired with the expectation that their primary activity will be research and their secondary activity teaching, while at the colleges it is vice versa. Thus, the expectations of new hires at the universities are primarily focused on their research record. The colleges' academic faculty are expected primarily to teach, and research is considered as a secondary priority. Therefore, the teaching obligation per week in universities is 8 hours as compared to 12–16 hours in colleges.

The real cutting point for getting into the tenure track takes place after approximately five years from the nomination as a lecturer on a temporary contract basis. Based on the achievements of the lecturer—most particularly, research achievements—it is decided whether the faculty member is promoted to a senior-lecturer rank and gets into the tenure track or is fired. About 20 percent of the lecturers do not enter the tenure track. After one gets into the tenure track, it is basically a permanent appointment for life until retirement at the age of 68 years. This is the age of retirement for professors in Israel (for both women and men). The retirement age in all other work sectors is 67 for men and 64 for women.

Hiring practices and negotiations are different at private institutions, which are much more flexible in hiring academic faculty from Israel or from abroad. They offer each one an individual contract. Each contract might be different in its terms and length, as opposed to the universities and public colleges, which are bound to offer exactly the same contracts in each rank, and are also restricted by the Council for Higher Education on the number of academic faculty they are entitled to employ.

The promotion at all universities is mainly influenced by research productivity. The promotion to a higher rank is judged by a professional ad hoc committee composed of four to six professors, who send the research works and curriculum vitae of the candidate to referees both in Israel and abroad. For the ranks of associate professor and full professor, it is obligatory to have at least three referees from abroad. The professional committee decides, on the basis of the evaluations, whether the candidate is eligible to be promoted to a higher rank.

The procedure of rank promotion at public colleges is more relaxed, compared to the universities, and is conducted by a special committee appointed by the Council of Higher Education. The achievements are evaluated both in teaching and in research. Though all of the academic ranks (from lecturer to full professor) do exist in colleges, they are not entitled to receive the fringe benefits of sabbatical funds and research funds for overseas travel, as will be explained further on. Academics are entitled to compete for research funds and to "buy" teaching time through such funds—thus, they can decrease their teaching load by obtaining external research funds.

Universities and public colleges in Israel lack the ability to compete for faculty by offering better salaries or fringe benefits. Universities are unable to compete for faculty since there is a uniform pay scale that applies to all academics in all universities. This results in little mobility of academic faculty during their careers. Many academics left Israel in the last decades to work abroad, particularly to the United States, and the brain-drain phenomenon has become an acute problem. In 2009, a special initiative was approved to return Israeli academics by establishing 30 research-excellence centers where special conditions will be offered.

Academic Salaries

Academic salaries in Israel are determined according to a uniform pay scale within the framework of collective wage bargaining agreements between the country's finance minister and the union representing senior faculty. There is no

Table 15.1 Academic faculty in Israel: Monthly salary distribution in NIS

Career rank	Monthly salary Top of scale	Monthly salary Middle of scale	Monthly salary Bottom of scale
Lecturer	13,920	13,065	12,946
Senior lecturer	16,279	16,024	14,487
Associate professor	19,621	17,648	16,802
Full professor	28,183	23,634	20,431

Source: Data based on information provided by the Israeli Council for Higher Education in May 2010 and updated until December 2009.

Note: US$1.00 = NIS 3.65, in February 2011.

differentiation between various disciplines or according to the productivity of a faculty member. Business school professors earn the same as Hebrew-language professors, and high-productive professors earn the same as low-productive professors. Two separate unions represent academic faculty at universities and at public colleges. Academic salaries in the private colleges are based on individual negotiations. The basic salary ladder of the four academic ranks is identical at both universities and colleges. However, only the academic faculty in universities enjoy meaningful fringe benefits of sabbatical funds and a special fund for scientific activities abroad, which the faculty in colleges are not entitled to. Rank and seniority (length of service) are the primary factors distinguishing between paychecks. Table 15.1 presents the academic salaries in Israeli universities and public colleges.

Table 15.1 shows the slight differences between the salaries of the three ranks of lecturer, senior lecturer, and associate professors due to seniority, but a significant contrast exists between salaries at various ranks. A full professor at the top of the scale, as defined in a study (Rumbley, Pacheco, and Altbach 2008), earns more than twice as much as a lecturer—NIS 28,183 (US$8,000) for a professor at the top of scale as compared to NIS 13,920 (US$4,000) for a lecturer (Council for Higher Education, n.d.).

In addition to the four categories of academic faculty ranks, additional ranks were created for faculty who are mainly designated to teach rather than to engage in research. There is a "parallel track" that includes the posts of "teacher" and "senior teacher"; their salaries are similar to that of a lecturer or a senior lecturer. In addition, several ranks for junior academic staff cover teaching and research assistants to teaching and research associates who possess doctoral degrees; and a growing number of part-time adjunct faculty exist, coming either from other higher education institutions, in which they are usually full-time employed, or from relevant professional fields. A separate salary scale is available for part-time faculty—ranging from professionals, who do not necessarily hold doctoral degrees (in professional fields like nursing, engineering, etc.), to full professors from other universities. The salaries are significantly lower for part-time faculty, as

Table 15.2 Distribution of academic personnel at Israeli universities and public colleges, 2007–8

Type of faculty	Universities	Funded colleges
Academic faculty	5,814	1,573
External part-time teachers	5,346	4,629
Junior faculty	2,334	274
Other	173	287
Total	13,667	6,763

Source: Data based on Central Bureau of Statistics 2009, 420.

compared to full-time employed faculty; the external faculty do not receive social benefits and are employed on a four-month (one semester) or eight-month (two semesters) basis. Table 15.2 presents the distribution of academic personnel at universities and public colleges.

As shown in Table 15.2, a large number of part-time faculty are responsible for teaching at the universities, particularly at colleges, and a large number of junior faculty are employed at universities, mainly as teaching associates.

As discussed, salaries of academics in Israeli higher education institutions are uniform and not based on merit. However, academic faculty at universities, in particular, can gain a significant increase in their salaries, if they are responsible for receiving external research grants. The increase can range from 6 percent, if the researcher is entitled to get less than US$12,000 per year from a research grant, to 50 percent, if the researcher is entitled to get over US$75,000 per year based on the terms for the leading researcher in a research grant (Council for Higher Education, n.d.). Furthermore, academic faculty who hold temporary administrative positions—such as deans, heads of departments, vice presidents, and so forth—are entitled to get increases that might range from 15 percent to 50 percent of their salary. The rule is that, altogether, remuneration for academic posts or for research grants should not exceed 90 percent of the basic salary.

Nonsalary (Fringe) Benefits

Significant fringe benefits are associated with salaries of academic faculty in Israel, particularly at the universities. The fringe benefits include sabbatical funds, a fund for overseas scientific activities, and a unique apparatus of "excellence criteria." All academic faculty in Israel are entitled by law to a health plan, paid vacations, and a retirement savings plan.

The sabbatical fund is a unique Israeli mechanism. From the initial stage of the state of Israel's establishment in 1948, Israeli academics have been encouraged to launch collaborative research ventures with colleagues outside Israel and to participate regularly in international academic conferences, workshops, and symposia. The sabbatical funds are given to all of the academic faculty at universities. For each year of work, the academic faculty are entitled to two months of sabbatical that might be accumulated. Currently, the payment for a month sabbatical for a lecturer is US$3,173; for a senior lecturer—US$3,876; for an associate professor—US$4,926; and for a full professor—US$6,104 (sabbatical funds are allocated in US$). All of these figures relate to payments before taxes (which reach after an initial sum of US$3,000 per month, a tax of 45 percent) and are also subject to modifications based on seniority. During the sabbatical period, academic faculty members stop getting their salaries and get sabbatical funds. If academic faculty have accumulated many sabbatical months and are unable to use them, they are not entitled to any compensation. They just lose their eligibility to go on a sabbatical. The sabbatical funds of university faculty are greatly envied by the academic faculty at colleges and frequently contested in various forums.

A special fund for participation on a yearly basis in conferences and research activities is also a unique fringe benefit granted only to universities' academic faculty. The overseas scientific fund ranges from US$3,883 for a lecturer to US$9,626 for a full professor. These funds might be used for participating in academic conferences, buying a laptop or computer, financing a translation of a paper, or other options.

The excellence criteria constitute an additional unique remuneration for academic faculty in Israel. Following a vigorous and long strike of the academic faculty at universities in 1994, it was agreed that an excellence criteria mechanism will be established, which might raise their salaries by up to 27 percent. Half of this compensation, 13.5 percent, is given automatically to faculty who do not practice more than a 50 percent teaching load at another higher education institution or do not earn more than 70 percent of an average salary in Israel, in addition to their university salary. Another 13.5 percent are awarded on the basis of research productivity and a variety of other criteria. The estimate is that nearly 90 percent of the academic faculty at universities may receive the "excellence criteria."

Supplementary Employment

In addition to their full employment at a university or college, many academics in Israel work as external part-time faculty in other higher education institutions. As shown in Table 15.2, 5,346 part-time external faculty were employed at universities and 4,629 were employed at public colleges in 2007–8 (Central Bureau of Statistics 2009, 420). Over 60 percent of the academic faculty in universities work on a part-time basis at another higher education institution, sometimes at even more than one other institution. While a less frequent career, consulting and working in nonacademic jobs (outside academia) are more typical in specific areas, such as law, business administration, computer science, accountancy, and marketing.

Supplementary employment is even more common at private colleges. Many of the teaching staff are part-timers. In 2007–8, nine private colleges reported a total of 465 full-time academic faculty (Council for Higher Education, n.d.)—a relatively small number, since the majority of their faculty are employed on a part-time basis and quite frequently originate from the universities.

In order to discourage the intensive supplementary employment, some compensating procedures were initiated for university faculty who devote most of their time to their home institutions. As mentioned above, a special apparatus of excellence criteria has been initiated following a long strike carried out by senior academic faculty at universities in 1994. Awarding 13.5 percent to those who teach not more than 50 percent at another higher education institution is supposed to restrict the supplementary employment. However, the admission that performing a 50 percent teaching load in another higher education institution (plus a 100 percent teaching load at the home institution) highlights the fact that this practice is viewed nearly as norm, given that academics in Israel cannot live comfortably based on one academic salary. Such a situation greatly restricts the time that academic faculty can devote to research.

Qualifications

The minimum qualification to enter the academic track at universities and colleges in Israel is earning a PhD degree. Many PhD holders are currently employed as junior academic staff, on a temporary term, mainly at universities. In 2007–8, as shown in Table 15.2, 2,334 junior academic staff were employed at the universities, compared to only 274 junior academic staff at public colleges. The employment contracts of the junior academic staff are renewed every year. Until 2008, they were employed for short terms of four months (a semester) or eight months (two semesters), fired after each period, and contracted anew at the start of each academic year or semester. Following a long strike in 2007, a new collective agreement was signed in January 2008 between the junior academic staff at all universities and the universities' heads, which changed their employment conditions. Nowadays, junior academic staff are employed on the basis of a yearly (12-month) contract but still for a period of just one year, and every year their contract should be considered for renewal. The year-long employment entitles the junior academic staff to obtain all social benefits associated with full-time employment.

Appointed lecturers are given a span of five years to prove their eligibility for entering the tenure track. The main requirement constitutes evidence of fruitful research work. If these lecturers are found eligible for obtaining a senior lecturer position, they enter the tenure track at universities (except the Open University, which does not provide a tenure track), as well as in many colleges, which entitles them to a permanent appointment until retirement.

As shown in Table 15.1, promotion is based mainly on seniority (years of service) and, particularly, on academic achievements of getting promoted to a more senior rank. When promoted, not only the salary increases but also all of the other associated fringe benefits—such as sabbatical funds and support for overseas research, as well as retirement funds and some other benefits.

In most private colleges, academic faculty are composed of a handful of renowned professors who retired, or were near to retirement at universities, and young faculty members. The renowned professors gain a much higher salary, as compared to their salary at universities (sometimes double or triple the comparable university salaries), but most of the young academic faculty at the private colleges get salaries that are quite similar to those at universities or public colleges.

International Competition

Along with the growing scarcity of academic positions in the last decades—as well as an inadequate infrastructure of research laboratories—the relatively low academic salaries in Israel have encouraged many Israeli faculty to pursue academic positions abroad. Dan Ben-David (2008) noted that academic salaries in Israel, as compared to those in the United States, have fallen behind in the three last decades. Furthermore, salaries in competing sectors within Israel (e.g., the high-tech industry) rose by a considerable amount in the last years, only enhancing the relative erosion of academic income. The flight of Israeli academics to institutions of higher education worldwide, particularly to leading American research universities, has intensified in the last decade (Saltzman 2010).

Ben-David (2008) conducted a series of studies related to the brain-drain phenomenon in Israeli academia. The number of European academics in U.S. universities, as a percentage of the academic faculty in different national jurisdictions, ranged in 2003–4 from 1.3 percent in Spain to 4.3 percent in the Netherlands. However, the number of Israeli academics residing in U.S. universities in 2003–4 represented 24.9 percent of the entire academic staff in Israel's academic institutions that year—over five times the ratio in other developed countries. The group with the greatest proportional representation of Israeli academics in top American universities is in the field of computer science—33 percent of the contingent remaining in Israel.

This enormous problem, which has been widely debated in the last decade in political and academic forums, has resulted in a centralized effort to lure the Israeli academics back to Israel. A plan devised by an interministerial committee aims to "coax back 500 of these talents between 2010 and 2014 at a pace of 100 a year" (Bassok 2009). The aim is to bring back talented Israelis in three areas: industry, the public sector, and academia. Subcommittees working under the auspices of the Absorption Ministry have been formed in each area. The core of the program is providing financial incentives for Israelis who will repatriate.

Following this plan, the Israeli government approved a NIS 1.3 billion initiative in March 2010—the creation of 30 research-excellence centers, aimed at attracting leading scientists who have left Israel to conduct research abroad. The centers will be established at a number of universities over the next five years. One-third of the funding will come from the state and the rest from academic institutions and private donations from abroad. A pilot of four excellence centers will begin during 2011. These centers will focus on advanced topics in computer sciences; advanced approaches in cognitive science; systems-level analysis of molecular basis for human diseases; renewable and sustainable sources of energy—areas in which Israeli scientists have made significant contributions to international research (Kashti 2010). The program was put together by Manuel Trajtenberg, chairman of the Council for Higher Education's Planning and Budgeting Committee, as part of a five-year development plan.

Together with these four excellence centers to be established in 2011, the fields of study for the other 26 centers will be determined later, in conjunction with university representatives. While the research facilities will only operate within university campuses, faculty members affiliated with colleges will also be eligible to conduct research there. The choice of which universities will host the research-excellence centers will be based on criteria including research capabilities in the fields in question, as well as their ability to devote resources to the centers and operate international advanced-degree programs taught in English.

The universities will also be asked to present a detailed list of Israeli researchers teaching abroad who could potentially be drawn back to the country to work and teach at one of the centers. There is an estimate of 1,000 to 3,000 potential Israeli researchers currently living abroad.

Conclusion

This chapter presented the salary and remuneration system of academic faculty in Israeli higher education. The clear distinction between the 8 universities and all of the other 58 higher education institutions results in differential fringe-benefit mechanisms for academic faculty at universities that are not granted to academic faculty in colleges as well as a differential teaching load in universities versus colleges. The uniform pay scale in all public higher education institutions in Israel, universities and colleges alike, restricts greatly the ability of universities—particularly leading research universities such as the Technion and Hebrew University—to compete for able and talented faculty. Such a situation combined with growing budgetary cuts, the inability to absorb large numbers of young PhDs, and a gradual deterioration of the working conditions of the academic faculty in the last decades have led to an immense brain-drain phenomenon. A new initiative of the Council for Higher Education in 2010, to establish 30 research excellence centers, purports to lure leading Israeli researchers to return back to Israel.

References

Bassok, Moti. 2009. "Israel seeks to overcome brain drain with 1.6 billion plan." *HaAretz* (August 17).

Ben-David, Dan. 2008. *Brain drained: A tale of two countries. CEPR Discussion Paper*, no. 6717.

Central Bureau of Statistics. 2009. *Education and culture: Selected data,* no. 60. Jerusalem: Central Bureau of Statistics.

Council for Higher Education. n.d. http://www.che.org.il. Accessed June 15, 2010.

Guri-Rosenblit, Sarah. 1996. "Trends in access to Israeli higher education 1981–1996: From a privilege to a right." *European Journal of Education* 31 (3): 321–40.

Kashti, Or. 2010. "Cabinet approves NIS 1.3b plan to reserve Israeli brain drain." *HaAretz* (March 14).

Rumbley, Laura E., Iván F. Pacheco, and Philip G. Altbach. 2008. *International comparison of academic salaries: An exploratory study.* Chestnut Hill, MA: Center for International Higher Education, Boston College.

Saltzman, Ilai. 2010. "The brain drain we don't hear about." *HaAretz* (May 13).

Stav, Steven, and Galit Eizman. 2008. "Trends in Israel." In *Privatization in higher education,* ed. Nadav Liron, 88–104. Haifa, Israel: Samuel Neaman.

16

ITALY

From Bureaucratic Legacy to Reform of the Profession

Giliberto Capano and Gianfranco Rebora

This chapter explains the shortcomings of the Italian university-system reforms, based on academics' salaries and terms of employment. New rules have been established over the last 20 years, designed to make universities more internationally competitive. The system of recruiting academics has repeatedly been changed, but reforms have failed to modify a highly inflexible wage structure or to introduce a manageable career system. Weak governance has prevented the central bureaucracy and academic management from making real use of the evaluation and assessment procedures introduced recently at both systemic and institutional levels. A new reform package approved at the end of 2010 is designed to deal with those problems inherited from the past and to pursue a more meritocratic system of academic pay and promotion, although some observers remain skeptical about the efficacy of such reforms.

A General Overview of the Italian University System

Unlike other countries, higher education in Italy is constituted only by the university sector. Italian higher education is a mass system, with over 50 percent of the country's 19-year-olds enrolling at a university. The system is composed of 95 institutions, 67 of which are public, 28 are private, and 11 of the latter are online universities. There were 65 (11 private) institutions at the beginning of the 1990s.

In the 2009–10 academic year, 1,780,033 students were enrolled at Italian universities compared with 300,000 in 1960, 718,000 in 1970, 1,060,000 in 1980, 1,457,000 in 1990, and 1,689,000 in 2000. The upward trend in the number of academics employed by the Italian higher education system has been of a different scale. Whereas in 1960 there were about 25,000 academics with a tenured position, by 1970 this figure had risen to 36,000, by 1980 to 43,000, and by 1990 to about 52,000. In 2000, however, the number fell slightly to 51,000 but by 2008 had risen to around 63,000.

Given the national higher education policy, Italy has tried to change the traditional method of steering higher education, based upon the dominance of central bureaucracy and the academic guilds. Such reforms have been predicated on the principles of evaluation, institutional autonomy, accountability, competition, and transparency. However, the strategy has been blighted by a series of problems and shortcomings. First, there is a weakness of governance at the institutional level. In fact, universities have failed to implement the new strategy, due to the persistence of democratic and corporative methods of self-government (Capano 2008; Rebora and Turri 2009). Secondly, there is the problem of how evaluation is integrated (Capano 2010; Rebora and Turri 2010). All too often, evaluation at both institutional and systemic levels has little effect and functions basically more as a rhetorical device. Third, there is a financial crisis. In the last few years, public funding of universities has fallen in real terms. Finally, against the background of this already rather depressed financial situation, the 2010 budget decreed that all academic salaries (as well as those of all other public employees) remain frozen until 2013.

New reforms have recently been approved (December 2010)—providing changes to institutional governance, the system of recruitment and promotion of academics, the structure of academic salaries, and the mechanism of public funding. This new reform package somewhat complicates the presentation of the Italian case, since the new law has yet to come into effect. Thus, the chapter covers the situation prior to the introduction of these new reforms and briefly mentions the new legislative provisions.

Academic Qualifications

Up until the new law was approved, at the end of 2010, the system constituted three levels of tenured positions in Italian universities—namely, full professor, associate professor, and researcher. All these appointments were permanent positions, from the time of hiring. Italian law provides open public competitions for all tenured positions. The 2010 law has now changed the status of researchers. In fact, the post of researcher has been transformed into a temporary one, based on a quasi-tenure-track mechanism (three to two years). After five years, researchers can obtain tenure (as associate professor) if they have achieved national "entitlement" to this position, although universities are not obliged to hire them on a permanent basis.

In Italy, since the academic profession is regulated by public law, the career path of academics, together with the mechanisms underlying their recruitment, is the same for both public and private universities.

At present, individuals who wish to enter the profession do not necessarily need to possess a PhD (despite the fact that in almost all fields, all applicants do).

The PhD degree was only introduced into the Italian system in 1980, and the first PhD degrees were awarded in 1988. Consequently, all those who entered the academic profession before this date did not possess a PhD (with the exception of the few people who got a PhD abroad). So, generally speaking, the majority of Italian academics younger than 50 to 52 years have a PhD, while older academics do not.

In 2009, 72 percent of full professors were over the age of 55, while 42 percent of all associate professors were also older than 55 years. Finally, the over-55 category of researchers accounted for 19 percent of the total (Ministry of Education, Universities and Research 2010). A recent comparative survey confirms that 48 percent of Italian academic staff possess a PhD, whereas only 34 percent of professionals did, compared with 69 percent of researchers (Bennion and Locke 2010).

At present, candidates applying for posts as researchers require a master's degree. Although most applicants do in fact possess a PhD, no such formal requirements apply to candidates for professorial posts. However, from 2011 on, under the new rule established by the recent reforms of 2010, a PhD will be required in order to apply for the new untenured position of a researcher.

Academic Contracts

Employment in Italy's universities is regulated by public law; thus, Italian academics enjoy civil-servant status. This means that all the rules concerning their employment (hiring, promotion, salaries, etc.) are dictated by law. At present, the fundamental regulations are provided by a law dating from 1980.

The regulations on recruitment and promotion were amended in 1998, before being partially changed, in 2005. Academic staff with tenure (in both public and private universities) are recruited through the use of an open public competition, organized on behalf of the specific subject area by the university. Since 1980, the content and boundaries of academic subjects in Italy's universities have been established by law. At present, there are some 350 legal academic sectors, but they should be reduced, following the 2010 university law. Each member of the academic staff belongs to one single academic sector. Up until 1998, such public competitions were organized along national lines, while the winners were selected by a commission elected by the professors affiliated to that specific subject area. Since 1998, universities have been empowered to organize their own competitions. The 2010 law has introduced a new mechanism—a national competition enabling candidates to obtain "entitlement" to became associate or full professors, after which individual universities call for applications to available professorial posts from those with the national qualification. This procedure involves both the recruitment of external academics and the promotion of internal members of staff. In fact, from the legal frame of reference, no concept of upgrading exists—instead, there is simply one of covering a vacant post. This means that if a university wants to promote one of its own members of staff, it is obliged to organize an open public competition, and thus many other applicants may apply for the post offered. Thus, since Italian universities are not empowered to independently decide internal promotions, they have no power over one fundamental aspect of the management of academic human resources (Moscati 2001; Capano 2008; Perotti 2008).

However, the new law establishes different rules for the recruitment of researchers. The national competition is in fact replaced by individual universities requesting applications for vacant posts, whereby the departmental committee itself has the power to choose the winning applicant.

Furthermore, as national regulations specify all material and financial terms and conditions of each academic post, the (public) universities have no room to maneuver. There is no leeway for any specific incentives or fringe benefits, and officially no opportunity to reduce teaching obligations, for example, of academics holding institutional positions (rector, dean, director of departments) or of those who excel in the research field although the new 2010 law has opened up such an opportunity. However, until the required governmental regulations have been approved, it is not clear whether, or how, this new mechanism will work.

The existing situation varies, as Italy's universities have independently started reducing the teaching load of their deans and directors (chairs) of departments (while rectors are completely exempt from teaching duties). Furthermore, in some universities, academics who have won substantial research grants (from the European Union Framework Programs, for example) are permitted to teach fewer hours.

National regulations establish that tenured academics are to teach and carry out research. Teaching posts, however, are only temporary and underpaid. Legal provisions state that a professor (full or associate) needs to spend at least 350 hours each year carrying out teaching activities (lectures, tutoring, supervising theses, meeting students, etc.), of which at least 120 hours should be spent lecturing. Until 2005, academics were required to teach one course only, amounting to a total of 60 hours as a rule. Researchers are not obliged to teach, but they can do so if they wish and may be appointed as adjunct lecturers.

Thus, in the current system, public universities lack the ability to reward academics who excel in the research or teaching fields. Although teaching is evaluated by the students, there is no institutional feedback. The productivity of research work is evaluated in some universities, to allocate individual research funds; however, due to the deep financial crisis affecting Italian universities in recent years, funds distributed in this manner are very limited. The new 2010 law, however, provides the triannual evaluation of individual academics' research performance by their universities, on the basis of the general parameters established by the National Agency of University Evaluation. Based on this triannual individual evaluation, underperforming academics may be denied salary raises and may even be excluded by the national committees, which are in charge of the assessment of national qualifications for becoming professors. The real effect of this new provision will be evident in the future.

Universities can hire people directly from foreign countries. In this way they enjoy greater freedom to adopt an institutional strategy aimed at the development of human resources. Such posts are jointly financed by the Ministry of Education, Universities and Research. Furthermore, the ministry also jointly funds the transfer of tenured academics from one Italian university to another (provided that the hiring university is located in a different region from that of the original employer). This ministerial provision has been introduced in order to motivate academic staff mobility between Italian universities, which until now has been characterized by a high level of institutional inbreeding.

Private universities are obliged to comply with national regulations but are free to offer incentives and fringe benefits and to negotiate specific duties. Some universities pay additional benefits; in other universities, the most highly reputed academics can negotiate their teaching loads. However, of the 28 private universities currently in existence, few are actually prestigious enough to attract distinguished scholars from public universities.[1]

Italian universities' human resource policies are subject to a substantial number of restraints (and this situation has not been substantially affected by the 2010 reforms). They have no room to develop their own strategies; they are basically weak employers, since they cannot use any of the instruments that universities in other higher education systems can employ in order to attract the best scholars or reward and encourage their best academics.

At the same time, due to the nature of the legal framework and Italy's cultural-historical background, Italian academics' identification with their universities is extremely weak.[2] They do, of course, identify with their own specific subject areas; however, they believe in being free to do what they want, after having performed the teaching duties assigned by the faculty. In other words, they see themselves more as publicly employed professionals than as civil servants. As a result, academics employed by public universities often hold teaching posts at private universities, which means they are teaching for their primary employer's direct competitors.

Academic Salaries

Until the end of 2010, academic-salaries scales had been strictly controlled by law. Before recent reforms, salary raises had been based on seniority. Existing regulations established a scale based on biannual salary points. Each of the first six biannual points increased an academic's salary by 8 percent. Subsequent salary points increased pay by 2.5 percent. However, the new 2010 law provides for a system, whereby points are assigned every three years after the evaluation of individual academics' performance in research and teaching.

Italian law also provides another mechanism of collective pay raises; each year, the salary of academics is raised by the average pay raise rate for all public employees the year before. The annual salary consists of 13 monthly stipends (i.e., in December, Italian academics receive two such stipends). These pay mechanisms are compulsory for both public and private universities. However, in the case of two private universities (Bocconi and LUISS), there are provisions for the payment of additional benefits. In Italy's public universities, no fringe benefits may be paid. Furthermore, pensions are subject to state regulations—meaning that academics receive their pensions directly from the state—as are health insurance payments.

Italian universities' salary scales, valid until the end of 2010 (see Table 16.1), substantially reward seniority. This means that initial salaries are quite low compared to other similar jobs in the professional sphere, particularly given that academics tend to enter the profession at the age of around 32–35 years; in the humanities, researchers often begin their academic careers at the age of about 40 years. This is unfair to younger scholars, whose performance in the research and teaching fields is often better than that of older colleagues. However, the new 2010 law could change this feature of the salary system: the new rules provide salary scales based on an evaluation of merit and performance, although many observers believe that the new system could be implemented in a distributive manner—by setting low standards, so that everyone qualifies for the salary increase.

Generally speaking, Italian academic salaries are quite good, when compared with those of other similar professions, but only after academics have worked for about 20 years in a tenured position (i.e., when they have reached the age of about 55 years). However, due to the low salaries paid during the early and middle years of the career, compared with other similar professions, the general opinion is that

Table 16.1 Salaries in Italy, until the end of 2010

Title	Average monthly salary	Scales* within ranks and monthly salary (in euro)	
Professore ordinario (full professor)	7,000	Top of the scale	9,640
		Middle of the scale	7,423
		Bottom of the scale	4,678
Professore associato (associate professor)	5,500	Top of the scale	6,562
		Middle of the scale	5,468
		Bottom of the scale	3,523
Ricercatore (tenured lecturer)	3,800	Top of the scale	4,875
		Middle of the scale	4,094
		Bottom of the scale	2,709

Source: Presidential Decree no. 382/1980.

Notes: It should be pointed out that the transition to a three-year scale, approved in 2010, will not change the average of those salaries shown in the table. 1.00 euro = US$1.40, March 7, 2011.
*Top of the scale: after 30 years' service in that position.
Middle of the scale: after 16 years' service in that position.
Bottom of the scale: during the first two years' service in that position.

the academic profession has lost its financial appeal over the last 20 years or so. Thus, younger scholars may put off following an academic career, due to the low salaries being paid.

This legal framework has clearly constrained Italian universities' capacity to develop competitive strategies designed to attract highly reputed scholars. With salaries being based exclusively on seniority, universities have lacked a fundamentally important policy instrument, from the competitive point of view. Certain private universities, on the other hand, do possess this same instrument, and thus a competitive edge, and have attracted a number of highly distinguished scholars from public universities in recent years. Thus, it is that Italy's public universities are only able to attract such scholars on the basis of their own institutional reputation or because of the personal interests of the academics in question.

Supplementary Employment

It is difficult to quantify the number of Italian academics who also have other forms of employment. There are no official figures or surveys available, although anecdotal experience would seem to indicate that a substantial number of academics do in fact hold other jobs, especially those working in certain specific fields.

It should be pointed out, however, that Italian law permits full and associate professors working in other professional fields to opt for a part-time post with tenure within the university system. Unlike other countries, in Italy academics with tenure are individually entitled to opt for part-time status. The salary paid to people in this position is only one-third less than that paid to full-time academics. In Italy, only 8 percent of academics opt for a combination of jobs, which is somewhat lower than what one might expect; for example, in practice most law professors and lecturers also work as lawyers.

Regarding the issue of additional professional activities, it is necessary to distinguish between further teaching and professional/consultancy work. Academics may earn additional income by teaching more courses than required within their own university (although such extra teaching is poorly paid). Academics may also teach in other universities (often private ones), since this initiative is not forbidden by law. Yet, this practice must be approved by their own deans (who rarely refuse to give permission). Some rectors have tried to exercise moral suasion in an attempt to prevent such actions but have not been very successful. In other situations, the universities of the same region (public and private) stipulated formal agreements, aiming to regulate and restrict external teaching.

Academics can also earn an additional salary by providing professional/consultancy services. In order to do so they are required to have the permission of the employer university, but the new law has abolished this institutional authorization regarding external activities. Such services are often provided on the basis of individual contracts, which make it difficult to know the numbers of people involved. However, undoubtedly this happens more commonly in certain subject areas (such as economics, business and administration, social sciences, law, and engineering) than in others (the humanities or hard sciences). Academics may also be paid extra for professional/consultancy services, provided on the basis of contracts between the university and an external purchaser. However, the mechanism of allocating the money from the job order to the providers of the service is often unfair to academics actually providing the service (also from the fiscal point of view). As a result, academics usually try to obtain external contracts on an individual basis, despite the fact that the financial crisis is forcing many universities to encourage their scholars with reputations in the external market to perform their services in-house, especially in the field of applied research (Rostan 2010).

No official figures for academics' additional salaries exist. However, it is reasonable to presume that the percentage of academics receiving additional salaries is significant (35–40 percent), and the percentage of those being paid substantial extra amounts for these additional services is quite low.

Structural Constraints on International Competition

On the basis of the picture sketched above, it is quite clear that the pay structure of Italian academics does not encourage international mobility toward Italy's universities. At the same time, the workings of the overall recruitment system, together with the financial crisis affecting Italian universities, represent structural incentives for young scholars to look for employment abroad. While no empirical data are available regarding this question, the general perception is that this phenomenon is significant—that each year the number of Italian academics obtaining an early tenured position abroad is the same as those who obtain a similar position in Italy.

Furthermore, few scholars who have obtained a tenured position in Italy then decide to move to a foreign university, while some Italian scholars agree to return to Italy after having obtained a tenured position abroad (thanks in part to the policy of cofunding, adopted by the Italian ministry). Yet, such a decision is not based on a higher salary but rather on the individual's desire to return home.

Nevertheless, although salaries paid by Italian universities may not be enticing, the overall working conditions of Italian academics may well be. In fact, the compulsory duties of Italy's academics are not as demanding as those of academics in other countries. This difference could constitute a benefit, albeit a modest one, that may counterbalance the unappealing pay structure currently in place within higher education in Italy. However, this balancing factor may only be considered of decisive importance for those who for personal reasons wish to work as academics in Italy.

Conclusion

This chapter offers evidence of the fact that the development of the academic profession in Italy has been thwarted by a series of substantial constraints—namely, the rigid pay structure, limited room for performance-related rewards, merit-based promotions mixed with public recruitment procedures, and factors encouraging opportunistic behavior. Private universities have little advantage over public universities in terms of such limits, as they can only provide extra salaries or benefits from within their own budgets.

The current financial position of Italy's universities is a worrying issue. However, the situation could change in the future, following implementation of the university law approved at the end of 2010, which provides different forms of academic recruitment and a new mechanism governing academic salaries, based on the periodic evaluation of individual performance in teaching and research. Genuine, effective implementation of these new rules would represent a paradigmatic move away from the deeply rooted legacy of Italian academic careers and salaries, which have been substantially based on seniority rather than individual ability and performance.

Notes

1. The most important private universities are: Milan's Catholic University (a broad-based university); Milan's Bocconi University (specialized in economics and business administration); Rome's LUISS (specialized in law, economics, and political science); Milan's San Raffaele (specialized in medicine); and the LIUC (specialized in economics and law) in Castellanza, Varese.
2. However, it should be stressed that the institutional identification of academics is also quite weak in a comparative perspective (Cavalli and Moscati 2010).

References

Bennion, Alice, and William Locke. 2010. "The early career paths and employment conditions of the academic profession in 17 countries." *European Review* 18 (1): 7–33.

Capano, Giliberto. 2008. "Looking for serendipity: The problematical reform of government within Italy's Universities." *Higher Education* 55 (4): 481–504.

Capano, Giliberto. 2010. "A Sisyphean task: Evaluation and institutional accountability in Italian higher education." *Higher Education Policy* 23 (1): 39–62.

Cavalli, Alessandro, and Roberto Moscati. 2010. "Academic systems and professional conditions in five European countries." *European Review* 18 (1): 35–53.

Ministry of Education, Universities and Research (Ministero dell'Istruzione, Università e Ricerca Scientifica). 2010. *Notiziario Statistico* no. 3. Rome: Ministry of Education, Universities and Research.

Moscati, Roberto. 2001. "Italian university professors in transition." *Higher Education* 41 (1): 103–29.

Perotti, Roberto. 2008. *L'università truccata*. Torino, Italy: Einaudi.

Rebora, Gianfranco, and Matteo Turri. 2009. "Governance in higher education: An analysis of the Italian experience." In *International perspectives on the governance of higher education*, ed. Jeroen Huisman, 13–32. London: Routledge.

Rebora, Gianfranco, and Matteo Turri. 2010. "Critical factors in the use of evaluation in Italian universities." *Higher Education* 61 (5): 531–44.

Rostan, Michele. 2010. "Challenges to academic freedom: Some empirical evidence." *Economic Review* 18 (1): 71–88.

17

WORKING CONDITIONS AND SALARIES OF THE ACADEMIC PROFESSION IN JAPAN

Kazunori Shima

The Japanese academic profession is financially viable, and salaries relative to other sectors in the labor market have remained competitive over the last 30 years. But other elements—including work time, obtaining academic employment, and job stability—have gotten worse. So, the attractiveness of the academic profession has declined. This also means that salaries are not internationally competitive, especially for attracting worldwide leading scholars.

Japanese Higher Education

"Japan's higher education system in the modern era was introduced under the strong influence of the German university model, which was at the center of 19th century academia, and tailored to meet Japan's specific requirements. Through education reforms after World War II, Japan's postwar system of higher education institutions adopted a US-style university system" (MEXT 2003, 2). Consequently, the development of Japan's higher education system has been affected by both Germany and the United States.

The Japanese higher education system has three types of postsecondary institutions: universities (four year), junior colleges (two year), and colleges of technology (two year). There are 765 universities (86 national universities established by the national government, 90 public universities established by local governments, and 589 private universities), 417 junior colleges (2 national, 29 public, and 386 private), and 64 colleges of technology (55 national, 6 public, and 3 private)—as indicated in the *School Basic Survey* by the Ministry of Education, Culture, Sports, Science and Technology (MEXT 2008a). Universities enroll 2,836,127 students (including graduate students); junior colleges enroll 172,726; and colleges of technology, 59,446.

Japanese universities have experienced two periods of rapid expansion of undergraduate students: from 1955 to 1974 and from 1984 to 2000. On the other hand, in terms of graduate students, rapid expansion has been continuous since 1991. In 2008, the national universities enrolled 623,811 students (including 146,501 graduate students); the public universities, 131,970 students (14,071 graduate students); and the private universities, 2,080,346 students (79,081 graduate students). In terms of faculty, 61,019 faculty members work at national universities; 12,073 at public universities; and 96,822 at private universities. The proportion of private universities in Japan is high, both in terms of numbers of institutions (77 percent) and students (73.4 percent); but national universities provide most graduate education programs and are the primary centers of research activity.

Japanese universities now face two financial problems. One issue results from the decline of the 18-year-old cohort, the other from declining government subsidy, which is due to the difficult national financial situation. Together, these conditions create critical income problems and force universities to compete with each other in order to survive, especially concerning small, local, private universities.

Academic Profession: Positions and Qualifications

Positions and Roles

According to the School Education Law, both public and private universities shall have presidents, professors, associate professors, assistant professors, research associates, and clerical employees. In addition to that, universities can have vice presidents, lecturers, and technical employees—and other staff, when needed. For the purpose of this chapter, professors, associate professors, lecturers, and assistant professors are considered members of the academic profession. In the School Education Law, the roles of professor, associate professor, lecturer, and assistant professor are defined.

There are 67,699 professors, 40,352 associate professors, 19,819 lecturers, and 34,506 assistant professors in Japan. Professors are the most numerous (39.8 percent), followed by associate professors (23.7 percent) and assistant professors (20.3 percent)—based on the *School Teachers Survey,* which provides comprehensive data (MEXT 2007).

Qualifications

The Standards for the Establishment of Universities require all academic positions to hold, as a minimum, academic degrees: professors must have a doctoral degree; associate professors, lecturers, and assistant professors must have at least a master's degree. But exceptions are made to these rules. For example, people who are deemed to have research achievements equivalent to a doctoral degree can be appointed as professors. As a result—based on the *School Teachers Survey* (MEXT 2007)—45.5 percent of all faculty have a doctoral degree; 25.8 percent have a master's degree; and 23.2 percent have a bachelor's degree (these percentages refer to the highest degrees possessed).

In terms of sectors, the proportion of faculty in the national universities with doctoral degrees (51.8 percent) is higher than in the other sectors (public, 42.2 percent; private, 41.7 percent). In terms of disciplines, academics in the faculties of science have more doctoral degrees (66.9 percent) than those in other disciplines. At the other extreme, the lowest proportion of doctoral-degree holders is found in the faculties of art (8.7 percent); faculties of medicine have the largest proportions of bachelor's degrees (45.8 percent), largely because they include nursing and related subject areas. In terms of age cohort, older faculty are less likely to have doctoral degrees. In fact, the proportion of faculty with doctoral degrees has increased dramatically since 1971, when only 15.4 percent of all faculty members possessed a doctoral degree. Clearly, in terms of getting jobs and promotions, the need to possess a doctoral degree has increased, especially for young scholars.

Academic Employment and Contracts

The number of new appointments to the academic profession in universities has grown from 5,128 in 1971 to 11,528 in 2007; however, the number of students enrolled in doctoral programs has risen more rapidly from 13,140 to 74,811. In Japan, it is widely assumed that most doctoral graduates will seek academic employment. Obtaining academic employment is becoming increasingly difficult for young scholars. The percentage of the cohort obtaining an academic position at a university just after graduating from a doctoral program declined from about 35 percent during the 1970s to around 15 percent during the 2000s (Kato 2007). The average age of appointment as an assistant professor has risen from 28 years in 1971 to 32.7 years in 2004. Moreover, based on the *School Teachers Survey,* the number of scholars over 60 years old, who retired or left the national universities to take positions in private universities, also declined from 348 in 1989 to 235 in 2007. Clearly, the conditions for obtaining academic employment have deteriorated for both young and old scholars.

Employment Process and Public Advertising

No special regulations exist regarding governing the employment process of academic professionals. In recent years, public advertisement has become one of the most important methods of recruiting academic profession. Of the new hires, 43.3 percent result from public advertisements; the proportion of associate professors recruited through public advertisement is the highest (60.4 percent);

in contrast, the proportion of new assistant professors thus recruited is the lowest (32.1 percent) (MEXT 2008b). This trend adds to the difficulties of young scholars seeking jobs, in fact, in terms of the private universities, the proportion of new appointments of assistant professors through public advertisement is only 14.4 percent. Where appointments are made without advertisement, existing members of the faculty approach the person whom they expect to appoint; this procedure is called *Ippon zuri,* which means "the fisherman catches the fish with only one rod."

Fixed-Term Appointments

The number of fixed-term appointments (nontenured appointments) has been growing rapidly (MEXT 2008b). In Japan, tenure is effectively the same as an indefinite appointment, especially for positions above the lecturer level. In 1998, there were only 99 fixed-term members of faculty, following implementation of the law concerning fixed-term appointments of university faculty, in 1997. In 2008, there were 32,372 fixed-term members of faculty. This indicates that 20.1 percent of all faculty members are in fixed-term appointments and that a fixed-term job market for academics has been established. In terms of positions, fixed-term assistant professors are numerous (43.5 percent); on the other hand, the number of nontenured professors in this category is the lowest (11.2 percent), followed by associate professors (13.8 percent) and lecturers (25.4 percent). Even at the level of professors and associate professors, a substantial proportion of positions are increasingly nontenured, and it has become more difficult for academic staff at all levels to move from fixed-term to tenured positions.

In Japan, if staff are appointed to a regular lecturer or associate professor job, they obtain a de facto tenure from the beginning. Evaluation is required for a promotion, but it is highly unlikely that they would be obliged to leave their position—even if they are not promoted. But, in the case of an assistant professorship, even if they can get an indefinite appointment, the eventual expectation is to get academic employment at other universities. As result, appointment to an assistant professorship is not generally considered a tenure-track position.

Research and Education

Generally speaking, when academics are hired, it is rare that their contract would specify the allocation of their time or the number of classes they need to teach. Japanese academics generally appear to prefer research to teaching. The proportions of teaching-oriented faculty is only 27.5 percent—compared to Russia, 67.6 percent; the United States, 49.2 percent; and the United Kingdom, 44.3 percent. But there is recently a trend toward a greater emphasis on teaching (Ehara 1996, 153). In a 2007 questionnaire, respondents were asked about the time spent on professional activities: teaching, research, service, administration, and other academic activities in a typical week (Fukudome and Daizen 2009). In total, the average weekly time spent on each activity had become longer in 2007 than in 1992, except for research. The average time spent on research had decreased sharply from 21.6 hours to 17.6 hours. Time spent on other activities increased, particularly for teaching and administration—each by about 2 hours.

As a result, the working time in a typical week had become around 1.6 hours longer (53.5 hours in 1992 and 55.1 hours in 2007), and in 2007 the time in a typical week spent on education (21.8 hours) is longer than time spent on research (17.6 hours), during periods of scheduled teaching.

Academic Salary

The average monthly salary (payment before taxes and excluding allowances) is ¥565,100 (US$6,891) for professors, ¥453,500 (US$5,530) for associate professors, ¥392,100 (US$4,782) for lecturers, and ¥316,800 (US$3,863) for assistant professors. Professors earn nearly 1.8 times more than assistant professors (see Table 17.1).

Variations exist among sectors and within each position. For professors, associate professors, and lecturers, private universities' average salaries are the highest—¥579,100 (US$7,062), ¥471,000 (US$5,744), and ¥393,300 (US$4,796). On the other hand, for assistant professors, average salaries at private universities are the lowest—¥292,400 (US$3,566). In terms of gender, female academic staff—¥407,400 (US$4,968)—earn on average 86.1 percent of the salary of male academic staff—¥473,300 (US$5,772).

Table 17.1 Salaries of academic profession by sector and position

University	Academic positions	Monthly average salary (¥)	Monthly average salary (US$)
National university	Professor	542,300	6,613
	Associate professor	436,300	5,321
	Lecturer	390,800	4,766
	Assistant professor	334,000	4,073
Public university	Professor	548,400	6,688
	Associate professor	445,400	5,432
	Lecturer	386,500	4,713
	Assistant professor	355,900	4,340
Private university	Professor	579,100	7,062
	Associate professor	471,000	5,744
	Lecturer	393,300	4,796
	Assistant professor	292,400	3,566

Source: MEXT 2007.

Note: US$1.00 = ¥82 (January 18, 2011).

Table 17.2 Average payments to professor, associate professor, and lecturer

Academic position	School teachers survey	Basic survey on wage structure		
	Monthly salary[a] (A)	Monthly salary[b] (B)	Annual bonus (C)	Total annual payments[c] (D)
Professor	¥565,100	¥673,800	¥3,370,100	¥11,455,700
	$6,891	$8,217	$41,099	$139,704
Associate professor	¥453,500	¥538,500	¥2,461,700	¥8,923,700
	$5,530	$6,567	$30,021	$108,826
Lecturer	¥392,100	¥495,100	¥2,099,400	¥8,040,600
	$4,782	$6,038	$25,602	$98,056

Source: MEXT 2007; Ministry of Health, Labor and Welfare 2007.
Notes: US$1 = ¥82 (January 18, 2011), payments before taxes.
[a]Excluding allowances and bonus.
[b]Including allowances.
[c]Including allowances and bonus: (D) = (B) x 12 + (C).

Monthly salaries do not include bonuses; in this project, bonuses are included in fringe benefits (next section). However, in the Japanese context, bonuses constitute an integral part of annual salaries. For comparative purposes, it is useful to indicate the levels of annual bonuses in Japan. Unfortunately, the *School Teachers Survey* does not collect bonus data, but relevant data are available in the *Basic Survey on Wage Structure* (Ministry of Health, Labor and Welfare 2007), though this only shows the average salaries by sector of professor, associate professor, and lecturer.

Based on these data (see Table 17.2), professors can be estimated to receive around ¥108,700 (US$1,326) per month as allowances, including a commutation allowance, family allowance, and district allowance.[1] They also earn a bonus. As a result, their average annual pay amounts to ¥11,455,700 (US$137,704) in total, including a bonus of 23 percent. Consequently, comparison of Japanese academic salaries, excluding bonuses with those of other countries, will tend to underestimate their value. Figure 17.1 shows age–annual salary profiles of each position and clarifies that annual salary of each positions rises according to age (labor experience).

Salaries in Other Professions

A medical doctor's earnings are the highest, followed by journalists. Professors' earnings are almost as high as those of journalists (see Table 17.3). Medical doctors earn 1.56 times more than professors. On the other hand, high school teachers earn only 80 percent of professors' average earnings. The average earnings of male employees who are 50 to 54 years old are 60 percent of the average earnings of professors. Over time (1971–2007), the relative proportions of professorial earnings to those of male employees have remained unchanged.

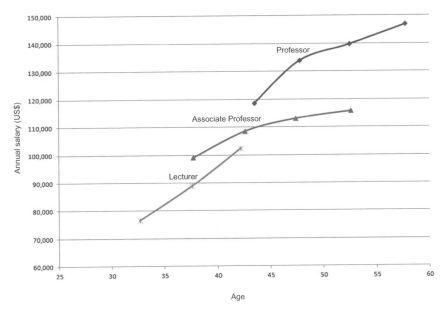

Figure 17.1 Age-annual salary profiles.

Source: Ministry of Health, Labor and Welfare 2007.

Note: Payments before taxes and including allowances and bonuses.

Table 17.3 Annual payments for five professions and average employees (male: 50–54 years old)

Profession	¥	US$	Multiples
Medical doctor	17,895,600	218,239	1.56
Journalist (newspaper)	11,966,500	145,933	1.04
Professor	11,459,200	139,746	1.00
Associate professor	9,492,100	115,757	0.83
High school teacher	9,224,100	112,489	0.80
Average employee	6,878,500	83,884	0.60

Source: Ministry of Health, Labor and Welfare 2007.

Note: US$1 = ¥82 (January 18, 2011), payments before taxes and including allowances and bonuses.

In summary, professors, with a full-time career at a single institution, receive competitive salaries. This is also true in the case of associate professors and lecturers. Data for assistant professors are not available from this survey; but, if they can get a promotion, they will receive an adequate salary. However, if they cannot get a promotion or find an alternative academic employment, they will face serious financial problems. This is true for graduate students, who cannot obtain an assistant professor position or postdoctoral fellowship; they will face more serious financial problems.

Determinants of Academic Salaries

All national universities have quite similar individual salary regulations. Generally, academic salaries in the national universities are mainly determined by a formula based on positions, years of experience, level of degree, and additional responsibilities (e.g., graduate student education). Annual negotiations take place between the national universities and the unions, but these strongly reflect recommendations of the National Personnel Authority, which determined salaries when academics in the national universities were employed as civil servants.

In the private universities, individual academic salaries are decided by each institution's own regulations, though many adopt procedures and regulations that also follow the provisions for salaries of civil servants. Salary rates at private universities are more dissimilar than those among national universities, and some traditional private universities offer higher salaries to their faculty than others.

As faculty evaluations are being introduced in most national universities, they are sometimes linked to academic salaries. It has been reported that 42.9 percent of national universities, 9.1 percent of public universities, and 15 percent of private universities use faculty evaluations to determine salaries, allowances, or special payments (Yonezawa 2000). In addition, 15.9 percent of national universities use faculty evaluations to determine bonus payments (Ohkawa and Okui 2007). Similarly, private universities use them to determine salaries (10.9 percent) or bonus payments (13.8 percent), according to a report of the Promotion and Mutual Aid Corporation for Private Schools of Japan (2009).

International Competition

National universities can, in principle, set their own salary regulations. The research universities, especially, are trying to recruit internationally recognized scholars from foreign countries. However, in general, Japanese academic salaries are not sufficiently attractive to draw leading scholars to Japanese universities. In fact, in 2007 only 3.4 percent of scholars were foreigners.

Given this situation, an interesting experiment is being conducted at the Tohoku University, a top national university. The university is attempting to recruit worldwide leading scholars by means of a procedure called the University Professor System. The system seeks to enhance the university by recruiting, as university professors, leading scholars who have the status of winners of the Nobel Prize, Fields Medal, Order of Culture, and so forth—by offering a salary equivalent to that of the university president (around ¥22.54 million [US$274,878]). As a result, the Tohoku University has succeeded in recruiting some internationally known scholars. Yet, such attempts to recruit overseas scholars represents a limited activity. Moreover, language still represents a major barrier to recruiting international scholars to Japanese universities. An alternative approach has been adopted by Aizu University, which used advertised positions internationally and also held bilingual faculty meetings in order to recruit foreign scholars (Ryu 2007). But this type of initiative also has limited impact; the salaries of Japanese academic professions are generally not sufficiently competitive to attract foreign scholars, and the problem of the language barrier remains significant.

Nonsalary (Fringe) Benefits

All academics in the national universities belong to the Federation of National Public Service Personnel Mutual Aid Association. The federation is subsidized, partially, by the government and supported by members through their annual payments. In return, it provides health insurance, accident and damage insurance, suspension of work insurance, retirement pension, and dependent relative survivor's pension. In addition, it provides discounted medical checkup packages and discounted hotel vouchers. These benefits are provided equally to all members and do not form part of negotiations for remuneration in the national universities. In the private universities, the Promotion and Mutual Aid Corporation for Private Schools of Japan provides similar services for all academics in the private universities.

In addition, national universities provide inexpensive housing for their staff or provide payments of around ¥27,000 (US$329) per month to staff who rent their residence privately. In private universities, similar payments depend on each individual university's regulations.

There are also separate retirement payments that are significant for all academics in Japan. The longer they work at one institution, the bigger these payments become. For example, in the case of a faculty member at Hiroshima University who has worked for 35 years, a university retirement payment will be equivalent to about 60 percent of monthly salaries (at the level reached at the time of retirement); some additional payment will also be provided, based on the faculty member's positions in the university. Those retirement payments will be paid in a lump sum to the faculty when he or she retires. In the case of faculty who have moved from one national university to another, their service periods are aggregated. However, in the case of those who have moved from a national university to a private university, their service periods are not aggregated. So, retirement payments are thought to affect faculty mobility from national universities to private universities or to universities in foreign countries before retirement.

While there are governmental funds for which academics can apply to do research in foreign countries, for a maximum period of two years, there are no general provisions for sabbatical leave in Japan.

Supplementary Employment

Data from the Changing Academic Profession 2007 survey[2] indicated that 18 percent of faculty also work part time at another higher education institution or research institute, 2.6 percent in a business organization, and 4.3 percent in a nonprofit organization or government entity outside of academia. These days, faculty are asked to do more social service, especially through contributions to industry, but the proportion of faculty working at business organizations outside the universities is still very low. In terms of restrictions on supplementary employment, the rules are determined by each university. At Hiroshima University, there is an upper limit of 15 hours per week, but with university approval, faculty may work longer. Apart from a minority of faculty, earnings from supplementary employment have little impact on average earnings.

Conclusion

The academic profession, as a full-time career at a single institution in Japan, is financially viable, and, with professors' salaries 1.67 times higher than those of average workers, the relative value has remained unchanged for the last 30 years. But academics' working hours have become longer, especially the time spent on teaching and administration. Obtaining academic employment has become more difficult, and appointments have become more precarious. In addition, academics are being more exposed by faculty evaluations. Overall, the real attractiveness of academic salaries is perceived to have declined, and internationally competitiveness is too weak to attract leading international scholars.

Notes

1. District allowance is provided based on the level of the average laborer's salary in the district.
2. The Changing Academic Profession 2007 survey was funded by the MEXT as a grant-in-aid for scientific research. It was intended to understand the nature and changes of the academic profession and an international research project consisting of more or less than 20 countries throughout the world.

References

Ehara, Takekazu. 1996. "Dilemma between teaching and research." In *International comparison of academic professions* [in Japanese], ed. Akira Arimoto and Takekazu Ehara, 147–65. Tokyo: Tamagawa University Press.

Fukudome, Hideto, and Tsukasa Daizen. 2009. "Education and research activities of the academic profession in Japan." In *The changing academic profession over 1992–2007: International, comparative, and quantitative perspectives,* edited by the Research Institute for Higher Education, Hiroshima University, 165–92. Hiroshima, Japan: Research Institute for Higher Education, Hiroshima University.

Kato, Takeshi. 2007. "Melting academic market place for young scholars." In *Academic marketplace in Japan* [in Japanese], ed. Yamanoi Atsunori, 289–316. Tokyo: Tamagawa University Press.

MEXT (Ministry of Education, Culture, Sports, Science, and Technology). 2003. *White paper on education, culture, sports, science, and technology FY2003.* Tokyo: MEXT.

MEXT (Ministry of Education, Culture, Sports, Science, and Technology). 2007. *School teachers survey* [in Japanese]. http://www.mext.go.jp/b_menu/toukei/chousa01/ky ouin/1268573.htm. Accessed December 26, 2011.

MEXT (Ministry of Education, Culture, Sports, Science, and Technology). 2008a. *School basic survey* [in Japanese]. http://www.mext.go.jp/b_menu/toukei/chousa01/kihon/ 1267995.htm. Accessed December 26, 2011.

MEXT (Ministry of Education, Culture, Sports, Science, and Technology). 2008b. *Survey on university reforms about contents and methods of education* [in Japanese]. Tokyo: MEXT.

Ministry of Health, Labor and Welfare. 2007. *Basic survey on wage structure.* http://www.e-stat.go.jp/SG1/estat/GL08020101.do?_toGL08020101_&tstatCode=000001011429& requestSender=dsearch. Accessed December 26, 2011.

Ohkawa, Kazuki, and Masaki Okui. 2007. "Condition of implementation for faculty evaluation in Japanese national universities" [in Japanese]. *University Evaluation Review* 6: 51–70.

Promotion and Mutual Aid Corporation for Private Schools of Japan. 2009. *Report on management improvement procedures of school foundations* [in Japanese]. Tokyo: Promotion and Mutual Aid Corporations of Private Schools of Japan.

Ryu, Shinu. 2007. "Internationalization of academic marketplace." In *Academic marketplace in Japan* [in Japanese], ed. Yamanoi Atsunori, 263–88. Tokyo: Tamagawa University Press.

Yonezawa, Akiyoshi, ed. 2000. *Trends and challenges of university evaluation* [in Japanese]. Hiroshima, Japan: Research Institute for Higher Education, Hiroshima University.

18

ACADEMIC SALARIES IN KAZAKHSTAN

Current Status and Perspectives

Sholpan Kalanova

While faculty of Kazakhstan are well educated and trained, substantial reforms need to be undertaken and ample funding provided in order to improve the positions of faculty and reach international standards in terms of teaching and research. Kazakhstan's faculty enjoy considerable social status; however, this does not translate into financial stability. To secure enough income, many professors need to work on more than one workload, which leads to the decrease of quality in the academic profession. Not enough time or funding is provided for research, and the majority of professors must concentrate more on teaching. The academic rank, seniority, and academic achievements determine the salary levels of faculty. There are four major ranks of faculty, ranging from assistant, to senior instructor, to associate professor, and to professor.

Overview of Kazakhstan's Higher Education

Kazakhstan's system of higher education is composed of universities, academies, and institutes, which train bachelor's degree students, specialists, master's degree students, and doctoral students (at the PhD level). Colleges that offer two-year vocational education are not part of the higher education system. Currently, there are 148 higher education institutions in Kazakhstan, and 93 are private. Only 20 years ago, during the epoch of the Soviet Union, the country had only 61 higher education institutions, all of them public (Kalanova and Omirbayev 2009). The enrollment of students over the last decade reflects the massification of higher education in Kazakhstan. Higher education is accessible to wide groups of the population; 43 percent of the age cohort from 18 to 24 years old study in higher education institutions (OECD and World Bank 2007).

Unfortunately, the academic profession is not very attractive today, especially for the younger generation. Relatively high salaries are offered only in a few top higher education institutions, which place high demands for employment. A noticeable brain drain occurred in the academic field about 10 to 20 years ago, when many young and ambitious professors switched to other spheres and were employed by national and foreign companies that offered much higher salaries than higher education institutions could offer.

The state regulation of higher education is strong in Kazakhstan. The Ministry of Education and Science regulates both public and private higher education institutions. Universities currently do not have much autonomy. Rectors of all public higher education institutions, except the national ones, are appointed by the Ministry of Education and Science. All education programs, their content and structure, are determined by the standards of the ministry, which apply to both public and private universities. However, changes are slowly taking place. For instance, according to the State Program of Education Development 2011–2020, the autonomy of all higher education institutions is to be instituted by 2018.

One of the numerous challenges in the higher education system of Kazakhstan involves the quality of higher education. Many families today opt to send their children to receive higher education in foreign countries—primarily, in North America, Europe, Russia, and also China and Malaysia, among others—because of the lack of confidence in local higher education. Another problem is the lack of funding for higher education. Kazakhstan has low levels of public funding for higher education. For example, only 10 percent of the education budget is appropriated to higher education. Few nonpublic sources of funding for higher education are provided, and they are limited in their scope. Some leading corporations offer grants for top students in those academic fields in which they have interest. However, this type of funding is often limited to top universities. A university-industry partnership operates only in its initial stage in Kazakhstan.

However, the overall situation is starting to change, for the better. The government has pledged to increase the budget for research by five times in the next several years, aiming to make it at least equal to 1 percent of the gross domestic product, from 0.2 percent today. More attention is being paid to lifelong learning, as more higher education institutions offer short-term professional programs in specific fields for individuals who want to update their qualifications. The current trend is to empower the higher education system, because more stakeholders realize the value of higher education for society and its necessity in fostering human capital to build a modern, knowledge-based, and innovative economy.

Academic Contracts

Academic contracts are mostly determined by the Law on Labor. There are unified requirements for both public and private higher education institutions. Usually a university president has complete authority and autonomy in hiring faculty and administrative staff at all levels, except for vice presidents. A university must have less than 45 percent of faculty who possess either a doctor of science, candidate of science, or PhD degree. For an institute, this proportion can be no less than 35 percent of faculty. The proportions are determined by regulatory requirements set by the Ministry of Education and Science and are necessary for the licensing of higher education institutions. Faculty at public universities are granted the civil-servant status by the Law on Education (2007a). However, this status only allows them to receive an additional monthly salary while on annual vacation (medical allowance). No other perquisites are offered—such as cofinancing of pensions by the government, for example. Private universities responded to this norm right away and also provide their faculty with a medical allowance.

Hiring of faculty at higher education institutions is accomplished through various means: classifieds are distributed in national and local newspapers concerning available vacancies, invitational letters are sent to notable faculty, and directors of departments offer their own candidates to the academic management. The status and prestige of a university, as well as its location, influence the potential to attract highly qualified faculty. Universities located in major cities, such as Astana or Almaty, find it easier to attract faculty, compared to regional universities. On the other hand, it is harder for regional universities to invite professors or associate professors from other universities; thus, they strive to provide more incentives for their own faculty to earn higher academic degrees. The management of such universities usually provides faculty with "creative vacations" of three to six months, with full salaries kept, so that a professor can work on his or her research to gain a higher academic degree. If such assistance is provided, the professor must then remain working at the university for at least three years.

The standard practice of hiring requires faculty to possess certain qualifications—such as an academic degree and title, experience of work in higher education institutions, academic achievements, and recommendations. Depending on the position that a professor is offered, an interview takes place with top management of the higher education institution or with the director of the department. It is generally easier to be admitted if prospective professors hold higher academic degrees, such as a PhD, as many universities are in need of highly qualified staff.

Employment contracts are regulated by the Labor Code and the Law on Labor. Academic contracts have similar characteristics with the contracts in other spheres, because the major contract requirements are mandated by the law. When hired by a university for the first time, a professor is usually offered an individual work contract for one year (Labor Code 2007; Law on Labor 1999). A professor can also be employed for a shorter-time period to teach a specific course or discipline for a partial workload, which has to be specified in the academic contract. After finishing the first year of the contract, if the professor has fulfilled all of the requirements and receives positive reviews from management, colleagues, and students; then, the university signs a new contract with the professor for an indefinite term. This policy holds true for all ranks. Academic contracts are similar in public and private universities, as they are both based on the same labor laws. If a university breaches the norms of the contract, professors have a right to file a petition against the violation with the Department of Labor, which is responsible for monitoring all organizations on their compliance to the labor laws.

When being hired for a job, a prospective professor cannot be discriminated against, on the basis of religion, ethnicity, sex, or age. For example, universities cannot refuse to employ women, even those who are planning to have children. Actually, there is a relative shortage of professors in Kazakhstan, possibly, because of lower wages in comparison with other industries, and universities are often in continuous search for qualified professors.

In the case that student enrollment diminishes dramatically and, thus, not enough of a teaching load exists, faculty can be fired regardless of whether their contract is for an indefinite time period. Usually, professors with lower academic degrees face a greater risk of being fired. A university's administration must inform the faculty member about the cutback—in writing, one month ahead—and must pay compensation based on a one-month salary, in compliance with the law. To understand such practices, it is necessary to see how the budget of higher education institutions is formed. There is no practice of endowment funds, as in the United States, which helps to maintain financial stability of higher education institutions. The main financing for universities is based on tuition fees paid by students. Statistical data for 2009 show that 76.6 percent of the students cover tuition fees on their own, while only 23.4 percent are funded with public grants (Agency of Statistics 2010). Faculty can also be fired for serious breaches of the contract, such as not attending lectures, corruption, inappropriate conduct, and other issues.

Faculty are expected to devote the majority of their work to teaching. Although research by faculty is welcomed by higher education institutions, not much time is allocated to such work. The main problem is funding and the fact that many professors work at several universities and thus lack time to dedicate to research. Public funds for research are usually appropriated to public higher education institutions, especially to national universities, while private higher education institutions are provided, rarely and in modest amounts, investments for research. Thus, research is mainly conducted in social sciences, which do not require as much funding. Such research is usually undertaken by faculty on their own means, often to earn an academic degree.

The results of research—in the form of publications or study guides for students—are among the indicators of effective work when faculty evaluations are conducted at the end of each academic year. However, specific levels of research productivity are not required at the majority of higher education institutions. Only a few universities, mostly national or top private ones, aim to place this performance into the international academic rankings and have started to provide for research in contracts, awarding additional bonuses to the salaries of

professors. However, to earn such bonuses, professors must produce concrete research results, such as having publications in highly ranked journals abroad and
in English.

Academic Salaries

The standard salaries of faculty in public higher education institutions are determined by state legal and regulatory documents, such as the decrees of the government. Salary levels of faculty are determined by academic rank, length of service,
and academic achievements. The salaries actually distributed are less than nominal
salaries by 20 percent, as 10 percent of the salaries cover individual income taxes
and another 10 percent contribute to pension funds.

The academic rank serves a major relevance on salary levels. For example, a
professor usually earns more than twice as much as an assistant. The one workload
monthly salary of a professor at a public university is about US$685, while that of
an assistant is US$308. Seniority emphasizes salary differences, but not by a high
margin. The salary of a professor with more than 20 years of experience is higher,
only by 7 percent, than that of a newcomer. Personal academic achievements also
play a significant role on salary levels, as today an increasing number of universities
hunt for the most productive faculty, usually regarding research potential, which
influences universities' ranking positions. Besides standard salaries, professors with
degrees such as candidate of science, doctor of science, and PhD receive additional
monthly bonuses for having these degrees.

Private higher education institutions usually offer salaries that are moderately
higher than those in public higher education institutions. For example, an associate professor at a public university receives one workload average monthly salary
of US$497, while his or her counterpart at a private university receives US$616.
However, working in private universities poses some risks, as well. Private higher
education institutions are commonly at a higher risk, given a diminishing number
of students. Students mainly prefer public universities, and when fewer students
are in the higher education system, private universities are more vulnerable. Besides, while public universities receive some public funding, private universities
can only receive public funding if students with public grants decide to enroll
there. Faculty at national universities enjoy higher salaries, as their salaries are
based on the coefficient of 1.75 to the standard salaries of faculty at other public
universities. Overall, the highest faculty salaries are provided at top private universities. There, a professor can earn one workload salary of as much as US$1,200
to US$1,500 per month.

When comparing the salaries of faculty with those of professionals in other
fields, representatives from other spheres with similar qualifications can earn up
to twice as much or more in natural resources and financial and other kinds of
corporations that operate in Kazakhstan. Even though the academic profession
has a high social status in Kazakhstan, faculty do not enjoy a high level of income.

However, measures to improve faculty salaries are being carried out. The government recently undertook steps to strengthen the financial positions of faculty at public institutions. In consequence of the Annual Address of the President to the People of Kazakhstan (2008), the salaries of faculty at public universities and other public servants were carried out, notwithstanding the consequences of the recent global economic crisis. Since the rise of faculty salaries at public universities, private universities had no other choice but to follow suit and raise the salaries of their faculty as well, in order to keep them.

Nonsalary (Fringe) Benefits

Professors of both public and private universities have a right for an annual paid vacation of two months, which provides two average monthly salaries and an additional average monthly salary as a medical allowance (Law on Education 2007b). One workload for faculty nominally features 36 hours per week. However, in real terms, the work period is usually shorter, because only about half of this time is for teaching classes while the other half is for preparation, research, and other functions. Thus, the faculty do not always need to be present at the workplace. The usual workload for other professions is 40 hours per week. Therefore, professors often manage to work for one-and-a-half workload periods at their primary university and even work part time at another university. More than half of the faculty in Kazakhstan are female, and their non-rigid work regime allows them to spend more time with their families. Higher education institutions sometimes offer fully covered housing to attract highly qualified faculty; however, this is not a frequent practice.

The government of Kazakhstan provides an annual state grant for top faculty—"the Best Professor of the Year." The grants are distributed among 200 leading professors in the country. Each grant amounts to US$20,000. The grant was instituted in 2005 to foster professional achievements and to improve qualifications of faculty (Ministry of Education and Science 2010). The grant is awarded based on teaching and research accomplishments, such as excelling in training PhD and master's students, having important research publications, acquiring patents, and other factors. A professor who wins the grant may reapply only three years later. The grant can be awarded to the faculty of both public and private higher education institutions in all fields; it has a specific purpose and is meant to be used for research internships abroad, writing monographs and textbooks, and engaging in research projects (Law on Education 2007c).

Supplementary Employment (Moonlighting)

A significant number of professors in Kazakhstan work in more than one higher education institution. Even at their primary university, professors often work for one-and-a-half workloads. While the exact portion of professors employed in several universities is unavailable, clearly, at least 50 percent of them have multiple positions in major cities—like Almaty, Astana, Shymkent, and Karagandy—which have many universities. Usually, these are the faculty with specialties such as business administration, law, English, information technology, and other common fields, because these programs are most popular among students. Additional workloads are common for faculty of both public and private universities. It is permissible by law to carry up to one-and-a-half workloads in one higher education institution. There are no prohibitions to work on half a workload at one or two other higher education institutions. The main reason for faculty to have additional workloads and work at several universities involves the need for additional salary, since the salary of one workload at a university is often not enough. Even teaching at several universities does not warrant a high level of income for the majority of faculty. However, working at several higher education institutions is not encouraged by the Ministry of Education and Science, as such a function has a detrimental effect on the quality of higher education.

Faculty can receive additional bonuses for participating in research projects. A professor may also hold an additional position in a higher education institution, such as directing a department. Supplementary positions and terms are added to an existing contract. Some faculty offer consultation services to public agencies, national corporations, and other organizations. However, this practice is not yet well developed in Kazakhstan and applies mostly to the faculty of top higher education institutions. It is also rare for faculty to engage in other forms of non-academic work; they usually work at several higher education institutions if they need to earn more. Only faculty of certain disciplines—for example, English faculty—can moonlight by offering language courses in their spare time.

Academic Rank and Qualification

As of 2010, there were 26,680 professors in public universities, of whom 1,873 held a doctor of science degree and 8,689 held a candidate of science degree. There were 12,057 professors in private universities, of whom 861 held a doctor of science degree and 4,326 held a candidate of science degree (Agency of Statistics 2010). The hierarchy of academic positions is the same in public and private higher education institutions. The hierarchy has four levels, with the fourth being the lowest and first the highest. To receive the position of an assistant, at the fourth level, a master's degree or a specialist degree is required (five-year higher education degree). The position of assistant is the lowest rank of faculty, which is an analogue to the United States. It is usually assigned to the incoming faculty, who has just graduated and started to teach at a university. For the position of senior instructor, at the third level, additional teaching experience is required. Usually, it takes several years to earn the position of senior instructor. For the position of associate professor (second level), it is necessary to have PhD or candidate of science degrees as well as to publish in national and foreign journals. To receive the position of professor (first level), PhD or doctor of science degrees are necessary, as well as to publish extensively in national and foreign journals and be a scientific supervisor to at least three PhD students. Academic promotion is based on academic degrees, experience, and academic achievements of the faculty. The degrees such as specialist (except for medical and veterinarian specialties), candidate of science, and doctor of sciences are not provided anymore, since 2011, because Kazakhstan switched to the Western system of bachelor's, master's, and PhD degrees. However, those degrees earned in the past are still recognized as valid.

International Competition

The relatively low level of salaries in higher education institutions of Kazakhstan does not promote the employment of foreign faculty. Few leading higher education institutions—such as the Kazakhstan Institute of Management, Economics and Strategic Research; Kazakh-British Technical University; and Al-Farabi Kazakh National University—employ foreign faculty who are paid salaries distinctly higher than those of local faculty. In the newly opened Nazarbayev University, which is aiming to reach the status of a world-class university, up to 75 percent of faculty are employed from high-level foreign higher education institutions. This university enjoys special funding to cover the salaries of faculty on the level of developed countries. It is not possible to precisely determine the number of faculty working abroad. However, it can be estimated that not many faculty have left to teach abroad, partly because of language barrier, as few professors are fluent in English. Recently, the state scholarship program, *Bolashak* (the future), which offers grants to students to study at top foreign universities, has expanded to provide grants to faculty to study or to attend research internships abroad. Also, the government has recently instituted a grant to invite 300 foreign professors to teach in Kazakhstan's universities each year. These exchanges are meant to improve international mobility and to raise qualifications of faculty.

Conclusion

The majority of faculty in Kazakhstan do not earn enough to enjoy a middle-class lifestyle, with the exception of faculty at the highest rank. Only faculty of the highest rank, such as professors, can be considered as part of the middle class, by Kazakhstan's standards. There is not a significant difference between faculty in public and private universities. Even though professors in public universities are civil servants, this provides them with no significant benefits in comparison to professors in private universities. For the majority of faculty, it is difficult to make a decent living on a single workload. Therefore, many professors strive to obtain a one-and-a-half workload and also moonlight at other universities for part-time loads, in order to earn sufficient income. Career advancement of faculty is not automatic. Generally, higher academic degrees are required, and a professor also has to prove his or her teaching proficiency, gain experience, engage in research, publish in scientific journals, and further options. International mobility is not developed, only a few top universities are able to employ foreign faculty. More funding is necessary to raise the level of teaching and research in higher education and to enhance the conditions and financial security of faculty. It is encouraging that the government has recently taken measures to improve the positions of faculty, as this is necessary for sustainable growth and progress of higher education in Kazakhstan—since the academic profession remains to be at the foundation of educational process.

References

Agency of Statistics of the Republic of Kazakhstan. 2010. "Education." http://www.stat.kz/publishing/Pages/Cocyalnaya_sfera%202010.aspx. Accessed August 5, 2010.

Annual Address by the President to the People of Kazakhstan. 2008. *Welfare growth of Kazakhstan's citizens is the primary goal of public policy*. http://www.akorda.kz/ru/speeches/addresses_of_the_president_of_kazakhstan/address_by_the_president_of_the_republic_of_kazakhstan. Accessed August 10, 2010.

Kalanova, Sholpan M., and Serik M. Omirbayev. 2009. *National system and educational standards of higher education in the Republic of Kazakhstan—Analytical report*. 2nd ed., updated. Moscow: Research Center for the Problems of Quality in Specialists' Training.

Labor Code of the Republic of Kazakhstan. 2007. Chapter 4, article 29.29. http://www.zakon.kz/141152-trudovojj-kodeks-respubliki-kazakhstan.html. Accessed August 15, 2010.

Law on Education of the Republic of Kazakhstan. 2007a. Chapter 7, article 50, clause 1. http://www.edu.gov.kz/fileadmin/user_upload/npa/zakoni/zakon_ob_obrazovanii.doc. Accessed August 12, 2010.

Law on Education of the Republic of Kazakhstan. 2007b. Chapter 7, article 53, clause 1. http://www.edu.gov.kz/fileasmin/user_upload/npa/zakoni/zakon_ob_obrazovanii.doc. Accessed August 18, 2010.

Law on Education of the Republic of Kazakhstan. 2007c. Chapter 7, article 53, clause 1. http://www.edu.gov.kz/fileadmin/user_upload/npa/zakoni/zakon_ob_obrazovanii.doc. Accessed August 21, 2010.

Law on Labor of the Republic of Kazakhstan. 1999. Chapter 2, article 10. http://www.kazpravda.kz/c/1008122401. Accessed August 27, 2010.

Ministry of Education and Science. 2010. "Higher education." http://www.edu.gov.kz//ru/dejatelnost/vysshee_i_poslevuzovskoe_obrazovanie/. Accessed August 23, 2010.

OECD (Organization for Economic Cooperation and Development) and World Bank. 2007. *Review of national policies for education—higher education in Kazakhstan*, 68. Bishkek, Kyrgyzstan: M. Maxima.

19

THE ACADEMIC SALARY SYSTEM

Conditions and Trends in Latvia

Tatjana Volkova

In the context of an economic downturn, the current challenges of postsecondary education in Latvia confront a heavy impact on the income structure of higher education institutions. The organization of academic work in Latvia is characterized by highly decentralized employment agreements. The current national data-gathering system is not sufficient for analyzing the conditions of faculty-staff employment and remuneration. There is no research currently available on the remuneration of faculty at higher education institutions in Latvia. The existing academic salary levels encourage competent faculty to look for possibilities abroad. Further data collection and analyses are required to properly analyze trends of academic salaries in Latvia.

Overview of Higher Education in Latvia

The chapter describes types of higher education institutions in Latvia, general trends of numbers of students enrolled, study programs offered by higher education institutions, and challenges of funding. Also, issues will be outlined related to the aging of the academic staff, reduced public funding, and the financial instability of the academic profession.

There are 31 higher education institutions in Latvia; 18 were founded by the state and 13 by private entities (2 are branches of foreign institutions). In addition, the system includes 26 colleges—18 founded by the state and 8 by private entities (Ministry of Education and Science 2008).

The relatively large number of higher education institutions in Latvia can be explained by the significant demand for higher education in recent years, following independence in 1991. After the fast growth of the higher education sector, the number of students has dropped for the fourth successive year. Due to demographic trends, the number of applicants will drop by an additional 50 percent from 2015 to 2017. The trend raises the issue of the sustainability of the full employment of academic staff available within the country. In addition to demographic trends, serious budget cuts in 2010 followed the economic recession.

An additional challenge in the higher education sector is the aging faculty. Almost half of the faculty are age 50 or older, which creates pressure to renew the staff in the coming years. Only 11 percent of current staff are younger than 30 years (Cabinet of Ministers, n.d.). In recent years the percentage of academic staff with scientific degrees has dropped and is currently 46 percent (down from 50 percent in 2002). Another disquieting trend is the reduction in the percentage of full professors in relation to the total academic staff—25 percent in 2005–6 but 22 percent in 2008–9 (Ministry of Education and Science 2010).

Types of Higher Education Institutions

Three main categories consist among postsecondary institutions in Latvia: universities, universities of applied science, and colleges. According to law, a university must meet the following criteria: offer undergraduate, postgraduate, and graduate study programs; graduate study programs have annual promotion; at least 50 percent of academic staff hold a doctoral degree; and scientific periodicals have been published in the fields of study offered. Scientific research is considered essential to qualify as a university (Law on Institutions of Higher Education 1995). A university of applied science must meet the following criteria: carry out academic and professional study programs at the undergraduate, postgraduate, and graduate levels; carry out research and artistic activities; and have at least 20 percent of academic staff with a doctoral degree (in some types of higher education institutions, at least 30 percent of the faculty are required to hold a doctoral degree). The colleges offer short-cycle professional education but are still considered higher education institutions. Yet, the colleges are allowed to offer only short-cycle higher education study programs that usually last two or three years. After college graduation, students get the fourth level professional qualification, according to the Latvian Law on Professional Education. Universities can also offer short-cycle higher education professional education programs. The academic degrees awarded by colleges are considered the same level as the similar degrees awarded by a university. Graduates of colleges are allowed to continue their studies at a university on the undergraduate level, entering typically into the third year of study—even if their college provided a three-year program.

Enrollment Trends

The statistical data of the Ministry of Education and Science show that the total number of students in the 2009–10 academic year was 125,350 (including at colleges); the matriculation of first-year students has dropped by 26 percent in general, compared with the previous year of studies. The majority of students (67 percent) studied in public higher education institutions, but 33 percent chose private institutions in the 2008–9 academic year (Ministry of Education and Science 2008). No significant changes have taken place in recent years in the distribution of students by fields of study. At present, approximately half of the students in Latvia are studying social sciences. It should also be noted that the percentage of students in engineering sciences, production, and construction—irrespective of the increase in the number of available places financed from the state budget—grows quite slowly (from 9.2 percent in 2004–5 to 11.1 percent in 2008–9). For the purposes of comparison, in 1997–98 the percentage was 20.5 percent. In recent years the percentage of students enrolled in health care and social welfare increased.

Higher Education Funding in Latvia

In an economic survey published in May 2010, the European University Association mentions that various European higher education systems experienced budget cuts less than 5 percent and some 5 percent to 10 percent (European University Association 2010). Due to the economic recession, the Latvian gross domestic product decreased by 18 percent, which led to severe budget cuts in every sector—including higher education. In the course of 2009, state funding for higher education was cut by 48 percent, compared to the budget originally anticipated; the cut to many research programs has been even larger, more than 50 percent. The initial cut was followed by a further 18 percent reduction in 2010 (European University Association 2010). Further budget cuts in 2011 are being negotiated by the Latvian government, European Commission, International Monetary Fund, World Bank, and other lenders.

In other words, universities are forced to cut their expenses drastically, which impacts their daily operation. Financing in Latvia covers only one-third of the entering students, mainly provided at state institutions; the other students pay tuition fees. Given the economic conditions, there is only a limited possibility to compensate budget cuts—through tuition fees. The total expenditure per student per annum was already significantly lower in Latvia compared to other European Union countries before the current crisis. According to data of Eurostat in Latvia, in 2007, the expenditure for full-time equivalent students (in both public and private institutions) averaged €4,544 per student per annum, which is the fourth-lowest rate in the European Union, following Estonia (€4,339 per student), Poland (€3,812 per student), and Bulgaria (€3,837) (Reis and Gheorghiu 2010).

Salary Trends

The academic profession could constitute a full-time career at a single institution that provides a middle-class lifestyle; but that depends on the level of the position, workload expected of academic staff, and the particular institution. Due to the declining number of students and decreasing public funding, a new group of "free-capacity" academic staff has appeared. Many higher education institutions can no longer provide full-time work for academic staff, which is why the academic profession generally does not provide a middle-class lifestyle. Due to severe budget cuts, public universities offer the minimum remuneration level for all academic positions, as set by the Cabinet of Ministers of Latvia.

The minimum salary for a lecturer is LVL 423 (US$850), but an average salary in the public sector in 2010 was only LVL 474 (US$952) (Ekonomika.lv. 2010). In order to increase their salary levels, faculty take part in training, research projects, or provide academic services in another higher education institution, nationally or internationally. It is difficult to estimate the additional income level from such activities, since it varies from case to case. These opportunities are available for all faculty staff, but different internal policies are set by each particular higher education institution. To accept an additional job, permission from the administration is required. There are fewer cases in which an academic staff member is also employed at a public or a private company. For example, due to the low academic workload, faculty could be employed in the commercial bank sector as a manager, become a research project manager for a private company, or provide training for adults.

Academic Hierarchy and Hiring Practices

In the higher education sector, the typical employee career ladder has the following ranks: assistant, lecturer, reader (docent), associate professor, and professor. Academics in all of these ranks have both teaching and research duties, but it is up to the higher education institution itself to determine the distribution of these activities—depending on the type of institution.

Academic hiring follows a standard practice in a public or private institution. The public announcement of a vacant position has to be placed on the website of the higher education institution and published in the central newspaper, *Latvijas Vestnesis*. The decision about the opening or the closure of a vacant position is a decision of the senate—the main governing body in higher education institutions. So, institutions have the autonomy to decide how many and which type of academic posts they need. After submission of the necessary application documents, the selection process follows established rules. For professors and associate professors, the decision as to whether the candidate meets the requirements for the position is made by the professors' council. The rules set by the Cabinet of Ministers in the Republic of Latvia describe the requirements to be promoted to the rank of associate professor and professor. In recent years, with the significant growth of students, there was no competition for faculty openings, due to demand. With the decreasing number of students, the impact of the economic recession and demographic challenges, the new trend is a greater degree of competition for each faculty position.

Academic Contract Types and Conditions

Academic and other staff in higher education do not have civil service status in Latvia. Tenure does not exist, and, thus, all academic positions are filled on a contract basis. Time limits exist on contracts for academic positions, limited to a maximum period of six years by law. The "unofficial" permanency might occur based on the final decisions about the election for academic positions made by the senate, which is mostly composed by academic staff.

The primary activity of faculty staff is teaching. Research activities are not considered the primary activity for permanent faculty staff but rather an integral part of the position. The involvement in research varies by the level of the academic position. For example, associate professors and full professors are required to do research, and the job description includes research as an obligatory part of their tasks. For positions such as readers and lecturers, the responsibility for research depends on the type of institution. At universities, providing academic-study programs and carrying out basic research, it is more common to include research activities for all levels of the academic staff. Research is assumed as the main purpose of a research position, with teaching as the secondary option.

It is not a common practice to specify in contracts how much time is allocated to teaching or research activities in Latvia. The contract specifies teaching hours, but research forms a less-expected activity. The situation is different when academic staff are carrying out the research activities financed by European Union grants. In such cases, the time allocations are specified for both activities.

Autonomy is granted to the higher education institution to hire the faculty. However, hiring of foreign faculty involves some restrictions placed on public higher education institutions by the Cabinet of Ministers of Latvia and requires Latvian-language skills for a full-time faculty member to be elected. In order to attract better academic staff to the particular higher education institution, the institution usually negotiates salary, benefits, reduced teaching obligations, and other conditions for the academic staff—possibly due to the full autonomy granted to each institution.

Academic Salaries

Academic salaries reflect the rank and workload assigned by a particular higher education institution. The principles of the salary system are set by the senate of the institution, and the level of salaries for particular academic positions cannot be lower than those set by the Cabinet of Ministers outlined in Table 19.1 (Ministry of Education and Science 2009).

Table 19.1 Minimum salary rates for academic staff, 2010–11

Academic rank	Minimum salary (LVL)*
Professor	826
Associate professor	661
Reader (docent)	529
Lecturer	423
Assistant	338

Source: Ministry of Education and Science 2009.
*US$1.00 = LVL 0.502.

The salary level of a particular faculty staff member is not stable from year to year, as the salary is dependent on teaching and research workload, number of students, level of the academic program taught, number of classes, and other issues. It is not the obligation of the higher education institution to provide a full-time workload for any particular academic staff member. The level of salary also depends on the public-financing policy at the state level for public higher education institutions, which reflects national economic conditions and thus creates fluctuations of the salaries in the institution.

In the face of current economic and demographic challenges, academic salaries—compared with other professionals with similar qualifications and level of education—could be considered less attractive. As indicated above, more than 75 percent of students are paying tuition fees in Latvia, which fluctuate year by year and constitute a rather big part of a higher education institution's budget. As a result, there are diverse possibilities at higher education institutions to reward faculty at salary levels. This depends on the number of students and courses taught. Differentiated salary systems exist, given that professors in some disciplines are better paid than others at the same institution.

It is up to the higher education institution to distribute teaching hours among the faculty. This depends on necessity—if enrollment is small, a staff member may deliver only one or a few courses; also, in some cases, academic staff members are involved only in the supervision of student diploma work. The university administration has the flexibility to work within a range of salaries, depending on the discipline and staff qualifications.

Public institutions receive funding based on a formula. The government is financing a certain number of student places; the rest of the students are paying tuition fees. Thus, the universities' income depends on the demand and purchasing power of students. Philanthropy, as a source of income, has very limited impact on the budget.

The main determinants of faculty salaries are formal qualifications and degrees; research activity and productivity can be rewarded with project grants. For example, if the faculty member is active and successful in submitting academic and research projects financed from outside the university (national research funds,

European Union structural funds, etc.), additional income is provided for the faculty. More typically, research activity is considered an integral part of academic activity and is not rewarded separately, although the practice exists at some institutions to reward staff for articles published in international journals, publication of academic books, and so forth.

Beyond Base Salary

Few benefits are offered as a part of an academic remuneration package. Benefits generally include paid vacation, usually eight weeks during the summer (July, August); health insurance is sometimes offered. Salary is the most important element in attracting faculty. No funds or benefits exist to compensate staff.

It is common for faculty to work in more than one higher education institution. In a smaller institution the practice is to combine the academic and administrative positions. In such cases, only one contract may exist, but salaries are indicated separately for each position (academic and administrative).

It is not easy to estimate how many professors are teaching in more than one institution. An attempt was made to develop a register of faculty working as full-time staff for a particular higher education institution, but due to the lack of support from institutions for such documentation, the register was not completed. Supplementary employment is common for staff at both types of higher education institutions—private and public institutions.

In the past, the legal restrictions on teaching at multiple institutions in some universities existed to maintain quality and to limit such teaching. In the current economic crisis, when the teaching workload is not too intense, such a limitation is not a common practice. There is, however, a requirement to inform and get permission from the administration of the higher education institution.

It is impossible to estimate the percentage of faculty members who supplement their academic salary with consulting and other nonacademic work. Such data do not exist. Usually it is not required to inform even the management of a higher education institution about consulting and other nonacademic activities. The most common activities are for staff in business-related fields.

Academic Qualifications and Promotion

The minimum degree required to enter the academic profession is a master's degree. The promotion of academic staff is based on degrees and evaluations of teaching or research productivity. There are limited vacancies for faculty staff in higher positions. Thus, even when a person holds a doctoral degree, promotion to the higher level may not occur, given the lack of vacant positions.

There is little difference between public and private institutions regarding promotion. The law on higher education regulates the minimum requirements for academic positions. To have a reader/docent position, a doctoral degree is required; but for professional study programs (with a more applied focus) at the undergraduate and graduate levels, a master's degree and seven years of professional experience in the particular field are the minimum requirements. For an associate professor and a professor, a doctoral degree is required for both academic and professional study programs.

To be appointed to the rank of professor for the first time, a person is required to have a doctoral degree and at least three years of experience in the position of associate professor. For the position of associate professor, a person needs to have a doctoral degree. In art sciences, when an individual's professional activities comply with the requirements set by the senate of a particular higher education institution, the person could be appointed despite not having a doctoral degree. The criteria are divided into several categories: scientific qualification, pedagogical qualification, and organizational competencies.

Scientific qualifications include publications in cited journals (five publications for a professor position and three for an associate professor position), participation or management in international projects or projects of the Scientific Council of Latvia, activities at the level of expert in international projects or programs, or received patents and licenses. The evaluated pedagogical activities serve supervising doctoral, master's, and bachelor's degree theses; offering study courses; making reports on academic conferences; lecturing abroad; publishing academic literature; and other procedures. Evaluated organizational competences include leading scientific or academic commissions, participating or organizing international conferences, participation in editorial boards of scientific journals, participating in organizational commissions of the international conferences, and other performances.

The right to evaluate candidates and elect them to "permanent" positions as associate professors or professors at an institution is given to the professors' councils by national legislation. To form such a council, the institution requires at least five full-time professors in a particular area of science. The decision to establish a professors' council is up to the senate of the higher education institution. The candidates for the council members must be approved also by the senate of a higher education institution. The positive decision of the professors' council is the only basis for the recruitment of professors at a particular higher education institution.

International Competition

Low academic salaries encourage high-level academic staff to look for possibilities abroad. The anticipation could involve spending a semester or academic year as a full- or part-time faculty member with salary paid by a foreign higher education institution. The salary level in Latvia is rather low, which limits possibilities for attracting foreign faculty. An additional barrier to attracting foreign faculty is a legislative requirement that to be elected as full-time academic staff foreign faculty members must pass a test of Latvian-language skills.

Private institutions have developed the policy to attract international scholars by offering salaries higher than those typically offered for local academic staff, but information is not publicly available on these cases. Due to the lack of data, it is difficult to estimate the number or percentage of professors who have left the country to teach abroad. Nevertheless, a growing number of professors would like to leave the country to teach abroad, given the insecurity of the Latvian salary system and the decreasing number of students in the coming years.

Conclusion

The academic salary system in Latvia is rather complex and reveals a necessity for further improvement. The main weaknesses of the system are insufficient financing for higher education, the unpredictability of budget allocations to higher education institutions for annual salaries, and insufficient funding for research activities. This last issue leads to a rather high teaching load for faculty, not leaving much time for research activities. These high loads also have an impact on the quality of teaching.

Almost half of the faculty are age 50 years or older, creating a growing necessity to renew the staff in the coming years. The aging of faculty threatens the sustainability of some academic programs. Since the salary level in Latvia of faculty staff is low, attracting international faculty is a rather challenging task. Another obstacle is the language barrier fortified by a test of Latvian-language skills required by law. Yet, there is a positive trend due to available European Union funding schemes, and the number of new doctoral students is growing and promises a good cadre of academic staff in the future.

References

Cabinet of Ministers of the Republic of Latvia. n.d. "Summary of activities plan regarding necessary reform in higher education and science 2010–2012." http://www.likumi.lv/doc.php?id=214704. Accessed December 1, 2010.

Ekonomika.lv. 2010. "Average salary in Latvia before taxes." http://www.ekonomika.lv/videja-darba-samaksa-latvija-pirms-nodoklu-nomaksas-444-lati/. Accessed December 1, 2010.

European University Association. 2010. "Economic monitoring report." http://www.eua.be/Newsletters/newsletter-archive/newsletter_9_21_may_2010.aspx. Accessed August 23, 2010.

Reis, Fernando, and Sorin Gheorghiu. 2010. *Population and social conditions.* Eurostat. epp. eurostat.ec.europa.eu/cache/ITY.../KS-QA-10-038-EN.PDF. Accessed August 23, 2010.

Law on Institutions of Higher Education. 1995. http://www.likumi.lv/doc.php?id=37967. Accessed December 1, 2010.

Ministry of Education and Science. 2008. *Report on the operation of higher education institutions.* Available at: http://izm.izm.gov.lv/registri-statistika/statistika-augstaka/parskats-2009.html. Accessed December 1, 2010.

Ministry of Education and Science. 2009. "The rules No. 836 by Cabinet of Ministers: Rules of remuneration of pedagogical staff." http://izm.izm.gov.lv/pedagogiem/darba-samaksa.html. Accessed August 23, 2010.

Ministry of Education and Science. 2010. *Report on necessary structural reforms in higher education and science for increasing Latvian competitiveness internationally.* http://izm.izm.gov.lv/pedagogiem/darba-samaksa.html. Accessed January 2, 2012.

20

ATTRACTIVENESS OF SALARIES AND REMUNERATION OF MALAYSIAN ACADEMICS

Muhamad Jantan

The salaries of academics in Malaysia are quite attractive, allowing for an upper-middle-class status—especially for academics with a full professor rank, which is possible for every academic. Further, these remunerations vary across disciplines, being most attractive for those in medical and related disciplines. The remunerations of academics in the public higher education institutions are better than their private counterparts due to the salary structure, nonfinancial benefits, tax arrangements, and retirement service. These factors have discouraged academics from leaving public institutions and minimize the need for supplementary employment.

Overview of Malaysian Higher Education

Malaysian higher education has seen dynamic changes in the last two decades—changes that have strained the resources necessary to ensure quality. Malaysian postsecondary education institutions include public and private ones in the form of community colleges, colleges, polytechnics, university colleges, and universities. The number of such institutions has grown tremendously in the last two decades; it now stands at 627, of which more than 90 percent are private (Ministry of Higher Education 2009) and 58 are degree conferring—20 public and 38 private.

The number of institutions grew as a consequence of the increasing demand for higher education, which is seen as a route for upward social mobility (Lee 2004). In 1985, over 85,000 students attended public institutions, increasing to more than 300,000 by 2005. Similarly, in 1985 only 15,000 students attended private colleges, but by 2006 these institutions enrolled more than 250,000 students (Tierney 2008).

The growth in the number of academics parallels that of enrollment, though at a slower pace. By 2009, it stood at almost 36,000 academics—65 percent in the public higher education institutions. For a long time, attracting individuals to join the academe was difficult due to the keen competition from the other sectors of the economy as well as the poor image of the academic profession (Jantan et al. 2006). The erosion of the professoriate's image stems from increased corporatization and bureaucratization of higher education (Tierney 2008; Lee 2004; Jantan and Sirat 2008), with little improvement in remunerations. In the 1990s, more corporate-management practices were introduced into the administration of public higher education institutions, and greater control by the Ministry of Higher Education was being exerted in many areas of academic pursuits. Academics, particularly in the public sector, have been subjected to performance-based evaluation, merit pay, and have had to compete for resources and research funds. Consequently, the profession ceased to be a destination of choice for fresh graduates. Steps are being taken to reverse this trend toward greater autonomy and better remuneration packages, particularly in the last five years.

Academic Contracts

Academic contracts, recruitment policies, and procedures vary across higher education institutions, particularly between public and private institutions, and between private institutions—whereas differences between public institutions are minimal. The invariance in the public sector is because the staff of public higher education institutions are members of the civil service in the country.

Faculty in the public institutions get inducted into the profession via direct entry or, indirectly, through academic staff-training schemes. In the latter, individuals with a bachelor's degree were invited to join academic-training programs with full financing to pursue doctoral-level education before joining the faculty. Direct recruitment involves postings in the mass media and on websites, followed by interviews undertaken by the university authorities. It is quite rare that candidates are required to give public seminars.

Contracts and remunerations in private institutions are determined by market forces and based on direct negotiation. In contrast, public-sector academics follow the civil service schemes, which are uniform across all public institutions. These schemes undergo changes from time to time, resulting from negotiations between the government and the civil service union. However, minor differences in hiring and entry-level salaries do occur, due to various interpretations by individual institutions of the ministry's policies.

The academic career in public institutions is permanent—with candidates needing to undergo a process of confirmation lasting from 1 to 3 years. Fixed-term contracts of 1 to 3 years only apply to retired academics and expatriates. Contracts exceeding 1 year, those for retirees exceeding the age of 65, and others for expatriates who have worked in the country for 10 consecutive years require the approval of the Ministry of Higher Education. In general, the employment of academics in private institutions is contractual, with contracts varying from 1 to 3 years, though some private institutions offer permanent positions. In some cases, the initial employment is on a contractual basis, before conversion to permanent positions. Besides contract duration, the content in terms of the expectations of the academics also differs between public and private institutions.

In public institutions, academics are expected to undertake research, teach, and provide services to the university and community. However, the specific time allocated for each of these functions may vary across institutions, between disciplines, and also among departments within faculties. Academics holding senior administrative positions focus almost entirely on their administrative duties. In the private institutions, the total teaching hours are sometimes stated explicitly in the contract. While in general teachers are expected to undertake research, the primary focus of private institutions is teaching, and the teaching load is typically double the requirement of their public counterparts. Data obtained from a Malaysian sample of 1,176 private- and public-sector academics who participated in the Changing Academic Profession study—involving 21 nations and coordinated by the University of Kassel, Germany—shows that on average about 18 hours a week are spent on teaching-related activities, 9 hours on research, and 5 hours on service when the institutions are in session. Yet, the hours for teaching reduce to about 10 hours and research increased to 14 hours when the institutions are not in session.

Academic Qualifications and Ranks

The academic hierarchy is typically made up of lecturer, senior lecturer, associate professor, and professor, although the position of assistant professor exists in one public institution. The entry-level academic position is the lecturer, for which the minimum qualification is a master's degree. The senior lecturer position is a more recent phenomenon, to allow candidates with a doctoral degree to enter the academe at a better remuneration level. Promotion from a lecturer to a senior-lecturer position is biased toward teaching ability, whereas promotion to associate professor and professor focuses more on research productivity and graduate supervision. The Changing Academic Profession study found that in 2008, 37 percent of Malaysian academics were PhD holders, with 73 percent senior-rank academics having a PhD compared to 29 percent of junior-ranked academics (Bennion and Locke 2010). At the top end of the hierarchy, it is rare for a professor not to have a doctoral degree or its equivalent.

Promotion in public institutions is based on five major criteria—namely, research and publication, teaching and supervision, academic leadership, consultancy, and services. Research productivity and academic leadership are prominent for promotion to professorship, while teaching and supervision feature more in promoting academics to senior lecturer. These domains and their associated weights vary across institutions in the public sector. The situation in the private institutions mirrors that of their public counterparts, though a small minority of private institutions do place a premium on seniority.

Academic Salaries

Salaries of academics in public and private higher education institutions are structured differently. For private institutions salaries are in gross form while in the public institutions gross salaries are made up of basic pay and allowances. The quantum and variety of allowances reflect the grade of the position in the civil service hierarchy. Fixed monthly allowances are given for housing and entertainment. Full professors enjoy additional monthly allowances, totaling MYR 2,634 (US$870), besides an annual house maintenance allowance of MYR 2,000 (US$661). For associate professors and lower, faculty enjoy a monthly cost-of-living allowance of MYR 300 (US$99). Professors performing clinician duties in medical- and health-related disciplines enjoy a monthly specialist allowance of MYR 2,400 (US$793). Moreover, a monetary incentive, called a "critical allowance," amounting to 5 percent of the basic pay, is given to associate professor academics and lower amounts in fields in short supply—including the professional disciplines of medicine, health care, pharmacy, and engineering. These allowances reflect the movement up the civil service ladder, as well as market demand for comparable expertise, and are enjoyed by all academics in the public institutions.

Table 20.1 provides the range of gross monthly salaries by rank in both the public and private institutions—excluding allowances applicable to specific disciplines, such as *critical* and *specialist* as well as allowances given on an annual basis. At the professor level, the quantum of allowances averages 43 percent of the gross amount; while at the associate professor, senior lecturer, and lecturer levels, the percentage is 21 percent, 19 percent, and 19 percent, respectively. The gaps in gross salaries between the ranks differ markedly between public and private institutions; gross salaries earned by an associate professor, senior lecturer, and lecturer are 40 percent, 37 percent, and 28 percent of the salary of a professor in the public institutions; and 70 percent, 45 percent, and 33 percent of the salary of a professor in the private institutions. The large gap between professor and associate professor contributes somewhat to movement of an academic from one institution to another. While the domains of assessment for promotion to professorship are the same across all public institutions, an academic may be found to be offered a full professorship in one institution after having failed to qualify in another. This is particularly true based on the movement from an established, research-intensive university to a newly established institution.

Differences in gross salaries also occur across disciplines. In public institutions, the basic-pay component of academics in the medical and dental disciplines is typically higher than academics in other disciplines. In addition, academics in

Table 20.1 Gross monthly salaries of academics, in 2009 (MYR)

Academic rank	Public			Private		
	Top scale	Middle scale	Bottom scale	Top scale	Middle scale	Bottom scale
Professor	24,024	15,250	11,896	19,204	16,184	12,991
Associate professor	9,448	7,920	6,842	14,146	11,424	8,396
Senior lecturer	8,629	7,252	6,173	9,778	7,173	5,195
Lecturer	7,614	5,478	4,046	7,190	5,339	3,650

Source: Government circulars obtained from the Human Resource Department of Universiti Sains Malaysia for the public higher education institutions and data from 8 private institutions, of the total of 38 private institutions in the survey.
Note: PPP US$1.00 = MYR 1.764 in 2009.

health-related disciplines, together with their counterparts in engineering, enjoy the critical allowance as well as the specialist allowance mentioned earlier. The salary ranges and variations across disciplines are determined by the ministry. In the private institutions, market forces dictate a similar scenario.

Determining the starting pay and annual increments in private institutions occurs primarily through private negotiations, as there is no union to engage in collective negotiation. In the case of public institutions, matters related to salary adjustments and bonuses are negotiated by the larger Civil Service Union at the federal level. The starting pay within the predetermined salary range for an individual joining the academe is largely determined by the institution, taking into consideration teaching experience, qualifications, and research productivity. However, for a candidate who is currently a civil servant, the last drawn salary is a major determinant.

Annual adjustments of salaries depend on the annual evaluation of perform-ance. In private institutions, evaluation is based on key performance indica-tors, typically involving teaching and research output and agreed upon by the individual and head of department at the beginning of the year. This assessment also determines the total bonuses and renewal of contracts. In the public sector, annual changes in basic pay are fixed by (a) not any increment, (b) normal incre-ment, and (c) extraordinary increment—depending on one immediate superior's as-sessment of the academic performance, on a scale of 1–100. The assessment covers teaching, research, and service activities agreed upon at the beginning of the year. Academics achieving a rating of less than 50 do not enjoy any increment, and a score of 85 or more entitles one to an extraordinary increment, while the rest receive the normal increment. Typically, no more than 2 percent of the workforce earn the extraordinary increment. Though student evaluation of teaching is conducted at the end of each semester, this is seldom considered when determining annual increments.

Salaries of academics compare favorably with the rest of the workforce. In 1999, the top 20 percent of Malaysian households have an average gross monthly income of MYR 6,268 (US$2,072), the middle 40 percent have an income of MYR 2,204 (US$728), while the bottom 40 percent have an average income of only MYR 865 (US$286) (Chakravaty and Roslan 2005). This has not improved much, as in 2007 only 4.9 percent of the 5.8 million households earned a gross monthly income exceeding MYR 10,000 (US$3,306), and only 20.7 percent exceeded MYR 5,000 (US$1,653) (Puah 2008). This supports the claim that salaries of academics in both public and private sectors enjoy a middle-class living.

After-tax salaries are notable considerations when comparing public- and private-sector salaries—as gross figures are misleading, due to the different salary structure and quantum of bonuses. Almost all the allowances (ranging from 19 percent to 46 percent of gross salaries) of public-sector academics are nontaxable income. The annual bonus given in the private sector is also structured with taxes in mind and typically ranges from three to five months of *gross* salaries, compared to one month of *basic* pay in the public sector. Factoring these considerations into the prevailing tax structure, the monthly after-tax salaries are about 91 percent to 96 percent of gross for the public-sector academics, compared to 72 percent to 86 percent for their private-sector counterparts—thus making salaries of public-sector academics more attractive than the salaries of their private-sector counterparts.

When compared to professionals in the other sectors of the economy, the salaries of academics are perceived as lower. Responses from 8 of 38 surveyed private higher education institutions estimate that the salaries of their academics are 10 to 20 percent lower than the market rate. However, the salaries of academics are better than those of most professionals in the other sectors of the economy. This trend is largely due to initiatives taken by the government over the last five years to improve salaries of academics in the public institutions. For example, if previously the salary of a full professor was limited to a specific level in the civil-service structure, it is now possible for a full professor to reach four additional (higher) levels. Also, the entry level for an academic with a doctoral degree is now at the senior lecturer's level, whereas previously it was only the lecturer level. Private higher education institutions followed suit in their attempt to attract qualified academics.

Nonsalary Fringe Benefits

An attraction of the academic profession in the public sector is the comprehensive fringe benefits provided to all civil servants, which include health care, retirement arrangements, paid vacations, and low-interest loans. Health-care benefits extend beyond retirement age and also apply to immediate family members including children younger than 18 years. Public-sector academics also enjoy 30 days (35 days for those who have served 10 years or more) of annual paid leave.

Unutilized days can be accumulated during the following year or be converted as a financial equivalent to be paid on retirement. Low-interest loans to purchase personal computers, cars, and houses are also provided to academics. Retirement programs come in the form of the employee-provident fund or the pension scheme. If the former program is chosen, it contributes 11 percent of gross salaries while the government contributes 12 percent throughout the working life and the accumulated contributions paid upon retirement. By contrast, academics choosing to be in the pension scheme enjoy a monthly stipend (amounting to 60 percent of the last-drawn basic pay) as well as a one-off gratuity payment (amounting to 7.5 percent of the last-drawn basic pay multiplied by the number of months served in the civil service). This pension is transferable to the spouse or school-attending children, upon death of the retiree.

Nonfinancial fringe benefits offered to academics in private institutions vary across all institutions. Most private institutions provide a health plan and some form of an employee-provident fund for their employees. The arrangement for the employees-provident fund is similar to that of the public-sector academics. Low-interest loans are not offered to academics. While paid leave is provided, the duration is much less in the public sector. In some private institutions, certain fringe benefits are only offered to academics of certain ranks. Apart from the benefits indicated above, there are other benefits, like travel subsidies for conferences and research grants, provided by both public and private institutions, though the quantum differs.

Supplementary Employment

Part-time employment is unusual, but it does occur. The Changing Academic Profession study indicated that only 2.43 percent of academics also work in another higher education institution, and 0.78 percent have part-time employment in business organizations. The same study also found that 68.9 percent of academics have spouses with full-time employment, and an additional 5.6 percent have a part-time job—thus reducing the need for a second employment.

Part-time academics from other public higher education institutions are usually employed to teach new programs for which the host institution does not have the expertise. This procedure usually occurs in newly established institutions, whereas part-time academics in more established public institutions are typically hired for adjunct and visiting positions that do not involve teaching. The situation is somewhat different in the private institutions, where the employment of part-time academics is a strategic consideration to enhance its efficiency in program delivery and to fill the shortage of expertise.

The Academic Performance Audit exercise, undertaken by the Malaysian Qualification Agency in 2009, indicated that the percentage of part-time academics in private institutions is about double the proportion in public institutions (11 percent to 5 percent). Also, the levels of part-time positions in the private institutions are highest for professors (18 percent) and lecturers (17 percent), compared to senior lecturers (less than 1 percent), indicating the two-prong strategy of utilizing expertise and enhancing efficiency at the lower levels.

Perceptions of Academics' Salaries and Remunerations

In general, widespread dissatisfaction still exists among academics regarding their salary and remuneration (Morris, Yaacob, and Wood 2003). Another study (IPPTN 2010) also revealed general dissatisfaction among public-institution academics with the pay and the remunerations provided, after accounting for their requisite qualification, the workload, and when compared to other professions with similar qualifications and experience. These negative perceptions are in some way contradictory to the quantitative analyses above. The situation in the private institutions is no different in the public institutions (Nair and Devi 2010; Lim 2010).

These dissatisfactions can be traced to the erosion of autonomy and the greater demand for accountability from governing authorities (Lee 2004; Hussein, Jantan, and Ansari 2002). Academics, particularly in research-intensive universities, are pressured to demonstrate enhanced research productivity, not only in terms of research publications but also in income-generating activities. This has led to more underperforming academics moving to private higher education institutions. Another study (IPPTN 2010) found that 53.2 percent of the respondents believe that each institution requires the autonomy to implement its own terms and conditions. Another concern is the rigid salary structure in the public sector, which does not allow for differentiation between institutions but is argued as being necessary if the nation is to nurture excellence in higher education (Hussein, Jantan, and Ansari 2002). Seven years on, about 60 percent of the respondents believe that academics in the research-intensive universities (the premiere universities in the public sector) should be given higher allowances together with critical allowances (IPPTN 2010).

Salaries in International Context

Relating salaries of Malaysian academics to their mobility, especially internationally, is difficult due to lack of data (IPPTN 2008). However, it was argued that Malaysian academics are generally less mobile (Tierney 2008). Using data from the Changing Academic Profession study, it has been found that 40.5 percent of academics surveyed have considered moving to another higher education institution in the country, but only 15.5 percent have taken concrete steps to do so; whereas, the similar percentages for movement to a foreign higher education institution are 25.61 percent and 6.54 percent, respectively, and percentages for moving out of education are 27.2 percent and 5.9 percent, respectively. Academic mobility among private-institution academics is higher than their public-sector counterparts (Nair and Devi 2010), as the academe is seen as a stepping stone to better-career opportunities (Jantan et al. 2006).

Even though the government has introduced programs to reduce brain drain and also initiatives to encourage Malaysians to return, no policy exists that differentiates salaries to be paid to foreign and local academics, particularly in public institutions. In fact, private institutions participating in the survey unanimously disagree with this policy of differential offerings to international scholars. However, the ministry has a provision to pay renowned scholars a monthly gross salary of MYR 60,000 (US$19,835). A recent study undertaken by the National Higher Education Research Institute (IPPTN 2010) found overwhelming support for such a differential remuneration package. It concludes that a more competitive remuneration, special incentives, tax rebates, a better health-care plan, as well as better research infrastructure are necessary to attract internationally renowned scholars to Malaysian higher education institutions.

Conclusion

The higher education sector in Malaysia has expanded rapidly over the last two decades, resulting in a shortage of suitably qualified academics to deliver the academic programs and other expectations of institutions. This shortage has been attributed to the salaries and remunerations that are perceived to be unattractive. The negative perceptions persist, largely due to the greater demand and expectations of the academic profession and the concomitant erosion of the traditional academic autonomy, in decisions related to academic activities. Greater flexibility in pay and remunerations management, particularly in the public higher education sector, is required if this shortage is to be effectively addressed, to ensure the quality of higher education.

References

Bennion, A., and W. Locke. 2010. "The early career paths and employment conditions of the academic profession in seventeen countries." *European Review* 18(1) Supplement no. 1: S7–S33.

Chakravaty, S. P., and Abdul-Hakim Roslan. 2005. "Ethnic nationalism and income distribution in Malaysia." *European Journal of Development Research* 17 (2): 270–88.

Hussein, S. A., M. Jantan, and M. A. Ansari. 2002. *Enhancing proportion of faculty with PhD in public universities*. Unpublished report submitted to the Ministry of Education.

IPPTN (National Higher Education Research Institute). 2008. "The global university model (part 5): How should Malaysia approach world class status." *IPPTN Global Updates 37* (August 15): 1–2.

IPPTN (National Higher Education Research Institute). 2010. *Memperkasa Institut Pengajian Tinggi dan Memartabatkan Ahli Akademik (Akademia)*. Unpublished report submitted to the Ministry of Higher Education.

Jantan, M., H. C. Chan, S. Shahnon, and S. Sibly, eds. 2006. *Enhancing the quality of faculty in private higher education in Malaysia*. Penang; IPPTN, Universiti Sains Malaysia.

Jantan, M., and M. Sirat. 2008. "Governance and decision making related to academic activities." In *The changing academic profession in international comparative and quantitative perspectives*. RIHE International Seminar Reports. Hiroshima, Japan: Hiroshima University.

Lee, M. N. N. 2004. "Global trends, national policies and institutional responses: Restructuring higher education in Malaysia." *Educational Research Policy and Practice* 3: 31–46.

Lim, B. T. 2010. "Nilai responses to PSPTN." In *Strategic roadmap for private higher education in Malaysia*. Unpublished report to the Ministry of Higher Education. IPPTN, Universiti Sains Malaysia.

Ministry of Higher Education. 2009. *Perangkaan Pengajian Tinggi Malaysia 2008*. Putrajaya, Malaysia: Ministry of Higher Education.

Morris, D., A. Yaacob, and G. Wood. 2003. "Attitudes towards pay and promotion in the Malaysian higher education sector." *Employee Relations* 26 (2): 137–50.

Nair, V., and B. Devi. 2010. "Human resources confrontation in private higher education: Challenges to become a full-fledged university." In *Strategic roadmap for private higher education in Malaysia*. Unpublished report to the Ministry of Higher Education. IPPTN, Universiti Sains Malaysia.

Puah, P. 2008. "Half of Malaysian households earn below RM 3,000 a month." *The Edge* (July 10).

Tierney, W. G. 2008. "The shifting boundaries of the academic profession: The Malaysian professoriate in comparative perspective." *Kemanusiaan* 15: 1–12.

21

MEXICAN FACULTY SALARIES TODAY

Once a Bagger, Always a Beggar?

Alma Maldonado-Maldonado

Mexican higher education may currently possess one of the most complex and stratified salary systems in the world. Since the first merit-pay and peer-review programs were established, in the mid-1980s, and especially from the early 1990s, no single faculty in the country earns the base salary established in his or her contract. Most faculty receive additional income—thanks to the existence of different merit-pay and peer-review programs at the institutional, state, or national level. Yet, these programs have created some collateral damage for the Mexican higher education system. Understanding this multifaceted context, this chapter faces several challenges in order to provide an accurate overview and analysis of salaries, remuneration, and contracts in Mexico.

Overview of the System

During recent decades, Mexican higher education has become larger, more diversified, and complex. According to the Ministry of Education (Secretaría de Educación Pública), the main source of all the national education information in 2009, the country had a total of 2,809 higher education institutions—905 public and 1,904 private (Ministry of Education 2010). The same year, 3,107,713 students were enrolled—3.4 percent in technical education programs (two-year programs), 89.1 percent in undergraduate programs (four years, or more), and about 7.5 percent in graduate education (master's degrees and PhDs). In terms of faculty members, the total number in 2009 was 300,251. The majority of faculty are hired on an hourly basis—86.7 percent at private institutions and 54.9 percent at public institutions. Full-time faculty at private institutions represent only 7.7 percent of the total, but at public institutions they represent 36.7 percent.

Among higher education institutions, the private ones have grown rapidly. In the past 13 years, 1,243 new private higher education institutions and 512 new public institutions were created, with a combined system growth rate of about 81 percent (Ministry of Education 2010). However, the distribution of enrollment between public and private higher education, in the same period, was 68 percent at public institutions and 32 percent at privates. So the largest number of students continues to attend public institutions in Mexico. The number of faculty members at private institutions increased by 116 percent, almost the same expansion as student enrollment. Faculty at public institutions grew by only 44 percent, about 20 percent less than the student-enrollment growth rate, implying an increased student/faculty ratio at public institutions.

From 2000 to 2003, 23.3 faculty positions were created nationally per day (Grediaga et al. 2004). This increase is indicative of the intensity of higher education development in Mexico. Naturally, this accelerated growth has created other issues related to improvisation, lack of experience, and professionalization (Gil-Antón 2002). Additionally, faculty are becoming older. According to two national surveys conducted in 1992 and 2007, the overall mean age of Mexican faculty increased by approximately nine years (Galaz-Fontes et al. 2009, 201). These situations have affected the salary situation of Mexican faculty.

Mexican Academic Salaries

There are at least eight subsystems in Mexican higher education institutions: public universities, private institutions, technological institutes (four-year institutions), polytechnic universities, technological universities (two-year institutions), teacher-training colleges (public and private), intercultural universities, and other public institutions (i.e., military schools). Indeed, the diversity and stratification of the Mexican higher education impacts faculty in terms of their salary, workload, benefits, types of contracts, and prestige. In addition to having a very stratified academic system, an extreme division consists between full-time and part-time faculty, with the latter having less stability, lower salaries, fewer benefits, and worse working conditions (Rondero López 2002, 216–17).

Analyzing faculty salaries within Mexico is difficult enough and not easily compared to salaries in other countries (Rumbley, Pacheco, and Altbach 2008). A major problem has involved obtaining information from private institutions. Information for this study was solicited from 50 institutions belonging to the most important association of private higher education institutions—Federation of Mexican Private Higher Education Institutions (Federación de Instituciones Mexicanas Particulares de Educación Superior); only 15 institutions answered, under the promise of anonymity. This custom created another layer of challenge when trying to make comparisons among private institutions as well as between the public and private sectors. One conclusion, though, is the immense range of salaries. The lowest monthly base salary in public institutions is US$356, while

Table 21.1 Average salaries in public and private universities (US$)

	Public institutions				Private institutions
Types of institution	Universities and research centers	Polytechnic universities	Technological institutes	Inter-cultural universities	
No. of institutions	47	17	14	5	15
Faculty categories	Salaries (US$)	Salaries (US$)	Salaries (US$)	Salaries (US$)	Salaries (US$)
Level 1 (top)	1,582	1,425	1,355	1,777	2,057
Level 2	1,399	1,306	1,258	1,716	2,218
Level 3	1,241	1,003	1,016	1,528	1,557
Level 4	1,112		923	1,537	1,152
Level 5	968		816	1,384	987
Level 6	887		740	1,225	

Source: Constructed by author, based on the salaries collected for this project. In the cases of polytechnic universities and private institutions, only three and five levels were possible to fulfill.

the highest is US$2,313—a difference of US$1,961. For private universities, the disparities are even larger—with the lowest salary at US$391 and the highest at US$4,008, a gap of US$3,617.

Another challenge is generalizing about private and public higher education institutions. Actually, public institutions include only 47 public universities and research centers, even though data on other types of institutions were also collected (see Table 21.1). Data included from private institutions reflect only those that replied on time.

All faculty at public universities and research centers participate in some type of merit pay/peer review programs. A major difference exists between the base salary and the "real salary," which includes the money received from these programs. So, the salaries included in the general tables do not reflect the total earnings received by faculty at these institutions. A salary that starts at US$356 monthly, which is also the current salary of a McDonald's or Wal-Mart employee or a lower-level secretary, is not actually the final salary received by a full-time faculty member. To calculate the real salary, anywhere from 15 percent to 75 percent additional wages would need to be added to the base salary—resulting from the merit-pay and peer-review programs. It is still shocking how low faculty-base salaries are at public institutions. However, the highest salary is US$2,313, although it does not form the "actual salary"—because faculty members earning this amount receive much more. Still, a base salary of US$2,313 is an adequate salary in Mexico, similar to what the district manager of a bank or a high-level accountant or administrator earns.

The main difference between public and private university salaries is that most private salaries presented in Table 21.1 are "actual salaries." Few private universities have special bonuses that would result in a drastic modification in these tables. Also, of all the private universities listed in 2009 (about 1,900 institutions), a large percentage of them are not able to hire full-time faculty. From the universities that responded to the survey, at least three institutions do not hire full-time faculty. These 15 institutions could be classified in four tiers; the first includes two prestigious national universities and one regional. The second tier numbers three regional universities with important prestige (although not at the top). The third tier contains one national demand–absorbing university and two regional demand-absorbing ones (one in and one outside the Mexico City metropolitan area). At the final tier, there are two lower-prestige universities located in Mexico City and three outside the city. Salaries from the first two groups increase the average for all private institutions. The lowest salary is US$385 monthly, close to the lowest at public institutions, but the highest is reported as US$4,008, which corresponds to the salary earned by a general manager of a national or international firm or even by a chief executive officer. The remaining question is: how many full-time faculty members were reported with access to the top salaries? The percentage is likely to be limited.

Finding information about public institutions is also problematic, despite the intention of laws demanding more transparency; there are several public universities that come up short on this obligation. Therefore, it is difficult to draw conclusions based on available numbers, especially in the case of intercultural universities, because the only five institutions that submitted information presented the highest salaries among these modalities.

Another basic problem is that polytechnic universities and intercultural universities do not have merit-pay or peer-review programs; so, most of the base salaries must be perceived as "actual salaries." Actually, technological institutions, which constitute the third-largest subsystem of higher education institutions in Mexico, present the lowest salaries in comparison to the other institution types. However, they do have merit pay/peer review programs, so this may be why they report lower-basic salaries than the other two.

Merit Pay/Peer Review Programs

Each institution defines its salary policies in general; however, state regulations involve "budget assignment and minimum wage," which affect both private and public institutions (Rondero López 2002, 211). Whenever an increase to the minimum wage is under way, which is normally a very small amount, the rest of the salaries in the country receive a corresponding increase.

As mentioned, most Mexican faculty members who participated in these merit-pay and peer-review programs received at least 50 percent of additional salary from them (federal or institutional) (Ibarrola 2005; Ordorika 2004; Galaz-Fontes, De la Cruz Santana, and Garcia 2009). The most prestigious of these programs is the National System of Researchers (Sistema Nacional de Investigadores). It was created in 1984 in response to the terrible economic situation of faculty and to mediate the brain drain, resulting from faculty going abroad or leaving public institutions for private ones. Within this program the productivity of scholars is evaluated periodically, and faculty receive an extra salary monthly.

One of the problems with the National System of Researchers is that only 4.7 percent of all Mexican faculty and 19 percent of full-time faculty belong to it. Among the system's scholars, only 7.9 percent belong to the highest-ranking level, making it the smallest group of members.

Describing the other merit-pay programs is a quite difficult task, given the diversity of programs; however, most of these programs follow the National System of Research mechanisms. The difference among merit-pay programs affects the level of sophistication in the evaluation of every single activity. Some programs may take into account mostly publications, among them the international ones; whereas others may consider further activities, such as administrative activities or teaching performances.

Many experts have studied the impact of merit-pay and peer-review programs in Mexico. Most of them agree concerning the negative impact of these programs, including that faculty do not consider retirement as a possibility, since they depend on external- or internal-merit-pay programs, which are not part of retirement income (Díaz Barriga 1997; Padilla González 2010; Pallán Figueroa 1994; Gil-Antón 2002).

Benefits

A faculty member in Mexico is hired into one of two categories. First, one can be hired as a wage earner or employee, which allows workers to obtain all the labor rights established in the Mexican Constitution. These labor rights cover social security, participation in a public federal mortgage credit system, participation in the public retirement fund program, eligibility for a Christmas bonus (at least 15 days of paid leave, called *aguinaldo*), vacations, and a respective bonus of 25 percent yearly. The second option is to be hired through "professional services," which is a type of private contract, similar to what is used when outsourcing services. Under this modality, institutions do not need to provide the labor rights because they are not retaining any tax (the individual has to pay them separately to the state). All faculty at public institutions are hired as wage earners, as well as at most private institutions. Of the 15 private universities that shared salary information for this study, only two report hiring full-time faculty through professional services.

Most faculty members at public institutions receive the benefits established by law, and differences in salary actually relate to the type of public institution. At public institutions, additional benefits are offered—such as coupons for pantry staples, a special bonus for Teacher's Day, help for child care, and funeral expenses. Professors also have the right to obtain a sabbatical semester or year (depending on seniority). The more prestigious the institution is, the better the benefits. For instance, faculty members can receive private health insurance, given the bad conditions of the public system; may have the support of research assistants; have a more flexible workload and less teaching; receive more days for the Christmas bonus (40 days); get more days of vacation bonus; and, in a research center, have the right to obtain 8,100 pesos (US$616) to buy books. A spacious, private office is also often a benefit of working at a research center.

Faculty members at the 13 private universities (of the 15 that answered the questions sent) that hire under the wage-earner system do receive the benefits prescribed by law. As with public institutions, the range of benefits is quite diverse and varied. The size and prestige of an institution matter a lot, with most demand-absorbing universities offering only those benefits required by law. Private institutions participating in this study offer a wide variety of benefits that include receiving two hard-cider bottles and a frozen turkey at Christmas; a celebratory breakfast for Teacher's Day; assistance with funeral services; life insurance; private health insurance; a marriage bonus (for a first marriage); a sabbatical semester (similar terms of the public institutions); or housing help. Benefits at private institutions are as stratified as the institutions themselves.

A more important characteristic, however, is that private institutions do not serve plans similar to the merit-pay/peer-review programs that exist at public institutions, and only five private institutions reported having something similar. One institution uses a point system in which faculty progress annually. Two institutions utilize an evaluation system that is more like faculty classification, and salaries depend on the position where someone is categorized. Among the remaining two institutions, one has a merit-pay system, but it only applies to hourly faculty, and the other has a similar system (more like a productivity system) that offers only a further, exceedingly small addition to the monthly salary. Only one of these institutions reported the percentage of full-time faculty who participate in these programs, which involves only 6.8 percent. This proportion is definitely lower than the average for public institutions. It is significant to mention that faculty at private institutions are able to participate in the National System of Researchers. However, family members' corresponding extra earnings are not provided directly from public funds but from their private universities, which have established that agreement with the National Council of Science and Technology (CONACYT). Still, these faculty receive the extra salary and the recognition as members of the National System of Researchers.

Faculty Contracts

The main differences among types of contracts include a professor's rank and type of institutions. In most autonomous public universities, faculty contracts are tied to the individual's rank, and every time a faculty member is promoted to another rank, a new contract is signed. The academic career system in Mexico constitutes a complex progression of ranks. Institutions may have six, seven, eight, or more levels, and normally it is not possible to skip levels in the progression through the ranks.

Another serious element to consider, regarding faculty contracts, is tenure *(definitividad)*. The tenure system in Mexico has its own particularities. In Mexican tenure, seniority tends to carry more weight than other criteria—such as, demonstrating abilities and improvements in research and teaching or evaluating of the overall academic production and achievements during a particular period of time. Another diversity of tenure systems in other countries is that, in Mexico, definitividad is not exclusive to full-time professors at public institutions. An hourly professor may achieve definitividad in a single course, which means this faculty member has the right to teach it as long as it is offered at the institution. Part-time faculty are also able to compete to obtain tenure. Finally, with few exceptions, nothing like tenure is available for the majority of faculty who work at the private sector in Mexico.

The diversity among Mexican higher education institutions creates a misconception about faculty contracts and their legal terms. Private higher education institutions may form a homogeneous sector, since most of them do not use any tenure system, and many private universities exercise nine-month contracts to avoid any commitment to their faculty in terms of labor rights.

Conclusion

Among other urgent challenges for Mexican higher education institutions is access for the expanding college-age population in the country. The second issue is to modify and transform evaluation mechanisms to improve the system instead of serving as additional salary providers. The government needs to create more institutional equity, given the tremendous institutional stratification, and to establish programs that not only distribute benefits among the already privileged. Furthermore, a more precise and efficient coordination is needed among institutions and subsystems, with more attention paid to the role of cross-border higher education and the role Mexican higher education plays in current internationalization processes (Maldonado-Maldonado 2006).

The most urgent challenge related to higher education faculty constitutes improving salaries and working conditions, gender equity, decreasing faculty dependence on the merit-pay and peer-review programs for total earnings, and establishing a dignified retirement process. Indeed, the dramatic reduction of Mexican faculty salaries has been documented by many scholars (Díaz Barriga 1997; Gil-Antón 1994; Ibarrola 1992; Ordorika 2004). Faculty salaries at the National Autonomous University of Mexico, one of the most representative universities in the country, were reduced in real terms by about 70 percent from 1976 to 1991 (Ordorika 2004). A slight recovery occurred from 1991 to 2003, with an increase of 6.2 percent, but the loss in purchasing power of these professionals over four decades has been stunning. It has also been estimated that, in 1987, income for full-time faculty reached the lowest point; in real terms (constant pesos), it was 35.4 percent of what they earned in 1981 in the same category, and 33.9 percent for the lowest categories. In 1991, salaries had recovered to only 46 percent of their value from 1981 (Ibarrola 1992).

To understand the current salary situation requires acknowledging the crisis of the past. Peaceful demonstrations drew public attention to the depth of the crisis nearly two decades ago. In one case, a group of National Autonomous University of Mexico professors, not children or teens, waited on a curb for a red traffic light to stop cars in front of them. A group of photographers also waited. When the cars stopped, the adults began cleaning windshields and accepted coins from the drivers, while the photographers snapped pictures. In a separate demonstration adults bagged groceries at a supermarket. In Mexico, children often do this in exchange for coins. Some of the adult baggers wore signs hanging from their necks; there were cameras flashing around this group, too. These two demonstrations took place in 1993 as part of a series of protests organized by National Autonomous University of Mexico professors. These events were staged to demonstrate just how low their salaries were. Protests over the working conditions and salaries of faculty were common during that period, but some professors found more dramatic ways to make their case to a broader public by conveying that even cleaning car windows or bagging groceries would yield supplemental income, in relation to their low salaries.

It is stimulating that, since 1993, faculty at public institutions have not organized additional protests against salary conditions. This is partly explained by the impact of merit-pay and peer-review programs in Mexico. In the case of private institutions, protests are rare, while they do have concerns about salaries or working conditions. However, the basic problems remain unresolved for faculty in both public and private sectors, and questions remain as to what extent the merit-pay and peer-review programs solved the salary problem and how sustainable the system will be for the long term. Faculty at public institutions have progressed from the need to bag groceries at supermarkets to collecting points for their curricula vitae to obtain extra salary, but there must be a better way to establish more dignified working conditions and salary. Publish or perish—plus getting an administrative position or performing activities valued by the merit-pay and peer-review programs—seem to be the current mechanism for survival. Meanwhile, expecting base salaries to be increased seems just a dream, at least for now.

References

Díaz Barriga, Angel. 1997. "Los programas de evaluación (estímulos) en la comunidad de investigadores: Un estudio en la UNAM." In *Universitarios: Institucionalización académica y evaluación,* A. Díaz Barriga and Teresa Pacheco. Mexico City: Centro de Estudios Superiores Universitarios.

Galaz-Fontes, Jesús, A. L. De la Cruz Santana, and R. Rodriguez Garcia. 2009. *El académico mexicano miembro del Sistema nacional de Investigación: Una primera exploración con base en los resultados de la encuesta la reconfiguración de la profesión académica en México.* Conference

Proceeding of the Seminario Internacional "El futuro de la profesión académica: Retos para los países emergentes." Buenos Aires, Argentina.

Galaz-Fontes, Jesús, Manuel Gil-Antón, Laura E. Padilla-González, Juan J. Sevilla-García, José L. Arcos-Vega, and Jorge G. Martínez-Stack. 2009. "The academic profession in Mexico: Changes, continuities and challenges derived from a comparison of two national surveys 15 years apart." *RIHE* (Research Institute for Higher Education, Hiroshima University) *International Seminar Reports* no. 13.

Gil-Antón, Manuel. 1994. *Los rasgos de la diversidad: Un estudio sobre los académicos mexicanos.* Mexico City: Universidad Autónoma Metropolitana-Azcapotzalco.

Gil-Antón, Manuel. 2002. "Big city love: The academic workplace in Mexico." In *The decline of the guru: The academic profession in developing and middle-income countries,* ed. Philip, G. Altbach. Chestnut Hill, MA: Center for International Higher Education, Boston College.

Grediaga Kuri, Rocío, Rodríguez Jiménez, José Raúl, Padilla González, and Laura Elena. 2004. *Políticas públicas y cambios en la profesión académica en México en la última década.* Mexico City: ANUIES-UAM (Asociación Nacional de Universidadese Instituciones de Educación Superior-Universidad Autónoma Metropolitana).

Ibarrola, María de. 1992. "Sistemas nacionales de incentivos al investigador: México: la experiencia de homologar y deshomologar las remuneraciones al trabajo académico." *Interciencia* 17 (6): 344–47.

Ibarrola, María de. 2005. *El Sistema Nacional de Investigadores a 20 años de su creación: Texto discutido en la mesa de diálogo sobre Políticas de deshomologación salarial y carrera académica en México del Segundo Encuentro de Auto-estudio de las Universidades públicas mexicanas.* Mexico City: CIICH-CESU-UNAM.

Maldonado-Maldonado, Alma. 2006. "Presidential politics and higher education reforms in Mexico." *International Higher Education* 45 (Fall): 3–4.

Ministry of Education (Secretaría de Educación Pública). 2010. *Base 911.* Mexico City: Secretaría de Educación Pública.

Ordorika, Imanol. 2004. "El mercado en la academia." In *La academia en jaque. Perspectivas políticas sobre la evaluación de la educación superior en México,* ed. Imanol Ordorika. Mexico City: CRIM-Miguel Ángel Porrúa.

Padilla González, Laura. 2010. *El académico mexicano miembro del Sistema Nacional de Investigadores: Su contexto institucional, uso del tiempo, productividad académica, e implicaciones salariales.* Conference Proceedings at the I Congreso de los Miembros del Sistema Nacional de Investigadores, Queretaro City, May 5–8.

Pallán Figueroa, Carlos. 1994. "Los procesos de evaluación y acreditación de las instituciones de educación superior en México en los últimos años." *Revista de la Educación Superior* 23, no. 3 (91): 7–40.

Rondero López, Norma. 2002. "El mercado académico en México: Reflexiones desde la sociología del trabajo." *Sociológica* 17 (49): 205–29.

Rumbley, Laura E., Iván F. Pacheco, and Philip G. Altbach. 2008. *International comparison of academic salaries: An exploratory study.* Chestnut Hill, MA: Center for International Higher Education, Boston College.

22

INTRODUCING MARKET FORCES IN ACADEMIC REMUNERATION

The Case of the Netherlands

Ben Jongbloed

With central government stepping back, academic institutions in the Netherlands have gained more room to negotiate salaries and working conditions for their staff. While there is still broad uniformity in terms of job classifications and sector-wide labor agreements for academia, a trend is also underway toward a more market-oriented and individualized appraisal and reward system.

Overview of the Dutch Higher Education System

In line with the general trend toward decentralization and steering from a distance, academic salaries and other terms of employment in the higher education system are nowadays settled in negotiations between academic institutions and labor unions representing academics. Since 1999, terms and conditions of employment are laid down in broad, system-wide collective labor agreements about academic salaries and job profiles. Therefore, academic institutions are mainly delegated to maintain the attractiveness of the academic workplace and ensuring academic productivity.

The higher education sector in the Netherlands can be broadly divided into two distinct domains: (a) The publicly funded sector, including 14 research universities and 40 universities of applied sciences; (b) the privately funded sector, consisting of 5 private universities (including a business school and 3 theological universities) and about 60 professional education institutions.

Research universities have about 220,000 students and about 23,400 academics. Their mission is teaching and academic research. Universities of applied sciences (382,000 students, 26,400 academics) are preparing students for specific professions and award, mostly, bachelor's degrees. Private higher education providers do not receive any government funding. Their programs are primarily in professional fields such as accountancy, business administration, and so forth. Data on private institutions are sketchy and largely unavailable. Student numbers are estimated at 60,000.

The research universities and the universities of applied sciences are governed by the same law, the Higher Education and Research Act of 1993. The act also governs personnel matters. All publicly funded research universities are members of the Association of Universities in the Netherlands. The universities of applied sciences are represented by the Netherlands Association of Universities of Applied Sciences.

The academic profession in the Netherlands is still seen as providing a decent existence, although the relative rewards and other working conditions have deteriorated compared to jobs in the private sector. Academics increasingly are hired on a temporary basis and may have to switch employment if their contracts end—with some leaving for a private-sector job. For the coming years, a substantial outflow of senior staff is predicted, given the age composition of academics. Age-conscious, human-resources policies are, thus, called for to ensure that staff are fully productive. Such policies include encouraging 60-plus age groups to remain in their jobs, while offering opportunities to all staff to get promotion or advance into other positions, by creating enhanced skills and competencies.

Academic Contracts

For tenure-stream faculty in research universities, the career ladder starts from the position of lecturer (*universitair docent,* comparable to "assistant professor"), with possible advancement to senior lecturer (*universitair hoofddocent,* equivalent to "associate professor") and, ultimately, the professor (*hoogleraar*). Academics in these ranks have both teaching and research duties, but it is left to individual universities and departments to determine how the different job tasks are to be assigned. In addition to these basic ranks, some (mostly nontenured) positions exist, such as research trainee (or PhD candidate, *assistent in opleiding*), postdoc, research and teaching associate, instructor, and others. Salaries increase by rank and seniority and are based on an assessment of merit, through an annual review of performance.

In the universities of applied sciences, the career ladder runs from instructor, to lecturer, and to lector. Here, the rank of professor does not exist. Positions are mostly teaching only. A lecturer has more responsibilities than an instructor, such as for developing courses and instructional material. The *lector* is a relatively new position, with a job profile that includes practice-oriented research and is the head of a so-called knowledge circle, where lecturers seek interaction with industry and professional networks. This may eventually bring in some additional (private and public) revenues. The number of lectors has increased quite substantially in recent years, introduced as part of a policy aiming at a professionalization of the staff in universities of applied sciences and improving their career perspectives.

Academic personnel are normally hired using a standard practice: the vacant position is advertised in newspapers, journals, or websites. A selection committee invites candidates based on a motivation letter, carries out interviews, and determines which candidate is preferred. The ultimate decision normally lies with the chair holder of the organizational unit. In the case of a full professor, procedures are slightly more elaborate, since other universities need to be consulted about appointments.

Universities have subscribed to a recruitment code, drawn up by the sector itself in 1979 (NVP 2006). The code offers some protection to an applicant during the course of the recruitment process. It ensures that an applicant has a fair chance at appointment (equal opportunity for equal ability), confidentiality is respected, and time limits are observed.

The universities and universities of applied sciences stick to a collective labor agreement (VSNU 2008; HBO-raad 2007). This agreement regulates the terms and conditions of staff in their workplace, their duties, and the duties of the employer. This arrangement is the result of a collective bargaining process between employers' organizations and the trade unions representing academic personnel. The agreement is deemed to be legally binding for the whole sector (universities and, respectively, universities of applied sciences). It sets out wage scales (see Table 22.1), working hours, training, health and safety, overtime, grievance mechanisms, and rights to participate in workplace or company affairs. In practice, the collective labor agreements for the universities and the universities of applied sciences do not differ substantially. The process toward a new agreement forms a fine tuning between the sectors. In order to stay competitive, private institutions normally do not deviate too much from the collective labor agreement.

The collective labor agreement applies to the contracts offered to academics for a determinate or an indeterminate period, depending on the job. For members of the academic/scientific staff, a temporary contract can be for a period up to a maximum of six years. This includes a maximum of two extensions of the contract. If academics are employed for an indeterminate period of time, such a position usually begins with a probationary period (usually two months). Doctoral candidates are offered a temporary employment contract for the expected duration of the doctoral candidate's PhD research (normally four years). After being awarded a PhD, some doctoral candidates continue in a postdoc position, while others may find a temporary or permanent position, either at their own university or somewhere else. *Doctoral candidate* is a distinct academic position that provides advanced research training through university research and, to a limited extent (less than 25 percent of working time), in teaching. Some universities have started to recruit PhD candidates as bursary students, providing them with a stipend and not a salary.

In publicly funded institutions, the legal status of staff constitutes civil servant. Debates have taken place to replace this standing by employment contracts under private law, but so far the civil-service status continues. Salary depends on the *job profile* and *job level* of the job-ranking system in the university or universities of applied sciences. A job profile comprises four components. First, relating to *job title,* it is noted that jobs are classified by content (i.e., objectives and result areas) and not solely by the title. Second, the *objective* of a job is a description of the aim of the post and is also the primary factor for deciding which job profile best suits a position. Third, the *context* of the job specifies the person who supervises the position and/or the person to whom the jobholder is responsible. Fourth, the *result areas* for a job comprise the associated activities that are geared toward the achievement of a specific result. For each jobholder, a decision is made on which result areas apply to the position.

A result area defines the core activity to be performed. However, the activity does not translate into concrete and measurable work agreements, as this can differ depending on a jobholder. Consequently, an academic's superior colleague needs to make concrete agreements with each new hire, on expected results. For example, if the option is published work (for education and research jobs), the employed academic is expected to meet the need for both the quantity and quality of publications, as well as the periodicals in which the articles are to appear. If the result area involves policy advising, it deals with policy recommendations and quality criteria to be met. In annual appraisal talks, the staff performance is evaluated, and continued poor performance eventually may lead to an academic being fired.

Higher education institutions have the autonomy to decide how many and which types of academic posts they wish to achieve. They are free to choose the individuals for these positions. Because they can negotiate the exact contents of the job profile with their academics, this freedom is used to attract teaching and research staff and prevent well-performing academic staff from leaving the institution. This constitutes a fair degree of competition for faculty. Apart from salaries, job-related aspects like working environment, laboratory facilities, composition of the research (or teaching) group, and mix of teaching and research tasks play a role here. Promotion—such as to the position of professor—is earned through applying for the job, usually in an open competition where the candidate's past performance plays a decisive role.

Academic Salaries

Publicly funded universities and universities of applied sciences negotiate collectively with trade unions about pay, salary increases, and conditions of service for their personnel, without any government involvement. There are separate bargaining rounds for universities and universities of applied sciences. Different universities, thus, will conform to the salary structure and pay raises that were agreed collectively. Collective labor agreements are normally valid for a period of a few years. There are 18 general salary grades (pay scales), plus a small number of job-specific salary scales (for doctoral candidates and professors). The salary tables include about 10 increments from the bottom to the top of the scale. As in most European countries, an overlap exists between the various salary scales; among other issues, the maximum wage for an assistant professor is higher than the minimum wage for an associate professor. The overlap between the scales allows employers some room for using the increments to reward differences in seniority and performance. Being promoted to a higher scale normally requires a formal procedure beyond the annual appraisal talks.

Salary differences occur between the university and universities of applied sciences because each sector has its own collective labor agreement that employs a labor market allowance instrument for responding to economic trends (for the recruitment and retention of employees with scarce and indispensable expertise). The decision to award a labor market allowance is made on a strictly individual basis for a temporary period of time. Overall, the salaries for professors are similar across disciplines. Some academics may receive a single allowance on top of their salary, as a reward for high productivity or if they have been deputizing (i.e., taking on the duties and responsibilities of an absent colleague).

Focused on labor-market problems, a ministerial working group (Van Rijn 2001) concluded that remuneration in the higher education sector is below the comparable positions in the private sector. However, one also needs to examine secondary benefits—employee benefits, such as arrangements for health insurance, disability income protection, retirement benefits, sick leave, vacation, and social security. Overall, these options are generally regarded as quite attractive to employees (see next section).

In terms of the determinants of faculty salaries, the job profile is crucial. Pursuant to the collective labor agreement, the job levels are linked to the agreed-salary structure. For individual academics, variations in salaries mostly relate to salary scales that apply to the ranks. In the university sector, an associate professor would have a salary based on salary grades 13 or 14. An assistant professor (or lecturer) is

Table 22.1 Median monthly salary of academic staff in 2008 (in euro)*

	UAS**	University
Professor	n.a.***	5,983
Lector	5,864	n.a.
Senior lecturer (associate professor; university)	n.a.	4,939
Lecturer (assistant professor; university)	n.a.	4,011
Lecturer (UAS)**	4,123	n.a.
Instructor (UAS)**	2,888	n.a.
Doctoral candidate (university)	n.a.	2,386

Source: VSNU 2008; HBO-raad 2007.

Notes: In 2008, US$1.00 = about EUR 0.68 (based on the European Central Bank).
*On average, the percentage of salary paid as taxes is 39 percent.
**UAS = universities of applied sciences.
***n.a. = not applicable.

placed in grades 11 or 12, while most temporary (and entry-level) positions (e.g., instructors and doctoral candidates) are in grade 10. The pay scales for full professors are equivalent to grades 16 to 18. For the universities of applied sciences, the grades for instructors are 8 to 10; lecturers are in 11 to 14; and lectors in 15 to 16. Table 22.1 shows the median gross monthly salaries of academics.

Nonsalary Benefits

Apart from salary, the compensation of academics includes bonuses, fringe benefits (both collective and individual), and nonsalary job characteristics. These are important elements to determine the attractiveness of academic jobs. For instance, part of the salary is paid by means of an end-of-year bonus in December (amounting to some 6 percent of annual salary, with a minimum of EUR 1,600 or US$2,350) and a holiday bonus (of about 8 percent of the annual salary) in May. Fringe benefits also exist in the shape of employer's pension contributions and schemes for parental leave. Most fringe benefits are uniform across all Dutch institutions and stipulated in the collective labor agreement.

Academics who lose their jobs are eligible for a state-unemployment benefit. In a case of an employee's illness or incapacity, social security regulations apply, ensuring the (temporary) continuation of pay during illness. Academics need to take out (obligatory) health insurance. All universities offer a collective insurance agreement, with a selected health insurance company. The employer will ensure a pension for its employees with the state pension fund. Pension-contribution premiums are shared between employer and employee.

To encourage academics to further develop their talents during each phase of their career, the collective labor agreement is allowing every employee a personal development budget. Such funds may also be used to prepare the employee for another job. For example, universities of applied sciences employees may be offered the opportunity to participate in exchange programs with businesses or enroll in a PhD track to enhance their career. For personnel development plans, each university has set aside a small percentage (1.4 percent) of its total payroll. The extent to which academics make use of personal development opportunities differs among individuals.

Thanks to an employment-conditions selection model, employees are allowed to determine part of their package of employment conditions, according to their own wishes and requirements. This model is a type of exchange system, in which sources (i.e., leave days, end-of-year bonus, and holiday allowances) can be exchanged for other employment conditions—the targets (i.e., reimbursement of travel expenses; extra pension, income, and leave; bicycle purchase; and trade-union contribution). It is also possible to save for a longer period of consecutive leave (a long-term savings model). The trend toward individual and flexible employment conditions is continuing. Such *schemes à la carte* are meant to help make working conditions in academia more attractive (de Weert 2004).

Supplementary Employment

An increasing number of academics have a part-time job. On average, for every full-time equivalent, 1.17 persons are employed. Holders of a part-time job are allowed to work in another university, but it is not quite common for academics to carry out this practice. If academics do serve more than one position, they most likely hold multiple job contracts.

Many lectors in the universities of applied sciences also serve a position in a research university, since these staff normally do not have full-time jobs. Also, the job profile involves a substantial degree of research activity. Multiple appointments are also more frequent in university hospitals and between universities and specialized government research institutes.

A higher number of academics in private institutions perform a second job, next to their academic position. However, it is quite rare for an academic to teach in both a public and a private institution.

In case academics hold multiple jobs or serve paid work outside their academic office hours, they are obliged to notify the organization and seek approval from the university. Normally, approval will be given, unless important institutional interests are at stake. In their *academic* office hours these workers are not allowed to claim or request reimbursements, remuneration, or donations from third parties, unless the employer grants permission. Such working conditions are not very common, however.

Dutch universities today are increasingly engaged in research commercialization and encouraged to do so by public authorities. Income from contract work has increased rapidly. For example, a rapid increase of *endowed professors* is funded by foundations and private organizations. Such positions are mostly temporary (not "structural") and on a part-time basis (mostly one day a week). Endowed chairs are inaugurated at the instigation of an external body and mostly cover specialized fields. In 2007, almost a quarter of all 5,481 chairs were directly or indirectly sponsored by external sources. To reduce concerns about excessive influence of the business sector on academic research, universities have subscribed a Code of Conduct for Scientific Practice to safeguard academic integrity.

Qualifications

The academic hierarchy, as described earlier, is the same in public and private universities. In teaching-only private institutions, the academic jobs are less differentiated. Both the university and the universities of applied sciences saw a complete restructuring of their classification, with functions converted into a new job-ranking system. In research universities, the system of University Job Classification took effect on April 1, 2003. The system is based on the so-called Hay method—developed by the HayGroup (a global management consulting firm)—and classifies academic jobs, not just on the basis of the tasks connected to the job profile but also on the job's result areas. Institutions in the universities of applied sciences sector can choose whether they utilize the HayGroup method or a system of job rating that awards scores to a number of criteria to arrive at the "weight" (salary) of each job type.

Depending on the position, the minimum degree required to enter a particular level in the job hierarchy differs. Job openings for doctoral candidates require a master's degree. A lecturer (or assistant professor) in a research university would need at least a master's degree. Yet, increasingly, a doctorate is required. Professors (chair holders) are required to have a PhD. More importantly, a good international (research) reputation, a large academic network, and good management skills are required.

In the universities of applied sciences, a lecturer rarely has a PhD. A master's degree is more common, but in quite a few cases the lecturer (or, one level below, the instructor) has the equivalent of a bachelor's degree. The lector position is the only one where a doctorate normally is required.

Universities have the discretion to set additional appointment requirements. For example, before being deemed eligible for a specific job or level, a person may need a doctorate or experience (e.g., a degree) in a specific area. Tenure in the previous job (seniority) or a good assessment usually is relevant, too.

In public research universities, promotion to higher ranks in the academic hierarchy is earned less and less on the basis of seniority and increasingly on performance in the result areas linked to the job. While this is also the case in the universities of applied sciences, seniority and experience still play a large role—likewise, in private universities.

Traditionally, a lecturer could only become senior lecturer or professor by applying for such a position with a vacancy. Today, to an increasing degree, the careers of young academic staff at research universities are based on *tenure-track* policy. This policy, which outlines the procedures and conditions for permanent employment, is primarily formulated at the level of the institution itself, with due consideration being given to the specific circumstances and the profile of the department or faculty concerned. Multiyear career-development objectives and agreements are laid down in an academic's personal development plan, with annual consultations taking place to evaluate performance.

The financial rewards and uncertain future prospects for tenure have led to a decline in research trainees, especially in fields with high private-sector demand. Institutional leaders and politicians are concerned about the declining attractiveness of the research system and the difficulty in retaining young researchers.

International Competition

The average remuneration of academics in the Netherlands exceeds the European average (EUR 40,000 or US$50,200 in 2006) and is roughly similar to the rate in the United States. A recent comparative study (Berkhout et al. 2007) went beyond gross salaries and incorporated tax rates (including the progressiveness of the tax system) and purchasing-power differentials between countries to sketch a fairer picture of the attractiveness of the academic profession.[1] It concluded that salaries of Dutch academics were indeed better than those in most European countries (e.g., Germany and France) but lagged behind the United Kingdom and the United States. Compared to Switzerland and the top UK and U.S. universities, the difference is even larger (see Figure 22.1).

While highly skilled migrants are generally driven by career and financial motives, incentives are slightly different for researchers. Attracting international scholars to a country does not only relate to salary levels or job security but depends on a mix of factors—including a competitive academic climate, decent career prospects in exchange for hard work, high levels of mobility, and openness to nonnationals. These factors are largely in place in the Netherlands. There are no policies to attract international scholars by means of offering them higher salaries than local researchers. However, the government has tried to remove administrative barriers (e.g., visa regulations) that stand in the way of foreigners wishing to work in Dutch academia.

In relative terms, more highly skilled migrants work in the research universities (5,000 persons in total, representing 20 percent of the staff) than in the universities of applied sciences (600 in total) (Grijpstra and Buiskool 2005). For universities, the majority are from Europe, followed by Asia/Australasia and North America. In particular, in the technical universities, the share of foreign academics is high (32 percent). Foreign staff primarily (77 percent) have temporary research jobs and are concentrated in the natural sciences, engineering, and agriculture.

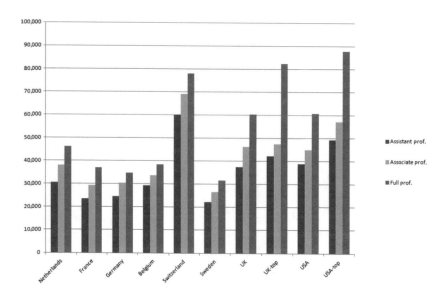

Figure 22.1 Reference salaries in public research universities, 2007.

Source: Berkhout et al. 2007.

Note: The salaries are based on net amounts, in euros. In 2007, EUR 1.00 = about US$1.37 (based on the European Central Bank).

Some universities attract a growing percentage of their graduate/PhD students from Asian and eastern European countries. In the universities of applied sciences, 3 percent of teaching staff are foreign, with most being employed in the schools specializing in creative arts.

Regarding Dutch academics going to foreign countries, statistics are rare and mostly deal with temporary stays abroad. Graduates going abroad after finishing their university degree mostly take up jobs in neighboring countries. Several initiatives have been taken to retain young promising academics, particularly for the science fields. Some universities are offering higher salaries for trainees, particularly in subject areas with projected faculty shortages, such as engineering. Other fields have introduced new types of appointments, such as tenure-track appointments and junior professorships. Some institutions have reduced the four-year PhD training period to make it more attractive for young people who want to speed up preparation for careers outside academia. Others introduced doctoral programs in cooperation with industry.

Conclusion

This sketch of academic salaries and working conditions in the Netherlands has shown that Dutch universities have been granted increasing room to negotiate the terms of employment for their academics. Collective labor agreements, negotiated without government involvement, are providing the framework for a single institution's remuneration policies and personal development plans for their academics. While salaries and nonsalary benefits are certainly above the European average and allow academics to lead a middle-class life, the fact that academics are increasingly evaluated on the basis of their performance means that there is less job security than in the past. For the future, the challenges will lie in securing the attractiveness of the academic workplace—an issue that is becoming increasingly urgent, given the "graying" of the academic population and the wish to retain talented people (young and old) for the country.

Notes

1. On average, an employee in the Netherlands pays 39 percent in terms of taxes and social security contributions.

References

Berkhout, Ernest, Maarten Biermans, Wiemer Salverda, and Kea Tijdens. 2007. *Internationale beloningsverschillen van wetenschappelijk personeel* [International comparison of salaries for scientists]. Amsterdam: SEO.
De Weert, Egbert. 2004. The academic workplace in the Netherlands. In *The international attractiveness of the academic workplace in Europe,* ed. Jürgen Enders and Egbert de Weert. Frankfurt/Main, Germany: Gewerkschaft Erziehung und Wissenschaft (GEW).

Grijpstra, Douwe, and Bert-Jan Buiskool. 2005. *De internationale mobiliteit van kenniswerkers in het hoger onderwijs* [The international mobility of knowledge workers in higher education]. Leiden, Netherlands: Research voor Beleid.

HBO-raad (Netherlands Association of Universities of Applied Sciences). 2007. *Collective employment agreement for the higher professional education sector. 1 August 2007 to 31 July 2010.* The Hague, Netherlands: HBO-raad.

NVP (Dutch Association for Personnel Management and Organizational Development). 2006. *NVP recruitment code.* Nieuwegein, Netherlands: NVP.

Van Rijn. 2001. *De arbeidsmarkt in de collectieve sector. Investeren in mensen en kwaliteit* [The labor market and the public sector: Investing in people and quality]. Den Haag, Netherlands: Ministerie van BZK.

VSNU (Association of Universities in the Netherlands). 2008. *Collective labour agreement Dutch universities, 1 September 2007 to 1 March 2010.* The Hague, Netherlands: VSNU.

23

NIGERIA

Toward an Open Market

Olufemi A. Bamiro

The Nigerian university system is a sector trapped by the three vectors: *access, quality,* and *cost.* The access problem is underscored by the fact that only one out of three qualified candidates seeking admissions into universities is admitted annually. The general quality of program delivery is negatively impacted by the shortfall in the number of academic staff, coupled with inadequate teaching and research facilities. Furthermore, most institutions are unable to fully recover operating costs, due to inadequate income from the various funding streams.

The ownership of the present 104 universities in the country is distributed as follows—federal government (27), state governments (36), and private (41). During the 2008–9 session—the public universities (federal and state) accounted for 95.2 percent of the 865,206 total student enrollments and 90.1 percent of the 25,065 total academic staff.

Over the years, staff salaries and conditions of service have been products of negotiations following confrontations between the federal government and the Academic Staff Unions of Universities, the umbrella union representing academic staff in public universities. The current Consolidated University Academic Salary Scheme, with considerable improvement in salaries, was driven by the need to compete in the African market for academic staff and curtail brain drain. This scheme, a federal government–approved scheme for federal universities, came into effect in July 2009. It is the benchmark for academic salaries in the Nigerian university system. Most state and private universities have adopted it while some others pay much less. Added to the salary scheme are incentives such as a one-year sabbatical, possibly with additional income after six years of continuous teaching and research; subsidized rent for accommodation; education for staff children from primary to secondary school levels; and promotion avenues, depending on the quality and quantity of individual research output. Nigerian academics are also given full-time pensionable employment with three-year probation, after which the appointment is confirmed according to the new statute—70 years of age for full professors and 65 years of age for other academic cadres.

The federal government has been grappling with the problem of access and quality through the establishment of more universities, the provision of a special fund to support junior academics pursuing doctoral programs, and special schemes—including salary supplementation—to attract Nigerians in diaspora and foreign staff to participate in teaching and research.

Overview of Higher Education

The Nigerian higher education system comprises the colleges of education, polytechnics/monotechnics, and universities. There are three categories of universities in the country, dictated by oversight—federal universities accountable to the federal government, state universities accountable to the state governments (36 federating states in the country), and private universities. From only one university in 1948, the number of universities increased steadily to 25 in 1985, followed by rapid growth to 104 in 2010. The 41 private universities, mainly faith-based, were established in response to the liberalization of the establishment of universities by the federal government, in 1995, to address the access problem. In the past few years, only about 250,000 places have been available for close to 750,000 qualified candidates who yearly seek admissions into universities. Current efforts to solve the access problem are predicated on the establishment of more private universities, the deployment of information and communications technologies for the operation of open and distance learning, and the opening up of the system to cross-border university education—relating to which, the National Universities Commission of Nigeria has already developed guidelines to attract international education service providers (www.nuc.edu.ng/pages/news). The commission is the regulatory agency established by the federal government for the regulation of key activities in the national university system.

Data on staff and students in the Nigerian university system were obtained from the National Universities Commission, with the data set for the 2008–9 session considered most comprehensive—based on information provided by 80 universities out of the 94 in existence. The total enrollment among different program levels in 2008–9 was 865,206 (717,014 full-time and 148,192 part-time students). The federal universities accounted for 61.8 percent of enrollment, state universities accounted for 33.4 percent, and private universities only 4.8 percent. Part-time programs take longer and are delivered through the open- and distance-learning mode supplemented with the traditional face-to-face mode of course delivery.

As shown in Table 23.1, there were 25,065 full-time academic staff—in federal universities, 15,569 (62.1 percent); in state universities, 7,019 (28.0 percent); and in private universities, 2,477 (9.9 percent). The highest-ranked cadre (professors

Table 23.1 Staff profile of the Nigerian university system, 2008–9

Item	Federal	State	Private	Total
No. of institutions covered	24	25	31	80
Level of employment				
Professors	2,097	663	278	3,038
Reader/associate professor	1,007	400	129	1,536
Senior lecturer	3,563	1,415	496	5,474
Lecturer II & I	8,902	4,541	1,574	15,017
Total full-time staff	15,569	7,019	2,477	25,065
Foreign staff	206	75	290	571
Visiting professors/sabbaticals	456	336	147	939

Source: Analysis of data obtained for this study from the Database of Staff and Students, maintained by the National Universities Commission of Nigeria.

and reader/associate professor) represented 18.2 percent, the senior lecturer cadre represented 21.8 percent, while lecturer cadre was 60 percent. The system had 571 foreign staff, with private universities accounting for half of them. Foreign staff are mainly from the United States, United Kingdom, India, eastern Europe (mainly Poland and Hungary), Turkey, and Africa (mainly Ghana, Egypt, and Cameroon).

Based on the National Universities Commission's student-teacher ratio for different programs in the system (varying from 10:1 to 15:1 for science-based programs and 30:1 for programs in humanities and social sciences), the commission estimated that the Nigerian university system had a shortfall of close to 5,000 academic staff in 2008–9; a situation that has negatively impacted the quality forming some of the programs.

Another dimension to the problem of access is created by the present typology of universities in the country—vis-à-vis fees being paid by students. Undergraduate students at federal universities pay between 50,000 naira (US$333) and 75,000 naira (US$500) per academic year due to heavy subsidy by the federal government. At private universities, undergraduate students pay between 300,000 naira (US$2,000) and 800,000 naira (US$5,333) for similar programs. State universities generally charge between 80,000 naira (US$533) and 180,000 naira (US$1,200) per academic year for undergraduate programs. Students pay much more for postgraduate programs in all the universities. As a consequence of the above, the Nigerian higher education sector is being squeezed by the three vectors of access, quality, and cost.

Academic Contracts

The entire national university system (federal, state, and private universities) operates three main cadres of staffing: the *lecturer* cadre (composed of lecturer grade II/lecturer grade I); the *senior lecturer* cadre; and the *professorial* cadre (composed of reader or associate professor and full professor). Faculty at federal universities in Nigeria are considered public servants and are, therefore, subject to a standardized payment scale now referred to as the Consolidated University Academic Salary. Although the staff in state universities are also public servants, their salary scales vary from one state to the other, given the significant differences in available resources to the state governments. Private universities also pay varying salaries to their staff. Almost all the staff in the system are employed on a full-time basis for teaching, research, and community service. While Nigerians do receive full-time pensionable appointments, non-Nigerians are given full-time contract appointments and, in line with government directive, such an appointment cannot stand below the rank of a senior lecturer.

Newly employed full-time Nigerian staff are typically placed on probation for three years. If after the period of probation they are found to be productive, their appointment is confirmed to the retirement age. Since the contract appointment of foreign staff is not pensionable, salary is normally adjusted upward (as high as 20 percent above the scale for that level).

In the Nigerian university system, staff generally enjoy a sabbatical of one year after working continuously for six full academic years. The sabbatical is designed to build the research capacity of staff. Staff on sabbatical are therefore expected to engage in research and limited teaching while spending the leave in any institution of their choice—subject to the approval of their university. Most significantly, staff on sabbatical enjoy payment of full salary in addition to financial support toward the cost of travel to and from the sabbatical venue. Thus, sabbatical is a period for additional earnings, depending on where the leave is spent and the remuneration package offered by the host institution. Yet, it is pertinent to note that in some cases staff are not able to proceed on sabbatical due to the shortage of staff in their departments. This happens in all the universities—federal, state, and private.

Academic staff are expected to retire, by statute, after attaining the age of 65 years, with payment of gratuity and regular pension, depending on their level of contribution under the Contributory Pension Scheme. All employers of labor in Nigeria—public or private—are, by law, expected to participate in this scheme for their workers. Under the Contributory Pension Scheme, workers contribute a percentage of their salaries (at least 7.5 percent of the basic salary), which is matched by their employers. Each staff chooses a Pension Fund Administrator to invest his or her contributions while still employed. Such an administrator is expected to invest the contributions and generate interest. However, access to the invested fund occurs only upon retirement. In response to the aging problem, with experienced professors leaving the university system in a significant number, the federal government has just increased the statutory retirement age to 70 years, for full professors only.

Overall, the federal government sets the pace for the university system in respect of staff salaries, allowances, and conditions of service. These issues are usually negotiated from time to time with the national staff unions at federal and state universities. Although staff in the private universities do not participate in the activities of the unions in the public universities, their management, however, takes due cognizance of the negotiated salary scales, especially for the federal universities, in setting their own scales to enable them to attract and retain staff. Also, while the federal government generally implements agreements reached with the national unions, state governments are not duty bound to carry out such accords. This has been creating problems in the system, as discussed below.

Academic Salaries

In 2001, the federal government, after negotiations with the staff unions, acknowledged certain scales of salaries and allowances. It was also agreed that salaries would be reviewed after three years (i.e., in 2004). This did not take place until a series of strikes leading to another round of negotiations in 2009. The Consolidated University Academic Salary Scheme, presented in Table 23.2, was the outcome of the negotiation between the federal government and the Academic Staff Unions of Universities, which became effective in July 2009.

The report of the Negotiation Committee offered the following comment:

> The Nigerian university academics represent critical mass of scholars in the society with the potential of transforming it. They, therefore, deserve unique conditions of service that would motivate them, like the intellectuals in other parts of the world ... and thereby stem the brain drain.
>
> *(Onosode and Awuzie 2009, 10)*

In line with the above declaration, the committee obtained information relating to the movement of Nigerian academics to other African countries, such as South Africa, Ghana, and Botswana as well as developed countries. The salary scales in Table 23.2 emanated from what the committee referred to as the "African Average"—that is, the average remuneration of academics in selected African countries, with which Nigeria potentially or effectively competes for the recruitment of academic staff.

Structurally, the Consolidated University Academic Salary Scheme has three components—basic salary (constituting about 54 percent), consolidated peculiar allowances (about 35 percent), and rent allowance (11 percent). At the end of each year, every staff member receives an automatic annual increment, depending on the level of employment, with the figure of monthly increase, indicated as "annual monthly increment" in Table 23.2. This annual increment is enjoyed until the staff reaches the top scale. At the end of the top scale, the staff stagnates until promoted to another level.

It is pertinent to note that the tax being paid by staff in a university is the product of negotiation between the university and the government of the state where the university is located. Overall, the taxes being paid by staff in the Nigerian

Table 23.2 Salary scale of staff in federal universities in local currency (naira)

Employment level		Monthly salary (Naira)*	No. of years to gain the top scale
Lecturer II	Bottom scale	137,459	
	Annual monthly increment	3,930	7
	Top scale	164,970	
Lecturer I	Bottom scale	173,333	
	Annual monthly increment	6,292	8
	Top scale	223,668	
Senior lecturer	Bottom scale	257,625	
	Annual monthly increment	9,472	12
	Top scale	371,292	
Reader/associate professor	Bottom scale	314,018	
	Annual monthly increment	11,449	9
	Top scale	417,063	
Professor	Bottom scale	381,696	
	Annual monthly increment	13,332	9
	Top scale	501,680	

Source: The analysis of data obtained for this study was from the report by the federal government of Nigeria and the Academic Staff Union of Universities (ASUU), July 2009.
*Exchange rate: 150 naira = US$1.00.

university system vary from 2 percent to 5 percent of the total salary. Furthermore, with the minimum wage of any worker in the public or private sector set by the government at 18,000 naira (US$120) per month; academic staff in the professorial grade and some at the senior lecturer grade, with a monthly salary between 300,000 and 500,000 naira, are undoubtedly within the middle class in the country.

Possibly, a new staff member may be appointed to a scale higher than the bottom scale, to reward proven productivity and experience. Also, a staff member, after spending the prescribed minimum of three years at a level, can be promoted to the next level—depending on the individual's level of productivity.

Information obtained from the National Universities Commission and the staff unions was to the effect that the Consolidated University Academic Salary Scheme, as presented in Table 23.2, has been incorporated at all the federal universities—about half of the state universities and most of the private universities. The staff unions in some of the state universities that have not yet implemented the scheme (still paying roughly 60 percent of the figures in Table 23.2 to their staff) have resorted to strikes to demand parity with their federal colleagues already enjoying the salary scheme. It is pertinent to note the existence of two state universities and four private universities paying roughly 10 percent to 20 percent more than the scheme. However, these are exceptions, with most state and private universities gravitating toward the implementation of the salary scheme, as shown in Table 23.2. Suffice it to say that the salaries and conditions of service in the federal universities will continue to serve as the benchmark for the university system in the country, with the state and private university owners trying to match the federal scales of salaries.

Nonsalary (Fringe) Benefits

A number of old federal universities provide accommodation for some of their staff with highly subsidized rents, in contrast to rents being paid outside the campuses. While staff in university accommodation statutorily forfeit the rent allowance component of their salaries (approximately 11 percent of the total salary), staff that have to rent accommodation outside the universities pay a lot more. This can be as high as 30 percent more than the allowance, or even more, depending on the university's location in the country.

Children of staff also enjoy almost free primary education and subsidized secondary school education. Most universities also provide staff and their dependents with free medical treatment for certain categories of ailments under the National Health Insurance Scheme.

Supplementary Employment (Moonlighting)

In the Nigerian university system, a significant number of staff, mostly in the public universities, do part-time teaching, particularly in the newly emerging private universities. Unfortunately, no data are available on the level of involvement of such staff, despite the fact that they are expected to obtain approval from their institutions to engage in part-time teaching in other institutions. Undoubtedly, part-time teaching by lecturers and senior lecturers was rampant a few years ago when the salaries of staff were indeed quite low. Remuneration from part-time teaching is based on the course load per semester and the staff cadre. Under the present dispensation, a professor handling a three-unit course (equivalent to 45 hours of teaching per semester) can earn between 50,000 naira (US$666) and 80,000 naira (US$1,000) per semester.

It is pertinent to note that universities in the country are being encouraged to establish consultancy services. A number of such outfits are successfully operating in some universities, attracting financial benefits to the consulting academics and their institutions. The operating profit-sharing formulae are designed by most institutions so that academic consultants do benefit financially and professionally. Anecdotal evidence exists of active professors earning close to 50 percent of their annual salary from consultancy activities.

Qualifications and Promotion Criteria

The minimum qualification to enter the academic profession as a lecturer grade II is a master's degree. In most universities, staff cannot progress beyond the lecturer grade, without the possession of a doctoral degree. One of the key issues generating debates in the higher education sector in Nigeria is the policy of the National Universities Commission—most, if not all, lecturers in the university system must possess a doctoral degree. In other words, the possession of a doctoral degree by lecturers has become the recognized currency to stay in academia in Nigeria. A survey of the programs operated in one of the top universities showed a significant variation in the percentage of academic staff having a doctoral degree from as low as 5 percent for medicine and law to the highest of close to 90 percent for education, social sciences, and agriculture (Bamiro and Adedeji 2010). Suffice it to note that the university system in Nigeria faces a serious academic human capital problem—both in quantity and quality. This is being addressed by encouraging older universities to embark on postgraduate-training programs to produce more doctorate graduates for the system. The Education Trust Fund, established by the federal government to intervene in the higher education sector, has been making an annual allocation of 50 million naira (US\$333,333) to each federal university, to support junior academics pursuing doctoral programs locally and abroad.

It is pertinent to note that promotion of staff in the system is based mainly on teaching and research outputs, in the form of publications. However, it is typically only after staff have spent a minimum of three years on a level that they are considered for promotion to the next level. Consequently, it will take a minimum of eight to nine years to move from lecturer I to senior lecturer to reader, and finally to full professor—assuming the candidate has satisfied the stipulated requirements of teaching and research outputs for each level. While some universities have developed instruments for quantitative measurement of teaching effectiveness, most universities in the system still rely on qualitative measurement. This has led to the general perception that the reward system has relegated teaching to the background in favor of research and publications. The level of research outputs is measured in terms of the quantity and quality of journal publications (with emphasis on the quality of outlet and dichotomy between onshore and offshore) and nonjournal publications (in the form of books, patents, technical reports, and conference proceedings). Some of the top universities in the country use a quantitative method of evaluation in which journal articles attract between 0 and 5 points, nonjournal articles between 0 and 3 points, with scholarly books and patents between 0 and 10 points. For a multiple-authorship publication, the contributing authors must indicate percentage contributions, which are factored into the determination of the effective score of each author for such publication. For promotion to the different levels, candidates must score not less than the following prescribed minimum points: lecturer I (8 points), senior lecturer (20 points), reader/associate professor (50 points), professor (70 points).

While there is no uniformity in the guidelines for promotion of academic staff in the Nigerian university system, in all cases of promotion of staff to the professorial grade in the system, candidates' publications are sent to at least three external assessors (chosen by the vice-chancellor of the university after due consultation) for assessment based on the guidelines prescribed by the institution. In some universities, at least one of the three assessors must belong to a recognized university outside the country. The final decision on the case is based on the reports of the assessors. Several instances of promotions are being turned down, based on negative assessor reports. It is also the norm that most academic staff get to the professorial grade before retiring from the system, while a considerable number move from one university (typically public) to the other (typically private) for career advancement.

International Competition

In the 1960s and 1970s, the few Nigerian universities in existence then could boast of a staff mix involving local and a significant number of foreign nationals. The conditions of service were excellent, due to the relatively adequate funding to support teaching and research. The foreign nationals earned good salaries while the environment was conducive to teaching, research, and learning. In the 1980s and 1990s, dominated by military rule, funding of universities dwindled so badly that few institutions could pay salaries that were globally competitive. A serious decay occurred in teaching and research facilities. This led to the exodus of lecturers (mainly from science-based faculties) to institutions abroad. Worst hit were the medical programs, with medical personnel leaving the country in the hundreds during the period. The country is still trying to recover, despite the gradual improvement in funding, since the return of civilian government in 1999. Although it may be too early to judge the impact of the new Consolidated University Academic Salary Scheme in attracting new staff and sustaining existing ones, it is worthy of note that the environment is improving gradually, with the university system having 571 foreign faculty out of close to 25,000 faculty, in 2009. The National Universities Commission established the Linkages with Experts and Academics in the Diaspora Scheme to attract Nigerians in diaspora to participate in teaching and research in the university system, for 3 to 12 months, through salary supplementation (National Universities Commission, n.d.). Actually, the inflow of international scholars could have improved significantly, with the exception of the general perception that the country is not safe. The security problem has unfortunately been discouraging foreign nationals, and even most Nigerians in the diaspora, from taking up appointments in the country. The government continues to pursue solutions to the problem.

Conclusion

There has undoubtedly been a significant improvement in the federal government–led salaries and conditions of service for academic staff in the Nigerian university system. However, a situation in which staff unions must resort to strikes that disrupt the academic calendars of universities, before government accepts to negotiate, is highly undesirable. This is symptomatic of a nation that still lacks a salaries and wages policy that takes due cognizance of the realities of the economic space and the appropriate indices of its people's standard of living. Furthermore, the significant differences in the financial resources available to the federal, state, and private universities call for a better balance of salaries and conditions of service for staff in the whole system.

References

Bamiro, O. A., and O. S. Adedeji. 2010. *Sustainable financing of higher education in Nigeria.* Ibadan, Nigeria: Ibadan University Press. http:www.ihen.org.ng/research-a-publica tions. Accessed March 10, 2011.

National Universities Commission. n.d. http://www.nuc.edu.ng/specialprojects/Lead/. Accessed March 9, 2011.

Onosode, Gamaliel, and Ukachukwu Awuzie. 2009. *Agreement between the federal government of Nigeria and the Academic Staff Union of Universities.* Abuja, Nigeria: Ministry of Education.

24

ACADEMIC SALARIES IN NORWAY

Increasing Emphasis on Research Achievement

Svein Kyvik

Higher education institutions are deeply affected by their political, social, and cultural environments. Situated in a social democratic society, Norwegian universities and colleges have stronger traditions for implementing egalitarian institutional policy measures than those in many other countries (Vabø and Aamodt 2009). This also applies to academic salaries, but over the last two decades market considerations and research achievements have increasingly affected wage policies. While all professors earlier had the same salary independent of discipline, seniority, research performance, and market value, there is now much more leeway for individual differentiation.

The Norwegian Higher Education System

Norway has a binary higher education system that broadly can be divided into a university and a college sector. The university sector is composed of eight public universities and eight specialized university institutions (economics and business administration, veterinary science, sport and physical education, music, architecture, and theology), of which three are private. The college sector is constituted by 21 state university colleges, primarily providing professional and vocational training at a bachelor's level but increasingly also at a master's level, and 7 other specialized public colleges. In addition, there are 21 small private higher education colleges. In 2008, Norway had about 215,000 students, of which 190,000 were enrolled in public universities and colleges and 25,000 in private institutions.

Since 1996, public universities and colleges have been regulated by a joint act that provides a common framework for the organization and governance of these institutions. Since 2003, this act has also encompassed private institutions.

In 2008, public universities and colleges had about 10,500 academic staff members in full-time permanent positions, of which nontenured staff amounted to more than 5,000 (primarily PhD students with a contract, and postdocs). Private institutions had about 800 staff members in full-time positions.

The binary system has come under pressure from colleges with university ambitions, and in recent years it has been discussed whether the binary divide should be abolished (Kyvik 2009b). In 2004, the government decided that colleges that fulfill certain minimum standards could apply for accreditation to university status, and three of the colleges have attained this status. Many of the other colleges are discussing how they can obtain university status, either by themselves, by merging with other university colleges to create larger entities, or by merging with a university (which one college did, in 2009).

Academic Career Structure

Since 1995, universities and university colleges have essentially practiced a common academic career structure with two different career tracks—a research-oriented and a teaching-oriented track (see Table 24.1). The research-oriented academic positions are associate professor and professor, while lecturer, senior lecturer, and docent are teaching-oriented positions, but they may possibly do research. The docent position is a newly established top position for senior lecturers. Individuals holding a PhD enter the research track directly as an associate professor; others normally enter the teaching track as a lecturer. The post of assistant professor was removed in 1995, but those still having this title are entitled to use it. Lecturer and senior lecturer are positions that are not widely used in the university sector. The college teacher position is used in practice-related professional programs, mainly in teacher training and health education, and the holders of this position do not have a master's degree. People appointed to all these positions obtain permanent employment right away. In addition, the universities have some positions for full-time researchers. Three types of temporary positions are found: research scholar (position for doctoral students), research assistant, and postdoc.

The criteria for appointment and promotion to teaching and research posts are laid down by the Ministry of Education and Research. Appointment as an associate professor normally requires a Norwegian doctoral degree in the subject area, or a foreign doctoral degree perceived as equivalent to a Norwegian doctoral degree. For appointment to lecturer and senior lecturer, a master's degree is the minimum requirement.

In total, 84 percent of the professors in public higher education institutions hold a doctorate. Formal research qualifications of academic staff in the colleges are generally low, compared to those of university staff, but higher than in similar colleges in other European countries (Kyvik and Lepori 2010). In 2008, 20 percent of the permanent teaching staff in the colleges had a doctorate. Only 6 percent were full professors, while more than 70 percent had the status as lecturer

Table 24.1 Academic staff in permanent positions in public universities* and in state university colleges, by rank, in 2008

	Universities		University colleges	
Rank	Number	Percent	Number	Percent
Professor	2,301	43	322	6
Associate professor	1,706	32	948	19
Assistant professor	168	3	75	1
Docent	9	—	30	—
Senior lecturer	174	3	570	11
Lecturer	723	14	2,488	50
Other tenured staff	240	4	135	3
College teacher	38	1	487	10
Total	5,359	100	5,055	100

Source: Nordic Institute for Studies in Innovation, Research and Education; Research Personnel Register.
*Including specialized university institutions.

or teacher (see Table 24.1). In contrast, more than 40 percent of the permanent academic staff in the universities were full professors.

Since 1993, associate professors in both universities and colleges may apply for promotion to full professor on the basis of their research competence (Olsen, Kyvik, and Hovdhaugen 2005). This reform made it possible to become a full professor in three different ways: (1) applying for a vacant professorship in open competition and becoming appointed as the best-qualified applicant; (2) applying for a vacant professorship in open competition, being found competent but not the best-qualified by the evaluation committee and then promoted to full professor at the department; and (3) by applying for promotion to full professor on the basis of research competence and being found competent by a unanimous peer review committee. The latter strategy now forms the most important way of becoming a full professor, while not many are appointed to an ordinary professorship due to few vacant positions.

Academic Contracts

In public higher education institutions, hiring procedures of academic staff are strictly regulated by the Ministry of Education and Research and individual institutions. Professors, associate professors, docents, senior lecturers, and lecturers are permanently appointed by their institutions, unless statutory authority exists for a temporary appointment. Appointments of temporary staff to permanent positions are permissible if no qualified applicants are available during a period of 3.5 years following appointment.

Norway does not have a tenure-track system, and the contracts do not specify expectations of research output. Thus, staff who do not do research, even though they might be expected to do so by their institution, will not be fired. Instead they are normally supposed to engage comparatively more in teaching or administrative work.

The contract with individual institutions lasts 12 months per year. Academic staff are subject to the same regulations as other state employees. This includes the right to salary during sickness, maternity and paternity leave, and occupational injury. The general retirement age is 67 years, but employees can retire as early as the age of 62 years and must retire by the age of 70 years. The official working week for academic staff is 37.5 hours, the same as for all public employees. Academic staff in the universities (not in the colleges) may normally apply for a sabbatical year after 6 years of teaching.

Vacant posts must, basically, be publicly advertised. In connection with the advertisement, a resolution must be passed concerning the content of the post, any qualifying period, the description of the post, and whether the post will be advertised nationally and/or in the Nordic countries and internationally.

A review committee is set up to evaluate the applicants and make a recommendation to the institution of an appointment to the vacant position. Normally, applicants for professorships should be assessed with respect to (a) academic qualifications, (b) other professional qualifications, (c) pedagogical qualifications, (d) achievements in dissemination of research and in contributions to societal debate, and (e) qualifications for management and administration. According to the Central Collective Agreement for the Civil Service, if two or more applicants are deemed to have approximately equal qualifications, a female applicant shall be ranked before a male applicant.

As a supplement to the evaluation by the committee, the highest-ranked applicants shall also be assessed with a view to their personal suitability for the post—for example, in relation to collaboration with colleagues and abilities as teachers and supervisors of students. Therefore, as a general rule, the applicant shall be called for an interview, and the faculty may further determine that trial lectures and other tests may be conducted.

Normally, private higher education institutions now partly follow these hiring procedures because private institutions are included in the common act on higher education, many of the private colleges receive state subsidies, and private establishments wish to appear as proper higher education colleges. This process can be regarded as a case of normative isomorphism, the socialization to predominating values in the higher education system in order to attract career-minded staff, and to be acknowledged as legitimate and reputable institutions (DiMaggio and Powell 1983).

As a rule of thumb, professors and associate professors in public higher education institutions should teach five hours a week (supervision not included) and use as much time for research as for teaching. Surveys of the use of academic staff time indicate that university staff spend on average about 30 percent of their total working time on research, a similar percentage on teaching, and less than

15 percent for supervision of graduate students (Kyvik and Smeby 2004), while state university college staff use, on average, 20 percent for research and development and 55 percent for teaching (Kyvik and Larsen 2010).

The government has made it clear that undertaking research is neither an individual duty nor a right but rather an institutional responsibility. The institution shall determine the distribution of time resources among the staff, according to constraints laid down by the Ministry of Education and Research, when determining the annual work program for each individual. In general, research-competent staff shall hold the opportunity to undertake research, while others should concentrate on keeping themselves abreast of recent research relevant to the skills students are to be taught. While in universities the practice seems to be that the staff might use as much time for research as for teaching, in state university colleges, time available for research differs much between individual staff members (Kyvik 2009a).

Academic Salaries

In Norway, academic salaries are basically determined in annual collective negotiations between trade unions and state authorities. These central negotiations regulate the general pay raise and the sum to be bargained in local negotiations. Every second year, revisions of the agreement that regulates working conditions in the state sector, besides salaries, are negotiated. This collective agreement contains regulations of working hours, salary during sick leave and maternity leave, overtime, pension rights, and other aspects. Trade unions play an important role in the system of wage negotiations and have more than 80 percent of the academic staff as members. Local negotiations take place at each institution between the institutional management and the local trade unions representing their members.

The academic rank is the primary determinant of salary level. Assistant professors, university and college lecturers, and college teachers are paid according to a scale based on seniority, but other criteria may also be applied. For the other positions, individual salaries are negotiated between unions and institutions within the limits of the pay scale based on a set of different criteria—mainly, the applicant's productivity in research, publishing, and market value. Most salaries for these latter positions tend to be at, or close to, the lowest level; but in recent years universities and colleges have increasingly applied the range of the pay scales to reward staff members and to attract staff from abroad.

Table 24.2 displays the distribution of monthly salaries for academic staff in public higher education institutions, in October 2008. The entrance level, as defined by the official pay scale, was 42,892 Norwegian kroner (NOK) (US\$7,500), and the maximum level was NOK 85,000 (US\$15,000). On average, a professor earned NOK 52,700 (US\$9,300), while the median salary was NOK 50,858 (US\$9,000).

Table 24.2 Monthly salary for academic staff in public higher education institutions, by October 2008

Rank	Average monthly salary		Scales within ranks	Monthly salary*	
	NOK	(US$)		NOK	US$
Professor	52,700	(9,300)	Top of scale	85,000	(15,000)
			Median	50,858	(8,900)
			Bottom of scale	42,892	(7,500)
Associate professor	41,300	(7,300)	Top of scale	52,175	(9,200)
			Median	40,592	(7,100)
			Bottom of scale	36,308	(6,400)
Senior lecturer	40,900	(7,200)	Top of scale	52,175	(9,200)
			Median	41,358	(7,300)
			Bottom of scale	36,308	(6,400)
Lecturer	38,600	(6,800)	Top of scale	45,308	(8,000)
			Median	39,058	(6,900)
			Bottom of scale	29,925	(5,300)

Sources: Statistics Norway and the Norwegian Association of Researchers.

Notes: NOK = Norwegian kroner; US$1.00 = NOK 5.70 (February 2011).

*Top of scale represents the highest possible monthly salary, bottom of scale the entry level, while the median is the most frequent salary level according to wage statistics.

A survey among academic staff shows that by December 2008, 5 percent of the professors had a monthly salary of NOK 44,440 (US$7,800) or lower, and 5 percent earned more than NOK 63,750 (US$11,200) (Forskerforbundet 2009). These figures indicate that the top of the scale is rarely used (if at all), and that the mean salary for professors is about 23 percent higher than the entrance level. Furthermore, the mean age of professors in 2008 was 56 years of age, indicating that the economic compensation for pursuing an academic career is relatively modest.

Although the pay scale is similar across all institutions and disciplines, professors have higher salaries in some disciplines than in others (see Table 24.3), but differences are relatively small. A survey among academic staff shows that by December 2008, 5 percent of the professors in economics had a monthly salary of less than NOK 46,500 (US$8,200), and 5 percent had more than NOK 67,500 (US$11,800); more than 5 percent of professors in the humanities were paid less than NOK 5,000 (US$900) (Forskerforbundet 2009). Data are not available for professors in law, but presumably this group has higher salaries than those shown in Table 24.3, due to the comparably high salaries in the private sector (Hægeland and Møen 2007).

Data on monthly salaries in private institutions are only available for one large specialized university institution in economics and business administration. The bottom level for professors is not that different from public institutions; 5 percent had a salary lower than NOK 49,200 (US$8,600), and median monthly salary was NOK 51,250 (US$9,000). However, 25 percent of the professors earned

Table 24.3 Monthly salary for professors in public higher education institutions, December 2008

	5% of professors earned less than:		Median monthly salary		Mean monthly salary		5% of professors earned more than:	
	NOK	(US$)	NOK	(US$)	NOK	(US$)	NOK	(US$)
Humanities	43,683	(7,700)	48,992	(8,600)	50,791	(8,900)	62,750	(11,000)
Natural sciences	44,442	(7,800)	50,858	(8,900)	52,289	(9,200)	63,750	(11,200)
Medicine	44,333	(7,800)	53,483	(9,400)	54,697	(9,600)	65,417	(11,500)
Economics	46,518	(8,200)	53,483	(9,400)	55,649	(9,600)	67,500	(11,900)

Source: Norwegian Association of Researchers.

Note: US$1.00 = NOK 5.70 (February 2011).

more than NOK 95,800 (US$16,800) per month, giving a mean of NOK 81,000 (US$14,200). Most of the other private institutions have a religious affiliation, and salaries probably compare to that of public colleges.

In general, academic staff in public higher education institutions have salaries that are slightly lower than those of civil servants in the state bureaucracy with comparable competence and seniority, although considerably lower than their counterparts in industry and the business sector. Moreover, these differences have increased over time (Røed and Schøne 2005). Nevertheless, an academic career seems to be attractive in subjects where a position in the public sector would be an alternative. Exceptions are subjects—such as medicine, dentistry, technology, economics, and law—where the job alternatives offer notably higher remuneration. Graduates possessing a higher degree and employed in industry or the business sector for some years, after leaving university, normally have higher salaries than their former professors. In some disciplines it is therefore a problem that some of the most talented graduates are not interested in a university career.

In an international perspective, Norway is attractive for PhD students because they are appointed to temporary posts for three or four years, and salaries commensurate with the first appointment in the public sector for candidates holding a master's degree. Also salaries for postdocs are competitive on the international academic market. Yet, salaries for professors are considered relatively low, compared to those of professors in the major scientific countries in the Western world, especially in subjects like medicine and technology.

Nonsalary Benefits and Supplementary Employment

In Norway, fringe benefits are not offered as part of academic remuneration at individual institutions, but all academic staff members are entitled to benefits like public health services, five-weeks vacation, and public pension.

With respect to pension, all academic staff members are compulsory members of the National Insurance Scheme and entitled to retirement pension, disability pension, and other services. Academic staff employed in state higher education institutions have mandatory membership, also in the Norwegian Public Service Pension Fund and are entitled to additional retirement pension. Membership in the latter fund implies a 2 percent deduction of the gross salary (a pension fee). In addition, the employer contributes substantially to the pension fund, and the percentage of the gross salary of an employee has been increasing over the last years due to an aging population. Thus, for the purpose of international comparison, membership in the latter pension fund can be regarded as a fringe benefit equivalent to at least 10 percent of the gross salary. The combined retirement pension for academic staff adds up to two-thirds of the salary at the time of retirement.

Many academic staff members have some sort of additional employment, but detailed statistical data on volume and earnings are not available. A professor or lecturer is entitled to take further employment, but the upper limit is 20 percent of a full-time position. Various surveys conducted among academic staff do provide some information on the scale of extra income and supplementary employment. According to their own estimates, in 2001, staff members in the university sector had an average working week of 49 hours, including 5 hours for activities that were not part of their duties as university employees (Kyvik and Smeby 2004). In the college sector, in 2005, the average working week was 43 hours, including 3 hours for external work (Kyvik and Larsen 2010). These activities involve teaching and examination work at other institutions; consultancy and professional practice as a lawyer, physician, dentist, and so forth; but also participation in professional associations, research councils, and work for journals as editor and referee. It is, thus, difficult to provide exact information on the scale of added income based on these time-survey data; but, in the university sector, three hours, on average, a week might form a qualified estimate and, in the college sector, two hours a week might.

In a survey undertaken in 2007–8 among academic staff in universities and colleges as part of an international comparative study (the Changing Academic Profession), one-third of the staff members reported they had a further form of employment (see Table 24.4), varying between one-fourth in the humanities and half of the staff in medicine and technology.

However, most academic staff earn more income, even if they do not have additional extra employment. This may include examination work at other institutions, honoraria for lectures, royalties for book publishing, and other factors.

Conclusion

In the Norwegian higher education system, career opportunities and pay raise—based on research achievements—have improved considerably over time. In the

Table 24.4 Academic staff in public higher education institutions with additional employer or remunerated work, 2007–8, in percentages

	Another higher education institution or research institute	Another employer outside academe	Self-employed	No other employment	Total
Humanities	7	3	12	78	100
Social sciences	22	5	6	67	100
Natural sciences	16	8	3	73	100
Technology	23	12	11	54	100
Medicine	17	17	18	48	100
Total	16	7	9	67	100

Source: Changing Academic Profession Project.

Note: The table includes 939 persons.

1990s, changes in the reward structure encouraged achievements in research. From 1993 on, associate professors have been entitled to apply for promotion to a full professorship on the basis of their research competence, irrespective of vacant professorships. Furthermore, the former central negotiation system of fixed salaries for professors, regardless of research production and scientific reputation, was changed into a system of combined central and local negotiations. The purpose of local negotiations basically regards to consider market value and to reward productivity and quality in research. These changes most likely have enhanced the research orientation, due to a closer link than earlier between research achievements, career development, and pay increase.

However, in many ways, international reports of increasing differentiation of the academic profession and increasing diversification of academic-staff working conditions do not relate well to developments in Norway. Egalitarian aspects of the Norwegian higher education system still prevail and have counteracted international trends and state initiatives to diversify working conditions among academic staff. At the system level, with the passing in 1995 of a common Act on Universities and Colleges, a process of homogenization (organization and management principles, funding structures, personnel policies, etc.) across the sectors was initiated (Kyvik 2009b). The academic profession has become more homogeneous, both with regard to career structure and working conditions. Nevertheless, individual salary differences have increased due to a stronger emphasis on market value and research performance.

References

DiMaggio, Paul J., and Walter W. Powell. 1983. "The iron cage revisited: Institutional isomorphism and collective rationality in organizational fields." *American Sociological Review* 48: 147–60.

Forskerforbundet. 2009. *Forskerforbundet: Lønnsstatistikk for statlig sektor.* Oslo, Norway: Norwegian Association of Researchers.

Hægeland, Torbjørn, and Jarle Møen. 2007. *Forskerrekruttering og opptrappingsplanen.* Notat 2007/37. Oslo: Statistics Norway.

Kyvik, Svein. 2009a. "Allocating time resources for research between academic staff: The case of Norwegian university colleges." *Higher Education Management and Policy* 21: 109–22.

Kyvik, Svein. 2009b. *The dynamics of change in higher education: Expansion and contraction in an organisational field.* Dordrecht, Netherlands: Springer.

Kyvik, Svein, and Ingvild M. Larsen. 2010. "Norway: Strong state support of research in university colleges." In *The research mission of higher education institutions outside the university sector,* ed. Svein Kyvik and Benedetto Lepori. Dordrecht, Netherlands: Springer.

Kyvik, Svein, and Benedetto Lepori. 2010. *The research mission of higher education institutions outside the university sector: Striving for differentiation.* Dordrecht, Netherlands: Springer.

Kyvik, Svein, and Jens-Christian Smeby. 2004. "The academic workplace: Country report Norway." In *The international attractiveness of the academic workplace in Europe,* ed. Jürgen Enders and Egbert de Weert. Frankfurt/Main, Germany: Gewerkschaft Erziehung und Wissenschaft.

Olsen, Terje B., Svein Kyvik, and Elisabeth Hovdhaugen. 2005. "The promotion to full professor—through competition or by individual competence?" *Tertiary Education and Management* 11: 299–316.

Røed, Marianne, and Pål Schøne. 2005. *Forskning eller høy lønn? Lønnsutviklingen for norske forskere 1997–2003.* Oslo, Norway: Institute for Social Research.

Vabø, Agnete, and Per Olaf Aamodt. 2009. "Nordic higher education in transition." In *Structuring mass higher education. The role of elite institutions,* ed. David Palfreyman and Ted Tapper. New York: Routledge.

25

RUSSIAN HIGHER EDUCATION

Salaries and Contracts

Gregory Androushchak and Maria Yudkevich

During the Soviet period, the academic profession was prestigious. It attracted the most-talented people and gave them good monetary and nonmonetary rewards, such as social status and an unusually high degree of personal freedom (compared to many other professions). In some disciplines (i.e., physics or mathematics), research was well integrated into world science, and in others, research was conducted in relative isolation. High standards were required to enter and stay in a profession and were maintained within the academic profession.

During the years of the post-Soviet transition, the situation changed drastically. Extremely low public financial support for higher education institutions caused adverse results. Since it was no longer possible to make a living in academia, the most talented and capable faculty left the academic profession for the incipient business sector or left the country, moving to U.S. and European universities. Faculty who decided to remain would need to teach at more than one university and engage in activities that provided immediate payoffs—at best private tutoring but more frequently working as salespersons, janitors, or other employees. These issues not only contributed to a decline of prestige for academic jobs but also undermined the self-esteem of the profession and weakened academic standards.

During recent years, the situation has begun to change, but only gradually. Current policy is to provide direct and indirect support from the Ministry of Education and Science to universities that attract better students and have substantial achievements in research. In these 30 to 40 universities, the level of remuneration is compatible with the alternatives in the labor market for highly qualified personnel and offers significantly more potential for creativity. Hopefully, examples of decent careers and the possibility of academic achievements, recognized in the international milieu by faculty of these universities, will contribute to the restoration of prestige to the academy in the coming years.

The National Context

The Russian system of higher education is represented by 662 public and 474 private institutions and slightly more than 1,600 regional branches—approximately two-thirds of which belong to public and one-third to private institutions.[1] There are 7.4 million students in the system of higher education, and 17 percent of them are enrolled in private universities. Only 45 percent of the total number of students in Russian higher education institutions are enrolled in full-time programs; 4 percent of students are enrolled in part-time studies; the rest are enrolled in some kind of distance-learning program.

The Range of Institutions

The context includes three types of higher education institutions—universities, academies, and institutes. Universities implement educational programs in a wide range of training and postgraduate programs (PhD and doctorate), conduct research, and develop new curriculum and methodologies in key areas of expertise. Academies differ from universities by providing a narrower range of programs and areas of research. Institutes are different from universities and academies, offering a narrow range of ongoing education programs and research activities.

The largest number of institutions—just over half of all public higher education institutions—are affiliated with the Ministry of Education and Science. There are 22 other ministries and agencies that have higher education institutions under their jurisdictions. Those with oversight for the largest number of institutions are the Ministry of Agriculture, the Ministry of Health and Social Development, the Ministry of Culture, the Ministry of Transport, and the Ministry of Sport and Tourism.

The average size of a Russian institution (that is, either an institution itself or its branch) is about 3,500 students, and at private institutions there are about 2,700 students. The number of full-time students per teacher is about 11, and the corresponding ratio is fixed by legislation.

The public higher education sector grew by 22 percent during the post-Soviet years, while the private higher education sector has grown from virtually zero over the past 15 years. While in the Soviet era only public institutions were permitted, the 1992 federal Law on Education provided a legal framework for the establishment and operation of private higher education institutions and resulted in an exponential growth in their number.

The dissimilarities between public and private institutions constitute their organizational and legal structures. Public universities receive public funding for training students who demonstrate high academic achievements on the entrance examinations, which since 2009 has been the State Unified Exam taken upon high school graduation. Public institutions are provided with buildings and basic infrastructure. A limited number of public universities receive public support to finance their research activities. The share of public funding to higher education increased during recent years and, according to the Federal State Statistics Service (Rosstat), currently constitutes approximately 60 percent of the total funds available to universities, as compared to about 40 percent at the beginning of 2000–2001.[2]

Private higher education institutions do not have access to public funding to cover the costs of enrolling even the most talented students or to support research activities. Typically, private institutions enroll weaker students, who are thought to be less willing to devote enough time and effort to their education and tend to be inclined toward simply earning a diploma. In this regard, private institutions are consistently associated with a segment of low-quality education.

A significant influence shaping the landscape and incentives for universities is that higher education today in Russia is considered a social imperative. Thus, in the year 2009, the percentage of the cohort of 17-year-olds admitted to higher education institutions reached 89.2 percent. The proportion of high school graduates admitted to universities during the year of graduation is about 65 percent.

Since 2006, there has been a 10 percent decline in the 17- to 18-year-old age cohort, whereas the reduction in the admission of publicly supported students was only 2 to 4 percent per year. As a result, the selectivity for publicly supported student places has been significantly diminished. Some institutions accept virtually all young people who apply to their programs, including those with an extremely low level of previous training and those with no motivation to learn.

Status of the Professoriate

While during the Soviet period a career as a faculty member implied comfortable financial circumstances, at the end of the 1980s the situation changed dramatically (for a general overview, see Smolentseva 2003). In 2008, the average monthly wage in the economy was approximately 17.3 thousand rubles, which was about US$700. The salary of young faculty is now about 70 percent of the average wage. The salary of professors mainly exceeds average wages in the economy by 20 to 25 percent, which, nevertheless, is still about 10 percent below the average wage of Russian workers with academic degrees.

Thus, university professors without additional employment are almost unable to reach the middle-class income level or to gain living conditions and opportunities comparable to people with similar abilities, education, and work experience who are employed outside the education sector.

Organizational Structure and Contracts

Academic positions within both public and private higher education institutions include assistants, lecturers, senior lecturers, associate professors (docents),

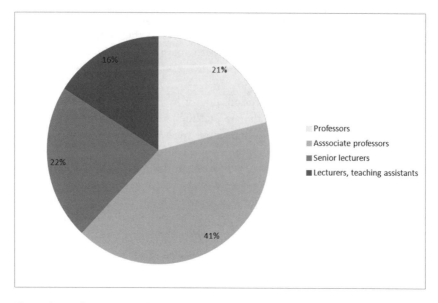

Figure 25.1 The structure of the teaching staff in the context of the academic hierarchy
Source: Federal State Statistics Service (Rosstat) 2009.

and professors.[3] The structure of the teaching staff in Russian higher education institutions is shown in Figure 25.1. The Russian academic system is quite hierarchical, and to advance in the career ladder means higher status and more opportunities.

A Set of Guidelines

Several specific organizational features are important in understanding the organization of faculty contracts in Russian higher education institutions:

> *Chairs (kafedras).* The chair is the unit in the organizational structure of a university responsible for decisions involving the teaching process (e.g., employment decisions regarding the academic position). The chair reflects a rather narrow scientific field of teaching and research. An average Russian public university encompasses about 15 chairs and a private university, about 10 chairs. The average number of academic staff belonging to a chair at public and private universities is 12 and 8 positions, respectively. Alternatively, some universities are organized into departments.
>
> *Teaching loads.* The main tool for coordination, planning, and monitoring of all teaching processes is an individual faculty workload (within a chair) and the total teaching load of the department—the volume of work related to teaching that a faculty member must assume within the academic year.

The teaching workload is calculated in hours (for a teaching assistant it corresponds to 750 hours and for a professor, 600 hours).

Scope of activities. Most teaching work is done in the form of lectures and seminars (classes). In addition to teaching classes, responsibilities include grading written assignments and examinations and the supervision of term papers, diploma papers, and theses. The practice of graders (students hired to grade written assignments) does not exist in the Russian academic practice; all the relevant work is required to be done by the faculty themselves.

Hiring Practices

Formally, all the positions are filled on a competitive basis, following a public announcement describing the vacant position. The head of the chair selects the most promising candidates and introduces them to the Academic Council, which approves the best one. However, competitive selection of teachers on the "open market" takes place only during the expansion of university educational programs into new areas or in the exceptionally rare cases of a faculty retirement.

In practice, however, heads of chairs, responsible for the employment decisions, tend to offer the posts of teaching assistants and full professors to their acquaintances, both in the academe and outside, who meet the formal requirements (degrees, working experience, etc.). Assistant and lecturer positions are usually filled by young people who graduated from the university or PhD students assigned to the chair.

Such practice leads to widespread inbreeding (about two-thirds of young faculty members graduated at the same university where they work), which is considered a normal characteristic within an academic community (Sivak and Yudkevich 2009; Horta, Veloso, and Grediaga 2007). Moreover, it is believed that an employment policy should benefit a university's own graduates (see Table 25.1).

Table 25.1 Heads of chairs opinions toward employment policy

University employment policy should be directed primarily on hiring	*Valid %*
Own graduates	62
Active researchers with research and teaching	48
Faculty with long teaching experience	39
Practitioners ready to combine work with teaching	15
Graduates from other universities	11
All who are ready to work full time	3
Total	99

Source: Kozmina, Panova, and Yudkevich 2007, conducted by the Laboratory of Institutional Analysis, at the Higher School of Economics.

Contracts

The duration of a standard employment contract includes one, three, or five years. Typically, the first contract is signed for one year and then extended for three years; and subsequently—unless some reservations exist (e.g., extremely low research productivity)—the contract is renewed every five years. No significant changes (in terms of teaching loads, remuneration, working conditions, etc.) are expected at renewal. There is no lifelong contract (such as tenure), but in the absence of any real competitive pressure and virtually automatic renewal of contracts, faculty consider their contracts as permanent and employment as rather secure. Meanwhile, the significant reduction of the 17 to 22 age cohort, during the next three to five years, will lead to a significant reduction in teaching positions and increased competition for them.

Salary, specified in the contract (signed between faculty member and university rector), usually include a budgetary component (some legally determined minimum wage—currently about no more than 25 percent of the average wage in the economy) and supplements (from both public and nonpublic funds, at the university's disposal). On average, the budgeted component of the salary package at public universities is about 65 to 70 percent of the average wage in the economy. Another 40 to 45 percent of earnings paid to teachers come from extrabudgetary funds.

While different in principle, real practices for hiring faculty and renewing their contracts are basically the same in public and private universities—except that at the latter, formal regulations are less important, due to a lower degree of accountability, in general. That fact, coupled with the orientation toward part-time programs, alters the composition of faculty at private universities.

At private universities, only a small number of teaching positions are core, full-time ones. Commonly, teachers at private universities in Russia work on short-term (part-time) contracts or are paid on an hourly basis, while being employed by public universities on a full-time basis. Such contracts are extended each year after a university confirms how many new students it enrolled for the next school year. The proportion of part-time faculty employed by other organizations (including public universities) amounts to 45 percent in private universities,[4] while in public higher education institutions it is about 20 percent.

Research

Despite the fact that the faculty's primary function is teaching, which is strictly regulated by the university curriculum, it is assumed that academics will do research as well (Levin-Stankevich and Saveliev 1996; Kuzminov and Yudkevich 2007). The volume of research activity (effort, time, etc.) and expected results (in terms of productivity) are not explicit in a contract.

High teaching loads, as well as additional employment, make research a mere formality for most faculty. According to the Monitoring of Education Markets and

Organizations, only about 20 percent of faculty participate in the type of research that implies remuneration, such as grants (Roshchina and Yudkevich 2009; Roshchina and Filippova 2006). On average, those who participate in research devote about 8 hours per week to it; whereas the actual amount of weekly classroom commitment is about 18 hours and preparation about 11 hours.

Research productivity as a competitive factor to influence the extension of contracts does not generally seem to work. Chairs and departments within universities report high rates of faculty engagement in activities related to research. The most popular indicator used is faculty publication rates. However, those are obscured by the inclusion of non-peer-reviewed internal publications, such as working-paper series run by chairs and departments, university-edited journals, and abstracts at departmental conferences and workshops.

Indicators like citation indices and impact factors of scholarly journals have not yet gained popularity among the authorities responsible for monitoring academic performance. The uncertainty faces the limited ways of checking the reliability of these indicators, given the unavailability and decentralization of this information. Thus, the evaluation of faculty research outcomes is scarcely included. Rather, universities and regulatory bodies monitor research activities.

Academic Salaries

During the 1990s and the beginning of the 2000s, earnings in the academic sector were 25 to 50 percent lower than average earnings in the economy. However, during the last five years, the gap has been decreasing, mostly due to a significant rise in public spending on higher education. By 2009, average earnings in the academic sector compared favorably (at slightly more than 110 percent) to average earnings in the broader economy. However, these days it is still noticeably lower than earnings of higher education specialists employed outside academia, let alone senior and middle managers (see Figure 25.2).

There are considerable variations in wages among academic fields, which reflect the calls for different degree programs. Therefore, the highest wages are in economics and social sciences, which are in the highest demand, while academic staff in the arts and natural sciences experience less demand and receive lower wages (see Figure 25.3).

The main determinants of teacher salaries in the university are teaching load, rank (which determines a budget category in the wage scale and, consequently, the magnitude of the budget component of wages), academic degree, and administrative services (see Figure 25.4). These factors on average add up to the 70 percent of academic salaries, and the corresponding share is referred to as basic component of salary. The rest of the salary is referred to as the stimulating component and constitutes about 30 percent of total salary.

In principle, universities have the legal and financial autonomy required for the individualization of teachers' salaries and competition for the best through higher

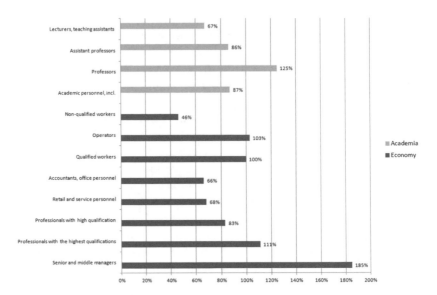

Figure 25.2. Earnings of workers of different professional groups and university professors, compared to the average wage in the economy.

Sources: Federal State Statistics Service (Rosstat) 2009; Monitoring of Education Markets and Organizations 2008.

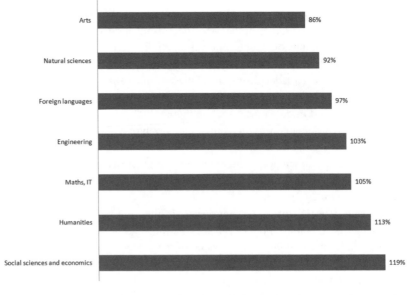

Figure 25.3 Ratio of average wages of teachers of various disciplines to an average salary paid teachers.

Source: Federal State Statistics Service (Rosstat) 2009; Monitoring of Education Markets and Organizations 2008.

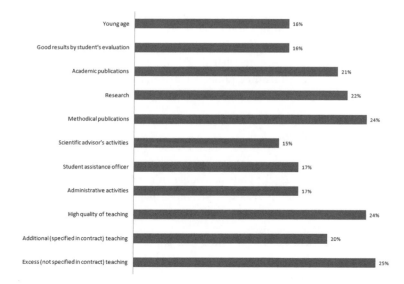

Figure 25.4 Share of teachers receiving allowances for certain activities.

Source: Federal State Statistics Service (Rosstat) 2009; Monitoring of Education Markets and Organizations 2008.

salaries, additional bonuses, and other items. What higher education institutions cannot do is to reduce a teacher's obligatory workload, given formal standards that correspond to rank and position. At the same time, despite the potential to compete for academic staff, universities actually do not do so. Reasons include: lack of extra financial capacity, no market for academic research (which would provide faculty and universities direct returns for their research reputation), and the high risk of social tensions within the university academic community.

Administrative positions are an important source of income for teachers. About 30 percent of faculty members have some administrative duties. The time that these academic staff spend on such activities is comparable to the average amount of classroom work and is about 18 hours per week. The earnings of academic staff who combine academic and administrative work are 50 percent higher than that of those who just teach and do research.

Nonsalary (Fringe) Benefits

Pension schemes and health care plans are guaranteed to all employees, including the university faculty, by law. As to other benefits for the faculty, beyond wages and a two-month annual paid leave, no other forms of remuneration are generally provided. In a small number of cases, a teacher may receive temporary housing at a university, and it may even be the primary incentive for working at a particular university, but these cases are rather exceptional.

It would, however, be incorrect to say that this long summer vacation is the only nonmonetary remuneration. Despite relatively low salaries, the professorial status at a public university—in conjunction with a sufficiently large amount of free time—is of great value, since that time can be monetized through tutoring, part-time teaching in other public or private universities, and other prospects.

Supplementary Employment

The practice of holding employment at several higher education institutions is rather common (Nazarova 2005). Thus, according to the Monitoring of Education Markets and Organizations' data in 2007, more than 22 percent of teachers worked simultaneously for more than one university. This percentage has remained rather stable in recent years.

In addition to their primarily contract responsibilities, it is common for individuals to teach in for-profit programs of a university—for example, a for-profit master of business administration program. Rates (paid per hour of instruction) for such programs are usually significantly higher than for the primary contract, and the possibility of teaching in these programs is often considered to compensate somewhat for low-paying activities at the basic rate.

No legal restrictions on teaching in several universities exist. While "multiple" employment is not directly encouraged, at a university that is interested in attracting and retaining strong faculty members and realizes the incapability to provide an adequate wage, management staff close their eyes to moonlighting. So, the following model is a rather typical one: a teacher receives low remuneration at a well-reputed public university that is his/her main full-time employment and has the possibility of using the reputation and status of that affiliation to give private lessons to university applicants and/or teach at a private university and be paid several times more than the main contract.

In recent years, the participation of teachers in paid research activities has significantly expanded. In 2006, about 14 percent of university faculty participated in such activities, and by 2008 the proportion of them has grown to 20 percent (see Figure 25.5).

Research activities increase faculty income by one-third. Monthly income in 2008 leveled at about 23,000 rubles, while remuneration for research constituted 6,600 rubles per month.[5] Average salary across all industries in Russia that year averaged 14,900 rubles per month.

Describing the system as a whole, faculty participation in paid research activities is more of an exception than the rule. Earnings that a public university receives for research and development activities constitute no more than 6 to 8 percent of the total income of a higher education institution, and most of this revenue (about 80 percent) is public funding. Public funding for research is directed mainly at about 30 to 40 of the leading Russian universities.

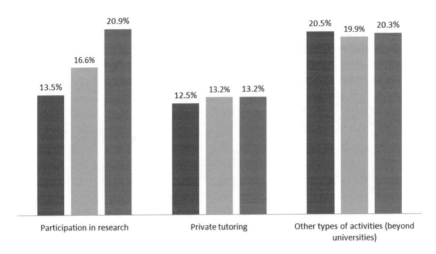

Figure 25.5 Additional paid work beyond teaching and associated activities (including administrative services).

Source: Federal State Statistics Service (Rosstat) 2009; Monitoring of Education Markets and Organizations 2008.

Qualifications

Virtually all faculty at Russian institutions have higher education credentials (see Table 25.2). About 64 percent of teachers have a candidate of science degree or a doctor of science degree. It is sufficient to have a diploma (bachelor's level and above) to begin an academic career at a university and to conduct seminars and tutorials. Lecturers should have (with rare exception) a PhD-equivalent degree. In the 1930s the Soviets adopted the German academic system of two levels of postgraduate degrees. The first level, candidate of sciences, is equivalent to a German *Doktor* degree and is mandatory for the associate professor position. The second level, doctor of sciences, equivalent to German habilitation, is required for the full professor position and various administrative posts in academia—such as heads of chairs, deans, vice-rectors, and rectors (see Table 25.2).

Promotions at lower academic ranks (e.g., from a senior lecturer to an assistant professor) are subject to obtaining a degree and formal qualification. At higher positions (e.g., professor), an emphasis is placed on work experience at an institution, in addition to a doctorate degree. The importance of experience is largely driven by low mobility of teachers between universities and the lack of competitive mechanisms for allocating positions.

Table 25.2 The highest degrees held by most professors at public universities

Public universities	Master's degree	Portion of public universities (%)*	Full-time faculty (%)**	Candidate of sciences degree (%)***	Doctor of sciences degree (%)***
Federal universities[a]	Degree granted	2.3	7.2	49.1	14.2
National research universities[b]	Degree granted	7.0	13.8	50.7	14.2
Technical and technological universities[c]	Degree granted	28.2	26.4	51.4	12.3
Socioeconomic, humanities, and pedagogical universities	Degree granted	28.2	31.6	52.8	11.4
Bachelor universities and colleges[e]	Degree not granted	34.3	21.1	51.7	9.3
Total/average		100	100	51.6	11.8

Source: Calculations by Higher School of Economics, using data from Federal Educational Portal "Russian Education" (2009), higher education institutions under jurisdiction of the Ministry of Education and Science of Russian Federation, http://www.edu.ru/.
*Among the total number of public universities.
**Among the total number of full-time faculty at public universities.
***Among the total number of full-time faculty in the corresponding universities.
[a]Leading large universities in each of the seven federal districts, and Moscow State University and Saint-Petersburg State University.
[b]Medium-size technical universities (with the exception of National Research University Higher School of Economics), usually working on in-depth research projects with generous financial support by the Ministry of Education and Science of Russia, in one or a few fields of studies.
[c]Technical and technological universities that have been provided with the status and additional funding for national research universities.
[d]Universities that specialize in socioeconomic studies, humanities, and pedagogical studies.
[e]Bachelor universities and colleges that provide students only bachelor degrees and former five-year specialist programs.

International Competition

In the transition period of the 1990s, a significant outflow of university professors took place. Such brain drain was quite common for universities in Moscow, St. Petersburg, major Russian university centers (such as Novosibirsk, Krasnoyarsk), and significantly weakened Russian higher education. However, today academic mobility usually takes place when young Russian academics decide which graduate school to apply to.

Salary levels at Russian higher education institutions continue to encourage brain drain. In the short term, this will encourage faculty to seek work in other countries, especially in disciplines where better working conditions are crucial (laboratories, technical staff, and equipment). In the longer term, the current situation causes an adverse selection, with weaker graduates choosing careers in academia.

With a few exceptions, no special policies are run by universities to attract candidates from the international academic job market. A recruitment initiative (financially supported by the Ministry for Education and Science), in 2009, was aimed at attracting leading international scientists. In 2010, Russians held the first competition for university-based "start-up" laboratories in Russia under the guidance of leading international scholars; and operating conditions involved substantial monetary awards to foreign researchers. However, participation in this program involves extremely high transaction costs and will have no system-wide impact in the near future.

Conclusion

The last 20 years have been a period of dramatic changes within the academic community in Russia. Many new higher education institutions (including private ones), of widely differing quality, emerged. Decreased public support for higher education institutions caused an erosion of academic values and led to adverse selection within the profession, which is supported by high demand for university diplomas in Russia, as higher education has become a social imperative.

Unification in academic salaries and employment contracts within academia (which existed in the Soviet period) gave way to diversity in academic contracts, incentive policies, and results. Income of university faculty cannot be reduced to the salary defined by an employment contract and should be considered as the sum of money coming from different activities. Remuneration coming from additional activities—such as private tutoring, teaching in other universities, consulting, and so forth—may be equivalent to or even higher than contract salary and in most cases have a substantial impact (often a negative one) on faculty incentives and efforts within the university.

In the coming years, measures will most likely be undertaken by the state and the academic community, to improve the quality of university programs, to support high-quality research within universities, and to restore the prestige of the academic profession in Russia.

Notes

1. This chapter focuses on higher education institutions only and does not consider academic contracts and salaries at research institutions affiliated with the Russian Academy of Sciences (which is, according to long-standing tradition, separate from the university sector in Russia).
2. The data on sources of income, except for public funding, of higher education institutions became available since 2006. By using the official chain price indices for tuition

and time series of the number of "commercial" students who either paid tuition themselves or for whom tuition was paid by their employer in 2000–2006, private funding of the universities was obtained and compared to public funding. Surveys by Higher School of Economics show that the share of private funding of research activities at universities was negligible during 2000–2008. *See* Shuvalova (2009, 66).

3. In this section the focus (unless told otherwise) is on faculty of public higher education institutions.

4. The yearly based Monitoring of Education Markets and Organizations study consists of representative surveys of students and their families, teachers (at schools) and faculty of colleges and universities, heads of colleges, and universities and employers. It does not currently have an English-language website. It is designed and administered by Higher School of Economics, under financial support of the Ministry of Education and Science of Russian Federation.

5. Again, data are based on the Monitoring of Education Markets and Organizations.

References

Federal State Statistics Service (Rosstat). 2009. http://www.gks.ru/wps/wcm/connect/rosstat/rosstatsite/main/population/wages/#. Accessed December 30, 2011.

Horta H., F. Veloso, and R. Grediaga. 2007. "Navel gazing: Academic inbreeding and scientific productivity." *Department of Engineering and Public Policy* 118. http://repository.cmu.edu/epp/118.

Kozmina Y. Y., A. A. Panova, and M. M. Yudkevich. 2007. *Survey of economic departments at St. Petersburg higher education institutions.* Moscow: Vershina.

Kuzminov, Y., and M. Yudkevich. 2007. "Academic freedom and university standards for teaching and research." Higher School of Economics working paper, WP10/2007/01.

Levin-Stankevich, L., and A. Saveliev. 1996. "The academic profession in Russia." In *The international academic profession: Portraits of fourteen countries,* ed. P. G. Altbach. Princeton, NJ: Carnegie Foundation.

Monitoring of Education Markets and Organizations. 2008. http://memo.hse.ru/published_ib. Accessed December 30, 2011.

Nazarova, I. 2005. *Teachers of economic disciplines: professional potential, employment and motivation* [in Russian]. Moscow: MAKS Press.

Roshchina, Y., and T. Filippova. 2006. "Teachers at the market for teaching services" [in Russian]. *Information Bulletin of the Monitoring of Education Markets and Organizations* 2 (20). Moscow: Higher School of Economics Publishing House.

Roshchina Y., and M. Yudkevich. 2009. "Determinants of research activity of university faculty: Administration policy, contract incompleteness or academic environments?" [in Russian]. *Voprosy Obrazovania* 3: 203–28.

Shuvalova, O. 2009. "Institutions of professional education: Human resources, economics and strategies" [in Russian]. *Information Bulletin of the Monitoring of Education Markets and Organizations* 1 (36): 20–80.

Sivak, L., and M. Yudkevich. 2009. "Academic inbreeding: Pro and contra" [in Russian]. *Oprosy Obrazovania* 1: 170–87.

Smolentseva, A. 2003. "Challenges to the Russian academic profession." *Higher Education* 45: 391–424.

26

FACULTY SALARY AND REMUNERATION IN THE KINGDOM OF SAUDI ARABIA

Mohammad Al-Ohali and Hamad Al-Mehrej

University faculty in Saudi universities enjoy generous remuneration. This perspective reflects policymakers' conviction that quality faculty members and teaching staff are the basis for advanced, excellent higher education and eventually for economic and social development. Salaries, various allowances, and incentives available to faculty members in the universities of the Kingdom of Saudi Arabia compare favorably on a global basis. This chapter examines faculty remuneration in Saudi Arabia. It also provides a basic idea about the type of academic contracts offered to faculty, their qualifications, and their positions at universities in Saudi Arabia.

The Higher Education System

Like many emerging countries, education in Saudi Arabia is dominated by the public sector. The Ministry of Higher Education is responsible for planning and overseeing all sectors of higher education. The government allocates 12 percent of the nation's budget for the development of universities and their staff. Due to this influx of resources, it is not surprising to observe an exponential growth in the number of students, faculty, and universities.

Over the last decade, through the support and guidance of the Ministry of Higher Education, a number of private universities and colleges have begun to offer degree programs. Since 2001, the number of private higher education institutions has grown to 8 universities and 25 colleges that cater to 55,000 students and employ about 1,900 local and expatriate staff.

Table 26.1 depicts the growth in higher education enrollment in the last decade (1999–2010). In 2010, the number of students in higher education (both public and private) had grown to more than one million students. More than half of the enrollments are female students (55 percent). The number of faculty members has experienced similar growth levels, as depicted in Table 26.2.

Table 26.1 The numbers of enrolled students in 1999, 2004, and 2010

Year	Male	Female	Total
1999	178,099	225,995	404,094
2004	253,551	350,216	603,767
2010	509,841	529,872	1,039,713

Sources: Ministry of Higher Education 2007; Ministry of Higher Education, Center for Higher Education Statistics, n.d.a, n.d.b.

Table 26.2 Number of faculty members in 1999, 2004, and 2010

Year	Male	Female	Total
1999	12,483	6,442	18,925
2004	17,813	8,753	26,566
2010	24,680	16,586	41,266

Sources: Ministry of Higher Education Statistics; Ministry of Higher Education, Deputyship for Planning and Statistics 2010.

The rapid expansion in higher education in Saudi Arabia in the last three decades challenged the tasks of preparing quality faculty and attracting world-class expatriate faculty. The Ministry of Higher Education has been working hard with public universities to ensure that the human resources policies in place are conducive to this goal; these policies give university rectors the authority to offer incentives to attract well-known scholars. Also, universities must be able to attract young Saudis and nourish them to become future faculty members. At the same time, universities need to offer competitive incentives and pay scales to attract the best foreign faculty from other countries. Due to excellent working conditions and competitive packages, faculty members, once hired at any level, mostly continue their life career in the same institution permanently. While universities may compete for similar resources from abroad, attrition and movement across universities within Saudi Arabia are not very common. There seems to be an understanding that new institutions will not be built by taking away talent and manpower from established ones.

Private Higher Education

In Saudi Arabia, private higher education has grown rapidly. Since 2001, the number of private higher education institutions has reached 8 universities and 25 colleges. Based on the differences between a private university and college, a university has four or more colleges while a college is a single unit. These private institutions have achieved distinction in the quality of their programs and the development plans according to which they operate.

The private higher education sector began with 550 male and female students. It has continued to expand—reaching approximately 55,000 male and female students in 2010. These universities and colleges work with the support and supervision of the Ministry of Higher Education. All of their programs must abide by the standards set by the National Commission for Academic Accreditation and Assessment. All the specializations of the private universities and colleges are linked to the current and future needs of the labor market. The degree programs they offer have been selected carefully to ensure the distinction of their graduates. Government support is tied to student performance and can reach full tuition each year for up to 50 percent of the newly admitted students in each private college or university. This policy requires students to have achieved at least a very good grade point average in order to be entitled to the full tuition support of the government, paid directly to the institution.

Academic Contracts

Saudi faculty members in Saudi Arabian public universities are considered to be public servants. Academic appointments are somewhat comparable to academic tenure in other countries. Saudi faculty hold a permanent position, with fixed, regular-annual increments and incentives, from the first day they are employed. Regulations, however, do exist for termination of employment—in case of poor or unacceptable performance (Ministry of Higher Education 2007). The mandatory retirement age for Saudi faculty is 60 years but can easily be extended up to age 65 if no health concerns prevent normal functions.

Expatriate faculty members are considered to be a point of strength and contribute to diversifying education and cultural experiences in Saudi higher education and universities. In 2010, there were approximately 10,000 expatriate faculty members—25 percent of the total faculty members—distributed in all universities and colleges in the country and from 31 nationalities around the globe. Expatriate faculty members work on renewable contracts and enjoy negotiable salaries and increments—based on their area of specialization, credentials, and market demand. These faculty do not have permanent positions, but contracts are generally renewed, except in the case of extremely poor performance. The renewal period is once in two years. Recently, some universities have awarded longer contracts to faculty who have maintained a high level of excellence in their performance. Each university develops its human resources policies and procedures in accordance with government regulations, but both public and private universities sign the contracts with their faculty.

Regulations governing the duties of university faculty members and other teaching staff, salary, and remuneration were introduced by a royal decree in 1980. All regulations have been set by the government and updated as needed to attract the best staff for higher education in Saudi Arabia. These regulations have been modified several times in order to make university jobs attractive to the best-qualified scientists and academics, by having a more competitive pay scale and incentives. A faculty member is expected to teach, carry out research, and contribute to community service activities. Promotion of faculty is linked to their research productivity, teaching load, and performance in community service, regardless of whether the university's emphasis is on research or teaching. Both public and private higher education institutions in the kingdom have an autonomy that allows them to compete for expatriate faculty members, offering them different benefits and incentives.

Qualifications

Regulations governing qualifications of faculty members and other teaching staff for universities across Saudi Arabia were also established by a royal decree in 1980. The decree specified five academic job titles: demonstrator (holds a bachelor's degree with a "very good" or higher grade point average, also known as graduate assistant in some universities); lecturer (holds at least a master's degree); assistant professor (holds a PhD or equivalent degree); associate professor; and full professor (Ministry of Education 2007). All professorial ranks require the minimum qualification of a doctoral degree.

Other teaching staff include graduate assistants and demonstrators who are hired after a bachelor's degree and take part in assisting in teaching, lectures, conducting of laboratories, and so forth. These staff are considered faculty members in training and enjoy all benefits and incentives. The time spent as demonstrators or graduate assistants is also counted as service years for their retirement. A demonstrator usually gets promoted to the level of a lecturer when he or she earns a master's degree. A lecturer is promoted to the position of an assistant professor when he or she earns a PhD degree or the equivalent. An assistant professor and an associate professor are promoted to the next rank after spending at least four years of service in the same rank and meeting several other requirements.

A demonstrator and lecturer are allowed a maximum of 10 years to advance to a higher academic degree, or they will be transferred to a nonacademic status. An assistant professor and an associate professor are promoted to the next rank after spending at least four years of service in the same rank and meeting other requirements. The promotion is granted based on presenting a number of refereed research papers, performance assessments in teaching, and contribution to community service. The scientific council in each university is the body responsible to recommend academic promotion, which has final approval from the university board.

Generally, Saudi faculty members are identified for a position at a university after their bachelor's degree. Upon graduation, qualified bachelor's degree holders who aspire to be a faculty member can apply as graduate assistants (or as demonstrators). Qualification means a high grade point average and good personal and communications skills. This is when their employment and training as faculty begin.

On an annual basis, universities identify job openings in different fields of study and recruit, accordingly. Graduate assistants are expected to complete their graduate studies, generally abroad in reputable and world-class institutions, and return to the university that employed them to begin their academic career. Most of them, especially in scientific fields, go abroad to pursue their master's and doctoral degrees. During their study, the employer university pays half of their current salary and, in addition, covers all their expenses including tuition, books, travel, and living expenses. Allowances for spouses and children (up to four children) are also available, and at times educational expenses of accompanying spouses are also provided.

Salaries, Benefits, and Incentives

This section deals with monetary and nonmonetary benefits given to the faculty across universities in Saudi Arabia.

Public university faculty members obtain an annual automatic raise by moving up 1 step, through 15 steps, in each rank, while they move upward from one level (rank) to another by upgrading their scholarly profile at the university. This scholarly upgrading is based on many accomplishments by faculty members, including research activities. Table 26.3 shows averages of the basic salary of public universities' faculty members and teaching staff for different positions and ranks, as

Table 26.3 Average monthly salaries (SR) for faculty (basic and new incentives)

Career rank[1]	Title	Scales within ranks	Basic monthly salary
Level 1	Full professor	Top scale	28,641
		Middle scale	23,529
		Bottom scale	18,417
Level 2	Associate professor	Top scale	25,334
		Middle scale	20,706
		Bottom scale	16,077
Level 3	Assistant professor	Top scale	20,735
		Middle scale	16,750
		Bottom scale	12,765
Level 4	Lecturer	Top scale	15,847
		Middle scale	12,305
		Bottom scale	8,763
Level 5	Demonstrator	Top scale	12,443
		Middle scale	9,545
		Bottom scale	6,647

Source: Ministry of Civil Services, n.d.

[1] In Saudi Riyals (SR); (US$1.00 = SR 3.75). Each rank consists of 15 steps. Top of scale is the average from the top 5 steps; middle of scale, the following 5; and bottom of scale, the bottom 5. The average for middle of scale is also the average for the 15 steps.

set by the royal decree in 2005 and modified in 2008 and 2010. Table 26.4 shows the average salary of faculty members in different ranks and fields—including a professor of medicine; a professor in a new university; and an associate professor of engineering. The clearly shown average of the basic salary per rank includes allocation of various percentages of basic salary to incentives such as the use of teaching aids, awards, and research and the new incentives introduced recently. A detailed discussion regarding incentives is in following sections.

Salaries of faculty in private universities are different from their counterparts in public universities, and in general their salaries are slightly higher than those of public universities. However, various private universities use different salary schemes, and private universities do not publish their salaries or make them otherwise public. Therefore, the following discussion is limited only to the remuneration of public university faculty members.

Nonsalary (Fringe) Benefits

Faculty members and teaching staff in Saudi universities enjoy various benefits, as stated in the Royal Decree no. 259 (in 2008). Faculty members are entitled to receive a one-month allowance for every year of service in higher education at retirement, an extra allowance for teaching more than their normal teaching load, sponsored scholarship for demonstrators and lecturers to pursue further higher education, training and housing allowances, and funds to attend conferences in and outside Saudi Arabia. In certain fields, such as medicine, faculty can make up to 70 percent of the basic salary, due to their extra medical services in the teaching hospitals or clinics. There are other benefits—such as a fully paid sabbatical leave, every five years. Faculty members can choose to spend their sabbatical at a university with an international reputation or at a research center. A faculty member at a professorial rank is eligible for a six-month to one-year sabbatical, after every five years of service with a university.

Incentives

Faculty members and teaching staff at Saudi universities also enjoy various additional monthly allowances, as incentives for better research and teaching activities, such as—10 to 30 percent of the basic salary for excellence, determined by receiving a local, regional, or international award; 20 to 40 percent of the basic salary, for rare specialties; 20 to 40 percent of the basic salary, for working in a newly established university; 40 percent of the basic salary for faculty staff who registered an invention; 25 percent of the basic salary for teaching a full schedule; 25 percent of the basic salary for staff who integrate advanced educational technology intensively in their teaching or research, such as advanced computer programs; and SR 1,500 to SR 2,500 (US$400–US$666) for holding a leadership position (such as dean or chairperson) in a college or department.

All faculty members are eligible for these incentives from the first day of their appointment. The numbers can vary, depending on the performance. Most faculty members qualify for the load compensation; in the case of incentives for using educational aids and computers, the decision is made after a committee review. Invariably, faculty with full teaching loads (of at least 10 teaching hours weekly for professors, 12 teaching hours weekly for associate professors, and 14 teaching hours weekly for assistant professors) are involved in recitations, serve as mentors to cooperative/summer training students, supervise master of science and PhD theses, serve as committee members, and take part in other academic activities. These activities are generally quantified; and the expected load can vary, depending on the rank of the faculty.

Overall, the incentives available in the Saudi system can enable faculty members to double their income. These incentives are available to all ranks, including the demonstrator, and are linked to performance. There are committees and instruments to assess eligibility for additional rewards, and, in fact, most Saudi faculty do double their basic salary.

Thus the total cost of a faculty member to the university, in addition to the basic salary, includes (a) the provided housing, generally a completely furnished villa with maintenance, utilities, and amenities covered and the size depending on both the rank of the professor and the size of the family; (b) allowances for teaching regular loads, utilization of computers and technology in teaching, and an extra allowance if the faculty are in disciplines facing shortages; (c) annual repatriation tickets (for foreign faculty and their family members); (d) schooling allowance; (e) medical support for the family; and (f) a 15 percent inflation allowance, and other items. Other payments include a transportation allowance, allowances for working in hazardous environments, and so forth. There is no income tax in Saudi Arabia. Faculty members in Saudi universities enjoy attractive salary packages, leading to better stability and a high rate of retention.

With these newly introduced incentives, in order to make the salary scale clear and meaningful, it is important to show examples of monthly income among university teaching faculty members, as in Table 26.4.

Supplementary Employment (Moonlighting)

Faculty members and teaching staff in Saudi universities are allowed to consult, teach, and carry out research for organizations, other than their own universities, to earn extra income. No detailed statistics are produced on the proportion of faculty who engage in work outside their universities. Each individual university keeps track of its faculty members. Although multiple appointments are rare, there is no restriction for faculty members and teaching staff to teach at other institutions.

As in most U.S. universities, faculty members work on campus for 10 months. Their annual salary is divided into 12 installments and is paid every month. For

Table 26.4 Monthly income of a sample http://www.bestbuyeyeglasses.com/marc-jacobs-mjacobs-324/3243244.html?cse=8&ci_src=14110944&ci_sku=3243244 of university teaching faculty members

Academic job titles		Average basic salary (SR)	Teaching allowance	Using teaching aids	Rare specialties	Working in a new university	Registering an invention	Receiving award	Medical field allowance	Transportation allowance	Total
% of basic salary		100%	25	25	Up to 40	Up to 40	40	30	70		
Professor of medicine	Upper range	28,641	6,226	6,226	9,962	n.a.	n.d.	n.d.	17,434	600	69,089
Professor of medicine	Lower range	18,417	4,004	4,004	6,406	n.a.	n.d.	n.d.	11,211	600	44,642
Professor of medicine in new university	Upper range	28,641	6,226	6,226	9,962	9,962	n.d.	n.d.	17,434	600	79,051
Professor of medicine in new university	Lower range	18,417	4,004	4,004	6,406	6,406	n.d.	n.d.	11,211	600	51,048
Associate professor of engineering	Upper range	25,335	5,808	5,808	8,812	n.a.	n.d.	n.d.	n.d.	600	46,363
Associate professor of engineering	Lower range	16,077	3,495	3,495	5,592	n.a.	n.d.	n.d.	n.d.	600	29,259
Associate professor of education	Mid range	18,005	4,501	4,501	n.a.	n.a.	n.d.	n.d.	n.d.	600	27,607

Source: Ministry of Civil Services, n.d.

Notes: Salaries in Saudi Riyals (SR)—US$1.00 = SR 3.75.

n.a. = not applicable.

n.d. = no data.

those intending to work during the summer term, an additional contract for one or two months is awarded. This can compensate teaching a course, developing a laboratory, or undertaking any academic development or research activity.

In addition, other options may supplement income—such as teaching in short courses offered to industry, involvement in short-term consultancy via funded projects, among others.

International Competition

The absence of reliable international data makes it hard to compare Saudi Arabia with other nations. This is also evident from the high demand for academic positions from Saudi and international academics and also from a limited number of early retirement of faculty members. However, it is worth mentioning that private industry offers a comparable or even better salary scale than academic salaries.

Conclusion

Higher education in Saudi Arabia is key to the country's transformation into a knowledge society; hence, the sector is receiving the highest-possible attention and support from the government. Saudi Arabia is among the top countries globally, in terms of salary scales. This status is as a result of policy to attract the best talent from both within and outside of the country. Allowances and incentives are extensive and attractive. While some motivations are based on performance, such as inventions, others are based on faculty working in remote areas or new universities; most of the allowances are provided to all faculty members (Saudis and non-Saudis).

References

Ministry of Civil Services. n.d. http://www.mcs.gov.sa/EmploymentInformation/EmploymentRights/SalariesLadders/Pages/default.aspx. Accessed May 1, 2011.

Ministry of Higher Education. 2007. *Rules and regulations of Higher Education Council.* 3rd ed. Saudi Arabia: Ministry of Higher Education.

Ministry of Higher Education, Center for Higher Education Statistics. n.d.a. http://www.mohe.gov.sa/en/Pages/default.aspx. Accessed May 3, 2011.

Ministry of Higher Education, Center for Higher Education Statistics. n.d.b. http://www.mohe.gov.sa/ar/Ministry/Deputy-Ministry-for-Planning-and-Information-affairs/HESC/Pages/ehsaat.aspx. Accessed May 2, 2011.

Ministry of Higher Education, Deputyship for Planning and Statistics—General Department for Planning and Statistics. 2010. *Current status of higher education in the Kingdom of Saudi Arabia.* Saudi Arabia: Ministry of Higher Education.

27

THE UNEQUAL PLAYING FIELD

Academic Remuneration in South Africa

Chika Trevor Sehoole

A 2010 survey of academic salaries, undertaken by the Association of Commonwealth Universities, shows South Africa's ranking as the second-best country, after Australia, in terms of academic remuneration levels. South Africa has the highest-salary scales relative to the national gross domestic product per capita; the overall average academic salary is seven times greater than the gross domestic product per capita (Maslen 2010). Thus, universities in general may offer competitive salaries, comparable to the best in the world. However, not revealed are inequalities in the universities, which are a legacy of the apartheid system. These inequalities have created an unequal playing field, where the best urban-based, research-intensive universities are able to compete for the best minds available in the country and the lower resource and smaller, rural-based or teaching universities are not able to offer such competitive salaries and, therefore, not able to compete.

The findings of this chapter are that—given the right qualifications, relevant skills, and experience—academic salaries and remuneration packages in South African universities afford academics opportunities for middle-class lives. Even though it is difficult to estimate the competition of the salaries and remuneration packages—relative to other professions with similar qualifications—the value of the academic life remains competitive and cannot be quantified simply in monetary terms. The benefits and allowances in terms of time, leave (vacation, maternity, paternity, research, compassionate, and travel), and flexibility far outweigh the monetary value offered by other professions.

For universities to thrive, they need to be adequately resourced through the right level of funding, production, and employment of quality staff. To remain competitive, universities should reward their academics in a way to ensure that they are able to attract and retain adequately qualified staff who will contribute to the achievement of the university's triple mission of teaching, research, and community engagement (HESA 2006). In the context of the inequalities highlighted above, more resources—both human and material—will need to be invested in smaller, rural-based and teaching universities, to put them at the same level of competitiveness as research-intensive, urban-based universities.

This study used primary data collected from government sources, interviews with government and university officials, and secondary data relevant to the topic. There are limited remuneration data available on private higher education institutions (universities), as there are no centralized data for private institutions as there are for public institutions.

An Overview of Higher Education

South Africa's public higher education has grown from one college, established in 1843, to 36 institutions—consisting of 21 universities and 15 *technikons* (polytechnics), by 2000. Through the merger policy passed in 2002, public higher education institutions were reduced from 36 to 23 universities—consisting of 11 traditional universities, 6 comprehensive universities, and 6 universities of technology (Department of Education 2001). In 2008, universities enrolled 799,387 students, with 500,717 enrolled for degree programs and 298,670 enrolled for certificate and diploma programs.

In 2008, South Africa spent 20 percent of state budget on education. About 2.3 percent of total state budget and 12 percent of the education budget (US$2.1 billion) was spent on university education (DHET 2010b). Universities also rely on student fees, private endowments, and contract research for their income.

Academic Hierarchy

The South African academic hierarchy is made up of five ranks of tenure-stream faculty—namely, junior lecturer, lecturer, senior lecturer, associate professor, and full professor. The title of assistant professor is not used, and its equivalent is probably a lecturer. Employment in universities requires a minimum of a master's degree. In 2007, 33 percent of academics had a PhD qualification (ASSAF 2010). This lower base of qualifications for staff is due to the fact that, prior to the merger of some technikons with universities, employment in technikons did not require a master's or doctoral degree qualification. With their conversion into universities, former technikons staff—some with qualifications lower than a master's degree and PhD—became part of the university system.

In 2008, public universities employed 41,738 staff, of which 20,203 were full time and 21,535 part time (Council for Higher Education, via email message, December 19, 2010). Of the full-time permanent staff 13 percent were full professors, 10 percent associate professors, 26 percent senior lecturers, 39 percent lecturers, and 7 percent junior lecturers; and the remaining 5 percent were undesignated.

Private Higher Education Institutions (Universities)

In 2010 there were 103 registered private higher education institutions in South Africa. These enrolled 73,827 students, of which 2,449 were graduate and 71,378 undergraduate students (DHET 2010a). The 2010 data shows that, of the 4,898 academic staff employed in these institutions, 3,135, or 64 percent, were part-time staff (Council for Higher Education, via email, December 19, 2010). Given the unavailability of data, a discussion on the remuneration practices in private institutions is limited and only referred to where relevant to the analysis, but not in comparison to public universities.

Salaries and Remuneration Practices

As mentioned earlier, the 2010 survey of academic salaries undertaken by the Association of Commonwealth Universities shows South Africa as ranking the second-best country after Australia, in terms of remuneration levels. However, South Africa also has had the highest level of growth in academic salary scales (51%) since the last survey (Maslen 2010). The high levels of growth in academic salaries should be understood in the light of the restructuring in education over the past eight years—as a result of mergers, which necessitated some changes in salary structures of merged institutions to achieve equity. For mergers to work, the government had to invest additional resources during the transition period in order cover extra expenses associated with these procedures. At the same time, a significant increase has occurred in government's budget allocation to universities, which has grown from R 9.8 billion (US$1.4 billion) in 2004 to R 14.923 billion (US$2.2 billion) in 2008. This represented an increase of 52 percent since 2004 (DHET 2009). This budget allocation further rose to R 19,537 (US$2.88 billion) in 2010 (DHET 2009), which is 100 percent more than the 2004 allocation. It can be inferred from the outcomes of this survey that academics have been beneficiaries from the increased government allocations to universities over the past six years.

Universities in South Africa are established in terms of the Higher Education Act, no. 101 of 1997 and deemed as legal entities enjoying autonomy from the state. This act makes provision for the appointment of the University Council, which is entrusted with the governance of the institution (Department of Education 1997b). As autonomous institutions, universities have the legal authority to hire its employees and determine the conditions of their employment. Academics are not civil servants. Their employment is regulated by the institutional statutes passed by the University Council. Negotiations regarding salaries are the purview of institutional councils and are normally delegated to the institutional human resource committee for implementation. Salaries are negotiated on an individual basis between the institution and the candidate during the recruitment process, and thereafter salary increases are based on the outcomes of negotiations between university management and unions. Even though some campus-based unions are affiliated to national bodies, salary negotiations are concluded at institutional levels. In some institutions these negotiations do not cover part-time staff, whose contracts and conditions of service are negotiated on an individual basis.

The government makes annual allocations to universities based on a funding formula (Department of Education 2003), and it is not involved in the determination of remuneration practices. However, it requires that universities should be able to account for how they spend public funds (Department of Education 1997a). To ensure good remuneration practices, universities have adopted remuneration policies and practices that include the use of at least two reliable sources for external benchmarking of organizations in a similar industry, of similar size and complexity. Universities participate in annual-salary surveys that are used as a basis for benchmarking salaries. Each institution develops its own criteria—based on a number of variables, including the discipline where a vacancy exists and the scarcity or availability of skills in that field. The use of external benchmarks is not to equalize salaries, but rather to get a sense of what the market pays for various positions, in order to make an informed decision regarding offers to new recruits. These benchmarks also help to ensure equity within the organization, in terms of the different levels of remuneration (HESA 2006).

The common practice in most universities is to structure pay as a remuneration package. This amount is then divided into basic pensionable pay, contributions to retirements and medical schemes, performance reward (variables dependent on performance), and up to a maximum amount of money stated in the package overall. The performance reward is given on an individual basis and includes meeting or exceeding performance targets (HESA 2006).

Table 27.1 shows average remuneration packages of academic staff, including the actual minimum and maximum salaries paid across the system. What these figures obscure are the variations in remuneration between traditional universities and universities of technology and those that also exist between urban and rural universities, as shown in Tables 27.2 and 27.3.

Table 27.1 Annual salaries of academics, including lowest and maximum salary (R)

| Rank | Average salaries for all institutions | | | Actual lowest and highest salaries | |
	Minimum	*Average*	*Maximum*	*Minimum*	*Maximum*
Professor	404,982	525,845	700,722	208,567	998,279
Associate professor	322,942	436,017	616,618	201,520	955,491
Senior lecturer	246,758	372,104	542,650	106,626	983,772
Lecturer	190,317	302,867	438,883	93,484	595,525
Junior lecturer	150,882	220,604	326,815	88,273	480,797

Source: Hemis data, Department of Higher Education and Training.

Note: Exchange rate US$1.00 = R 7.00.

Table 27.2 Minimum and maximum salaries of traditional universities and universities of technology

	All (average)	Traditional (minimum)	UOTs* (minimum)	Traditional (maximum)	UOTs* (maximum)
Professor	525,845	208,567	383,672	998,279	792,897
Associate	436,017	201,520	268,249	955,491	674,032
Senior lecturer	372,104	106,626	176,909	983,772	647,836
Lecturer	302,867	93,484	163,325	595,525	484,789

Source: Hemis data, Department of Higher Education and Training, 2010.
Note: Exchange rate US$1.00 = R 7.00.
*UOTs = universities of technology.

Some universities pay special allowances for involvement in management positions—such as head of department or dean posts—that are short-term appointments. Some institutions offer salary increment on confirmation of a relevant higher degree or a research-incentive bonus upon confirmation of a doctoral degree.

With respect to normative salary structure and internal pay equity, debate involves about what constitutes best practice. Also, there is no single approach to establishing equity in the internal pay line, owing mainly to such factors as the current levels of remuneration, organizational affordability, and organizational health (HESA 2006). For example, a big research university may offer a good remuneration package to a senior professor who is further enhanced by benefits—such as provision of good research infrastructure, opportunities for conference attendance, and overseas travel. On the other hand, a smaller, rural-based teaching institution may not be able to afford similar benefits. In this regard, organizational affordability and financial health influence the extent to which the smaller universities are able to compete with larger institutions for qualified staff. Table 27.3 shows that, in the categories of professor and associate professor, urban-based universities offer better remuneration than smaller, rural-based universities. The professoriate in universities is key in attracting research contracts and production of graduate students, which all contribute to the competitiveness of an institution.

Compared to rural-based universities, these urban-based universities are more able to attract public funding and private endowments—based on the strength of their research capacity and output, teaching output, and program offerings that are aligned to the needs of the economy. This is part of the heritage of apartheid that still needs to be redressed in order to achieve equity in higher education. The competitiveness of academic salaries is a contributory factor to South Africa, which is a destination of choice for many academics from the rest of the African continent who come to South Africa to further their careers—thereby contributing to brain drain in the region.

Table 27.3 Comparison of remuneration packages of urban-based universities in Gauteng Province and rural-based universities

	All	Urban (Gauteng) minimum	Rural minimum	Urban (Gauteng) maximum	Rural maximum
Professor	525,845	326,650	208,567	998,279	686,145
Associate professor	436,017	254,310	230,662	736,277	717,000
Senior lecturer	372,104	106,626	112,275	983,772	760,875
Lecturer	302,867	117,358	141,642	595,525	451,314

Source: Hemis data, Department of Higher Education and Training, 2010.
Note: Exchange rate US$1.00 = R 7.00.

Hiring and Promotion

South African universities have a tenure system in which academics are initially employed on probation and are subsequently offered a tenured, permanent position, after satisfying the stipulated criteria. The probation period varies across institutions and can last from one to three years.

The hiring of new staff entails public advertisement of positions in the media and via the Internet, interviews, and the candidate may be invited to give a seminar. The minimum qualification for a lecturer is a master's degree or PhD and for an associate professor and a full professor, a PhD plus teaching and research experience. For appointment of strategic value to the institution, some universities use search committees to attract the right candidates. Universities offer various types of contracts that may be permanent (full time and part time) or temporary (full time and part time).

Criteria used for promotion of staff vary across institutions. For example, promotion from lecturer to senior lecturer requires a completion of a PhD, evidence of teaching outputs, and supervision of graduate students. Promotion from senior lecturer to associate professor requires evidence of supervision of master's and doctoral students to completion, book publications, and publications in accredited journals. Promotions from associate professor to full professor requires evidence of sustained teaching and research outputs—in the form of successful supervision of master's and doctoral students to completion, a sustained publication record as evidenced by book and journal articles, and a standing in research as demonstrated by obtaining a rating by the National Research Foundation.

South Africa has a peer review rating system of researchers, which is based on the evaluation of the research outputs of academics. Three rating categories (A, B, and C) are awarded, depending on the quality and impact of the research output. An academic whose research enjoys national standing and recognition would be awarded a C rating; one whose research enjoys international recognition would be awarded a B rating; and those who are renowned world leaders in their fields are awarded an A rating (National Research Foundation, n.d.).

Rated researchers are sought by universities, as the quality and calibre of a university is measured by the number of rated researchers employed. The National Research Foundation provides incentives to rated researchers in the form of awards, which may vary from US$7,000 for C-rated researchers to US$18,000 for A-rated researchers.

The use of indicators such as qualifications, experience, skills scarcity, satisfying requirements for internal equity and fairness, strategic priority, market profile of an individual, employment equity, and benchmarks in the recruitment and hiring of academics suggests that, in general, remuneration levels and practices in universities are competitive and are geared toward attracting the best staff. While all institutions try to be competitive, they also ensure that remuneration should be affordable to the institution and sustainable over time. These principles and framework are applicable in public universities and private higher education institutions. In interviews with officials of selected private institutions, it was indicated that they also use reliable sources for external benchmarking of organizations in a similar industry, as well as external advisers to recruit staff and to determine remuneration levels. Sometimes there is diversion from this practice, as many private institutions are for-profit and rely mainly on part-time and contract staff; their remuneration levels are also influenced by the nature of requests for training they receive and the price the client is willing to pay.

There were no available data to allow comparison of salaries paid by universities (private and public), government sector, and private industry. However, in interviews with human-resources practitioners of some institutions, it was indicated that universities try to match salaries offered by the private industry. Furthermore, in areas of critical, scarce skills—such as medicine, accounting, and engineering—universities are not able to match the salaries; and favorable working conditions include permission to do private outside work, to compensate for the shortfall in salaries that universities pay.

Benefits

South African universities offer benefits that also determine remuneration levels and are based on value proposition and benefits that include flexible working hours, travel grants, leave (conference attendance), vacation (42 days a year for academics), maternity and paternity leave, sick leave, research infrastructure, research support, research assistants, incentives for research output, and allowance for rated researchers. These benefits, especially those related to research support, are mainly applicable to major research universities. Smaller teaching universities would mainly offer higher salaries in the form of hard cash in order to attract quality staff. However, the monetary value would normally pale against the benefits offered by bigger research institutions, resulting in research institutions having an edge over teaching institutions in recruiting staff.

Benefits—such as, medical aid or medical insurance, group life, relocation costs, study opportunity for dependents and self—are a common practice in many public universities. In particular, study opportunities for dependents are said to be a popular benefit for staff. The study opportunity benefit is limited to dependents studying at the institution where the staff member is working, unless the intended study program is not offered at the home university. The benefit mainly covers tuition but sometimes boarding and lodging as well. A settling fee to have children in schools and taking over bursary commitments (sometimes equivalent to an annual salary) are additional benefits offered by some institutions.

Special provisions are made to attract staff in areas of scarce skills. The criteria used to qualify for scarce skills are based on a turnover rate, which is the amount of effort put into recruiting and filling the post. Categories of scarce skills include engineers, specialist veterinarians, certificated financial accountants, chartered accountants, internal auditors, mathematicians linked to focus on school teaching, and industrial psychologists. Other factors considered in determining rare skills include experience, exposure, and specific attraction.

Special provisions made to attract these skills for staff include provision for outside work and consultancy. Many universities have a restraint of trade policy, where staff is not allowed to do outside work unless special permission is obtained from the head of department or dean. Some universities encourage staff to be involved in private work, as it helps them to be exposed to the latest technology and knowledge in their fields. This also helps to promote the image and profile of the institution. Although no data are available to measure the extent of involvement of academics in private work, it is common knowledge that many of them are involved in private work to supplement their salaries. In South Africa, higher education is said to be a low-risk environment and, thus, attractive to academics who have a heart for teaching and research, even though better jobs with better financial rewards may be available elsewhere. There is no monetary value that can be attached to many of the advantages of the academic profession.

Conclusion

This chapter has provided an overview of trends in salaries and remuneration in higher education in South Africa, showing the competitive nature of the profession and remuneration practices in the context of inequalities between institutions. The playing field is not level and gives advantages to bigger research institutions to attract the best available talent as they are endowed with resources relative to other institutions. In this regard, the chapter has shown that the academic remuneration practice is characterized by the scramble among institutions for the best available minds and skills in the field. If academics are productive in terms of teaching and research and the category of critical, scarce skills, they can lead a comfortable, middle-class life, comparable to colleagues in other professions with similar qualifications. While in monetary terms the academic profession may not compete with the private sector, the benefits and flexibility that academia provides make up for the shortfall that academia may experience.

There are variations within the system, based on differences in actual minimum and maximum salaries between urban-based and rural-based universities and also between major traditional universities and universities of technology. The chapter has not been able to shed sufficient light on remuneration practices in private higher education because of a lack of data. Yet, it can be safely assumed that practices in public higher education do not differ much from those in the private sector, except that the latter relies much on part-time staff, whereas the former relies on full-time staff.

References

ASSAF (Academy of Science of South Africa). 2010. *The PhD study: An evidence based study on how to meet the demands of high-level skills in an emerging economy.* Pretoria, South Africa: ASSAF.

Department of Education. 1997a. "Education white paper 3: A framework for the transformation of higher education." Pretoria, South Africa: Government Printers.

Department of Education. 1997b. Higher Education Act, no. 101, 1997. Pretoria, South Africa: Government Printers.

Department of Education. 2001. *National plan for higher education, Pretoria, Ministry of Education.* Pretoria, South Africa: Government Printers.

Department of Education. 2003. *Funding of public higher education.* Pretoria, Department of Education.

Department of Higher Education and Training. 2009. *Ministerial statement on higher education funding 2009/10 to 2011/12.* Pretoria, South Africa: Ministry of Education and Training.

Department of Higher Education and Training. 2010a. *Register of private higher education institutions.* Pretoria, South Africa: Department of Higher Education and Training.

Department of Higher Education and Training. 2010b. *Information on state budget for universities.* Pretoria, South Africa: Department of Higher Education and Training.

HESA (Higher Education South Africa). 2006. *Good governance of senior staff remuneration in South African higher education.* Pretoria, South Africa: HESA.

Maslen, G. 2010. Australia and South Africa pay top salaries. *University World News* (December 20): 152. http://www.universityworldnews.com/article.php?story=20101217224942899. Accessed December 20, 2010.

National Research Foundation. n.d. "Evaluation and rating." http://www.nrf.ac.za/projects.php?pid=33. Accessed February 23, 2011.

28

REMUNERATION OF ACADEMIC STAFF IN TURKISH UNIVERSITIES

Kemal Gürüz

The Turkish higher education system includes state universities and nonprofit private institutions. Academic staff in state universities have civil-servant status, and those in the professor and docent positions have tenure. The number of academic positions in state universities, as well as the remuneration of academic staff, are strictly regulated by legislation. Requirements for and procedures to be followed in appointments and promotions, as well as job descriptions for each rank, are specified by law; there are no individual contracts. The gross monthly income of a full-time academic staff member, in general, consists of the gross monthly salary plus additional payments for extra-teaching load, consultancy, contract research and services, basic research, and commercial activities in university *technoparks*. In practice, however, the income of the vast majority of the academic staff—especially those in disciplines other than medicine, engineering, business, and law—consists only of the gross monthly salary and additional payment for extra-teaching load. In some cases, these latter means can be quite significant.

Private universities have to comply with all of the academic requirements pertaining to conditions and procedures for appointments and promotions in state universities, but they are completely free in establishing positions, setting pay scales, and stipulating job descriptions and conditions of employment in individual contracts, which vary widely between universities and academic staff.

Detailed information is provided on the remuneration of academic staff in state universities, while only anecdotal information is available for private universities, where such information is confidential.

Overview of the System

Turkish higher education is a unified system, similar to the American system, in governance and academic structure (Law no. 2547; Law no. 2809). The Council of Higher Education is a constitutional body charged with planning, coordination, and governance of all higher education institutions. The Interuniversity Council is an academic advisory body to the Council of Higher Education.

A university (including private universities) is a corporate body founded by an act of the Parliament and, in general, comprises faculties, graduate schools, conservatories, four-year higher (vocationally oriented) schools, and two-year vocational schools. Each faculty and school comprises a number of departments. Degrees offered are in line with the requirements of the Bologna process.

Nonprofit institutions of higher education can be founded by charitable foundations. They are governed by their own boards of trustees and are completely autonomous financially and administratively but have to comply with the academic regulations related to state universities.

The main income stream of state universities is the state budget, which is a separate act of the Parliament for each state university. Students pay a contribution fee, which is centrally set by the government for each degree program in state universities. A revolving fund is established in each state university, where income from contract research, consultancy, patient care, and other services performed by the staff is collected. Private universities have complete freedom in setting tuition fees.

Academic Organization and Enrollment

The system currently comprises 102 state and 54 private universities and 9 independent, private, two-year vocational schools.

Enrollment in the 2009–10 academic year was 3.5 million students, with a gross enrollment ratio of 54 percent (ÖSYM 2010). An analysis of the component parts of student enrollment, according to the level of study, included: associate level, 30 percent; bachelor level, 64 percent; and graduate level, 6 percent. Forty-three percent of students were enrolled in distance-education programs. Despite their relatively large number, only 5 percent of students were in private institutions.

In 1992, an additional fee-paying track was established at associate and bachelor levels in state universities, where students pay tuition fees approximately equal to full cost (Law no. 3843). Currently, 13 percent of undergraduates are full-fee-paying students.

Qualifications and Appointment of Academic Staff

Academic staff include professors, docents, assistant docents, research assistants, lecturers, instructors, educational planners, translators, and specialists. Minimum criteria for appointment to each position and job descriptions are specified in laws (Law no. 2547; Law no. 2914). These apply to both state and private universities.

The professor rank is equivalent to full professor, docent to associate professor, and assistant docent to assistant professor—as in the American system. These three ranks constitute faculty members, and the rest are designated as auxiliary academic staff. The total number of academic staff in 2009–10 was 105,427; 9,556 of these were in private universities. The total academic staff comprised 63,246 auxiliary academic staff and 42,181 faculty members. Private institutions employed 5,940 auxiliary staff and 3,616 faculty members (ÖSYM 2010).

The same job description applies to professors, docents, and assistant docents and includes teaching, basic and applied research, thesis supervision, seminars, services (such as consulting), contract research and patient care, and student counseling. The number of positions for each rank of academic staff in state universities are determined by individual acts of the Parliament.

Private universities have freedom in establishing academic-staff positions and the procedures to be followed in inviting candidates. They must, however, comply with the minimum requirements that apply to each academic-staff rank in state universities.

Minimum requirements for appointment to the three ranks of faculty-member positions are separately specified in laws. At the assistant docent level, these requirements include doctoral-level degree and foreign-language proficiency. The docent title is similar to the German habilitation and the French aggregation. It is awarded nationally by the Interuniversity Council and must be obtained before one can apply to a docent position. A doctoral-level degree is required to apply for the docent title, but one does not have to go through the assistant professor stage to qualify for the docent title. On the other hand, after the docent title, at least five years of work experience, in or outside of a university, and internationally recognized publications are explicitly specified in laws as minimum requirements for applying to full professor positions.

All vacant faculty-member positions need to be advertised nationally and are thus open to candidates from outside the institution as well. Candidates for each position are evaluated by committees of internal and external academics, appointed by the university—at least one of whom must be external. Evaluation is increasingly based mainly on research and publications and, to a lesser extent, on teaching experience. The appointment is made by the university rector, based on recommendations of the committee and the head of the academic unit. Clearly, promotion from one faculty-member rank to another is not automatic and, in principle, not based on seniority.

Only Turkish citizens can be appointed as faculty members in state universities. Those appointed to professor and docent positions in state universities have tenure until the compulsory retirement age of 67 years. Assistant professors are appointed for a two- or three-year term, with a maximum total appointment period of 12 years. If they are not appointed as docents within 12 years, they are required to leave. Termination of the employment of a civil servant is a contentious and yet unresolved issue in the Turkish legal system. In practice, at the end of 12 years, those assistant docents who have not been appointed as docents are usually transferred to lecturer or instructor positions.

Those who have obtained professor, docent, or assistant docent titles, or their equivalents abroad, are evaluated by the Interuniversity Council, and if their titles are determined to be equivalent, they can apply for appointment to vacant positions in Turkish universities.

Most private universities do not use a tenure system and employ academic staff on individual contracts. Private universities also are not bound by the compulsory retirement age of 67 years, and can employ foreign nationals at all ranks.

The minimum requirement for appointment to an auxiliary staff position is a bachelor's degree. Research assistants are normally students in graduate-level programs; they assist faculty members in teaching and research. Applicants are evaluated on the basis of their cumulative grade-point averages, the score in a Graduate Record Examination–type nationwide examination, and foreign-language proficiency.

Lecturers and instructors are employed for teaching courses that require specialized knowledge and expertise. Applicants are required to provide evidence for their expertise, such as work experience and/or publications. Lecturers and instructors are normally appointed to teach a particular course and are paid on an hourly basis. In cases where no faculty members may teach a particular subject, they can be appointed for a maximum fixed term of two years, which can be renewed. Permanent appointments can be made for lecturer and instructor positions in vocational schools and conservatories.

Minimum requirements for and procedures to be followed in making appointments to auxiliary academic staff positions are also specified separately based on laws. These positions do not need to be advertised nationally, and committees that evaluate applicants do not need to include external members. Appointments are made by the university rector, upon recommendations of committees and the heads of the academic units concerned. Appointments to research assistantships in medical-specialty training programs directly follow results of a nationwide test, based on medical curricula.

Employment of research assistants is normally terminated when they receive their doctoral or medical-specialty degrees to prevent inbreeding. Thus, a research assistantship is the first step toward obtaining a faculty-member position but normally in a different university. However, these arrangements are still challenged by courts.

Lecturer, instructor, educational planner, translator, and specialist positions are normally terminal positions in the Turkish system, unless one receives a doctoral degree and applies to a vacant assistant docent position, or if one has a doctoral degree as well as a docent degree and applies to a vacant docent position.

In summary, the entry point to the academic profession is normally the assistant professor level, which requires a doctoral degree. In principle, seniority is not a factor in appointments and promotions. Publications in journals, covered by citation indices, are increasingly the major factor. However, the tendency to prefer someone already employed in that institution is widespread. Academic staff in private universities are employed on individual contracts that vary in scope, status, and conditions. Such contracts are confidential, and no information could be obtained regarding their details.

Remuneration of Academic Staff in State Universities

All academic staff in state universities are paid according to a general pay scale that sets basic monthly salaries. The general pay scale in the law on civil servants (Law no. 657) consists of some 15 vertical levels, with level 15 at the bottom and level 1 at the top and a number of horizontal steps at each level. Vertical levels reflect positions and posts, as well as years spent there, while horizontal steps reflect only years. The total monthly salary of a civil servant consists of the basic salary plus supplemental payments. The basic scale for supplemental payments to academic staff is set forth in the law on academic staff (Law no. 2914). Basic gross monthly salaries of academic staff as of May 2010 are shown in Table 28.1.

Monthly salaries of academic staff in state universities are specified every fiscal year, within the state budget, and an adjustment is made in July that reflects inflation. All academic staff in a given rank receive the same salary, regardless of their field.

According to the recent change in legislation (Law no. 5947), academic staff in state universities are normally employed on a full-time basis. This entails eight hours per day and five days in a week of work within the institution. On the basis of a subsequent ruling by the Constitutional Court (Decision no. 2010/21), professors and docents are allowed to engage in private practice after-hours—after 5 p.m. during weekdays and over weekends—and to receive income. However, a state of confusion exists, as to how the said ruling of the Constitutional Court will be reconciled with the wording of Law no. 5947.

Table 28.1 Gross monthly salaries (TL) of academic staff in state universities

Academic staff rank	Basic gross monthly salary	Total gross monthly salary	
		Minimum	Maximum
Professor	1,818	4,137	4,744
Docent	1,343	2,953	3,500
Assistant docent	1,233	2,769	2,782
Research assistant	802	2,275	2,342
Lecturer	1,020	2,437	2,626
Instructor	1,020	2,424	2,619
Education planner	881	2,319	2,516
Translator	1,020	2,316	2,492
Specialist	1,054	2,490	2,633

Source: Middle East Technical University Personnel Department, May 2010 (private communication).
Note: US$ 1.00 = TL 1.55 (in May 2010).

It is possible for state universities to employ foreign academic staff on fixed-term individual contracts and pay them up to six times the salary of a Turkish staff of the same position. However, the bureaucracy involved is so cumbersome and thus it is so time-consuming to complete the formalities that it is nearly impossible to use this channel effectively. Furthermore, interpretation of the term *salary* by the state bureaucracy eliminates possibilities of supplemental income and fringe benefits for foreign academic staff.

Additional Remuneration

There are several channels for additional remuneration. The first is an extra-teaching load in one's own institution. By law, the minimum teaching load in fall and spring semesters is 10 hours per week for faculty members and 12 hours for lecturers and instructors. Lecture hours, laboratory work, seminars, and supervision of graduate students all count toward the required minimum teaching load. Only faculty members, instructors, and lecturers get paid on an hourly basis for any extra teaching. Hourly extra-teaching rates are annually specified within the state budget. As of May 2010, the hourly extra-teaching rate is TL 9 (US$5.80) for lecturers and instructors, TL 11 (US$7.10) for assistant docents, TL 14 (US$9.00) for docents, and TL 17 (US$11.00) for professors teaching in regular programs.

These rates are multiplied by 3.2 for extra-teaching load in full-fee-paying programs and by 5 for teaching in a summer school. For additional payment purposes, there is, however, a cap of 20 hours of extra teaching per week, or 80 hours of extra teaching per month in regular programs, and 10 hours per week or 40 hours per month in full-fee-paying programs. Thus, it is possible for a professor to receive an additional monthly gross income of up to TL 4,076 (US$2,630) during the fall and spring semesters (TL 1,360 plus TL 2,176, giving a total of TL 4,076). The corresponding monthly amounts would be TL 2,912 (US$1,879) for a docent, TL 2,288 (US$1,476) for an assistant docent, and TL 1,872 (US$1,208) for a lecturer or an instructor.

Gross payments for extra-teaching load in regular programs made to academic staff at Middle East Technical University (METU) in Ankara in April 2010 are shown in Table 28.2.

Table 28.2 An example of monthly income (TL) from extra teaching load

Rank/Payment	Lowest	Median	Highest
Professor	688	1,030	1,371
Docent	574	861	1,148
Assistant docent	459	689	918
Lecturer and instructor	441	588	734

Source: Middle East Technical University Personnel Department, May 2010 (private communication).
Note: US$1.00 = TL 1.55 (in May 2010).

There are no required minimum teaching loads and caps on payments in summer schools, which means that all teaching receives extra pay. Few universities have summer semesters. Some state universities also have full-fee-paying master-level programs by courses carried out in evenings and over weekends. A few state universities also have dual-diploma programs, carried out jointly with universities abroad. Middle East Technical University, for example, has no full-fee-paying programs at the bachelor level but has full-fee-paying master-level programs by courses and dual-diploma programs with the State University of New York, Delft University, and Humboldt University. Extra-teaching-load (hourly) rates in these two types of programs can be as high as 10 times of the rates in regular programs—TL 170 (US$110) for professors—with a cap of 40 hours per month. It is thus possible for a professor to make an additional monthly rate of TL 6,800 (US$4,387) for teaching in these two types of programs. Teaching in these programs is treated as teaching in full-fee-paying programs for additional payment purposes. Gross payments made to academic staff in full-fee-paying track programs at Middle East Technical University in the month of April 2010 are shown in Table 28.3.

Academic staff who have opted not to engage in private practice after hours are allowed to carry out contract research, consultancy, and other services. Revenues from such activities as well as from patient care in university hospitals, including overhead, are collected in the university's revolving fund. Academic staff can receive additional income from a revolving fund, depending on their contributions to the activities and revenues in that category. The ceiling on such payments is normally eight times the basic gross monthly salary; if such activities are carried out after 5 p.m., the ceiling becomes 12 times the basic gross monthly salary. The latter case, however, is rare, even in university hospitals. Thus, in principle, a professor can receive an additional maximum gross monthly income of TL 18,180 (US$11,729), and an assistant docent can receive TL 12,330 (US$7,955) from activities performed through the revolving fund.

The following rates are the gross monthly payments made to academic staff in the Faculty of Medicine of Ankara University in the month of April 2010: professor, TL 3,669 (US$2,367); docent, TL 2,722 (US$1,756); assistant docent, TL 2,475

Table 28.3 Monthly income (TL) from teaching in full-fee-paying track programs

Rank/Payment	Lowest	Median	Highest
Professor	689	3,788	6,887
Docent	574	3,156	5,738
Assistant docent	459	2,525	4,590
Lecturer and instructor	367	2,020	3,672

Source: Middle East Technical University Personnel Department, May 2010 (private communication).
Note: US$1.00 = TL 1.55 (in May 2010).

(US$1,584); research assistant, TL 797 (US$514); specialist, TL 817 (US$527). In the same month, 20 professors in the Ankara University Faculty of Medicine were paid the maximum and then allowed for medical services performed after hours.

It should be pointed out that academic staff, only in faculties of medicine and dentistry, receive additional income on a more-or-less regular basis throughout the year, and even those monthly payments vary depending on hospital income. On the other hand, in a university without a faculty of medicine, like the Middle East Technical University, academic staff receive additional income from a revolving fund—only throughout the duration of a contract for a service, applied research, or consultancy. It is, therefore, not realistic to report additional monthly income figures through revolving funds as regular income, on a continual basis, outside of faculties of medicine and dentistry.

The Scientific and Technical Research Council of Turkey (Turkish acronym, TÜBİTAK) funds basic and applied university research on a contract basis. Universities are not allowed to charge overhead for TÜBİTAK-supported research and research projects funded through the European Union framework programs. Academic staff involved in such projects can receive additional monthly income of up to 75 percent of their monthly gross salaries—for a professor, TL 4,744 × 0.75 = TL 3,558 (US$2,295).

Academic staff in state universities in less-developed regions of the country are paid an additional monthly supplement that varies from 15 to 200 percent of the basic gross monthly salary, depending on the region. On the other hand, no additional payment is made to cover the higher cost of living in cities like Istanbul.

An additional income channel has been created by the law on technology development zones (Law no. 4691), enacted in 2001. There are now technoparks in 36 universities. Academic staff in state universities can provide consultancy services to companies in technoparks; they can also set up their own companies with the approval of the university administration. The two-largest technoparks are located in the campuses of METU and Istanbul Technical University. In May 2010, the METU technopark hosted 260 companies, with 25 of these founded by METU academic staff. The number of METU academic staff engaged in the technopark was 464, compared to the total of 2,424 academic staff employed by METU.

There is no ceiling on additional income that academic staff receive from activities in technoparks. Such payments can be potentially significant in some universities, but are confidential. Thus, when this last income channel is also taken into account, in principle, no limit is made to the monthly income of academic staff in a Turkish state university. The practical situation, however, is quite different. Staff with heavy teaching loads have little time for contract research. Only so many patients can be treated in university hospitals. One can get involved in only so many research projects, and so forth.

Deductions from gross monthly salary include income tax and contribution to the retirement-pension fund and health-benefits scheme for civil servants. The income tax rate is progressive and depends on the gross annual income that includes all types of payments mentioned previously. For academic staff with little or no additional income—from extra-teaching load, revolving funds, and the other sources mentioned previously—the net monthly salary, on average, corresponds to around 75 percent of the total gross monthly salary.

Fringe Benefits in State Universities

Health benefits in state universities include free medical care for staff as well as their dependents. They are only required to pay 25 percent of the cost of prescriptions, full costs of some prosthetic devices, and additional costs charged by private hospitals if they choose to go there rather than to a public hospital.

All academic staff are entitled to one month of a paid vacation every year. Additionally, professors and docents are entitled to one year of sabbatical with full pay for every six years of service.

The compulsory retirement period for academic staff is the age of 67 years. Female staff can retire, after at least 20 years of service, at 55 years of age. The corresponding limits for male academic staff are 25 years of service and 58 years of age. Upon retirement, each staff member receives a lump-sum payment—called the "seniority bonus"—calculated by multiplying the years of service by a fraction of the total gross monthly salary last received. In May 2010, the seniority bonus varied between TL 38,000 and TL 63,000 (US$24,516 to US$40,645), for those who have served for at least the minimum-required years. In addition, retired staff continue to receive a monthly salary, fairly close to the salary before, and the same health benefits.

In summary, monthly salary is the main income of academic staff in Turkish state universities. Most faculty members, lecturers, and instructors receive more-or-less regular income for extra teaching throughout the fall and the spring semesters, and a smaller number for teaching in summer schools. Thus, extra teaching is the second source of income. Academic staff in state universities can be seconded to teach in private universities on an hourly basis and are allowed to receive additional income only if they fulfill the required minimum weekly teaching loads. Income from activities performed under the revolving fund is the other major source of additional income, which can be as high as several times the total gross monthly salary. But, academic staff only in faculties of medicine and dentistry receive additional income from this source, on a more-or-less regular basis throughout the year. Additional income from research projects supported by TÜBİTAK and the European Union, and, particularly, from technopark activities can be quite significant. However, only relatively few academic staff are involved in such activities, and they are mostly in the research-intensive older universities.

Remuneration of Staff in Private Universities

Private universities have complete freedom in financial matters, such as setting tuition fees and establishing pay scales for their staff. Pay-scale information in private universities is confidential, and universities' administrations do not furnish such information, even to the Council of Higher Education. Thus, what is provided below is only anecdotal information.

There are basically two categories of private universities: (1) those that have significant research activity and aspire to internationally competitive world-class status and (2) those that are mainly teaching institutions catering to local demand. Private universities in the first group pay internationally competitive salaries to staff with internationally recognized credentials, and this can be as high as US$100,000 per year. Those in the second group pay full-time staff no more than twice the gross monthly salary for a given rank in a state university and rely mostly on staff retired or seconded from state universities on an hourly basis.

All staff are employed on individual, fixed-term contracts, and few tenured staff are employed. Even those private universities in the first group rarely employ research assistants in a status similar to that in state universities to avoid taxes and legal problems of employment upon completion of degrees. Rather, they offer scholarships and tuition-fee waivers to graduate students as payment for their services, without any commitment for future employment.

Conclusion

Salaries in state universities not supplemented by income, from the other channels mentioned previously, are compatible with equivalent positions in the civil service. Unsupplemented salaries in state universities, however, are not only internationally noncompetitive but also insufficient to maintain a comfortable standard of living, especially in the three big cities—Istanbul, Ankara, and Izmir. Anecdotal evidence indicates that this is clearly not the case for academic staff in private universities.

References

Constitutional Court Decision No. 2010/21. 2010. *Official Gazette* (July 22): www.memurlar. net/haber/172437. Accessed February 12, 2011.

Law no. 657. Law on civil servants. www.memurlar.net/common/documents/3402/657. htm. Accessed May 25, 2010.

Law no. 2547. Higher education law. www.yok.gov.tr/content/view/435/1831/lang,tr/. Accessed May 25, 2010.

Law no. 2809. Academic organization law. www.yok.gov.tr/content/view/434/1831/ lang,tr/. Accessed May 25, 2010.

Law no. 2914. Higher education employee law. www.yok.gov.tr/content/view/436/1831/ lang,tr/. Accessed May 25, 2010.

Law no. 3843. Law on dual education. www.yok.gov.tr/content/view/433/1831/lang,tr/. Accessed May 25, 2010.

Law no. 4691. Law on technology development zones. http://mevzuat.basbakanlik.gov.tr/ Metin.Aspx?MevzuatKod=1.5.4691&sourceXmlSearch=&MevzuatIliski=0. Accessed on January 1, 2012.

Law no. 5947. Law on full-time employment. www.resulkurt.com/haber.php?haber_id= 2415. Accessed February 12, 2011.

ÖSYM. 2010. *Higher Education Statistics 2009–2010.* http://www.osym.gov.tr/belge/ 1–12038/2009-2010-ogretim-yili-yuksekogretim-istatistikleri-kit-.html. Accessed May 30, 2010.

29

ACADEMIC SALARY IN THE UNITED KINGDOM

Marketization and National Policy Development

Fumi Kitagawa

All UK universities receiving public funding have comparable legal rights to appoint whomever they choose, within broadly comparable salary ranges. Since the mid-1980s, universities have been competing to recruit high-quality academic staff with better salaries and terms of employment as well as by offering additional inducements. Each university has different hiring practices, rewards, promotion criteria and policies/practices, and nonsalary benefits. Recent years have witnessed a substantial improvement in academic salaries and benefits. However, due to the recent financial crisis and subsequent cuts in public funding, UK universities have faced a different economic environment, and the continued affordability of these salaries and benefits has become questionable. The ability to secure high-level academics in the future will pose a major challenge to the UK higher education system.

Overview of the UK Higher Education System

The structure of the UK higher education system, the activities of UK academics, and the nature of their work and profession have substantially changed over the past three decades. In short, the sector has been facing increasing competition and continuous marketization. Academic career structures have been changing, as well. One of the key developments in UK higher education during the last 30 years has been the emergence of regular assessments of the quality of research in universities—something that has affected academic pay, promotion, and rewards structures. In this chapter, the main focus is on salary and other benefits of academic staff involved in both teaching and research activities (i.e., lecturer, senior lecturer, reader, and professor), rather than positions designated for research or teaching only (i.e., research fellows or teaching fellows). The data related to academic salary are derived through a variety of sources—including those from the Universities UK database, the Higher Education Statistical Agency, and the Universities and Colleges Employers Association.

The higher education sector in the United Kingdom has been transformed into a "diversified and increasingly stratified sector" (Brennan, Locke, and Naidoo 2007, 175). A main source is the change from an elite to a mass system of higher education (McNay 2006; Scott 2010). The number of 18- to 30-year-olds in higher education rose to 42 percent by 2006, four times the numbers reported 25 years ago (PMSU 2006). The number of universities has also increased, due in part to the policy implemented over the past decade, designed to relax the definition of a university. As of August 2010, there were 165 higher education institutions in the United Kingdom, of which 131 were located in England (Universities UK 2010). In 2008–9, the total number of academic staff was 179,040, of which 117,465 were employed full time (65.6%) (Universities UK 2010).

Most higher education institutions are publicly funded, but there are a few notable exceptions. Buckingham University was founded in 1976 as an independent private university. Recently, new private providers of higher education are emerging. For example, in July 2010, BPP University College of Professional Studies was granted university college status, being the first private provider to gain university status in 30 years (Hubble 2010).

The entire sector has relied heavily on public funding in the past. However, this dependence is lessening and is significantly lower for some institutions. In 2008–9, 56.4 percent of income of the higher education institutions was derived from public sources (Morgan 2010). All public institutions, whatever their level of public funding, are subject to public accountability requirements and a range of other regulations (e.g., publicly funded student numbers and a certain level of academic quality). Various policy levers encourage higher education institutions to support the implementation of government policies as a part of their public-service role.

The present structure of the UK higher education sector is said to be the result of the 1992 Further and Higher Education Act. This act abolished the binary divide between universities and polytechnics and established a single unified system of universities and higher education colleges, whereby additional institutions gained university status. Changes in 1999 and the revised criteria for university titles, permitted by the 2004 Higher Education Act, led to the creation of yet another group of new universities (sometimes referred to as "post-2004" universities). The 2004 act eliminated the requirement for research-degree-awarding powers, among other measures, which was designed to relax the definition of a university.

Institutions are competing more to attract students, staff, research grants, commercial income, and donations. The effects of the devolution of authority for higher education, research funding, and management of tuition fees are a growing area of policy concern. Oversight for higher education has been devolved in Scotland and Northern Ireland as well and in Wales, to a lesser extent

(Universities UK 2008). The funding of research remains a matter for the UK government, through the funding bodies and research councils. In England, a 6 percent reduction in the central government's allocation for teaching at universities for the 2010–11 academic year was announced in December 2010. In addition, in England, the government has recently approved plans to allow universities to charge undergraduate students up to £9,000 (US$14,116) per year, raising the cap from the current level of £3,290 (US$5,160). This is going to influence the funding landscape of higher education in the United Kingdom.

Academic Contract and Pay Structure

Universities are autonomous organizations, and the employment contract is made between individual institutions and the members of the academic staff. Staff members do not have civil-servant status. The 1980s witnessed major changes in the academic contracts of university staff in the United Kingdom, stimulated by the Thatcher government. Following the sharp reductions in funding imposed in 1981 and demands for ongoing efficiency gains; and the move toward more proactive management by university governing bodies—see the 1985 report by Sir Alex Jarratt (Steering Committee for Efficiency Studies in Universities 1985)—the government acted to reform the conditions affecting the employment of academic staff.

Tenure had been a cornerstone of employment, perceived to offer important protection to academic staff. However, the Education Reform Act of 1988 removed tenure, which meant that all staff appointed or promoted after November 20, 1987, could be dismissed if considered redundant. For some academic staff, this step reflected an attack on their status, job security, and academic freedom. Thereafter, financial viability and individual staff performance became key factors influencing the ongoing employment of academic staff. Further, the Research Assessment Exercise, introduced in 1986, has placed institutions in competition with each other for research-active academics and for a place in league tables. Universities have been competing to recruit leading researchers with better salaries and terms of employment, as well as nonmonetary rewards—such as investment in equipments and laboratories.

Since the early 1990s, a number of national-policy developments have geared toward shifts in human-resource management at higher education institutions (Strike and Taylor 2009). The Committee of Vice-Chancellors and Principals' report—"Promoting People," also known as the 1993 Fender Report—set out to provide a framework for the development of staff at universities and was heavily influenced by private-sector management trends. Successive governments from the late 1990s have been concerned about the role of universities in society, their level of autonomy, and the way in which they are managed. At the national level, for example, the Higher Education Role Analysis has been developed, with the aim that institutions will implement more transparent and unified pay and grading structures. The National Academic Role Profiles was agreed by the Joint Negotiating Committee for Higher Education Staff to provide new single pay and grading structure for all university staff.

In 2008–9, the total number of academic staff was 179,040, of which 117,465 were employed full time (65.6%) (Universities UK 2010). The proportion of staff with part-time contracts has increased over the last three years. Holders of permanent or open-ended contracts represent 61 to 65 percent of the total academic staff. The proportion of female staff on fixed-term and part-time contracts are higher than those of male staff (HESA 2009). Today, academics employed on non-standard contracts are a larger part of the labor market in higher education (Locke and Bennion 2010).

Although the focus of this chapter is on the academic salary of staff engaged in both teaching and research, the diversification of academic career structures has to be noted. The traditional academic career structure in a research-intensive university tended to be *a single ladder* from lecturer to senior lecturer and, then, from reader to professor. More recently, an emergent academic career model seems to have *parallel pathways* in addition to traditional career models—including research, teaching, and administration career progression. These teaching or research-only positions are found at both old pre-1992 universities and newer post-1992 universities. However, a number of remaining issues concern the sustainability and career development of contract research staff. For instance, a recent study notes "dissatisfaction with promotion criteria, particularly the lack of transparency and the fact that part-time and fixed-contract staff were excluded from staff development and promotion opportunities" (Metcalf et al. 2005, 28).

Academic Salary

Currently, most university employees are paid according to an incremental pay scale known as a "continuous spine." The pay scale corresponds to a grading structure with the 51-point pay spine/scale (UCEA 2008b) and the allocation of staff to grades. This only applies to the limit of £55,259 (US$88,674) per annum, awarded to senior lecturers. In terms of academic responsibilities and professional prestige, the lecturer position in the United Kingdom is almost identical to assistant professor in North America. Most lecturers in the United Kingdom have a doctorate (e.g., PhD, DPhil), which is increasingly considered to be a prerequisite for an appointment at that level; but there are differences between fields. Lecturer salaries range from about £30,870 to £35,646 (US$48,420–US$55,911) per annum (lecturer A) and from about £36,715 to £43,840 (US$57,587–US$68,763) per annum (lecturer B). Within the same salary ranges, individuals can negotiate their salaries. The average professor's annual salary was £69,870 (US$111,562) in 2007–8. Senior lecturers received on average £46,319 (US$73,958) and lecturers £38,105 (US$60,842), respectively, in 2007–8 (HESA 2009; *THE* 2009). Quite often, however, salaries for appointments at the professorial level are advertised as a "Competitive Professorial Package," in order to attract excellent academics.

There are differences in salaries and titles offered by various institutions. Universities established before 1992 and those that became universities after 1992 have important differences. Post-1992 universities have a title of principal lecturer, which corresponds to senior lecturer at pre-1992 institutions. The recent Higher Education Statistical Agency's figures reveal that, in general, academics employed at research-intensive institutions earn more than their counterparts at new post-1992 universities (Fearn 2009).

Recent years have witnessed a substantial improvement in academic salary in the United Kingdom. It appears that UK academic salaries were increasing at a faster rate than at any other countries, until 2009. This is partly explained by the proportion of full-time academics awarded the title of professor, which increased from 10.9 percent to 19.3 percent between 1995–96 and 2006–7 (Rumbley, Pacheco, and Altbach 2008, 62). Pay scales were negotiated in 2006 and increased 13.1 percent between 2006 and 2009, across the three years (UCEA 2008a). HESA data (2009) show that the average professor's salary in 2007–8, compared with 2006–7, increased by 5.4 percent. United Kingdom academics on average earned £43,486 a year in 2007–8, meaning a 7 percent increase from an average salary of £41,128 in 2006–7. By comparison, British workers nationally saw pay rises of 4 percent (Fearn 2009). This has placed the salary of university academics ahead of some of their professional counterparts in the United Kingdom. Thus, the UK higher education sector generally seems to have experienced little difficulty in recruiting and retaining staff, except where private-sector salaries and external earnings potential are quite high and where the labor market has been buoyant (Beer 2009) (e.g., medicine, engineering, computing, the law, accountancy, and some other business fields). However, due to the recent financial crisis and subsequent cuts in public funding, UK universities face a different economic environment, and the affordability of this level of pay and benefits has become questionable. After much negotiation, university salaries were increased by just 0.5 percent in August 2009 (Harris 2010).

International comparisons of academic pay are not easy to conduct, but the limited overall picture indicated that UK academic salaries (on a purchasing power parity basis), in general, appear competitive in the international context (JNCHES 2008). As of 2005–6, the average monthly entry-level (lecturer) salary is US$3,345 (World Bank PPP US$), whereas a top-level (professor) average monthly salary is US$5,589 (World Bank PPP US$). Across all grades, average monthly salary at the UK higher education institutions is US$4,343 (World Bank PPP US$) (Rumbley, Pacheco, and Altbach 2008). These U.S.-dollar monthly salary figures are based on the World Bank purchasing power parity index. However, both at the top level and the entry level, the salaries are lower than in Australia, Canada, and the United States (Rumbley, Pacheco, and Altbach 2008).

Hiring Procedures

Apart from the salary, the key differentiation stems from the ability of each university to attract staff of the highest quality, by offering additional inducements. Each university has different hiring practices, rewards, promotion criteria and policies/practices, and nonsalary benefits. All UK universities have the same legal rights to appoint whomever they choose, within broadly the same salary ranges. The key purpose of the Higher Education Role Analysis (HERA) is to describe the activities and responsibilities required to perform a specific job, allowing the post to be graded accordingly. Thus, when a job is opening, the university department identifies the HERA role and grade for the vacancy. For academic, research, or teaching posts, the standard HERA roles identify each grade salary and spine point.

The academic positions open to external candidates are advertised through public posting on university websites, on specialized websites (e.g., www.jobs.ac.uk), in national newspapers, and in specialized publications (e.g., *Times Higher Education*). Since April 2009, all vacancies at grade 6 and above are advertised on the Jobcentre Plus website as well as on each university's own job pages and on www.jobs.ac.uk. This new initiative is required by the government rules, which stipulate that, when the employer applies for non–European Union individuals to be given permission to work in the United Kingdom, the vacancy has to be advertised through Jobcentre Plus. For the non–European Union citizens, it is required for the potential employer to demonstrate that no suitable candidates are available in the European Union to take up the position, and a certain period of time for advertisement is required for the specific position.

Overall, more academics are coming into the United Kingdom than leaving to work abroad. This is particularly the case at the more junior ranks. There is some outflow at the more senior levels, including professors. In 2007–8, 38,420 academic staff were non-UK nationals, representing 22 percent of the total UK academic population (Universities UK 2010), and this proportion has increased significantly in recent years. According to the statistics, 27 percent of full-time academic staff appointed in 2007–8 came from outside the United Kingdom (Locke 2010). A recent survey of higher education institutions found that the most common region for the recruitment of all levels of academic staff was the European Union. For professors and lecturers, the next most common region was North America, and for researchers it was East Asia (Locke 2010). The recent change in immigration policy and visa requirements for foreign nationals is expected to adversely affect the recruitment patterns of academic hiring.

Benefits

Pensions are a significant and costly element of the overall remuneration of many employees in higher education. There is a range of pension provisions in

UK higher education. The University Superannuation Scheme is the national final salary pension scheme for eligible university employees throughout the United Kingdom. Membership in the scheme is continuous if academics transfer to another participating institute; providing the break in employment is less than one month. Entry to the scheme is automatic upon appointment. Proposed changes to the University Superannuation Scheme are currently being debated, and the main issue concerns the economic sustainability of the pension scheme.

Apart from pension schemes, each university offers different benefits packages. Many institutions seem to have family-related benefits—such as maternity, paternity and parental leaves; child-care provisions; and other benefits including work-life balance schemes, loans, and cycle schemes. Academics enjoy the additional benefits of about 35 days of annual leave. In general, medical care is covered by National Health Service, and academics may benefit from its provisions.

Rewards and Promotions

A common theme running through the last 30 years in UK higher education has been a growing emphasis on performance and assessment. This has had important consequences for academic staff. While staff appointments are open and subject to legal constraints, especially regarding equal opportunities, targeting key staff and head-hunting are quite common. Universities, especially those institutions with the most resources, are often adept at securing the services of key individuals. Generous rewards, both financial and nonfinancial, may be available.

One of the main areas of change relates to staff promotions. In the 1980s, universities had been constrained by a fixed proportion of senior staff, effectively imposing a quota of promotions each year. Academic staff moved up the salary scale in annual increments, which were normally automatic and awarded with the minimum of scrutiny. Today, by contrast, formal restrictions on the number of senior staff have been removed, replaced by constraints of financial viability. In most cases, automatic progression has been replaced by annual performance reviews and accelerated promotions; additional increments and other forms of rewards are now commonplace. Most universities have introduced elements of performance-related pay, especially for senior academic staff.

The University and Colleges Employers Association's report (UCEA 2005, 26) pointed out that *nonfinancial rewards* act as intrinsic motivators/rewards to tackle difficulties in attracting new staff and in retaining key personnel. These factors include increased time and resources for research, the recognition of teaching contribution, better access to training and development, mentoring schemes, and improved communications. Universities are also exploring mechanisms to recognize and reward the diversity of academic and related activities within existing systems for the recruitment, appraisal, and promotion of staff by introducing workload models and voluntary schemes, for example.

Supplementary Employment

Universities are also more aware than before of the opportunities that staff obtain for external employment. Such activities may be controlled but are often encouraged as a means of raising overall earnings. In some academic fields, in particular, conducting consultancy is an attraction to academic staff. United Kingdom academics take on consultancy in two ways—through either independently led or institution-led models. There is normally a limit placed upon the length of consultancy activities, such as 25 working days a year. Other nonfinancial incentives for consultancy works may include tax exemption, insurance coverage, and administrative support.

Not much information is available regarding differences across disciplines—in terms of the amount of consultancy activity conducted, levels of income, or related institutional practices (Universities UK and AURIL 2001). This includes information on reward and promotion for individuals related to consultancy activity and institutional strategies and the overall benefits, rewards, and motivation related to such activity at the institutional level. Among other undocumented forms of supplementary employment, there is a dearth of information regarding academics providing teaching services at multiple institutions.

Conclusion

The higher education sector in the United Kingdom is at a crossroads. The sector is facing a substantial decrease in government funding. A number of higher education institutions have recently taken measures, such as early retirement and voluntary severance schemes, in order to make a saving on annual operating costs. Several departments have been closed down and, as a result, redundancies cannot be avoided. Academic staff face growing pressure in order to retain their positions and to accept the increased workload to combat job insecurity. Individual institutions and the higher education sector as a whole need to reconsider what it takes to attract, retain, and reward a diverse range of individuals with the right qualifications and experience. Strategic actions are required at the institutional level to attract and retain the best academic staff for the institution, deliver on institutional missions, and find new markets in a rapidly changing global landscape of higher education.

Despite relatively unfavorable pay conditions, the UK higher education sector has always attracted academic talent from the rest of the world. This is clearly not just because of academic salary and other benefits and rewards, but also due to the recognized excellence in research activities and the reputation of a system open to researchers from all over the world. Due to the demographic changes within the sector—with the retirement of a large number of prominent senior academics in years to come—and also due to the recent stricter immigration policy, the ability to secure high-level academics in the future will continue to pose a major challenge to the UK higher education system. A competitive salary is necessary but is probably not a sufficient factor by itself.

References

Beer, J. 2009. "Key issues facing UK HE: Staff quality, experiences, skills and skills gaps." http://www.jisc.ac.uk/media/documents/aboutus/strategy/janet%20essay.pdf. Accessed March 14, 2011.

Brennan, J., W. Locke, and R. Naidoo. 2007. United Kingdom: An increasingly stratified profession. In *The changing conditions for academic work and careers in select countries,* ed. W. Locke and U. Teichler Kassel, 163–76. Germany: International Centre for Higher Education Research.

Fearn, H. 2009. "Pay packets of excellence." *Times Higher Education* (March 19). http://www.timeshighereducation.co.uk/story.asp?storycode=405805. Accessed February 14, 2011.

Harris, N. 2010. "Academic benefits." http://www.jobs.ac.uk/career-tools-and-advice/careers-advice/1388/academic-benefits. Accessed March 19, 2010.

HESA (Higher Education Statistics Agency). 2009. *Resources of higher education institutions, 2007/08.* May.

Hubble, S. 2010. "The Browne review of higher education funding and student finance, House of Commons Library." http://www.parliament.uk/briefingpapers/commons/lib/research/briefings/snsp-pdf. Accessed February 14, 2011.

JNCHES (Joint Negotiating Committee for Higher Education Staff). 2008. "Review of higher education finance & pay data—Final report." December. http://www.ucea.ac.uk/en/New_JNCHES/jnches-review-of-finance-and-pay-data/. Accessed February 14, 2011.

Locke, W. 2010. "The changing academic profession in the UK and beyond." www.universitiesuk.ac.uk/ ... /The%20Changing%20HE%20Profession.pdf. Accessed December 30, 2010.

Locke, W., and A. Bennion. 2010. *The changing academic profession in the UK and beyond.* London: Universities UK. http://www.universitiesuk.ac.uk/Events/Documents/The%20Changing%20Academic%20Profession%20in%20the%20UK%20and%20Beyond%2022%20June%202010%20_Final_.pdf. Accessed February 14, 2011.

McNay, I. 2006. "Delivering mass higher education: The reality of policy in practice." In *Beyond mass higher education: Building on experience,* ed. Ian McNay. Maidenhead, UK: Society for Research in Higher Education/Open University.

Metcalf, H., H. Rolfe, P. Stevens, and M. Weale. 2005. *Recruitment and retention of academic staff in higher education.* London: National Institute of Economic and Social Research.

Morgan, J. 2010. "V-Cs outrank generals when it comes to pay gap over those in the trenches." *Times Higher Education* (December 9).

PMSU (Prime Minister's Strategy Unit). 2006. "Strategic priorities for the UK: The policy review." November 23. http://image.guardian.co.uk/sys-files/Politics/documents/2006/11/24/policy_review.pdf. Accessed March 20, 2010.

Rumbley, L. E., I. F. Pacheco, and P. G. Altbach. 2008. *International comparison of academic salaries.* Chestnut Hill, MA: Boston College, Center for International Higher Education.

Scott, P. 2010. "Structural changes in higher education: The case of the United Kingdom." In *Structuring mass higher education: The role of elite institutions,* ed. David Palfreyman and Ted Tapper. New York: Routledge.

Steering Committee for Efficiency Studies in Universities. 1985. *Report (Chairman Sir Alex Jarratt)*. London: Committee of Vice-Chancellors and Principals.

Strike, T., and J. Taylor. 2009. "The career perceptions of academic staff and human resource discourses in English higher education." *Higher Education Quarterly* 63 (2) 177–95.

THE (Times Higher Education). 2009. "Average salary of full-time academic staff, 2007–08." http://www.timeshighereducation.co.uk/Journals/THE/THE/19 March 2009/attachments/Tables 01.pdf. Accessed February 14, 2011.

UCEA (Universities and Colleges Employers Association). 2005. "Recruitment and retention of staff in higher education 2005." http://www.ucea.ac.uk/ucea/filemanager/root/site_assets/publications/rr_summary_2005.pdf. Accessed March 20, 2010.

UCEA (Universities and Colleges Employers Association). 2008a. "A review of the implementation of the framework agreement for the modernization of pay structures in higher education." http://www.ucea.ac.uk/en/Publications/index.cfm?1=1&obj_id=B081E802-D500–4AF2-B86E6023782866E4. Accessed December 23, 2010.

UCEA (Universities and Colleges Employers Association). 2008b. "Where are we now? The benefits of working in HE." http://www.ucea.ac.uk/objects_store/where_are_we_now._the_benefits_of_working_in_he.pdf. Accessed February 14, 2011.

Universities UK. 2008. *Devolution and higher education: Impact and future trends.* London: Universities UK.

Universities UK. 2010. "Higher education in facts and figures, summer 2010." http://www.universitiesuk.ac.uk/Publications/Documents/HigherEducationInFactsAndFiguresSummer2010.pdf. Accessed December 23, 2010.

Universities UK and AURIL (Association for University Research and Industry Links). 2001. *Optimising consultancy.* London: Universities UK.

30

THE POWER OF INSTITUTIONAL AND DISCIPLINARY MARKETS

Academic Salaries in the United States

Martin J. Finkelstein

In the United States, institutional base salary is the primary component of academic compensation. Indeed, institutions of higher education define the trajectory along which academic careers are pursued (as the norm, promotion through the ranks *within* the same institution) and control the level of compensation. Thus, the institutional type (ranging from research university to small, private college) is one of two primary determinants of how much a professor is paid. The second element is academic field: faculty compensation varies substantially at the same institution among faculty in different fields—depending largely on the market for members of that field outside the university. Within institutional types and academic fields, salaries vary intentionally by academic rank and seniority and, unintentionally, by gender. Academics in the United States are well paid in international comparisons, and salaries grew modestly in real dollars during the last quarter of the 20th century. Yet, salaries have leveled off over the past decade or two, and the salary disadvantage of academics versus other professionals in the United States has been growing.

Overview of Higher Education

The higher education system in the United States is a large and highly decentralized one, with some 4,000 institutions offering instruction at the postsecondary level to some 17 million students, by about 1.1 million faculty members (600,000 of whom are full time). The system is a bifurcated along two major axes. First, in terms of *mission* and *degree level,* approximately half the system (2,000 institutions and 9 million students) is oriented to vocational or workforce preparation and offers either two-year degrees or nondegree certificate options. The other half, the focus of this chapter, provides traditional baccalaureate and graduate degree–level instruction in four-year colleges and universities (Gumport 2000). A second axis of institutional bifurcation is between *publicly* and *privately sponsored* (funded) institutions. While private four-year colleges and universities outnumber public ones by 2:1, they enroll only about one-third of four-year college and university students.

Over the past decade or two, this highly decentralized American system has encountered many of the same challenges encountered by nations worldwide: increased demands for access and growing constraints in public revenues/appropriations (Marginson and Rhoades 2002). This has fueled several trends that have become typical globally: increasing focus on institutional performance and accountability measures; increasing privatization in the public sector; and increasing reliance on contingent academic staff (Black 2004). With declining baseline institutional support, academic staffs are under increasing pressure to generate revenue from instructional, research, and service activities. In terms of instructional staffing, it has led many four-year institutions to resort to contingent staffing. Indeed, in the last 20 years, fully half of the new academic staff hired by four-year institutions have been to such limited-term appointments, subject to renewal but *not* eligible for permanent tenure (Schuster and Finkelstein 2006).

Academic Contracts, Hiring, and Promotion Processes

Hiring for full-time, academic-staff positions—whether in the public or private sector—is decentralized to the level of the individual institution. Individual academic units (departments and even programs) within the college or university, acting through ad hoc faculty search committees,[1] identify and screen candidates, and recommendations are made from the committee to the academic dean supervising the unit in question and, ultimately, to the campus chief academic officer (Matier 1991). Two aspects of these searches are particularly important: their scope and the legal parameters within which they operate. Regarding scope, most full-time-faculty searches at four-year institutions are national in scope—that is, they seek to identify and recruit the most-qualified candidates in the United States in the field or subfield in question. At major research universities, the scope of such searches is increasingly international in scope (Bair 2003). In reality, searches at lesser institutions and searches for limited-term appointments (even at the research-oriented universities) may be conducted less systematically and may be largely regional or even local in scope. All searches are conducted within the parameters of U.S. federal government's nondiscrimination policies, reflected in civil rights legislation over the past half century, including nondiscrimination on the basis of gender, race/ethnicity, age, sexual orientation, and other factors. Typically, institutional human-resource (personnel) office staffs have prepared recruitment guidelines as to scope of advertising, strategies for identification of women and minority candidates, permissible questions to ask at interviews, and so forth (Twombly 2005).

In terms of procedure, a hiring academic unit through its search committee would recommend several candidates to the academic dean supervising that unit (often in some kind of rank order). Then, the dean would make the actual hiring decision, not only including which candidate should be selected but also negotiating terms and conditions of employment (e.g., rank and salary) directly with the candidate (Twombly 2005).

At the point of initial authorization for recruitment to an academic staff vacancy, the *type of contract* or appointment is usually clearly specified: either eligible for the award of tenure after a probationary period or a limited-term contract that may or may not be renewable for one or more succeeding terms (Clark and Ma 2005). Irrespective of the type of full-time appointment (tenure eligible or limited contract), the actual length of the initial employment contract may vary between one to three years. A type of annual review is usually mandated, although it may be somewhat perfunctory for limited-term appointees. For tenure-eligible appointments, a review typically takes the form of annual assessments of progress to tenure (Twombly 2005). The major high-stakes review for tenure-eligible faculty comes one year before the end of the entire probationary period, at which time a decision is made as to whether to award tenure. That decision is based on an assessment of the performance of academic staff members in their teaching, research, and service responsibilities. At research universities, research performance as reflected in publications and grant awards are emphasized, while at four-year institutions that have a predominantly teaching mission, teaching performance is likely to be a more central consideration (although some sort of research performance is expected). Typically, in the U.S. system, a negative tenure decision is tantamount to a nonreappointment decision. For limited-contract academic staff, major evaluations and reappointment decisions are made in the middle of the year, preceding the final year of the contract.

Beyond the duration of their appointments and their eligibility for the award of tenure, fixed-term faculty typically differ from tenure-eligible faculty in terms of both their academic credentials and the scope of their work responsibilities. In terms of credentials, roughly 90 percent of all tenure-eligible appointees to the entry-level rank of assistant professor hold the PhD degree at four-year colleges and universities. Moreover, they are likely to be new or recent graduates of leading doctoral programs in the United States (Clark and Ma 2005). The figure for fixed-term contract faculty would be about 50 percent. With respect to work responsibilities, tenure-eligible academic staff are typically expected to perform all three basic academic functions of teaching, research, and service—the latter including administration, institutional, and/or external professional service to their academic field or the larger community. Indeed, they likely would have been hired in no small part, on the basis of their potential for developing a productive research career—at least at the research universities (Matier 1991). Fixed-contract faculty, typically, have a much more specialized function and are hired to perform one principal function—most often, teaching (especially for lower-division or introductory undergraduate courses)—but sometimes, research (typically on an external government or private foundation grant) or administration (typically as director of an academic program that may be based off the main campus or digital/distance).

Academic Salaries

Overall, academic salaries in the United States are among the highest in the world. In a recent study by the Center for International Higher Education at Boston College (Rumbley, Pacheco, and Altbach 2008), the United States was fifth in the world—behind only Saudi Arabia, Hong Kong, Canada, and Japan. Together with reasonable availability of positions, such relatively high salaries in the United States serve as something of a magnet for academics in Europe (most recently, from the United Kingdom and France) and Asia (especially China and India, where many recruits to U.S. doctoral education in the sciences and engineering stay to pursue academic careers) (Bhandari and Laughlin 2009).

While comparatively high overall, the available data suggest that academic salaries in the United States do vary by type of appointment. Overall, they are generally higher for tenure-eligible, full-time faculty than for fixed-contract faculty— although in some professional schools, fixed-contract appointments actually receive a salary supplement as a kind of reward for forsaking tenure eligibility (Chait and Trower 1997). Given that the evidence is not definitive and, furthermore, given the focus of this study on faculty in career-ladder appointments, the following discussion focuses on salaries of full-time faculty in tenure-eligible appointments.[2]

In the United States, the salaries of full-time, tenure-eligible academic staff are determined exclusively by the institutional employer, subject to competitive-market conditions. They vary substantially by type of institution/employer and by academic field.

Salary Variations by Institutional Type

Table 30.1 shows average salaries of U.S. academic staff, as they vary by type of institution and academic rank. In terms of institutional type, the higher levels of

Table 30.1 Average salary by academic rank, institutional degree level, and control, 2008–9

| | Salary (US$) | | | | | |
| | Doctoral | | Master's | | Baccalaureate | |
Academic rank	Public	Private	Public	Private	Public	Private
Professor	115,553	147,286	88,298	94,760	84,502	88,092
Associate	80,013	93,317	70,233	72,522	68,121	66,703
Assistant	68,072	79,915	59,397	60,069	56,883	54,945

Source: American Association of University Professors 2009.

degrees offered by an institution (BA, MA, PhD/MD), the higher the salary it pays its academic staff. That premium tends to increase with academic rank—that is, it is less discernable at the entry level and much larger at the senior ranks. At the entry level, research-university faculty earn about 20 percent more than entry-level faculty at baccalaureate colleges, and at the full professor rank they may earn as much as 50 percent more, on average. There are substantial disparities between public and private institutions: salary scales at public institutions tend to be scrutinized by government officials and may also be subject to regulations for public employees. They are consistently both lower and less flexible than among private institutions. Salaries are on average about 10 percent to 20 percent higher at private institutions, and that disparity, again, tends to grow larger at the senior ranks. Among private institutions, church-related colleges tend to offer, on average, lower salaries than private institutions with no religious affiliation.

The Market Value of Academic Fields

In the United States, there are wide disparities in salaries by academic field—relating to the market value of a particular field outside the university in the broader economy. That is, in order to compete with business and industry (and even government) in recruiting academic talent in fields such as law, engineering, business, chemistry, microbiology, and others, academic institutions must offer salaries that are higher than for some fields—such as English, philosophy, sociology, and others—that have fewer lucrative opportunities outside the university. The distribution of fields, by their outside market value, roughly parallels the proportion of PhD recipients nationally that are employed outside academe. Table 30.2 shows the average salary for selected academic fields as a percentage of the average salary of professors of English language and literature (one of the three liberal arts fields displayed in the table).

The data suggest several observations. First, it is found that the salary premium for the professions ranges from just above one-quarter in business (27.4% in the public sector, 25.9% in the private sector) to about two-thirds in law (69.1% in the public sector, 60.7% in the private sector) with engineering at about 40 percent (38% in the public sector, 50.7% in the private sector) and health professions at over 50 percent in the public sector and nearly equaling law (above 60%) in the private sector. These are substantial differences: faculty in law and the health professions are earning about 1.5 times more than their liberal arts colleagues in the humanities. English language and literature are compared to chemistry, computer science, and psychology—three fields within the traditional liberal arts on American campuses. The salary premium for natural scientists (chemistry and computer science) is discovered as over literature professors by about 15 percent across both the public and private sectors, and the salary for social science faculty (e.g., psychology) is under 10 percent. Taken together, these data suggest substantial disparities between the traditional liberal arts and the professions in the United States.

Table 30.2 Average salaries in selected fields as a percentage of the average salary in English fields

	University faculty			
	Public		Private	
Discipline	Salary (US$)	Difference vs. English (%)	Salary (US$)	Difference vs. English (%)
Business teachers, postsecondary	$82,970	+27.4	$84,940	+25.9
Computer science teachers, postsecondary	$75,670	+16.1	$76,260	+13
Engineering teachers, postsecondary	$89,920	+38.0	$101,690	+50.7
English language and literature teachers, postsecondary	$65,150	0	$67,460	0
Chemistry teachers, postsecondary	$77,230	+18.5	$77,580	+15
Psychology teachers, postsecondary	$72,500	+11.3	$71,570	+6.1
Health specialties teachers, postsecondary	$99,750	+53.1	$107,380	+59.2

Source: U.S. Department of Labor 2009.

Moreover, within the traditional liberal arts, more modest, but consistent, differences refrain favoring the natural sciences.

It is significant to note that interfield differences persist across both the public and private sectors at roughly the same magnitude, with two notable exceptions: in both engineering and the health professions, the salary premiums are somewhat greater in the private than in the public sector.

Other Factors: Rank, Seniority, and Gender

Within institutions and academic fields, the prime determinant of salary is academic rank (see Table 30.1). Almost all institutions—private as well as public—have some kind of salary scale organized by academic rank. There is typically a floor and ceiling for the ranks of assistant, associate, and full professor and several "steps"—perhaps four to six—within each rank. Promotion to the next higher rank commonly carries with it a substantial salary increase from the then current step within the previous rank to the lowest step on the next higher rank. For tenure-eligible academic staff in the United States, this step typically involves promotion to associate professor, with tenure after the six- or seven-year probationary period.

Within academic ranks, salary is set primarily by seniority, although perform-ance factors may enter into the equation. Annual expansions at most institutions tend to be "across the board, cost-of-living" increases (Perna 2001). Where merit pay is added, it usually constitutes only a small or secondary component of an-nual increments. It tends to be based on research productivity, as reflected in peer-reviewed publications, rather than on teaching performance—as reflected in student course evaluations.

Two other determinants of salary deserve attention. The first is gender. Histo-rically, female academic staff have earned about 80 percent of male academic staff's salaries, with similar qualifications/credentials and performance records—controlling for institutional type, academic field, and academic rank. It appears that this gap has closed to roughly 90 percent over the past decade, as sex-discrimination liti-gation and the results of gender-equity salary studies have documented residual gender differences. It appears that at the entry level, these variations are diminish-ing even further (Perna 2001).

The second element regarding salary gaps is collective bargaining and the un-ionization of academic staff. Approximately one-third of academic staff in U.S. four-year colleges and universities are unionized (Rhoades 1998). Following an explosion of such activity in the late 1960s and 1970s, attendant on federal and subsequent state enabling legislation, the pace of academic unionization has atrophied—as it has in the general U.S. economy, where only 15 percent of work-ers are represented by a union. Most of the unionized faculty are represented by either their local, state, or municipal employees' union or by one of the national unions representing elementary- and secondary-school teachers, which may be part of a larger industrial worker union (e.g., the American Federation of Teach-ers). These academic staff are primarily located in the public sector. The available evidence, as of 2004, suggests that union membership is associated with modestly higher salary levels than with nonunion membership (Rhoades 1998; Schuster and Finkelstein 2006).

The 9- or 10-Month Contract

It is important to clarify that most academic staff in the United States are em-ployed on 9- or 10-month (academic year) rather than 12-month (calendar year) contracts; so that salary reports are referring to *base* salaries for a maximal 10 month, or academic year, contract (Clark and Ma 2005). Practically speak-ing, this means that base salary figures tend to underestimate actual academic staff compensation. Many faculty teach additional courses in the summer, work on research grants, or engage in other income-producing activities that result in supplemental compensation from their employing institution (Bair 2003). They may also engage in overload teaching and other special assignments during the academic year, for which they receive supplementary compensation from their employing institution. The point is that most faculty earn at least 5 percent of their base salary in summer or other supplemental compensation from their employing institution—beyond any supplemental employment derived from outside their employing institution. This supplementary income typically allows faculty to manage economically the two- or three-month period, in which they are not receiving regular monthly payments from their institution.

Academics Compared to Other Professionals

In 1999, academic staff in the United States earned 74.5 percent of the weighted average salary of other highly educated professionals, ranging from about half in the case of lawyers and physicians to about 90 percent in the case of engineers and computer scientists. By 2003, the U.S. Bureau of Labor Statistics reported that the academic salary disadvantage had increased slightly from 25.5 percent to 27.7 percent (Schuster and Finkelstein 2006). If one focuses on the point of career entry, the case of the newly hired assistant professor, the market is found signaling a long-standing salary disadvantage for at least the last quarter century. In 1975, entry-level salaries for assistant professors exceeded the median family income in the United States as a whole, by 3 percent. By 2000, entry-level assistant professor salaries had declined to about 92 percent of median family income. Yet, it should be noted, a portion of that decline may be attributable simply to the rise in the proportion of two-income families, effectively inflating median family income and deflating entry-level salaries. Those entry-level differences tend to widen—even considerably, at the more advanced career stages—when attorneys are moving into partnerships and physicians into group practices.

In general, then, while the salaries of academic staff in the United States are good relative to those of academic staff in other nations, their relative position in terms of compensation in their own national context is less favorable—and apparently declining (Schuster and Finkelstein 2006).

Fringe Benefits

In addition to salary, all institutions in the United States provide their academic staff with an array of nonsalary compensation, typically referred to as "fringe benefits." These almost always include health insurance for the staff member and his or her family (to which the staff member may be required to contribute a portion) and an institutional contribution to a retirement plan (which usually requires a matching individual contribution) (Clark and Ma 2005). Beyond these basics, many institutions include some kind of tuition benefit for academic staff, their spouses, and children. Given the costs of higher education in the United States, especially in the private sector, such a benefit can amount to a substantial portion of annual salary—during the years it is used by a staff member or his or her immediate family. While salary is nearly always the primary component of compensation, health insurance, retirement contribution, and tuition benefits form the key aspects of the overall compensation package. Most institutions estimate the actual costs to them of fringe benefits as about 30 percent of an academic staff member's base salary (Leslie and Slaughter 1995).

Supplementary Employment

According to the 2004 National Study of Postsecondary Faculty (U.S. Department of Education 2007), just over half of all full-time faculty (whether term appointees or tenure eligible) reported receiving supplementary salary from the employing institution beyond their contractual base salary. That base salary supplement usually takes the form of overload or summer teaching, although it may also serve as special stipends for undertaking administrative assignments or of pass-through funds from external grants. Beyond such modal supplementary employment at their home institutions, about one-third of academic staff report receiving income from consulting or freelance work in their academic field outside their employing institution. This includes royalties and other income from intellectual property as well as specific short-term consulting assignments. It may also include income from another institution of higher education (usually teaching part time on another campus). Indeed, about one-fifth of the faculty report receiving income from other (presumably nonacademic) employment outside their home institution.

While about the same proportion of academic staff earn these different categories of income in the public versus the private sector, some public-private distinction exists in the actual amounts of outside income earned. Academic staff in the public sector earn an average of about 11 percent of their institutional base salary in total outside income and about 6 percent of their institutional base salary from outside employment income (including consulting). The corresponding figures for academic staff in the private sector are 14 percent and 7 percent, respectively, of institutional base salaries, which are 20 percent higher to begin with.

All in all, these data clearly suggest that in the United States institutional base salary is by far the major component of academic compensation, especially when fringe benefits are included. While income from outside sources varies by type of institution and academic field, nonetheless it remains, proportionately speaking, a minor component of the total professional income of academic staff.

Conclusion

While academic staff in the United States are not civil servants and are, legally speaking, corporate employees of the college or university that pays them, a significant majority have benefited historically from the protection conferred by academic tenure (i.e., the relative security of a continuous appointment.)[3] Increasingly large proportions of U.S. academic staff, however—more than half of all new full-time appointments over the past generation—are being appointed off the tenure track and, ipso facto, do not enjoy those protections. While academic staff in the United States are currently pressed by the challenging economy of 2008–09, their compensation compares favorably to that of academic staff in other countries overall. However, their relative position among other learned professions at home does not seem as favorable as their international position.

For U.S. academic staff, the base institutional salary constitutes the major portion of their total compensation. That salary is determined exclusively by the home institution in the context of the broader academic marketplace competition for faculty talent and in accordance with institutional salary scales. An important basis for the level of compensation is academic rank and experience—in line with the situation in other countries. Unlike many other countries, however, salaries in U.S. institutions are shaped significantly by market forces: the relative value of academic fields outside the academy is reflected in wide variation among academic staffs, by field, inside the academy. Generally speaking, academic staff in the professions—especially in medicine, law, and business—are paid 1.5 or 2 times as much as their counterparts in the liberal arts, and scientists modestly out-earn humanists. Moreover, unlike many other nations, salaries in the private sector are frequently higher than those in the public sector. There is also significant variation in salary by type of institution, with faculty at the major research universities, especially the private ones, and at the senior ranks, earning 50 percent more that those in baccalaureate institutions.

Nevertheless, academic salaries in the United States in 2010 barely afford incumbents a middle-class lifestyle, especially for those working in expensive urban centers with high housing costs. Indeed, half of all U.S. faculty seek supplemental compensation from the home institution, and one-third work outside their primary employing institution. Many depend on the secondary income of working spouses, often themselves professionals or academics. In many respects, like all workers in the global economy, academic workers in the United States are coming to depend less on their employing organizations and increasingly developing themselves as entrepreneurs in the knowledge economy.

Notes

1. Search committees tend to be dominated by faculty members in the hiring department, although they may include members from related departments. They are typically position specific and lapse once the position is filled. Their contact with the academic dean is mainly mediated by the department chair. For a good description of U.S. faculty search procedures, see Musselin (2010).
2. A systematic comparative study is currently under way in the United States of differences between salaries of tenure eligible versus fixed-contract, full-time appointees, according to John Curtis, director of the Research, American Association of University Professors.
3. Tenure in the United States is best defined as a judicialized dismissal procedure. Tenured academic staff on continuous appointments can only be dismissed "for cause" and

subject to peer review in a procedure that ensures "due process." Such cause, however, beyond incompetence, nonperformance, or moral turpitude, may include "financial exigency" of the employer or program elimination (Finkelstein 2002).

References

American Association of University Professors. 2009. "On the brink: The annual report on the economic status of the profession." *Academe* 95 (March/April): 14–28.

Bair, J. 2003. "Hiring practices in finance education: Linkages among top-ranked graduate programs." *Journal of Economics & Sociology* 62 (2): 429–43.

Bhandari, Rajika, and Shepherd Laughlin, eds. 2009. *Higher Education on the move: New developments in global mobility.* New York: Institute for International Education.

Black, Jim N. 2004. *The freefall of the American university: How our colleges are corrupting the minds and morals of the next generation.* Nashville, TN: WND Books.

Chait, Richard, and Cathy Trower. 1997. *Where tenure does not reign: Colleges with contract systems.* New Pathways in Academic Careers. Washington, DC: American Association for Higher Education.

Clark, Robert, and Jennifer Ma, eds. 2005. *Recruitment, retention, and retirement in higher education: Building and managing the faculty of the future.* Northampton, MA: Edward Elgar.

Finkelstein, Martin J. 2002. "Tenure." In *Higher education in the United States: An encyclopedia,* ed. J. F. Forest and K. Kinser. Santa Barbara, CA: ABC-CLIO.

Gumport, Patricia. 2000. "Academic restructuring: Organizational change and institutional imperatives." *Higher Education* 39: 67–91.

Leslie, Larry, and Sheila Slaughter. 1995. "The development and current status of market mechanisms in United States postsecondary education." *Higher Education Policy* 10: 239–52

Marginson, Simon, and Gary Rhoades. 2002. "Beyond national states, markets, and the systems of higher education: A glonacal agency heuristic." *Higher Education* 43: 281–309.

Matier, Michael. 1991. "Recruiting faculty: Complementary tales from 2 campuses." *Research in Higher Education* 32 (1): 31–44.

Musselin, Christine. 2010. *The market for academics.* New York and London: Routledge.

Perna, Laura W. 2001. "Sex and race differences in faculty tenure and promotion." *Research in Higher Education* 42 (5): 541–67.

Rhoades, Gary. 1998. *Managed professionals: Unionized faculty and restructuring academic labor.* Albany: State University of New York Press.

Rumbley, Laura E., Iván F. Pacheco, and Philip G. Altbach. 2008. *International comparison of academic salaries: An exploratory study.* Chestnut Hill, MA: Boston College, Center for International Higher Education.

Schuster, Jack H., and Martin J. Finkelstein. 2006. *The American faculty: The restructuring of academic work and careers.* Baltimore: Johns Hopkins University Press.

Twombly, Susan B. 2005. "Values, policies and practices affecting the hiring process for full-time arts and sciences faculty in community colleges." *Journal of Higher Education* 76: 423–47.

U.S. Department of Education. 2007. *The national study of postsecondary faculty 2004.* Washington, DC: National Center for Education Statistics.

U.S. Department of Labor. 2009. *National occupational employment and wage estimates survey, May 2009.* Washington, DC: Department of Occupational Employment Statistics.

PART 3
Reflections

31

ACADEMIC COMMUNITY AND CONTRACTS

Modern Challenges and Responses

Yaroslav Kuzminov

The position of researchers and teachers who are at the main core of the modern university has been seriously affected by economic trends and the expansion and increasing complexity of academic institutions worldwide. Are professorial positions simply losing their unique character in the labor market today or is the decay of the traditional university model being witnessed?

This book compares and examines trends in salaries and remuneration for the work of the academic profession. It considers the quantitative and qualitative elements of academic contracts across 28 countries in order to speculate about how contracts are determined—regarding global influences, peculiarities of national institutions, and the level of economic and social development of the host country.

The Academic Profession in a Changing Labor Market

A Middle-Class Person

Historically, university teachers belonged to the middle class. The course of events toward the end of the 20th century lowered the bar; yet, no doubt, many university teachers belong to the middle class. This means that their income allows them a wide choice in terms of consumption and lifestyle. But academic staff are a subset of a larger middle class. Traditionally, professors tended to favor intellectual consumption over mass culture, and their work style combined a high degree of independence and self-regulation, when even free time was devoted to creative professional goals.

A reasonable basis is to regard the increase of faculty income as normal and appropriate, not a result of competition with others, and rarely provoking the envy of colleagues. The deterioration in salary and working conditions is considered an abnormal state, treated by faculty as a temporary misfortune (rarely affecting their professional and working behavior) or (when it exists for a long period of time) as a sign of a university crisis.

A Creative Person

Starting from Karl Marx's definition of work alienation, university teachers have always been associated (and have always associated themselves) with self-stimulating, creative work. Russian physicist Lev Artsimovich was quoted as saying, "Can you imagine, these guys let me do such an interesting job and even pay me for it?" The inevitable routine, such as grading or examinations, was treated as unavoidable but might even permit the expression of a professor's unique personality.

In the national labor market, a professor's position has been characterized as receiving a fine (or reasonable, in local terms) remuneration package plus significant autonomy in exchange for high qualifications and specialized skills. When the rewards of academic labor seemed adequate, universities did not experience a shortage of young people willing to pursue this path.

The Price of Freedom

As members of the creative professions increased in numbers during the second half of the 20th century, another advantage of the academic position came to the fore. While teachers might not have earned much (at least during the first 10 years of their career), they had more free time available than their better-paid colleagues at commercial firms. Academics acquire two months of freedom during the summer term (or even more), compared to a three-week vacation, sabbaticals plus fewer externally specified and monitored working hours—factors that outweighed the higher income provided in other sectors. Professors had a guaranteed living and a comfortable life in retirement. Thus, nonpecuniary benefits included both working conditions and extra free time.

Global Networks—Global Market?

Just like the field of science, the academic profession is international in its nature. Universities' restrictions on academic positions—to hire local nationals only—causes a decrease in the quality of research and teaching and, in the end, undermines the institutions and the country's competitive intellectual power. Today, as English has become a language for international and academic communication, universities from countries with a low-English-language capacity are in a disadvantaged position. Universities in which research and instruction cannot be provided in English are not considered seriously as players in a global competition at the academic labor market. The example of China and a number of other countries shows that a state must invest significant resources in order to overcome such a situation.

In addition, university teachers without a good command of English for professional communication are shut off from the global market and, moreover, find themselves with limited access to the larger professional community and recent advances in their disciplinary fields.

Academic Equilibrium: Stable Universities and Efficient Contracts

The status of a university is to a large extent defined by the quality of its faculty. This is true both for a university's teaching and research activities. Academic stability or instability depends on whether a university's key academic professionals—that is, teachers—work toward achieving the larger goals implied by their labor contracts or just perform their duties while distracted by additional employment, or "moonlighting," made necessary by poor salaries or decreased purchasing power. If the latter happens, a university functions, but there is a decline in the quality of services—including teaching and research—which are, after all, the very reasons a society supports its universities. In the end, universities with low educational and research performance begin a downward spiral in which they lose in the competition with other institutions, their income is diminished, and talented students begin to enroll elsewhere.

A stable organization requires efficient contracts. A contract seems to be efficient when conditions ensure the possibility for both parties to achieve the goals outlined in the contract with minimum costs. An efficient university teacher's contract assumes that a faculty member has the knowledge and skills required and priorities including research, communication with students and colleagues, teaching and consultations to students, productive use of free time, and an ability for the self-regulation of one's work. Satisfaction resulting from this kind of work one may call "academic remuneration." In other words, a university teacher, usually considered by the academic community as a proper one, appreciates the nonpecuniary benefits of his or her work and attaches value to it—so that it counterbalances the lower relative income offered in relation to others with comparable qualifications in other sectors of the professional labor market.

An efficient contract system has to provide pecuniary and other kinds of material benefits, both when a person is accepting an academic position and throughout his or her career, so that the person does not feel the lack of material and cultural goods and can support a family at a reasonable level. Yet, remuneration should not be too high. If it is extravagant, an adverse selection will emerge, and a teaching career might attract people who cease to appreciate academic remuneration and see their work simply as a source of income.

Crises, Quality, and Professional Communities

There should be professional communities uniting researchers and creative practitioners, both within universities and beyond, who are ready and willing to assess their colleagues' teaching and research quality. Indeed, education that is produced by universities is a classic example of a credence good.[1] That means, it is either impossible or difficult for consumers themselves to evaluate the quality directly—either *ex ante* (before an applicant makes a college choice) or *ex post* (when a graduate leaves university for the labor market). University "clients" and donors—such as the government, local community, entrepreneurs, students, and their parents—are only able to give a formal evaluation. The help of professional communities is required to become more reliable on university quality. Thus, the quality of professional community (standards that they maintain, enforcement for opportunistic behavior, etc.) becomes crucial.

However, recent decades offer examples of university crises and the decline of quality, which were caused in part by a disregard of the prerequisites for an efficient contract. Changes within professional communities, or even their destruction by totalitarian states, inevitably led to quality downturns. This concern is especially clear in the example of the humanities and social sciences in Communist bloc countries.

The example of the Soviet Union and post-Soviet countries also demonstrates other ways in which values that provide the basis of academic contracts can be eroded. On the one hand, in the late Soviet period, the combination of material and other benefits provided by universities and research institutes[2] turned out to be significantly higher in comparison with alternatives for educated human capital (in industry, administrative work, etc.)—in terms of free time and the freedom of self-organization, which were among the scarcest workplace benefits in the USSR. Combined with a low control from professional communities, this led to research institutes being filled with people of rather poor professional abilities, who got jobs through personal networks and were not so much interested in research itself.[3]

Contracts failed to achieve needed results again in the 1990s, when university faculty and research employees saw their salaries shrink, up to four times in terms of purchasing power, in post-Soviet countries. In conjunction with opened borders and a rapid growth of the commercial sector, this condition led to the flight of most-qualified academics—either to foreign universities or commercial firms (doing mostly noncore work, in the latter). Nonetheless, new teachers were joining universities.

The New Generation of Academic Hires

By providing low salaries (noncompetitive, in comparison to global academic markets and the national labor market), universities attracted three types of people.

The first type is the professional, whose preference for the benefit of academic life was enough to sacrifice many material benefits. It cannot be denied that such people do exist, but it also cannot be assumed that their numbers are sufficient to support a university system of high quality. In any case, basing policy on the presumption that individuals are willing to make this kind of personal compromise would be an illusion for any university.

The second type of a professional who enters a poorly remunerated profession is a person with a low self-esteem, who is probably not competitive in other markets due to limited professional training, accomplishment, or intelligence. Academic remuneration makes less difference for them.

The third type consists of people who are uninterested in academic remuneration but whose aim is to derive maximum private incomes by leveraging the status of their academic position. In this case, the interests of the university and its students are unscrupulously ignored, even when the infractions of the formal rules become obvious. This can imply corruption or the neglect of one's duties.

The examples shown above are the most visible infractions of the efficient contract. The environment is by far more serious when (a) insufficient income is supplemented by secondary employment, which abuses the privileges of freedom and flexibility and affects performance; and (b) the professional community's limited influence on employment and quality control, which in turn diminishes the university's academic activities and leads to academic provincialism— one key feature is the contraction of references in publications to one's native language only.

Framing Successful (and Unsuccessful) Contracts

An efficient contract can exist in different legal forms. For example, research results presented in this book indicate that when faculty hold the status of civil servants or are employed by a university directly, the university is their employer, and in both cases, conditions of the efficient contract can be met. Most of the country chapters demonstrate that a variety of contracts exist—the basic formula boiling down to a ratio between the scope of employment duties,[4] material and nonmaterial benefits, and compensation levels for professionals in the nonacademic labor market.

The easiest way to view this is in the form of remuneration tiers. Remuneration levels in different countries range between the highest nonentrepreneurial wages (i.e., doctors, journalists, and senior government officials) and average market wages of university-degree specialists (i.e., engineers and civil servants). At the same time, in countries with stable universities, midcareer remuneration never falls to a lower-middle-class level (i.e., school teachers, welfare workers, etc.).

Still, it would be an oversimplification to assert that a university's equilibrium (stable) is just a result of an efficient contract with its teachers. Equilibrium can easily be upset if the university's responsibilities decline or expand drastically. The latter can be even more disturbing because, even if a university's funding for faculty remuneration keeps pace, it is too expensive to attract people for tenure-track or tenured positions. Thus, the university compromises and hires people only to teach.[5]

The Human Capital Revolution and Resulting Challenges

Universities have been challenged by a second wave for greater access to higher education programs. The first explosion of demand (by an order of magnitude, from several percentages to 15%–25% of the youth cohort) happened in the middle of the 20th century—based on a high demand for educated professionals (engineers, manufacturing technicians, and managers). This, in turn, was caused by the increasing purchasing power of large sections of the population (or, in other words, by the middle class asserting itself as a dominant social group). The society and the economy demanded mass services both in terms of final consumption (health care, education, and consulting) and production (development laboratories, engineering inspection departments, marketing bureaus, etc.). Additionally, during this period, the rate of young people finishing high school grew from 20–30 percent to 50–60 percent.

Practically all the countries examined in this present study experienced a three- or even fourfold increase in the number of students during the past two to three decades. The main features of growth in the modern higher education are:

1. A large-scale expansion of enrollment, covering 40–80 percent of a birth cohort;
2. The first level (bachelor level) is no longer strictly related to a specific profession;[6]
3. Access, which becomes gradually more equitable and less determined by a family's social status.

The most typical consequences of this process are:

1. Per-student-funding decline—the society's willingness to appropriate additional funds to education grows more slowly than the population's demand for higher education. Some of our researchers point out that funding for faculty wages has decreased slightly over the past decades and their income dropped in relative terms.
2. The decline in student quality and motivation for studying due to an expanding participation across birth cohorts, it is not only excellent school graduates who enter universities but ordinary ones, too (and in some cases, those who only just mastered the secondary school program).
3. A growing number of higher education institutions—these are less oriented to research and analysis and more oriented to developing common social skills and/or ready-to-use techniques (both materiel and social).

All of these consequences affect the faculty profile and their working conditions. It is mainly the most developed countries that are witnessing a decline of guaranteed academic income. While school teachers normally react on that by a substantial increase in teaching loads, university professors quite often prefer lower incomes, while keeping the same level of loads.

In some cases, within stable university systems, the salaries of teachers at the beginning of an academic career are lower than what is required for a middle-class lifestyle. It can be assumed that this is a kind of filter for selecting those who appreciate academic remuneration. Indeed, a teacher might settle for several years with a smaller salary if there is a prospect of reaching to the next salary level in due time. But, for those who are blind to the benefits of the structure of academic life, it will seem too low even for a starting salary. Moreover, a low-entry-level salary (in relation to the definition of middle class) may create disincentives for weak teachers (who will not be promoted) to stay at the university in the same position. They will have to give way to new candidates.

"Pure Teachers"

Nevertheless, universities are experiencing a growth in the ratio of professors for whom the condition to participate actively in research is not required. While such teachers may appreciate an academic remuneration, this group's size (in comparison with the pecuniary group) can differ significantly from that of active research-ers. In particular, the radius of one's professional acknowledgment is much smaller. Staff who only teach can just be evaluated and recognized by his or her students and closest colleagues, while an active researcher gets recognized by colleagues from other universities, other countries, or sometimes even by future generations. The motivation for this group (teaching staff) resembles that of a school teacher, or the former is somewhere in between a school teacher and a teaching researcher.

It is highly probable that the emergence of a group of pure teaching positions is a reflection of an increasing teaching load under the first years of university undergraduate programs, which are characterized by a large number of students who are very close to high school students, both in psychology and motivation. Teaching core courses for a large audience and giving seminars for an audience that is mostly uninterested in the subject are hard challenges for a researcher. This is probably why universities hire staff only to teach, even if they might be replaced by professionals with higher research standards from the external labor market. Also, sometimes staff who only teach get promoted and earn higher salaries.

The advantage for the university (and their fellow researchers) of having staff hired only to teach is that, if necessary, they may be more inclined to extend their working time by adding more contact hours or agreeing to grade more papers. Therefore, this type of staff makes universities more flexible and resistant to vari-ous external circumstances.

Still, a university that wants a position in global rankings (and national recognition as an elite institution) will always be bound to limit the rate of staff hired only to teach, at no more than 10 percent to 20 percent of all faculty. This forces universities to employ other methods of covering teaching obligations to new, larger enrollments.

Engaging Students: Teaching Assistants

Universities in many countries extensively use graduate students as teaching assistants. In some countries this practice is used to attract a rather cheap and, at the same time, highly skilled labor force to educational production. In some other university systems (with a rather high level of inbreeding), this practice is also used for screening and training potential faculty members.

Despite the frequent jokes about leading American universities being "places where Indian students teach Chinese students," the quality of education generally stays high. The fact is that teaching assistants usually perform parts of a teacher's workload, which can be called routine—grading student papers, giving support to weaker students, and providing procedural support during lab operations. This routine work may be the least-attractive part of senior staff's workload, and experienced members of faculty may start to perform these duties mechanically. Yet, for students, these tasks are not trivial, and they consider this job quite seriously as a good and respected way to support their studies.

New, Attractive Opportunities Outside the Ivory Tower

The biggest challenge to the modern university may not be extensive enrollment growth but, rather, competition from the intellectual labor market. For 50 years, universities basically enjoyed a monopoly over highly trained intellectual capital, providing adequate salaries but with the freedom and flexibility implied by "academic remuneration"; yet, the situation has changed dramatically.

The intellectual, technical, and creative shifts in the economy gave rise to a large number of new positions benefiting freelancers and business people and that also provided a substantial part of what "academic remuneration" implies. Once an exclusive benefit of academic life, today jobs in consulting, marketing, design, journalism, Web projects, nonprofit projects, or engineering compete with university employment in terms of the freedom of self-organization at work, a stimulating professional environment, a high share of creative work, and external social prestige.

Moreover, a number of traditional ways of managing intellectual labor in industry and public administration have changed significantly. Nowadays, firms and organizations give creative workers more independence at work and are less likely to control work protocol, including office attendance. Various new forms of employment have emerged, due to the Internet revolution, which provide a high degree of freedom with the options for working off-site and a flexible schedule.

Few of the nonpecuniary benefits are exclusive advantages of university work. Among them are (a) high self-esteem, constantly kept up through the feeling of the importance of one's work, and (b) security and a low risk of losing a job due to circumstances beyond the employee's control.

We can conclude that the value of academic remuneration decreases as the share of intellectual and creative work in the broader economy grows. The absolute size of an academic remuneration might stay the same or even increase, but similar advantages will be increasingly available outside the university.

Several decades ago, academics were comfortable in their positions, and any salary disadvantage might be remediated by other advantages of academic life. However, present-day universities experience serious competition in the competition for the best young professionals. A possible hypothesis is that a university's economic stability in the next decade will require that remuneration (including salaries and extra benefits) must be competitive with other creative professional opportunities in the labor market. The time when universities had a monopoly on freedom and creativity is now gone. We believe that this contributes to why academicians in many countries feel dissatisfied with the current level of their salaries and benefits, as shown in many parts of this book.

Notes

1. For definition, see M. R. Darby and E. Karni, "Free Competition and Optimal Amount of Fraud," *Journal of Law and Economics* 16 (1) (1973): 67–88.
2. In the USSR and post-Soviet countries, academic organizations are divided into mainly educational ones (higher education institutions) and mainly research ones (research institutes). In the latter, the educational component consisted of PhD programs only.
3. It would be interesting to know to what extent this is true for the academic markets in developing countries. Unfortunately, our latest results provide no answer for that.
4. In particular, this concerns the regulated amount of workload, teacher's formal status requirements (PhD), and research-results requirements (publications).
5. See, for example, I. Khovanskaya, K. Sonin, and M. Yudkevich, "Budget Uncertainty and Faculty Contracts: A Dynamic Framework for Comparative Analysis," CEPR DP 6744, 2008.
6. With the exception of medicine and law.

APPENDIX

Table A.1 Academic hierarchy, titles by rank in descending order

Country	Top rank	2nd rank	3rd rank	4th rank	5th rank	6th rank
Argentina	Full professor	Associate professor	Assistant professor	Senior assistant	Assistant	Teaching assistant[1]
Armenia	Professor	Docent	Assistant	Lecturer		
Australia	Professor + associate professor	Associate professor	Senior lecturer	Lecturer B	Lecturer A	Associate lecturer
Brazil	Titular (full professor)	Associado (associate)	Adjunto (adjunct)	Assistente (assistant)	Auxliar (auxiliary personnel)	n.a.
Canada	Full professor	Associate professor	Assistant professor	Other (ranks below assistant professor)	n.a.	n.a.
China	Professor	Associate professor	Lecturer	Teaching assistant	n.a.	n.a.
Colombia	Profesor titular	Profesor asociado	Profesor asistente	Profesor auxiliar	Instructor	n.a.
Czech Republic	Professor	Associated professor	Senior assistant	Assistant	Lecturer	Others[2]
Ethiopia	Full professor	Associate professor	Assistant professor	Lecturer	Assistant lecturer	Graduate assistant
France	Professor	Maitre de conference	Secondary teachers working in higher education[3]	Untenured lecturers[4]	n.a.	n.a.
Germany	Professors: C4/W3: full professors or chair holders	Professors: C2/C3/W2: equivalent to associate professor	Professors: C1/W1: equivalent to assistant professor	Researchers and lecturers	Junior staff, teaching only positions	n.a.
India	Professor	Associate professor	Assistant professor	n.a.	n.a.	n.a.
Israel	Full professor	Associate professor	Senior lecturer	Lecturer	n.a.	n.a.
Italy	Professore ordinario	Professore associato	Ricercatore	n.a.	n.a.	n.a.
Japan	Professor	Associate professor	Lecturer	Assistant professor	Research assistant	n.a.
Kazakhstan	Professor	Associate professor	Senior teacher	Assistant	n.a.	n.a.

Latvia	Professor	Associate professor	Reader	Lecturer	Assistant of professor	n.a.
Malaysia	Professor	Associate professor	Senior lecturer	Lecturer	n.a.	n.a.
Mexico	Profesor/ investigador Titular C	Profesor/ investigador Titular B	Profesor/ investigador Titular A	Profesor/ investigador Asociado C	Profesor/ investigador Asociado B	Profesor/ investigador Asociado A
Netherlands	Professor	Senior lecturer	Lecturer	Instructor; doctoral candidate	n.a.	n.a.
Nigeria	Professor	Reader/associate professor	Senior lecturer	Lecturer	n.a.	n.a.
Norway	Professor	Associate professor	Senior lecturer	Lecturer	n.a.	n.a.
Russia	Professor	Associate professor	Senior lecturer	Lecturer, assistant lecturer	n.a.	n.a.
Saudi Arabia	Full professor	Associate professor	Assistant professor	Lecturer	Demonstrator	n.a.
South Africa	Professor	Associate professor	Senior lecturer	Lecturer	Junior lecturer	n.a.
Turkey	Professor	Docent	Assistant docent	Research assistant	Lecturers and instructors	Educational Planners, translators, and specialists
United Kingdom	Professor	Reader	Senior lecturer	Lecturer	n.a.	n.a.
United States	Professor	Associate professor	Assistant professor	n.a.	n.a.	n.a.

Source: All data reported in the Appendix are compiled from the country case studies.

Notes: n.a. = not applicable.

[1]Teaching assistants are volunteer advanced students.

[2]"Others" does not mean the lowest Level but the category stipulated by the higher education act as "research and development workers taking part in pedagogical activities." This category does not exist at all higher education institutions and makes only a very small percentage from the total academic staff.

[3]Level 3 is not part of the academic career as such: no progression available without a PhD.

[4]Level 4 mainly consists in PhD students that are paid during their PhD.

Table A.2 Academic salaries at public universities, PPP US$*

Country	Average monthly salary of university faculty					
	Top rank	Rank 2	Rank 3	Rank 4	Rank 5	Rank 6
Argentina	4,385	4,029	3,453	3,151	n.a.	n.a.
Armenia	665	595	486	405	n.a.	n.a.
Australia	7,499	n.d.	6,240	5,183	3,930	n.a.
Brazil	4,550	4,226	3,190	2,073	1,858	n.a.
Canada	9,485	7,424	6,140	5,733	n.a.	n.a.
China	1,107	803	712	259	n.a.	n.a.
Colombia	4,058	3,047	2,374	2,064	1,965	n.a.
Czech Republic	3,967	3,058	2,087	1,642	1,655	2,562
Ethiopia	1,580	1,378	1,191	1,022	864	n.a.
France	4,775	3,705	1,973	n.a.	n.a.	n.a.
Germany	6,383	5,184	4,326	4,927	4,885	n.a.
India	7,433	6,823	3,954	n.a.	n.a.	n.a.
Israel	6,377	4,762	4,323	3,525	n.a.	n.a.
Italy	9,118	6,717	5,029	n.a.	n.a.	n.a.
Japan	4,604	3,704	3,322	2,837	2,897	n.a.
Kazakhstan	2,304	1,671	1,198	1,037	n.a.	n.a.
Latvia	2,654	2,124	1,699	1,359	1,087	n.a.
Malaysia	7,864	4,084	3,739	2,824	n.a.	n.a.
Mexico	2,730	2,282	2,017	1,793	1,488	1,336
Netherlands	7,123	5,880	4,775	3,472	n.a.	n.a.
Nigeria	6,229	5,158	4,369	2,758	n.a.	n.a.
Norway	5,847	4,667	4,755	4,491	n.a.	n.a.
Russia	910	650	476	433	n.a.	n.a.
Saudi Arabia	8,524	7,501	6,068	4,458	3,457	n.a.
South Africa	9,330	7,680	6,490	5,228	3,927	n.a.
Turkey	3,898	2,832	2,436	2,027	2,216	2,173
United Kingdom	8,369	6,050	5,276	4,077	n.a.	n.a.
United States	7,358	5,853	4,950	n.a.	n.a.	n.a.

Source: All data reported in the Appendix are compiled from the country case studies.

Notes: n.a. = not applicable; n.d. = no data available.

*Converted from local currency units by using PPP conversion rates retrieved from Penn World Tables 7.0 Database (June 3, 2011). For countries with 2010 salary PPP conversion rates for 2009 were used due to data availability issues. For countries with 2009–10 academic year salary data PPP conversion rates for 2009 were used due to data availability issues. For countries with salary data for academic rather than calendar years the latter calendar year PPP conversion rates were used, since in most countries that corresponds for the lengthier part of the academic year (e.g., for the United Kingdom, 2006 PPP conversion rates were used).

Table A.3 Academic salaries at private universities, PPP US$*

Country	Year	Average Monthly Salary of University Faculty					
		Rank 1	Rank 2	Rank 3	Rank 4	Rank 5	Rank 6
Armenia	2009/10	915	467	350	n.a.	n.a.	n.a.
Colombia	2008	5,110	4,088	3,380	2,555	1,690	n.a.
Ethiopia	2008	1,784	1,598	1,508	1,150	884	486
France	2009	13,939	n.a.	2,228	n.a.	n.a.	n.a.
Italy	2009	9,118	6,717	5,029	n.a.	n.a.	n.a.
Japan	2007	4,919	4,001	3,339	2,481	2,438	n.a.
Kazakhstan	2010	2,304	2,074	1,498	1,152	n.a.	n.a.
Latvia	2009/10	2,169	1,615	1,302	1,036	815	n.a.
Malaysia	2008	8,346	5,891	3,699	n.a.	n.a.	n.a.
Mexico	2009	3,533	3,465	2,722	1,719	1,413	n.a.
Nigeria	2009	4,242	3,490	2,863	1,927	n.a.	n.a.
United States	2008/2009	7,897	6,044	5,006	n.a.	n.a.	n.a.

Source: All data reported in the Appendix are compiled from the country case studies.

Note: n.a. = not applicable.

* Converted from local currency units by using PPP convertson rates retrieved from Penn World Tables 7.0 Database (June 3, 2011). For countries with 2010 salary PPP conversion rates for 2009 were used due to data availability issues. For countries with 2009–10 academic year salary data PPP conversion rates for 2009 were used due to data availability issues. For countries with salary data for academic rather than calendar years the latter calendar year PPP conversion rates were used, since in most countries that corresponds for the lengthier part of the academic year (e.g., for the UK 2006 PPP conversion rates were used). Only countries included are those where academic salaries in private universities were provided by country authors.

Table A.4 Supplementary contract benefits at public universities*

Country	Housing	Low-interest loans	Paid vacations	Retirement funds	Other benefits**
Argentina	5	5	1	1	1
Armenia	5	5	1	1	5
Australia	5	5	5	1	3
Brazil	5	5	1	1	1
Canada	4	3	1	2	3
China	2	3	2	2	2
Colombia	5	5	1	1	1
Czech Republic	5	5	1	1	5
Ethiopia	4	5	4	1	2
France	5	4	5	1	5
Germany	5	5	1	1	5
India	1	5	1	1	1
Israel	5	4	1	1	5
Italy	5	5	1	1	5
Japan	4	5	1	1	5
Kazakhstan	3	5	1	5	1
Latvia	1	1	5	1	5
Malaysia	5	1	1	1	2
Mexico	5	4	1	1	2
Netherlands	5	5	1	1	1
Nigeria	1	5	1	1	1
Norway	5	5	1	1	5
Russia	5	5	1	1	2
Saudi Arabia	2	5	1	1	2
South Africa	4	4	3	1	5
Turkey	3	5	1	1	5
United Kingdom	4	4	1	2	5
United States	5	5	5	1	1

Source: All data reported in the Appendix are compiled from the country case studies.

Notes: The contract benefits in the column cells are as follows: 1 = provided to all employees by law; 2 = widely used to attract best faculty; 3 = important part of contract negotiations; 4 = not influential in contract negotiations; and 5 = not offered as part of an academic contract.

* Weight assigned to the importance of each benefit was based on the experience and expertise of country experts.

** Child benefits, subsidized or free education for children, salary bonuses, traveling and conference allowances, social security plans (including disability, separate pension plans, health plans, in addition to those provided by law), allowances for participation in research.

Table A.5 Sources of faculty income at public universities*

Country	Salary from the university	Teaching in other institutions	Consulting activities	Nonacademic jobs**	Other sources of income***
Argentina	1	3	3	5	2
Armenia	1	2	4	4	2
Australia	1	4	3	3	3
Brazil	1	3	2	5	1
Canada	1	4	2	3	3
China	1	2	2	5	5
Colombia	1	3	3	4	4
Czech Republic	1	2	3	2	2
Ethiopia	2	1	1	2	2
France	1	3	3	5	5
Germany	1	4	3	5	5
India	1	5	5	5	3
Israel	1	3	4	4	5
Italy	1	4	2	5	5
Japan	1	3	3	3	3
Kazakhstan	1	2	2	3	3
Latvia	1	2	3	2	2
Malaysia	1	4	3	5	4
Mexico	2	2	3	3	1
Netherlands	1	4	4	4	4
Nigeria	1	4	2	3	3
Norway	1	3	3	4	4
Russia	1	2	4	2	5
Saudi Arabia	1	2	2	5	1
South Africa	1	4	2	5	5
Turkey	1	4	2	5	2
United Kingdom	1	3	2	5	5
United States	1	4	3	3	3

Source: All data reported in the Appendix are compiled from the country case studies.

Notes: The numbers in the column cells are as follows 1 = the most important component for academic's income; 2 = very important; 3 = not so important; 4 = very little importance; and 5 = not applicable in the country.

*Value assigned to different sources of income was based on the experience and expertise of country experts.

**Entrepreneurial activities, private consulting, journalism.

*** Private tutoring, publications, research, honoraria for guest lecturing, royalty from publishers for publications, income from intellectual property rights, scholarships.

CONTRIBUTORS

Editors

Philip G. Altbach is J. Donald Monan S.J. University Professor and director of the Center for International Higher Education at Boston College, in the United States. He was the 2004–6 Distinguished Scholar Leader for the New Century Scholars initiative of the Fulbright program. He has taught at Harvard University, the University of Wisconsin–Madison, and the State University of New York at Buffalo, and has been a visiting scholar at the SciencesPo, Paris, France; the University of Bombay, India; and is a guest professor at Peking University, China.

Gregory Androushchak is adviser to the rector of National Research University–Higher School of Economics for economics of education and a researcher at the Laboratory for Institutional Analysis. He is an adviser to the government of the Russian Federation and Ministry of Education and Science regarding policies of public funding of higher education and measures to estimate and enhance the efficiency of Russian universities.

Iván F. Pacheco is research assistant at the Center for International Higher Education at Boston College, in the United States. Trained in Colombia as a lawyer, he has been a visiting scholar at Oxford, an intern at LASPAU-Harvard, and has been Director of Quality Assurance for the Colombian Ministry of Education, acting Vice Minister of Higher Education, and board member for more than 10 Colombian public universities.

Liz Reisberg is research associate at the Center for International Higher Education at Boston College, in the United States, where she coordinates several grant-funded projects, engages in research, and contributes to Center publications. She is also an independent consultant working with ministries of education and universities on strategies for improving higher education. She was the founder and former executive director of the MBA Tour, a company that organizes professional recruitment tours throughout the world.

Maria Yudkevich is vice rector for research at the Economics Department at the National Research University–Higher School of Economics in Moscow, Russia (HSE) and a director for academic development for HSE. She also chairs a Laboratory for Institutional Analysis at HSE. The main areas of her interest and research work are contract theory with a special reference to faculty contracts, universities, and markets for higher education.

Authors

Hamad Al-Mehrej is head of the General Administration at the University Enhancement Program in the Ministry of Higher Education, Saudi Arabia. He has served as associate professor and vice dean for research at Imam Mohammad Bin Saud University, in Riyadh, and as Saudi cultural attaché in Kuwait and the United Kingdom. He holds a PhD in measurement and statistics from the University of Kansas.

Mohammad Al-Ohali is deputy minister for educational affairs in the ministry of Higher Education of the Government of Saudi Arabia. He served as project manager for the plan on the future of higher education in the Kingdom (AFAQ). He has served as dean of the Faculty of Graduate Studies at the King Fahd University of Petroleum and Minerals and in other leadership roles. A physicist, he is author of 42 research publications in refereed scientific journals.

Elizabeth Ayalew is assistant professor at College of Education, Addis Ababa University, in Ethiopia. She has served as the associate dean (graduate programs) and assistant dean (undergraduate programs) of the college between 2003 and 2006. Her research interest generally includes higher education, teacher education, gender and language education, information systems, and knowledge management.

Olufemi A. Bamiro is vice-chancellor and professor in the Department of Mechanical Engineering, Faculty of Technology, University of Ibadan, in Nigeria. He has over 35 years of teaching and research experience in the areas of mechanical engineering, science and technology policy studies, software development, and environmental impact assessment. Dr. Bamiro served as secretary of the panel that produced the energy policy for Nigeria in 1984 and in other positions. He is currently involved with the project on sustainable financing of higher education in Nigeria sponsored by the Partnership of Higher Education in Africa, the MacArthur Foundation, and the World Bank.

Giliberto Capano is professor of political science and public policy in the Department of Political Science of Bologna University, Italy. He has been dean of

Bologna University's II Faculty of Political Science. His main research interests are: theories of public policy, higher education policy, legislative behavior, public administration reforms, and the policymaking role of interests' groups.

Martin J. Finkelstein is professor of higher education at Seton Hall University, South Orange, New Jersey, United States. He has taught at the University of Denver and Teacher's College, Columbia University; and has served as a visiting scholar at the Claremont Graduate University, the Research Institute for Higher Education, Hiroshima University, Japan, and visiting professor at the University of Hong Kong. He is author, with Jack Schuster, of *The American Faculty: The Restructuring of Academic Work and Careers.*

Ana García de Fanelli is the director of the Center for the Study of State and Society (CEDES), in Buenos Aires, Argentina. She is senior researcher of the National Council of Research in Science and Technology at the Higher Education Department of CEDES, and is professor at the University of Buenos Aires and at San Andres University.

Gaële Goastellec is head of a research unit at the Observatoire Science, Policy and Society, University of Lausanne, Switzerland. She works on higher education policies in an international comparative perspective, taking as foci both the issues of equity in access and academic careers. Her research includes fieldwork in France, the United States, Indonesia, South Africa, and Switzerland.

Sarah Guri-Rosenblit is the director of international academic outreach and the head of graduate studies in education, at the Open University of Israel. Her areas of expertise are focused on comparative research of higher education systems, distance education, and e-learning. She was selected as one of the 2005–6 30 New Century Scholars in the Fulbright Program on: Higher Education in the 21st Century.

Kemal Gürüz is retired professor of chemical engineering at the Middle East Technical University and the former president of the Council of Higher Education of the Republic of Turkey, a national board of governors for all institutions of higher education in the country, which now comprises over 140 universities with a total enrollment of 3 million students. His previous posts and positions include president of the Turkish National Science Foundation and fellow at the Weatherhead Center for International Affairs at Harvard University.

Marius Herzog is research assistant at the International Centre for Higher Education Research of Kassel University, in Germany; he is involved in the EUROAC-Project (the Academic Profession in Europe: Responses to Societal Challenges). He studied sociology at the Free University of Berlin, where he got his diploma.

Muhamad Jantan is director of corporate and sustainability development at the Universiti Sains Malaysia, in Penang, Malaysia. In 1990, he joined the School of Management, Universiti Sains Malaysia. He has been the head of Department of

Statistics and Operations Research, head of Department of Operations Management, deputy dean of Research and Graduate Studies at the School of Management, acting director of IPPTN (National Higher Research Institute of Malaysia).

Narayana Jayaram is professor of research methodology and dean, School of Social Sciences at the Tata Institute of Social Sciences, in Mumbai, India. He has taught sociology in various capacities at Bangalore University (1972–99) and Goa University (1999–2003). He was director of the Institute for Social and Economic Change, in Bangalore. He was visiting professor of Indian Studies at the University of the West Indies.

Glen A. Jones is the Ontario Research Chair in Postsecondary Education Policy and Measurement and the associate dean, academic, at the Ontario Institute for Studies in Education at the University of Toronto, in Canada. He has been an Erasmus Mundus Scholar at the University of Oslo and a visiting professor at Fudan University. He received the Distinguished Research Award from the Canadian Society for the Study of Higher Education in 2001.

Ben Jongbloed is a senior research associate at the Center for Higher Education Policy Studies of the University of Twente, in Enschede, the Netherlands. He has been involved in a large number of international research and consultancy projects, many of them dealing with issues of reform and restructuring.

Sholpan Kalanova is deputy director of the Department of Strategic Analysis at the Administration of the President of the Republic of Kazakhstan and is a scientific supervisor at the Independent Kazakhstan Quality Assurance Agency for Education. She was vice president of academic affairs at the Kyzylorda State University and Taraz State University. She worked as deputy director of the Department of Governmental Inspection and Administrative Department at the Ministry of Education and Science of the Republic of Kazakhstan and was a director of National Accreditation Center at the Ministry of Education and Science. She then moved on to work as the president of the Independent Kazakhstan Quality Assurance Agency for Education.

Barbara M. Kehm is a professor of higher education research at the University of Kassel, in Germany. She is also managing director of the International Centre for Higher Education Research of Kassel University and coordinator of an international master's program Higher Education Research and Development. Her special fields of expertise are internationalization in higher education, the Bologna Process, new forms of governance in higher education, and emerging forms of professionalization in higher education institutions.

Fumi Kitagawa is based at the University of Bristol in the United Kingdom. She is completing NCCPE-ESRC research synthesis 2009 "Academic promotion criteria for third stream activity" focusing on the UK higher education sector. Previously she worked at CIRCLE (Centre for Innovation, Research and

Competence in the Learning Economy) at Lund University in Sweden as assistant professor and at the Higher Education Research Division in the National Institute for Educational Policy Research in Japan as Research Fellow. She has held Jean Monnet Fellowship at European University Institute to work on the role of universities in innovation systems.

Yaroslav Kuzminov is a rector of the National Research University Higher School of Economics, Head of the Department of Institutional Economics, Academic Supervisor of the Laboratory for Institutional Analysis of Economic Reforms of the Higher School of Economics, Moscow, Russia. He is a member of the Presidential Council for Facilitating the Development of Civil Society Institutions and Human Rights and a member of the Public Council at the Ministry of Education and Science of the Russian Federation.

Svein Kyvik is senior researcher at NIFU STEP (Norwegian Institute for Studies in Innovation, Research and Education) in Oslo, Norway. For over more than three decades he has undertaken research in the fields of sociology of science, academic careers, and higher education policy.

Wanhua Ma is professor at the Graduate School of Education and director of the Center for International Higher Education at Peking University, in Beijing, China. She has been a visiting professor at the University of California, Berkeley, teaching an undergraduate course on economic reform and education change in China. She has also been a consultant at East-West Center at Hawaii University and was selected as a Fulbright New Century Scholar, carrying out a research project on the formation of global research universities. In the fall of 2008, she was invited as Erasmus Mundus professor to Finland and Norway. She has published extensively on reforms of Chinese higher education and the formation of American research universities. Her current research focuses on internationalization of Chinese higher education and capacity building of research universities both in the United States and China.

Alma Maldonado-Maldonado is a researcher at the Educational Research Department [Departamento de Investigaciones Educativas] of the Center for Advanced Research of the National Polytechnic Institute [Centro de Investigaciones Avanzadas del Instituto Politécnico Nacional]. Previously, she was an assistant professor at the University of Arizona's Center for the Study of Higher Education in the United States. Her research focuses on comparative higher education, international organizations, higher education policy and research on Latin America and particularly on Mexico and issues regarding globalization, mobility, and internationalization of higher education (institutions, faculty, and students).

Arevik Ohanyan is a junior faculty member at Eurasia International University. She has been a visiting scholar at the Center for International Higher Education at

Boston College courtesy of the Junior Faculty Development Program established by Bureau of Educational and Cultural Affairs of the U.S. Department of State.

Gianfranco Rebora is professor at the University Carlo Cattaneo of Castellanza, in Italy, and director of the Department of Management. He has also served as rector and as dean of the Faculty of Economics of the University Carlo Cattaneo. Since 1994, he has been full professor in business administration at the University Carlo Cattaneo. He earlier was full professor of business administration at the State University of Brescia and associate professor of business strategy at the Bocconi University of Milan.

Simon Schwartzman is the president of Instituto de Estudos do Trabalho e Sociedade in Rio de Janeiro, in Brazil, and a Fulbright New Century Scholar for 2009–10. He is a member of the Brazilian Academy of Sciences and a recipient of the Brazilian Order of Scientific Merit. He has also served as president of the Brazilian Institute for Geography and Statistics, Brazil's census office.

Helena Sebkova is the director of the Centre for Higher Education Studies in Prague, in the Czech Republic. The main areas of her interest and research work focus on quality assurance and quality culture, internationalization with respect to the Bologna process and its priorities, higher education management and governance, respectively, collaboration of higher education institutions with external stakeholders in general and employers in particular. In 2004–2008, she was the national coordinator of the multinational OECD project, Thematic Review of Tertiary Education.

Chika Trevor Sehoole is associate professor in the Department of Education Management and Policy Studies at the University of Pretoria, in South Africa. In 2003, he was a visiting postdoctoral fellow at the University of Illinois, at Urbana Champaign, in the United States. In 2005, Professor Sehoole had a Fulbright New Century Scholar fellowship, through which he conducted research on global student mobility. He has worked in the National Department of Education in South Africa, where he was involved in higher education policy making and management activities. This entailed work in the planning, funding, research management, and regulations of private higher education. He writes and publishes in the areas of higher education policy, internationalization of higher education, and trade in education.

Kazunori Shima is associate professor at the Research Institute for Higher Education, Hiroshima University, in Japan. His research focuses on the impact of recent developments in the National Universities in Japan.

Tatjana Volkova is professor of strategic management and rector of BA School of Business and Finance, in Riga, Latvia; and a member of Board of the Association of Professors of Latvia. She is national editor of *Baltic Journal of Management,* an expert for the "National Development Plan of Latvia 2007–2013." She also is a former President of Rector's Conference of Latvia, and former Member of European University Association Council.

Julian Weinrib is a doctoral candidate in the Department of Theory and Policy Studies in Education at the Ontario Institute for Studies in Education at the University of Toronto, in Canada. His research interests focus on the internationalization and globalization of higher education systems and institutions.

Anthony Welch is professor of education, University of Sydney, in Australia. His numerous publications address reforms, principally within Australia and the Asia-Pacific. He has been a visiting professor in the United States, United Kingdom, Germany, France, Japan, and Hong Kong (China). He was Fulbright New Century Scholar.

Jianbo Wen is a PhD student at the Graduate School of Education, Peking University, in Beijing, China; and an English lecturer in the School of Foreign Languages of the Central University of Finance and Economics, Beijing.

INDEX